RURAL FINANCIAL MARKETS IN ASIA: POLICIES, PARADIGMS, AND PERFORMANCE

by

Richard L. Meyer
and
Geetha Nagarajan

OXFORD

UNIVERSITY PRESS

OXFORD

UNIVERSITY PRESS

Oxford University Press is a department of the University of Oxford.
It furthers the University's objective of excellence in research, scholarship,
and education by publishing worldwide in

Oxford New York

Athens Auckland Bangkok Bogotá Buenos Aires Calcutta
Cape Town Chennai Dar es Salaam Delhi Florence Hong Kong Istanbul
Karachi Kuala Lumpur Madrid Melbourne Mexico City Mumbai
Nairobi Paris São Paulo Singapore Taipei Tokyo Toronto Warsaw

with associated companies in Berlin Ibadan

Oxford is a registered trade mark of Oxford University Press

Published in the United States by Oxford University Press Inc., New York

First published 2000
This impression (lowest digit)
1 3 5 7 9 10 8 6 4 2

Published for the Asian Development Bank by
Oxford University Press

British Library Cataloguing in Publication Data
available

Library of Congress Cataloging-in-Publication Data
available

ISBN 0 19 592452 5   (Paperback)
ISBN 0 19 592451 7   (Hardback)

Printed in Hong Kong
Published by Oxford University Press (China) Ltd
18th Floor, Warwick House East, Taikoo Place, 979 King's Road, Quarry Bay
Hong Kong

CONTENTS

FOREWORD

An economic transformation has occurred in much of rural Asia since the Asian Development Bank (ADB) last undertook a survey of the region in 1976. The rural economy has become increasingly linked to a rapidly integrating world economy and rural society in Asia faces new opportunities and challenges.

The transformation of rural Asia has also been accompanied by some troubling developments. While large parts of the region have prospered, Asia remains home to the majority of the world's poor. Growing inequalities and rising expectations in many parts of rural Asia have increased the urgency of tackling the problems of rural poverty. The rapid exploitation of natural resources is threatening the sustainability of the drive for higher productivity and incomes in some parts of rural Asia and is, in general, affecting the quality of life in the entire region.

These developments have altered the concept of rural development to encompass concerns that go well beyond improvements in growth, income, and output. The concerns include an assessment of changes in the quality of life, broadly defined to include improvements in health and nutrition, education, environmentally safe living conditions, and reduction in gender and income inequalities. At the same time, the policy environment has changed dramatically. Thus, there has arisen a need to identify ways in which governments, the development community at large, and the ADB in particular, can offer more effective financial and policy support for Asian rural development in the new century.

Therefore, the ADB decided to undertake a study to examine the achievements and prospects of rural Asia and to provide a vision for the future of agriculture and rural development in Asia into the next century. The objective of the Study was to identify, for the ADB's developing member countries in Asia, policy and investment priorities that will promote sustainable development and improve economic and social conditions in the rural sector.

The Study was designed as a team effort, using ADB Staff and international experts under the guidance of an ADB interdepartmental steering committee. To address the diverse issues satisfactorily and in a comprehensive manner, five thematic subject areas were identified to provide the analytical and empirical background on which the Study's recommendations would be based. Working groups comprising ADB staff were set up to define broadly the scope and coverage of each of the themes. The five working groups acted as counterparts to international experts recruited to prepare the background reports, providing guidance to the experts and reviewing their work to ensure high quality output.

A panel of external advisers from the international research community was constituted to review and comment on the approach and methodology of the study and the terms of reference for each of these background reports. The external advisers also reviewed the drafts of the reports. In addition, external reviewers, prominent members of academe and senior policymakers, were appointed to review each of the background reports and to provide expert guidance.

The preparation of the background reports included four workshops held at the ADB's headquarters in Manila: an inception workshop in May 1998; two interim workshops, in November 1998 and January 1999, respectively, to review progress; and a final workshop in March 1999, at which the background reports were presented by their authors to a large group of participants comprising senior policymakers from the ADB's developing member countries, international organizations, international and locally based nongovernment organizations, donor agencies, members of academe, and ADB staff.

The five background reports, of which this volume is one, have now been published by Oxford University Press. The titles and authors of the other volumes are:

Transforming the Rural Asian Economy: the Unfinished Revolution
Mark W. Rosegrant and Peter B. R. Hazell

The Growth and Sustainability of Agriculture in Asia
Mingsarn Santikarn Kaosa-ard and Benjavan Rerkasem, with contributions by Shelley Grasty, Apichart Kaosa-ard, Sunil S. Pednekar, Kanok Rerkasem, and Paul Auger

The Quality of Life in Rural Asia
David Bloom, Patricia Craig, and Pia Malaney

The Evolving Roles of State, Private, and Local Actors in Rural Asia
Ammar Siamwalla with contributions by Alex Brillantes, Somsak Chunharas, Colin MacAndrews, Andrew MacIntyre, and Frederick Roche

The results and recommendations from the Study were presented at a seminar during the ADB's 32nd Annual Meeting in Manila. These have since been published by the ADB as a book titled *Rural Asia: Beyond the Green Revolution*.

The findings from the Study will provide a basis for future discussion between the ADB and its developing member countries on ways to eradicate poverty and improve the quality of life in rural Asia. The volumes in this series should prove useful to all those concerned with improving the economic and social conditions of rural populations in Asia through sustainable development.

Tadao Chino
TADAO CHINO
President
Asian Development Bank

PREFACE

We wish to acknowledge the many people without whom this work would not have been completed. First, we appreciate the effort and commitment of the senior Asian Development Bank (ADB) managers for supporting the entire research project and giving it so much of their personal attention and time. Next, we want to thank Bradford Philips and Shahid Zahid of ADB for their careful leadership, continuous encouragement, and the professional way they managed the entire project. Nimal Fernando and the other members of ADB's Working Group on this topic deserve special recognition for their constant encouragement, guidance, criticism, and information provided to us. They always kept us focused on the central objective. The external advisers provided useful insights and suggestions about what the study should address. Nimal Sandernate and J. D. Von Pischke thoroughly read the first draft and provided a highly detailed comprehensive and professional critique that helped shape subsequent drafts. Their vast Asian experience was clearly reflected in their review.

Many people were very generous with their time, data, papers, and suggestions. At the risk of overlooking someone, we want to specifically mention the following: Saroj Aungsumalin, Lynn Bennett, Enjiang Cheng, Kim Cooling, Terry Dunphy, Gershon Feder, Prabhu Ghate, Wu Guabao, Jikun Huang, Baqui Khalily, Ross McLeod, Bagavathi S. Nagarajan, Tongroj Onchan, Albert Park, Dick Patten, Rama Rao, Richard Roberts, Marguerite Robinson, Scott Rozelle, Wang Sangui, Ammar Siamwalla, Satish Suryanarayana, John

Whittle, Sylvia Wisniwski, and Jacob Yaron. Several of them went to great effort to obtain and send information crucial to writing the case studies and provided detailed comments on our drafts.

We appreciated the collegiality of the members of the other study teams. We also acknowledge our OSU colleagues Dale W Adams, Claudio Gonzalez-Vega, and Douglas H. Graham whose research and ideas have shaped our thinking over the years.

Joan Weber managed the project in her usual careful and efficient manner and was absolutely indispensable in managing the workflow and word processing the drafts and final product. We appreciate her ability to be cheerful and upbeat while under pressure to meet competing demands. Lori Karn once again did her fine professional job of word processing for yet another one of our writing projects filled with last minute deadlines. Jay Maclean provided careful professional editing that corrected many errors and made the manuscript read much better. Members of the project secretariat within ADB were always willing to assist us in all aspects of the study.

Finally, we thank our spouses, Carol and Shiva, for their encouragement and patience. They were pleased when we undertook this research and were even happier when it was finished.

RICHARD L. MEYER
and GEETHA NAGARAJAN

I INTRODUCTION

BACKGROUND

Rural financial markets in Asia are ill-prepared for the twenty-first century. That is the undeniable conclusion of this study.

Asian rural financial markets have been buffeted by several major forces during the past three decades. Policymakers have tried to direct them to meet economic and social objectives, first to support the green revolution and, more recently, to aid in poverty alleviation. Massive amounts of subsidized funds have been supplied for these purposes. New specialized development finance institutions have been created to deliver credit to targeted clients when commercial lenders failed to serve the intended clients adequately. The transition economies have been forced to dismantle their planned allocation of resources and now struggle to create market-oriented financial institutions. The market economies have removed some of the most repressive features of their urban-biased policies, but both entrepreneurs and financial institutions have much to learn about how to succeed in the new environment.

The result of these many changes and government interventions is a fragile financial system with limited outreach. Many institutions have failed, many have been recapitalized, and many are weak with large nonperforming portfolios. Few countries have strong, self-sustaining institutions with the capacity to serve large numbers of rural farm and nonfarm clients, including the poorest members of the rural economy.

A positive feature is the large amount of experimentation that has occurred in many countries, especially by nongovernmental organizations (NGOs), to break the barriers faced by the poor in accessing formal finance. These innovations appear to be more promising than previous attempts to induce lenders to serve this clientele group.

While Asian financial markets have been struggling, the rural areas in much of the region have undergone a major transformation. This transformation was caused by an unprecedented technological and economic revolution that raised agricultural productivity and helped the region escape the worst cycles of hunger and despair faced by previous generations. The scientific breakthroughs of the green revolution induced major changes in farm and nonfarm production systems, resulting in new sources of employment in rural areas.

Public institutions created the technology, adapted it to local environments, and disseminated it to farmers. Complementary investments were made in irrigation, roads, and distribution systems such that farmers could access the water, seed, fertilizer, and chemicals needed for production. Markets emerged to handle the inputs and expanded production in many countries. Private traders and cooperatives performed the marketing functions in several countries, while governments and parastatal agencies were dominant in others. Policymakers created major subsidized credit programs as part of the technological package extended to farmers to encourage the rapid adoption of the new technology.

In the 1970s, many studies were undertaken of rural financial systems, often with the objective of determining whether farmers were receiving the funds targeted for them and whether the funding affected the adoption of technology and improved rural income. There has been no comprehensive survey of rural finance in the region, however, to analyze the role of the financial system in the transformation process and to assess the status of the system today. This study fills that void and furnishes important lessons about the appropriate role of finance in rural development. It analyses how rural financial markets in Asia evolved during this period of rapid rural transformation. It is one of five studies for a major research project commissioned by the Asian Development Bank (ADB) in 1998 entitled A Study of Rural Asia. The objective of the project was to identify, for the Bank's developing member countries, policy and investment priorities that will promote sustainable development and improve economic and social conditions in the rural sector. It represented a follow-up study to two earlier regional studies of rural Asia that the ADB undertook in the 1960s and 1970s, respectively.

The five studies review developments in the Asian rural economy to gain an understanding of the causes and consequences of economic performance during the last two decades, and to identify possibilities and constraints to furthering the transformation into the next century. The five studies identify strategies and priorities for Asian developing countries and for the international donor community. Within the ADB, they provide background information and material for the formulation of its rural development strategy and the basis for its future operations in agriculture and rural development. The intended audience for the published reports of these studies is professionals and policymakers involved in efforts to improve conditions in rural Asia.

METHODOLOGY

The primary objective of this study was to examine the provision and use of financial services in Asia's rural economy since the last survey by ADB, published in 1978, and to identify the relationship between the transformation of the rural economy and the rural financial system. Asia is a vast region composed of many heterogeneous countries that have employed a variety of policies and programs since the 1970s to improve rural finance. To narrow the task to manageable proportions, six countries were selected for detailed study–Bangladesh, People's Republic of China (PRC), India, Indonesia, the Kyrgyz Republic, and Thailand. Bangladesh was chosen because of the key role that microfinance organizations have come to play in the country. India and the PRC were selected because they represent huge countries with a long history of heavy governmental intervention in their financial markets. The Kyrgyz Republic is one of the transition economies and has rapidly implemented major economic reforms. Indonesia and Thailand represent countries in which market forces have been allowed to play a larger role in shaping the financial system.

All the relevant literature that could be identified for these six countries was assembled, and a limited amount of primary data was obtained with the help of nationals in the countries. The key literature on rural financial markets in other developing countries was also consulted.

Since the study was based largely on existing literature, key details were often not available on specific topics such as total rural loans made or outstanding; the characteristics of the participants in formal and informal rural financial markets; the terms and conditions of financial transactions; financial policies and supporting financial infrastructure; the details of the design and operations of formal financial institutions and informal financial arrangements; and the perceptions of policymakers, bank employees, farmers, and nonfarm entrepreneurs. This limitation meant that the current status of rural finance and its evolution since the 1970s were constructed from fragmentary and incomplete information. Fortunately, several commentators on various drafts helped clarify specific points and correct possible misinterpretations.

ORGANIZATION

This volume is divided into two main parts. The first part consists of five chapters that present the study's objectives, the conceptual framework, and the principal findings. The second part presents a short overview of the six countries followed by the detailed case study of each.

Chapter II summarizes the nature of the economic transformation that has occurred in Asia since the 1970s, explains the structural changes that occurred in the rural economy, and identifies the opportunities and challenges that these changes present for rural financial markets. It draws heavily on a companion volume by Rosegrant and Hazell (1999).

Chapter III provides the conceptual framework used to analyze financial markets. It presents a lengthy review of the evolution in views that has occurred about the role of financial markets in economic development, and the costs and risks of providing rural financial services. It describes the approach governments took to rural finance in the 1970s and 1980s, the problems identified with this approach, and the resulting shift from the old directed credit approach to the new market-oriented paradigm for developing financial markets. The emergence of microfinance and its contribution to the new paradigm are explored. The problems of creating financial markets in transition economies are discussed as well as the new understanding of the role of information in finance. The chapter concludes with a three-pronged strategy for building rural financial markets based on the new paradigm: creating the policy environment, building financial infrastructure, and institutional development.

The first section of Chapter IV traces the history of rural finance in Asia since the 1970s and summarizes the current status. It begins with a description of the perspective of rural finance held at the time of the previous rural Asia studies conducted by ADB in the 1960s and 1970s. It discusses why directed credit may have made a more positive contribution in some Asian countries than elsewhere, but also describes how financial problems contributed to the financial and economic crisis in Asia that began in 1997. The section ends with the status of rural finance in the region today. Three financial institutions in the region have been identified as flagship institutions because of their relatively good performance compared to most rural financial institutions in developing countries. The second section summarizes the experience of these flagship institutions: the Bank for Agriculture and Agricultural Cooperatives in

Thailand, the unit desa system of Bank Rakyat Indonesia, and the Grameen Bank in Bangladesh. The key factors that determined their relative success are identified.

Chapter V summarizes the key findings of the study and identifies priority actions to be taken to strengthen rural financial markets in Asia. It describes some of the special problems that complicate the task and discusses how the financial crisis may influence the process. It identifies the key policy areas that demand attention, the financial infrastructure that is weak or missing, and the need for institutional development, especially regarding failing institutions and microfinance organizations. Major issues for donors are identified. The chapter ends with a statement of the financial market challenges the region faces as it enters the twenty-first century.

The detailed case studies follow a similar outline, but the details presented vary because of differences in the available information. The studies explain the general strategy that each country has followed in its financial sector and how the rural sector has been treated in term of policies and institutions. To the extent possible, information is presented on the nature of formal and informal rural financial transactions. The evolution of microfinance is discussed, describing its expanding role in making small loans to farm and nonfarm enterprises. The outreach and sustainability of financial institutions are emphasized because of the poor performance of many countries in these key performance measures. Recommendations for improvements in rural financial markets are presented at the end of each country study.

II Economic Transformation and Rural Financial Markets in Asia

R ural Asia has undergone a fundamental economic transformation during the past three decades. Economic growth rates have been particularly high in East and Southeast Asia, but even the slower growing countries have made progress. Growth has been accompanied by a rapid structural transformation of the rural economy, reflected in a decline in the relative importance of agriculture, increased use of sophisticated capital inputs in agricultural production, a greater specialization in production on large farms while small farms diversified their income sources, an explosion in the growth of rural cities and towns, and the emergence of a heterogeneous, rural nonfarm economy.

These changes created major new opportunities for rural financial markets and increased the demand for financial services. Here a brief summary of these changes is provided, drawing heavily on the empirical evidence presented in a companion volume (Rosegrant and Hazell, 1999), and the effect on financial markets of the changes is discussed. The role of finance in economic development is discussed in more detail in Chapter III and detailed accounts of how rural financial markets responded to these opportunities are presented in the six case studies.

THE ECONOMIC TRANSFORMATION OF ASIA

Before the financial and economic crisis that began in 1997, many Asian economies recorded spectacular growth. The rapidly growing economies of the PRC, Indonesia, Republic of Korea, Malaysia, and Thailand experienced annual GDP growth rates of 5 to 10 percent over the entire period of 1967 to 1995 (Rosegrant and Hazell, 1999). The South Asian countries of Bangladesh, India, Nepal, Pakistan, and Sri Lanka grew at rates in the 3 to 5 percent range. Myanmar and the Philippines were in the slow growth category of less than 3 percent per annum. With high growth rates, many Asian economies were able to generate substantial increases in per capita income.

Various explanations have been given for the rapid growth rates achieved by Asian countries, but there is little consensus among the analysts. Some analysts focus on the sound macroeconomic policies followed by East Asian economies, which had relatively small fiscal deficits, moderate inflation rates, realistic exchange rates, and stable real interest rates. Market-oriented policies and openness to international trade also characterize these countries, while a number of slower growing economies followed a more protectionist policy framework. Industrial policies in Japan, Republic of Korea, and Taipei,China, particularly concerning credit and exports, contributed to rapid and equitable growth, but questions have been raised about the transferability of this model to other economies. Investments in education and efficient bureaucracies have been identified as important in some economies, but the recent financial and economic crisis in Asia revealed large institutional weaknesses in corporate and financial governance.

STRUCTURAL TRANSFORMATION AND THE ROLE OF AGRICULTURE

Economic development involves a fundamental structural transformation of the economy. The size of the nonagricultural sector rises relative to that of the agricultural sector, agricultural employment declines relative to nonagricultural employment, and expenditures on agricultural products fall relative to products and services produced by the industrial and service sectors. These changes occur because of the low income elasticity of demand for food and other products produced in agriculture, and because of specialization, in which many economic functions carried out by farm households in the countryside are transferred to specialist producers in towns (Tomich, Kilby, and Johnston, 1995).

Asian agriculture has contributed to the structural transformation process in several ways (Rosegrant and Hazell, 1999). First, as agricultural incomes rose, demand increased for products and services produced in the nonfarm sector. Second, through savings and taxation, large amounts of capital were transferred from the agricultural sector to finance the nonagricultural sector. Third, agricultural growth contributed to the emergence of the agro-industry sector, rural manufacturing, and the rural nonfarm economy. Fourth, productivity increases permitted the release of agricultural labor to the emerging rural nonfarm economy and urban industries. Fifth, agricultural growth generated foreign exchange, through increased exports or reduced imports, needed for industrialization.

Agriculture had to undergo a productivity revolution to increase output and efficiency in order to perform these functions successfully. The countries most successful in stimulating agricultural growth were those that promoted technological change, improved rural infrastructure, and employed a set of policies that did not overly tax or discriminate against the agricultural sector. Economies with massive state intervention, weak infrastructure, or with more inward- than outward-looking policies were least successful in achieving an agricultural revolution to stimulate a broader economic transformation.

The decline in the relative size of agriculture has been especially rapid in some Asian countries. For example, the share of agriculture value added in total GDP in the Republic of Korea fell from 34 percent in 1966 to about 6.5 percent in 1995 (Rosegrant and Hazell, 1999). In the same period, the agriculture share fell dramatically from 51 to 17 percent in Indonesia, from 33 to 11 percent in Thailand, and from 28 to 13 percent in

Malaysia. In slower growing countries, the declines were from 45 to 28 percent in India, 37 to 26 percent in Pakistan, and 26 to 22 percent in the Philippines. In Myanmar, the agricultural share in GDP actually rose during the same period.

There has also been a significant decline in agricultural labor relative to the total labor force. The agricultural labor share in the Republic of Korea fell from 54 percent in 1966 to 14 percent in 1995, and from 58 to 23 percent in Malaysia in the same period. In 1995, the agricultural labor share in Indonesia, Pakistan, the Philippines, and Sri Lanka was relatively high at approximately 40 to 50 percent. It was 60 to 70 percent in Bangladesh, PRC, India, and Thailand, and over 70 percent in Myanmar and Nepal.

The fact that the agricultural labor share in the economy is higher than the agricultural output share implies lower per capita incomes in agriculture than in the nonagricultural sector. One way that many Asian farm households have narrowed this gap is to engage in multiple economic activities combining nonfarm activities with farm work. The emergence of a dynamic rural nonfarm economy has facilitated this process.

THE EMERGENCE OF RURAL NONFARM ACTIVITIES: ONE FOOT ON THE FARM AND ONE IN TOWN

The specialization of economic functions that occurred as part of the structural transformation created an explosion in rural nonfarm activities. Specialized nonfarm firms have emerged to supply seeds, fertilizers, foods, household utensils, clothing, and other goods previously made on farms. Blacksmith and equipment repair shops produce and repair farm machines and implements. Transport and trade services increase in importance as marketable surpluses rise on farms. Moreover, some of these rural firms produce goods sold in urban and export markets.

This growth of the rural nonfarm sector has often been overlooked by policymakers but its importance is becoming more widely recognized through the results of much new research (e.g. Dorosh, Haggblade, and Hazell, 1998; Hazell and Reardon, 1998; Reardon, et al., 1998). The nonfarm economy in Asia is now reported to account for 40 to 60 percent of total national employment and 20 to 50 percent of total rural employment (Rosegrant and Hazell, 1999). Income data from household surveys reveal that nonfarm activities are even more important than suggested by the employment data because the income estimates include some nonfarm work preformed by farm households. Some members of farm families engage in nonfarm enterprises on the farm (e.g. food processing, weaving, and basketry), while others find seasonal and part-time employment in towns. Furthermore, the nonfarm income share is rising, especially for poorer rural households. Many rural landless or near landless households rely on nonfarm earnings, including both low-investment manufacturing and service activities, and unskilled farm and nonfarm wage labor. Often nonfarm work generates earnings during off-peak farm seasons so it contributes to income stabilization and consumption smoothing over the year.

Farm households also export labor to urban centers for full-time and seasonal employment. Some of these persons become overseas workers and send large amounts of remittances to households on farms and in small towns to help sustain household consumption and contribute to onfarm investments. These income flows and remittances are especially important in rural areas that lack insurance and financial markets.

THE COMMERCIALIZATION OF AGRICULTURE

The green-revolution technologies, involving the introduction in the late 1960s of high-yielding varieties of wheat and rice, application of chemical fertilizers and modern pest control methods, coupled with increased capital investments on farms and in institutional infrastructure, fueled the structural transformation of rural areas. The new technologies expanded agricultural production and induced demand for fertilizers, chemicals, and other purchased inputs. The commercialization of production had two impacts. First, the rise in marketable surpluses led to increased marketing of agricultural inputs and outputs. Cash incomes rose for many farm households, market exchanges substituted for barter, and the rise in use of money as the medium of exchange helped integrate the rural with the urban economy. Second, decisions about product choice and input use evolved from a subsistence to a profit maximization orientation (Pingali and Rosegrant, 1995). On some farms, integrated farming systems were replaced with more specialized crop and livestock enterprises. Highly specialized large-scale plantation systems have been developed for fruit, sugar, tea, and rubber. Smaller farms combine farm and nonfarm enterprises to increase incomes and diversify their income sources.

Structural transformation has also been accompanied by an evolution in food production systems (Table II.1). At low levels of economic development, most farms produce for subsistence, with the exception of export crops produced on plantations. Food self-sufficiency is the farmer's primary objective, most inputs (labor, seeds, manure) are nontradable, and a wide range of diversified products is produced. Income is derived largely from agricultural sources but, because production is low and mostly consumed, little cash income is generated.

With new biological technologies, production rises and marketable surpluses begin to emerge, particularly in regions with better infrastructure. Semi-commercial farms regularly produce surpluses and use a mix of tradable and nontradable inputs. Some specialization in production occurs at this stage, and farm households begin to earn larger amounts of nonagricultural incomes from onfarm sources (e.g. wage labor for other more specialized farms) and nonfarm sources. Semi-commercial farms engage in many cash transactions. The last group of farms is fully commercialized; they operate almost exclusively in the market economy, and employ the full range of financial instruments to facilitate transactions of goods and services.

Table II.1: Characteristics of Food Production Systems with
Increasing Commercialization

Level of market orientation	Farmer's objective	Sources of inputs	Product mix	Household income sources
Subsistence systems	Food self-sufficiency	Household-generated (nontraded) inputs	Wide range	Predominantly agricultural
Semi-commercial systems	Surplus generation	Mix of traded and nontraded inputs	Moderately specialized	Agricultural and nonagricultural
Commercial systems	Profit maximization	Predominantly traded inputs	Highly specialized	Predominantly nonagricultural

Source: Pingali and Rosegrant (1995).

MARKETS AND THE CRITICAL ROLE OF FINANCE

The Emergence of Markets

The structural transformation process requires supportive institutions. Markets are required in order to enable a greater division of labor, by which a producer specializes in one activity and trades with others who have different specializations. Markets integrate these specialized producers and consumers, allowing them to engage in transactions involving an increasingly heterogeneous set of goods and services produced across space and time. As structural transformation begins to occur, markets for land, labor, capital, and finance emerge, multiply in number, and become more complex in response to the greater variety of goods and services demanded. Markets with varying degrees of efficiency have emerged in the developing market economies of Asia. The transition economies in the region, however, are experiencing difficulties in creating markets and supportive institutions such that agriculture is constrained in its ability to contribute to economic growth. Therefore, the transformation process is retarded. In the extreme, there are producers in the transition economies who have actually reverted to subsistence production and barter exchanges.

The Role of Finance

The theoretical literature on finance describes why financial contracts, markets, and institutions emerge in a market economy and contribute to economic growth. Levine (1997) summarized this comprehensive literature. The costs of acquiring information[1] and making transactions create incentives for the emergence of financial markets and institutions. The financial system has the primary role of facilitating the allocation of resources across space and time in an uncertain environment. This primary role consists of five basic functions: ameliatoring risk, allocating resources, monitoring managers and exerting corporate control, mobilizing savings, and facilitating the exchange of goods and services. When these functions are performed well, they contribute to economic growth through two channels: capital accumulation and technological innovation (Figure II.1). The emergence of financial systems, and especially banking can, therefore, be expected to influence the speed and pattern of capital accumulation and technological innovation in rural areas. The empirical question concerns whether or not financial markets have contributed to or retarded economic growth in rural Asia.

Policymaker Perceptions about Rural Finance

Policymakers have long perceived the potentially important role for credit in agriculture. The authors of the Asian Development Bank (ADB) study on rural Asia in 1977 (ADB, 1978, p. 91) noted that the development of credit programs up

---

[1] The crucial role of information in contributing to efficient financial markets is discussed in Chapter III.

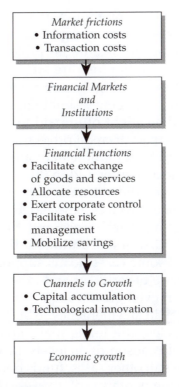

Source: Adapted from Levine (1997).

Figure II.1: A Theoretical View of Finance and Growth

to that time reflected, first, the concern for accelerating agricultural (especially food) production; second, the growth potential of agriculture by widespread adoption of high-yielding varieties and, third, recognition of the role of credit in the development of small farm agriculture

Many Asian policymakers at that time did not believe that a farmer's ability to self-finance investments would lead to a socially optimum rate of growth. They perceived that the potential of the green revolution would not be realized unless farmers could access an elastic supply of funds at more reasonable interest rates than available from informal sources. These views provided the rationale used by many Asian countries to develop targeted and subsidized agricultural credit programs along with strong support for input- and output-marketing projects to encourage the adoption of green-revolution technologies. The Bimas project in Indonesia and Masagana 99 in the Philippines are archetypal models of this strategy. They provided highly subsidized loans to farmers who agreed to adopt the new technologies; later, both projects collapsed under the weight of unpaid loans.

The precise impact of credit projects is difficult to measure and the results of impact studies are ambiguous, as will be discussed in the next chapter and in the case studies. While it is fairly clear that credit did not make as important a contribution to technological change as was expected, the policies employed to push banking into rural areas and the large amount of subsidized funds disbursed undoubtedly had diverse and diffuse results. In some cases, loans supposedly borrowed to finance the purchase of fertilizer and other production inputs may have made an even greater impact because the borrower diverted the money in an emergency to buy medicine for a sick child. In other cases, the loans may have helped families maintain household consumption levels during the lean season before harvest. In still other cases, funds borrowed for farming leaked into financing nonfarm enterprises. The point is not that the credit had no impact, but rather that the Asian financial systems could have played an even more important role if the financial policies had focused less on subsidized loans for specific purposes. Moreover, the economic transformation might have evolved in a more equitable fashion. The existence of subsidized credit institutions discouraged the emergence of market-based institutions in rural areas and contributed to the disparity between households and firms that gained access to formal finance and those that were denied access.

The following chapters will explain how the well-intentioned credit projects did not produce the desired results. The projects had less impact on adoption of the new technologies than expected, especially for farmers who were convinced about the expected profitability of adoption and used self-finance or informal loans to finance technological change. However, the projects seriously impaired the banks, cooperatives, and specialized agricultural development banks that tried to implement them. Moreover, the strategy employed was usually fundamentally flawed because it failed to provide savings, insurance, money transfer, and other financial services demanded by farmers.[2] Policymakers did not fully understand the concept of a financial market and the multiple ways it contributes to economic growth, and pursued a strategy excessively oriented towards providing cheap loans to farmers.[3]

Finance and Welfare Outcomes

The way financial markets perform can be an important determinant of the welfare outcome of increased commercialization in agriculture (von Braun, 1995). First, contrary to their intent, credit policies have often been biased against the poor. For example, subsidized interest rates, supposedly designed to help the poor, actually benefit the rich who successfully compete to obtain the scarce funds (Gonzalez-Vega, 1984). If access to credit really accelerates adoption of technology, then the late adopters who face credit constraints may face lower profits and miss most of the benefits of the new technology.

Second, smallholders who adopt the new commercial orientation often maintain some low-return subsistence food production as insurance in a risky environment. The poor are most likely to adopt this strategy. The development of sustainable financial institutions may encourage these producers to abandon this strategy, if they are assured of borrowing for consumption expenditures in the event of crop

---

[2] A comprehensive review of the literature on donor and government experience with programs and policies to expand agricultural credit and marketing services in low-income countries can be found in Meyer and Larson (1997).

[3] However, Adams (1988a) noted that several Asian countries employed more of a financial intermediation approach to finance and mobilized more rural savings than many other low-income countries.

failure. Moreover, farmers may choose to hold their borrowing capacity with a reliable financial institution in reserve and allocate their own resources to more risky and more profitable enterprises, knowing that credit will be available if needed (Zeller et al., 1997).

Third, the rural financial system can improve the ability of households to save and build up productive assets. This is particularly true where agricultural commercialization leads to the receipt of large payments of cash a few times during a year. Through efficient savings and borrowing opportunities, households can smooth their cash flows (Meyer and Alicbusan, 1984); resources that are surplus for one household at one point in time in one location can be intermediated to another household in another location that faces a deficit in desired funds. The problem is that most government credit projects ignored the savings side of financial intermediation and did not facilitate the accumulation of rural savings.

Rural financial markets can also be important in shaping the emergence and evolution of nonfarm enterprises (Meyer, 1999). However, most of the targeted agricultural credit programs were restricted to farm producers and some even prevented financial institutions from serving nonfarm enterprises. This meant that liquidity-constrained enterprises were limited to their own resources, to informal finance, or to borrowed funds diverted from other purposes. In these situations, firms that supply farm inputs or processing services and market farm outputs may be constrained in offering efficient service. Suppliers' credit and advance payments provided by larger urban firms may reduce the severity of this problem, but these arrangements that tie credit to marketing may also limit competition, resulting in higher costs and lower prices for farmers.

RURAL FINANCIAL MARKET POLICIES IN ASIA

The conclusion of this analysis is that economic growth in rural Asia during the past two or three decades has often occurred in spite of, rather than because of, rural financial policies. In fact, financial policies may have distorted economic outcomes and contributed to some of the inter- and intra-regional inequalities in income and wealth observed between and within countries in the region.

We analyze in the following chapters how views concerning rural finance have evolved, especially during the 1980s and 1990s. Financial policies have improved in some countries, especially Indonesia and Thailand, since the ADB's 1977 survey (ADB, 1978). Unfortunately, many countries, especially in South Asia and in the transition economies, are still a long way from having strong and viable market-based financial institutions. Many countries still cling to the old paradigm of directed and subsidized farm credit.

The following chapters will demonstrate how appropriate financial market policies contribute to structural transformation and agricultural growth. They will also show how growth in rural areas stimulates the demand for financial services. The role of the State is also analyzed. On the one hand, the appropriate role for government is to create a conducive environment in which competitive financial institutions can emerge, build financial infrastructure, and support institutional development. Among other things, this means macroeconomic stability, reasonably low levels of inflation, procedures to enforce contracts, the protection of property rights, and a regulatory and supervisory system to ensure prudent financial operations. On the other hand, governments must avoid the temptation of inappropriately using financial institutions for social policies such as subsidizing particular economic activities or groups within society or alleviating social problems following major conflicts or disasters. Financial market interventions are a poor second-best approach for solving important social problems that require direct policies to encourage human capital formation and improve access to productive assets. A new paradigm of financial market development has emerged to substitute for the largely failed directed credit approach to rural finance. It involves a three-pronged framework for building financial markets as discussed in the next chapter.

III Development of Rural Financial Markets

This chapter presents a discussion of why the development of viable and efficient rural financial markets is important for rural Asia, summarizes major issues about government involvement in creating these markets, and presents an improved strategy for developing financial markets and institutions. The development of rural finance is placed in the broader perspective of financial markets. The chapter also provides a framework for analyzing the Asian approach to promoting rural finance discussed in the next chapter, for organizing the six country studies presented in Part B, and for formulating the recommendations presented in Chapter V.

The chapter consists of three main sections. The first section contains a discussion about the relationships between economic development and the financial sector. The financial system is defined and the special challenges of providing financial services in rural areas are identified. Government intervention in financial markets is discussed in the second section. Some of the key debates about the appropriate role of government are highlighted, including the paradigm shift that has occurred in the approach advocated for developing rural finance. The section also briefly describes how new thinking about knowledge and information is contributing to the debate about the appropriate role of the State and donors in the development of financial markets. A three-pronged framework for building rural financial markets is introduced in the third section; it includes creating the policy environment, building financial infrastructure, and developing institutions. The topic of developing institutions includes one subsection that

summarizes lessons learned from microfinance, and another
that deals with the problematic issue of agricultural
development banks. These two topics are especially relevant
for several Asian countries.

THE FINANCIAL SYSTEM AND ECONOMIC DEVELOPMENT

Finance and Economic Development

The efficient functioning of markets affects the pace, speed,
and pattern of economic development. Financial institutions–
formal, semi-formal, and informal–represent an essential part
of the institutional infrastructure required for an efficient market
economy. Financial systems provide vital services in an economy
as noted earlier (Levine, 1997; World Bank, 1989). They provide
payment services; they mobilize savings and allocate credit;
and they price, pool, and trade risks. In this way they make it
cheaper and less risky to trade goods and services and to borrow
and lend. Without finance, economies would be reduced to the
inefficiency of barter. Investors would be limited to self-
financing their investments. Households with surpluses, but
without good investment alternatives, would be forced to store
their savings under the mattress or hold them in less productive
assets. Limited access to financial services due to inefficient
financial markets constrains economic development (Fry, 1988).
For these reasons, governments and donors have devoted vast
resources to developing financial systems in low-income
countries during the past three decades.

There has been considerable debate about the role of
financial markets and economic growth, and the appropriate
role of the State in regulating financial systems. Shaw (1973)
and McKinnon (1973) pioneered the view that repressed
financial systems constrain economic growth. Countries that
have held interest rates at artificially low real rates were found
to experience lower growth rates than those that have adopted

market rates (World Bank, 1989). Although competing views still exist, the preponderance of theoretical and empirical evidence today firmly suggests a positive relationship between financial development and economic growth (Levine, 1997). In recent years, the debate has increasingly focused on what the State should and should not do, and the impact of financial policies in the specific case of the "East Asian Miracle". One view argues that suspected market failures are a rationale for government intervention to improve access to credit (Stiglitz, 1992). Another view, however, is that the state of empirical evidence makes it difficult, if not impossible, to determine situations in which intervention can be unequivocally prescribed and its consequences fully anticipated (Besley, 1994).

Rural Development and the Demand for Financial Services

Financial services are important for the development of rural areas. Rural transformation provides opportunities for investments in farm enterprises. Technological changes often require complementary investments that increase demand for working and investment capital. Some of this demand is self-financed, some is serviced by informal sources, but still others require longer-term loans provided by formal institutions. Supplying reasonably priced loans, therefore, can speed the adoption of technology, expand the production of food supplies, and increase farm incomes. When a reliable supply of formal finance is established, farmers may alter their perceptions about the risks of investing. They may choose to invest more of their own funds knowing that their unused borrowing capacity will be available to meet future cash needs (Zeller et al., 1997).

A wide variety of rural nonfarm enterprises also arises in response to new opportunities and demands for new goods and services that emerge with economic transformation (Rosegrant and Hazell, 1999). In the absence of financial services, income from nonfarm enterprises may provide funds for farm investments, but they also generate a demand for loanable funds that cannot always be met by savings or informal finance (Meyer, 1999). Taken together, farm and nonfarm enterprises with their diverse economic activities comprise a large and heterogeneous pool of potential customers for formal loans.

A safe and reliable place for savings is another important but largely overlooked financial service demanded in rural areas (Vogel, 1984). The widespread use of informal finance, self-help and village-level savings groups, and funeral funds is evidence of demand for savings services. All rural households must save; otherwise they would not survive seasons of the year when cash is in short supply or in bad years when crops fail and livestock die. They must also save for unexpected family emergencies of illnesses and death. Saving to make lumpy investments is also important. A recent study showed how access to loans and remunerative ways to save influenced the decision of poor farmers in India to undertake irreversible investments in digging wells for irrigation (Fafchamps and Pender, 1997).

Insurance markets do not exist in most developing countries so rural households employ a variety of strategies to cope with risks and smooth consumption over time (Zeller et al., 1997). Some households acquire assets that produce uncorrelated returns, and hold physical assets in the form of livestock that are easy to liquidate. But such liquidations may jeopardize the ability of households to recover after the emergency passes. Other households use risk-reducing strategies such as pesticides or engage in multiple and diverse income-earning enterprises. Those with access to financial services, however, have additional options of holding financial savings and borrowing in times of emergencies. As noted in Thailand, risk pooling occurs in villages through informal borrowing and lending (Townsend, 1995), but these traditional methods cannot easily accommodate large shocks, such as occurs with a major drought or a disease epidemic that simultaneously affects everyone in the village.

Another financial service demanded in rural areas is a safe and reliable method to transfer remittances. Transfers by family members who have emigrated are an important source of income for many small farm households. For example, a survey in poor Pakistani villages revealed that internal and external remittances represented 9 to 18 percent of annual per capita income over a five-year period in the late 1980s. They made an important contribution to rural investments (Richard Adams, 1998). It was estimated that between 1977 and 1986, Bangladesh earned about $3.3 billion[1] in foreign exchange through remittances, an amount equal to about 5.6 percent of GDP, 43 percent of the foreign aid received, and 74 percent of the country's export earnings. About three quarters of this total came from Middle Eastern countries where thousands of Bangladeshi workers were employed. The main informal method of sending money into the country is through the *hundi* system. The migrant overseas gives the foreign exchange to a hundi agent with an associate in Bangladesh who gives the equivalent amount in taka to the specified recipient. This informal arrangement is attractive because a higher exchange rate is obtained, and the recipient avoids the confusion and poor service of the banks and the potential fraud in banks and post offices. The most frequent uses of the remittances were reported as constructing housing and buying land (Bakht and Mahmood, 1988).

The users of financial services in rural areas are heterogeneous and include farm households, plantations, agribusinesses, rural nonfarm enterprises, and landless workers. Households and firms of all income and wealth levels demand financial services. Their demand includes short-term working capital and long-term investment loans, small quickly disbursed loans for emergencies, consumption loans, secure places to hold deposits, and efficient banking mechanisms to transfer payments and remittances.

Farm households employ a variety of methods to manage their cash inflows and outflows over time (Meyer and Alicbusan, 1984). Some have financial surpluses just at the

---

[1] $ means US$ throughout the text.

time that others face deficits. This provides opportunities for financial intermediation within rural areas in spite of apparent similarities in the seasonality of farm enterprises. The covariance of incomes earned on some farms, however, and a local financial institution's vulnerability to the systemic risks that farmers face can impede financial intermediation (Binswanger and McIntire, 1987).

The Structure of the Financial System

The financial system consists of many institutions, instruments, and markets (World Bank, 1989) including formal, semi-informal and informal financial arrangements and institutions. In rural Asia formal financial institutions include commercial banks, development banks, specialized savings banks, postal savings systems, cooperative banks, and unit and regional rural banks. Semi-formal financial systems are composed of farmers' associations, credit cooperatives, credit unions, village banks, self-help groups, integrated rural development programs, and nongovernmental organization (NGO) financial programs. Communal and savings clubs, mutual aid societies, rotating savings and credit associations (RoSCAs), input suppliers, storekeepers, trader/farmer/agent lenders, moneylenders, and friends and relatives comprise a heterogeneous category referred to as informal finance (Meyer and Nagarajan, 1992). In financial markets, specialized institutions such as savings banks that only mobilize deposits co-exist with purely credit-dispensing government and NGO programs, full service banks, member-owned cooperatives and credit unions, and informal sources.

The suppliers and users of financial services come together in markets and are matched through various types of instruments, the most frequent being loans and deposits. While most formal lenders make only short-term loans for production purposes (for agricultural and nonfarm activities), a few also experiment with consumption and term loans. Most financial NGOs specialize in making short-term loans that can be used by the borrowers for any purpose. The majority of traditional banks provide only collateral-based loans but some banks and most NGOs offer innovative noncollateral-based loans.

Markets are often segmented, with some sources specializing in offering limited instruments to specific types of clients (e.g., Yadav, Otsuka, and David, 1992; Nagarajan, Meyer, and Hushak, 1995). Users of services may be able to meet all their demands from one source, but frequently more than one source is used. Formal loans generally carry lower interest rates but impose higher transaction costs than informal sources, such that borrowers in rural Asia often seek large formal production loans and small informal loans for consumption and emergencies. The formal and informal systems are linked when a trader borrows from a bank and on-lends to producers as contract farmers, or when a self-help group or NGO collects savings in a village and deposits them in a neighboring bank.

Several countries are attempting to exploit the comparative advantage of each type of finance by strengthening the links between them. For example, the case studies presented later describe German-funded projects designed to link self-help groups and NGOs with formal financial institutions. Because of information problems and high transaction costs, the residents of specific geographic areas may have access to only a small number of suppliers of services. Remote areas with poor transportation may lack access to formal financial institutions. This is why Asian policymakers have tried to induce banks into broadening their rural outreach, and why many NGOs target households with little or no access to formal finance.

A major contentious issue has been the extent to which informal loans, especially from moneylenders, are exploitative. The term usurious interest rates is often used with respect to informal finance, but there is relatively little firm evidence to evaluate whether or not the observed high informal lending rates exceed the costs and risks of lending. Several studies have noted that a large number of moneylenders operate in a market and each makes a fairly small number of loans (e.g., Aleem, 1993). The evidence of many lenders has often been used to argue that competitive conditions exist such that interest rates, although high, reflect costs. The number of lenders in itself does not conclusively demonstrate contestable markets, however, because of market segmentation. Any given borrower may be limited to only a few informal lenders who have the liquidity and the information about a client to make a loan (Esguerra, Nagarajan, and Meyer, 1991).

The Costs and Risks of Providing Financial Services

The provision of financial services consumes resources in the economy. Building an efficient financial system is expensive and supplying services imposes costs on both providers and users. The costs of developing the formal financial system involve the direct costs of building, equipping, and staffing networks of banks, cooperatives, and financial institutions. There are also important indirect costs in developing and operating courts, legal systems, and regulatory and supervisory bodies, as well as the communication, information, and transportation systems needed within banking networks, and between banks, clients, and supervisory authorities.

Transaction Costs for Providers and Users

Finance is an information-intensive industry. Providing services requires significant expense in collecting, processing, storing, and manipulating vast amounts of information on clients, loans, and savings accounts. Institutions must learn how to use this information effectively to determine what services to provide, to whom, and at what price. They must design, monitor, and enforce financial contracts, and earn enough income to cover the costs of staff, the use of capital, taxes, adhering to regulations, and the cost of loan losses (World Bank, 1989). Formal institutions must systematically collect and evaluate information needed for screening clients, making loan decisions, and monitoring borrower performance, and they must conform to rules set by owners, directors, and regulators.

Informal rural moneylenders and traders have an advantage because they can access local information about their clients efficiently through living and working in villages. They have the freedom to decide whom to serve or not serve without being held accountable to others.

The users of financial services also bear transaction costs including the value of time lost, travel costs, and other noninterest costs in getting and repaying loans and making deposits. Borrowers often have to visit distant bank offices to apply for loans, to provide documents and information demanded by the lender, and to make payments. Likewise, depositors incur travel costs and the opportunity cost of time in waiting to deposit and withdraw funds. Financial institutions have experimented with different methods to reduce costs. For example, Viet Nam uses mobile banking and several countries are experimenting with making loans through lines of credit. Many NGOs make group rather than individual loans to reduce costs.

Surveys in several developing countries reveal that rural formal loans cost borrowers 1 to 30 percent of the loan amount in transaction costs (Meyer and Cuevas, 1992). The largest percentages were found for small loans in Bangladesh. Underdeveloped support institutions, financial regulations, small institutions, small loan sizes, and lack of innovation contribute to these costs. One study found that the high reporting requirements for donor funds raised the transaction costs to lenders and borrowers (Cuevas and Graham, 1984). Due to high transaction costs, borrowers tend to use informal sources for small consumption loans even though the interest rates may be higher than for formal loans.

Risks of Providing and Using Financial Services

Providers and users of financial services face multiple risks that increase costs. Lenders face the credit risk that borrowers may default. They face price risks due to unexpected changes in interest rates and foreign exchange risks if they have liabilities in foreign currencies. There is systemic risk in which the default of one or a few large borrowers may endanger the whole financial system (World Bank, 1989). The current financial and economic crisis in Asia illustrates the demonstration-effect risk in which investors question the risk of doing business in one country due to problems in another. Localized lenders with portfolios concentrated in small geographic rural areas are exposed to covariant income risk: that their clients will be simultaneously affected by a local drought or disease epidemic. Formal financial institutions with broader coverage have greater capacity to withstand the effects of highly localized shocks and can provide the liquidity needed by affected households and firms for recovery.

Information asymmetries create lending risks because borrowers have more information about their projects and intentions than do lenders (Stiglitz and Weiss, 1981). Lenders attempt to reduce credit risk by improving their expertise in collecting and analyzing information about borrowers and their projects. The use of loan collateral is the most common method for reducing credit risks. This does not work efficiently in countries such as Bangladesh, however, where many intended clients do not have acceptable collateral, and expensive and time-consuming legal procedures prevent effective realization of legal claims on collateral. Therefore, the well-known Grameen Bank and many NGOs in Bangladesh use a group-liability lending technology to induce borrowers to use their local information to screen persons selected into the groups and to apply peer pressure to encourage delinquent members to repay.

The legal constraints that impede financial transactions in developing and transition economies are just beginning to be understood. Laws on movable collateral, for example, impede businesses from using machinery inventories as collateral for loans. Accounts receivable are also not acceptable collateral in some countries. This constrains the ability of equipment dealers to borrow for their businesses and provide suppliers' credits to their clients (Fleisig, 1995). The indirect channel of linking financial institutions to small borrowers is broken, access to credit is restricted, and interest rates are pushed upward.

Lenders typically raise interest rates to cover risks, but there are several limitations to this approach. Some countries have usury laws that prohibit setting rates high enough to cover the costs of serving the riskiest clients. For example, India imposes a ceiling of a 4-percent nominal interest rate on loans made to the weaker segments of the population, and commercial banks are required to make one percent of their total priority sector loans to those segments. In the extreme case, raising rates can be self-defeating because of adverse selection: high rates may discourage the more creditworthy customers from borrowing, leaving the lender with the most risky clients. Furthermore, there is the risk of moral hazard: clients may take on riskier projects to cover high interest costs (World Bank, 1989). There may be social resistance to charging higher rates for poorer clients to cover the transaction costs and risks of servicing their small loans and deposit accounts. For example, NGOs in Pakistan and other countries that oppose high interest rates use hidden fees to help cover their lending costs.

Financial savings also involve risks. Financial institutions face a potential liquidity mismatch when mobilizing short-term savings to make longer-term loans. They face potential bank runs when the liquidity problems of one institution cause panic among savers who then demand withdrawals from other institutions, as occurred recently during the financial and economic crisis in Asia. Savers face the potential loss of savings in uninsured institutions. Even if deposits are insured, savers may have to wait long periods before actually receiving their funds when an institution fails. The potential risk of poor people losing savings is a major policy issue in Bangladesh and other countries where unregulated NGOs engage in aggressive savings mobilization. Small localized institutions have a disadvantage compared to larger ones with more dispersed networks because, in the event of a localized problem such as drought, savers will demand to withdraw funds just at the time that borrowers want to borrow (Binswanger and McIntire, 1987).

Governments can adopt measures to reduce information costs and lending risks. For example, strengthening the accounting and auditing requirements improves the quality of information about large firms. Creating credit bureaus facilitates the exchange of information about borrowers. Investments in transportation and communication infrastructure reduce the costs of acquiring and sharing information. Forecasting information about commodity prices and market opportunities is especially helpful to agricultural lenders who have to project debt repayment capacity of farm borrowers. Improved prudential regulation and supervision of financial institutions reduces risks to depositors and systemic risks for the entire financial system. Loan guarantee schemes are frequently created to reduce lending risks but, as seen in India and the Philippines, they often have not worked well in reducing risks and have been sustained only through massive subsidies (Meyer and Nagarajan, 1996). Only in specific circumstances can guarantee schemes be expected to be effective in expanding rural lending (Gudger, 1998).

High Costs and Risks in Rural Areas

Rural areas present especially difficult and costly problems for the provision of financial services (FAO/GTZ, 1998). Rural bank clients are more dispersed than urban clients and often demand relatively small loans and savings accounts, so per unit transaction costs are high for financial institutions. Information costs for providers and users are higher because transportation and communication infrastructure is usually less well developed. Agricultural loans are often considered inherently risky because of production and marketing risks. Moreover, the returns on farm investments are often low because of urban-oriented agricultural policies. Loan repayment by farmers may be contingent on the borrowers' first meeting household consumption requirements. Many potential clients have little acceptable loan collateral, and property rights to mortgaged land may be uncertain and hard to enforce. Although farm households engage in a variety of enterprises, the concentration of crops and livestock in specific geographic locations results in high covariance of household incomes that makes localized institutions vulnerable to local disasters.

Recognition of these costs and risks provides a rationale for governments and donors to intervene in rural financial markets. This intervention, however, has often focused on the symptoms of the problems rather than the underlying causes. Most governments have underestimated the difficulties, costs, and risks of supplying rural financial services. Moreover, as noted in the case studies, politicians have used policy interventions as a way to appeal to voters. This situation is most obvious in the Bangladesh and India case studies.

EVOLUTION IN POLICIES AND APPROACHES TO RURAL FINANCE: MOVING FROM MANDATES TO MARKETS

Government Intervention in Financial Markets

Governments intervene several ways in financial markets. Historically, they have controlled the means of payment to guarantee soundness and collect seigniorage[2] (World Bank, 1989). More recently, they have attempted to influence credit allocation, the subject of the next section. Their primary concern has often been to ensure prudent behavior by banks. The impact of bank failure is especially important in developing countries because there are few alternative sources of finance for firms and households. Financial crises can occur when regulation fails, such as happened in the recent financial and economic crisis in Asia. Depositors lose confidence in the banking system in such circumstances so governments introduce deposit insurance and lender-of-last-resort facilities, and bail out failed institutions to prevent bank runs, reduce depositor losses, and restore confidence in the banking system. For example, due to a lack of confidence in banks during the crisis that began in 1997, Indonesians shifted deposits to State and foreign banks

---

[2] This refers to the profits earned by issuing currency.

that were perceived to be stronger (McLeod, 1998). The government eventually agreed to protect all depositors to calm the market.

Governments influence the growth in money supply and interest rates as part of overall macroeconomic management. Prudential regulation and supervision procedures are implemented to prevent fraud and excessive risk taking by financial institutions. These include minimum capital requirements, auditing and reporting requirements, and portfolio restrictions. The difficult task of regulation is one of balancing efficiency and innovation, which require freedom to act, and stability, which requires some regulation. A recent concern is the moral hazard problem that can occur when banks are not allowed to fail. If bank owners and managers are not required to pay for their mistakes, they may be induced to undertake risky investments in the future knowing that the government or an international agency will cover their losses.

Directed Credit

Most Asian countries have viewed control of finance as an important means to speed industrial development, expand exports, promote small business, fight poverty and assure cheap food supplies to urban areas. Rather than rely on financial institutions to use market mechanisms to mobilize savings and allocate resources, they have intervened in markets to direct credit for specific purposes. Five main types of interventions have been used: lending requirements and quotas imposed on banks, refinance schemes, loans at preferential interest rates, credit guarantees, and lending by development finance institutions. These actions are intended to increase lending by reducing the costs and risks to lenders of making loans to preferred clients and sectors. Loan waivers and forgiveness programs are also used to reduce the debt burden of priority borrowers.

The donor agencies have made substantial investments in directed credit projects and in agricultural development projects with credit components. The ADB approved 72 projects between 1970 and August 1991 for a total of almost $1.4 billion. Just over $1.0 billion went to 36 projects providing credit to crop farmers and cooperatives for the acquisition of equipment. Over 60 percent of the credit projects went to 13 market economy countries in the region (ADB, 1993).

Much has been written about the impact of directed credit but it is impossible to be precise about the impact in any given situation. While targeted firms and industries may receive more credit than they would without the directed credit, it is hard to determine if aggregate growth is affected. The problem is that credit subsidies are not free; someone must pay them. If regulations lead to cross-subsidization within banks, nonpriority borrowers pay some of the costs through higher interest rates. Bank owners may also experience lower returns on their capital. Moreover, the credit allocation may worsen income distribution if the credit is explicitly or inadvertently skewed in favor of larger firms. The clearest impact has been observed in the damage that directed credit inflicted on financial systems (World Bank, 1989). Many directed credits became nonperforming loans because cheap interest rates encouraged unprofitable investments. In some cases borrowers intentionally defaulted because they believed that governments would waive or forgive their loans or not take action against defaulters in priority sectors. Financial discipline was damaged and intermediaries weakened. The problem was particularly serious for Asian development finance institutions and many became insolvent and were closed or had to be recapitalized, in some cases, many times. Refinance schemes discouraged savings mobilization, leading to lower financial intermediation. Therefore, whatever economic benefits that countries realized due to directed credit imposed a high cost on the financial system.[3]

---

[3] In the late 1980s, Egaitsu (1988) concluded that directed agricultural credit had made a positive impact in expanding outreach but recognized that viability was a problem.

Doubts About the Directed Agricultural Credit Paradigm

Policymakers in the 1950s and 1960s assumed that farmers lacked access to formal credit, that informal lenders charged usurious interest rates, and that short-term high-cost informal loans were unsuitable for financing the productive investments considered essential for rapid technological change and sustainable rural development. Therefore, supply-leading directed agricultural credit policies were implemented to overcome perceived financial market imperfections. A major role was assigned to financial institutions to address numerous economic and social issues. The paradigm was based on the false idea that rural poverty could be addressed through credit alone (Adams, 1998). Donors helped formulate these ideas and funded many projects to expand financial and marketing services in rural areas (Meyer and Larson, 1997).

USAID Spring Review and FAO Conference

Two major events were instrumental in raising concerns about the directed credit paradigm used to rationalize agricultural credit projects in developing countries: the 1972/ 73 Spring Review of Small Farmer Credit by the United States Agency for International Development (USAID); and the 1975 World Conference on Credit for Farmers in Developing Countries held at the Food and Agriculture Organization of the United Nations (FAO) headquarters in Rome.

The Spring Review was a massive exercise. About 60 reports were prepared on specific farm credit programs in developing countries and 20 analytical papers were written. In total, it generated some 6,000 pages of reports. The Review involved considerable interaction among authors, academics, USAID personnel, and policymakers in workshops held in developing countries and a major final conference held in Washington DC. Finally, a book was published summarizing the results of the analysis and discussions (Donald, 1976). The FAO conference was preceded by a study conducted by a joint working group composed of staff from FAO and the Cassa di Risparmio delle Provincie Lombarde (CARIPLO) (FAO/ CARIPLO, 1975). The content of the group's report was tested in regional agricultural credit seminars, and it became the basic working document for the Conference.

The major findings of these two events implicitly challenged the directed credit approach. They offered a different vision captured in these ten points:

- Small farmer credit projects are part of a larger rural capital market.[4] Small farmers tend to have greater access to informal sources, and the major increases that occurred in formal finance have mainly gone to larger farmers.
- The introduction of special, subsidized agricultural credit programs inhibits commercial lenders from expanding into rural areas. This helps perpetuate the dualism observed in rural financial markets.
- Low interest rates (in both nominal and real terms) are the most contentious issue. Many analysts argue that low interest rate policies are a major factor determining the observed distorted patterns of credit allocation.
- Preferential interest rates for small farmers are especially detrimental to improving access to formal loans, and are not an effective way to transfer income to small farmers.
- Low interest rates are more important in determining the ability of institutions to cover costs and risks than they are in influencing farmer demand for loans. The profitability of new technology, the supply of related farm inputs, and the prices received by producers are more important in determining farmer adoption than access to low interest loans.

---

[4] The concept of a capital market was used for the first time in the discussion of agricultural credit. Later, the term financial market became more widely used.

- When interest and other subsidies are provided, they should be utilized to build up institutions rather than passed on to farmers in low interest loans. Savings mobilization should be given more emphasis in financial policies. The low interest rates paid on savings are detrimental to rural savings mobilization.
- Loan default rates are high and demand more attention, but crop and credit insurance and loan guarantees are not likely to be good solutions to the problem.
- The administrative costs of lending are high and require cost-reducing innovations such as partial service bank branches, mobile banks, village bank agents, and the creation of rural banks. Group lending contributes potentially more to cost reduction than to improving debt recovery.
- There is no single best type of institution to provide rural financial services. Commercial banks, agricultural development banks, and farm cooperatives have all experienced successes and failures in serving agriculture.
- The benefits of small farmer credit projects may not cover costs. When the conditions for successful credit projects are not met, other programs may be capable of raising small farmer welfare at lower costs.

In the ensuing years, much additional research was conducted on rural financial markets. Generally the results tended to support the critical observations made in the Spring Review and FAO conference. The Asian and Pacific Regional Agricultural Credit Association (APRACA) was established in October 1977. Through its auspices, studies were also prepared in the region and training was conducted on agricultural credit policies and programs. Many important studies were abstracted and published for use in training courses of the Economic Development Institute of the World Bank (Von Pischke, Adams, and Donald, 1983). All these efforts contributed to raising concerns about the wisdom of the old paradigm.

Colloquium on Rural Finance

The next major event in which agricultural credit policies and programs were debated by academics and policymakers was the Colloquium on Rural Finance in Low-Income Countries sponsored by USAID and the World Bank in Washington DC in 1981. A publication summarizing the research findings presented at the Colloquium became a focal point for discussions and debates around the world (Adams, Graham, and Von Pischke, 1984). The findings confirmed many of the arguments of the previous decade and provided several new insights. The central theme stated that "traditional thinking often leads to costly and sometimes counterproductive policies and that financial markets would make a much more positive contribution to rural development if appropriate policy changes were adopted" (p. 6). The specific key points included (p. 1-7):

- Agricultural credit is not a direct input in agricultural production, but is provided as the result of a process of financial intermediation. Financial services are as important to rural nonfarm enterprises as they are to farming.
- Credit is fungible and it is costly and difficult to effectively target end use.
- Maintaining positive real interest rates is the most important element in improving rural financial market performance.
- Financing loans out of savings will diminish or erase patronal relations that currently exist between borrowers, intermediaries, and financial authorities.
- Reducing dependency on external funds will reduce the politicization of rural financial markets.
- Broadening financial intermediation will increase competition among formal and informal lenders and reduce any monopoly profits that may exist.
- Analysis should build a better understanding of the factors affecting the performance of financial institutions

rather than attempt to measure credit needs or impact at the farm level.
- Reforms in financial market policies are more often blocked by political obstacles than by economic forces.

Many of the conclusions of this meeting were strikingly similar to the AID and FAO meetings held 10 years earlier. However, there were two new major contributions of the research reported in this volume. They concerned costs and politics. Papers were presented that measured the transaction costs incurred by lenders and borrowers, and the authors explained how these costs influence the behavior of both. Other papers reported how subsidized credit programs are part of a system of political patronage, and how subsidized interest rates for farmers fail to compensate for other policies that discriminate against agriculture. Unfortunately, the insights presented in these research results and disseminated in these meetings did not make a major impact on Asian policymakers, so credit projects in the region often continued to be designed and implemented under the directed credit paradigm.

The Microfinance Revolution: Fad and Fundamentals

Beginning in the 1970s, a new financial development began to emerge in developing countries that also contributed to changing views about the appropriate strategy for developing rural financial markets. This was the emergence of microfinance, mostly the granting of small loans, which began as a series of small experiments and mushroomed into a development fad. Many institutions, especially NGOs, make small loans as part of their programs to create employment, raise the income of the poor, provide emergency relief following natural disasters and conflicts, and improve rural health, education, and nutrition. Microfinance experiences in Bangladesh and Indonesia have made important contributions to the emergence of microfinance. In this section the highlights of this new approach to expanding the financial frontier are summarized and the lessons for rural financial markets identified.

The Origins of Microfinance

Agricultural credit policies had their origin in a desire to improve agricultural technology and speed agricultural growth. The rationale for making small loans or microloans sprang from three different development initiatives (Churchill, 1998). First, several countries promoted the establishment of small and medium enterprises (SMEs) and many donor projects contributed to this objective. Many of these projects enjoyed only modest success and the sustainability of the services provided to entrepreneurs was a chronic problem. Over time, the approach evolved into supporting microenterprise development through small loans, with or without training, because it was one way to provide sustainable support to micro and small enterprises.

Second, microlending or microcredit originated in projects to alleviate poverty. The objective of these projects is often income generation rather than enterprise development. Means tests or other criteria are used to identify the poorest of the poor who are the primary target groups. Once again, microloans to the poor offer some promise of sustainability in the face of declining subsidies. The Grameen Bank and the Bangladesh Rural Advancement Committee (BRAC) are recognized pioneer organizations in Asia with this orientation. Some of these organizations strive to self-finance the costs of their credit services while seeking subsidies for education, training, and technical assistance activities.

Third, many microfinance organizations (MFOs) emerged to provide financial services for firms and households not served by the conventional financial sector. ASA in Bangladesh and the unit desa system of Bank Rakyat Indonesia (BRI) fall into this category. They specialize in microloans and other financial services, but do not particularly target the poorest of the poor who may need more than credit to start and successfully manage a microenterprise (ADB, 1997f).

The early microlenders emerged in the late 1970s, and their efforts gained momentum during the 1980s. By the mid-1980s, researchers began to evaluate these experiences systematically and, by the early 1990s, suggestions for best practices emerged. Many of the pioneer microlenders had a far superior performance than the earlier agricultural credit projects in terms of outreach and loan recovery even in countries, such as Bangladesh, where the conditions were very unfavorable.

The Fundamentals of Microfinance: Lessons for Rural Finance

The microfinance experience is important to analyze because of the potential lessons for developing sustainable rural finance. The fact that the microfinance approach produced results superior to many of the old paradigm agricultural credit projects contributed to the development of a new paradigm. The MFOs managed to develop important innovations that enabled them to expand the financial frontier in developing countries. For the first time, large numbers of poor borrowers have access to formal financial services due to these innovations, which reduced lending costs and risks, and permitted MFOs to serve poor clients successfully without the collateral normally required by banks. The techniques that contributed to their success include:[5]

- Loan sizes - loans are small in size, and are made for only a few weeks or months to be used mostly for working capital purposes.
- Repeat loans - incentives are given to clients to maintain good repayment records by rewarding them with (almost automatic) repeat loans. For some lenders, the

---

[5] No single list of lessons or best practices exists. Many of the points listed here were discussed in Chaves and Gonzalez-Vega (1996), Christen et al. (1995), Churchill (1999), Donors Working Group (1995), Otero and Rhyne (1994), Rhyne and Rotblatt (1994), and Yaron et al. (1997).

size of the first and repeat loans is set according to a predetermined formula.

- Loan repayment schedules - frequent payments are required, often weekly or monthly, to enable close monitoring of borrower performance.
- Interest rates - interest rates and fees are high, usually much higher than those charged by conventional lenders, and are usually positive in real terms.
- Loan officer efficiency - loan officers frequently handle 75 to 100 borrower groups or 200 to 500 individual borrowers. Financial incentive schemes for employees stimulate high levels of efficiency.
- Loan collateral - many MFOs use a lending technology involving peer group formation and peer monitoring as a substitute for conventional loan collateral to reduce transaction costs and risks. MFOs that use the more conventional individual lending technology accept as collateral household goods and other assets with high use value to their clients.
- Decentralized lending procedures - the procedures for screening applicants and processing loans are simple, with considerable autonomy given to loan officers, who are required to maintain close contact with their clients.
- Loan delinquencies and losses - lenders frequently report loan recoveries of 95 percent or more. Computerized systems are often used to produce daily repayment reports so loan officers can take corrective action at the first hint of unexplained delay in their clients' payments. Some organizations offer interest rebates for on-time or early repayments, and others charge penalty interest for late payments.

These techniques are in sharp contrast with the old paradigm agricultural credit projects, and contribute to the success of microfinance. There are limitations, however, in the applicability of microlending technologies for rural finance. First, they appear to be best suited to urban enterprises or rural nonfarm households and firms with regular and frequent cash incomes. They have yet to be rigorously tested with specialized farmers who have highly seasonal cash flows or for medium- and long-term lending. Second, transaction costs for the financial institutions and their clients are likely to be higher in rural than in urban areas. The clients are more dispersed so travel costs are higher for loan officers and it is difficult for them to serve a large client load. Some MFOs reduce their transaction costs through group lending, but this raises borrower transaction costs. Moreover, peer pressure may not be as effective in sparsely populated areas where group members have less information about each other and peer monitoring is more costly.

The third limitation in microlending is that, except for some urban locations, financial markets for the poor are highly segmented with each microlender usually serving only a small market niche. Small MFOs have limitations similar to most informal lenders in serving only a local clientele because high information and transaction costs discourage competition and constrain them from rapidly expanding to serve new clients and regions. Being limited to local markets, they have concentrated portfolios with a large covariant risk. Fourth, most MFOs have paid little attention to providing savings services, but a safe and secure place to deposit savings may be more important than credit for farm households that need to smooth consumption in the absence of insurance markets. Many MFOs obtain their resources from subsidized sources, have little experience in mobilizing savings, and conclude that the cost of mobilizing resources from clients is high by comparison.

Since the microfinance field is fairly new with the oldest organizations having only 10 to 20 years of experience, many design questions still have to be resolved. For example, rural finance must deal with clients subject to the systematic risks of floods, drought, and disease, but relatively little is known about the capacity of MFOs to cope with such adversities. The 1998 floods in Bangladesh created liquidity problems for MFOs. Most have little capital and are dependent on donor or government sources that need to provide new funds to cover losses and supply liquidity. Emergency procedures to deal with this problem must be worked out in advance to enable MFOs operating in high risk areas to plan prudent levels of reserves. Nonfinancial services also present a challenge. Financial services alone are not sufficient to lift the poor out of poverty but cost recovery for these services presents a serious problem. Some poor people are not prepared to participate in group-based financial activities and a process of social intermediation may be required in order for them to be linked to financial markets (Bennett, Goldberg, and Von Pischke, 1998).

The Changing Paradigm for Developing Rural Financial Markets

Many developing countries continue to use the traditional directed credit approach toward agriculture, but a significant shift in views is occurring in some developing countries. The old paradigm of subsidized and targeted lending has been gradually replaced by the new paradigm oriented more towards financial market efficiency (Robinson, 1997; Vogel and Adams, 1997; Adams, 1998). The failure of most countries to develop a sustainable rural financial system using the old agricultural credit paradigm, coupled with the successes of a few MFOs, contributed to the emergence of a new paradigm. In Asia, the experiences of the unit desa system of BRI in Indonesia, of the Bank for Agriculture and Agricultural Cooperatives in Thailand, and of the Grameen Bank in Bangladesh, made important contributions to the new views. The main features of the old and new paradigms are summarized in Box III.1. The policies implemented in many developing countries today reflect the shift from a traditional supply-leading directed credit approach to more market-oriented, demand-leading financial services.

New Paradigm: Financial Market Approach

The shortcomings of targeted agricultural credit programs are well documented (e. g. Adams, Graham, and Von Pischke, 1984; Meyer and Larson, 1997; FAO/GTZ, 1998) and have been

Box III.1 Primary Features of the Old and New Paradigms

Features	Directed Credit Paradigm	Financial Market Paradigm
Problem definition	Overcome market imperfections	Lower risks and transaction costs
Role of financial markets	Promote new technology Stimulate production Implement State plans Help the poor	Intermediate resources more efficiently
View of users	Borrowers as beneficiaries selected by targeting	Borrowers and depositors as clients choosing products
Subsidies	Large subsidies through interest rates and loan default Create subsidy dependence	Few subsidies Create independent institutions
Sources of funds	Governments and donors	Mostly voluntary deposits
Associated information systems	Designed for donors	Designed for management
Sustainability	Largely ignored	A major concern
Evaluations	Credit impact on beneficiaries	Performance of financial institutions

Source: Adapted from Adams (1998).

summarized above. The results of negative evaluations coupled with the financial drain that subsidized programs imposed on government resources led to a gradual shift in financial policies in many countries beginning in the early 1980s. The early success of some microfinance projects, which operated on different assumptions and with different procedures, contributed to the change in paradigm (Otero and Rhyne, 1994).

The new financial market paradigm adopts the perspective of financial markets and limits their role to financial intermediation rather than being a tool to stimulate production, compensate for distortions in other markets, and alleviate poverty. These outcomes are expected to occur as a natural result of efficient intermediation rather than through specific mandated programs. Innovations to reduce transaction costs and the freedom to set interest rates high enough to cover costs are of primary importance. Borrowers and savers are not considered to be beneficiaries but rather valuable clients with whom relationships should be nurtured to help achieve long-term growth. Institutional sustainability, breadth and depth of outreach, and quality of services provided are emphasized as key performance measures (Adams, 1998).

The new paradigm is reflected in commitments by some governments to financial market liberalization, reduced targeting of loans, and better pricing of financial products. The financial frontier is being pushed outward to include several innovative financial institutions, programs, and products designed to service those previously excluded from formal finance (Von Pischke, 1991). The new paradigm emphasizes voluntary savings mobilization rather than funding from governments or donors, which is consistent with the objective of creating independent institutions. The information systems of the financial intermediaries can then be designed to serve the needs of management rather than of donors. The sustainability of the institution and its ability to grow are the major criteria for evaluating the performance of a financial institution. The recent emergence of a few sustainable MFOs offering financial services to clients outside the formal financial frontier is evidence that the new paradigm offers insights into a better way to expand finance into rural areas on a more sustainable basis. These issues are discussed in more detail in the next chapter as they relate to rural Asia. Evidence of the new thinking is found more frequently in microfinance than in rural finance policies, and this represents the serious policy challenge for decision makers in Asia today.

Expanding the Paradigm

This perspective of a changing paradigm for rural financial markets is useful in identifying key weaknesses in the policies and programs employed by many developing countries. It is also useful in comparing the policies commonly used in the past with more modern approaches employed in several countries today. However, it has some shortcomings as an analytical tool for determining the nature of problems that countries face in identifying and resolving constraints and bottlenecks in their rural financial markets. For example, the important issue of an appropriate regulatory and supervisory framework for rural finance and microfinance is not addressed. This issue is important because savings and deposits are increasingly substituting for government and donor funding. Deposit insurance may be the answer in some countries, but moral hazard problems must be resolved. Legal issues represent a second set of issues not addressed in the new paradigm. Microfinance can skirt some problems related to collateral and contract enforcement, but they are more serious in rural finance that involves land and other physical collateral. A third area of concern is institution building, and the appropriate method to subsidize institutional development without creating subsidy dependence. These issues are addressed in the framework presented at the end of this chapter, but first it is important to understand the special problems of transition economies and our new understanding of the key role of information in affecting financial market performance.

CREATING FINANCIAL MARKETS IN TRANSITION ECONOMIES

Creating sustainable finance in transition economies is an especially challenging problem. Transition involves a complex process of rapid transformation from a State-planned to a market-based economy; it means creating new institutions, adapting existing institutions, and dismantling inefficient institutions and overbuilt capacities (World Bank, 1996b). The Asian transition countries are heterogeneous. Some countries such as the PRC and Viet Nam have a long history, old institutions, and fairly well developed infrastructure. They embarked on a gradual transition in the 1980s with microeconomic reforms preceding macroeconomic reforms. The PRC, for instance, gives priority to agriculture and rural industries. Inflation is under control and the Government can concentrate on price reforms. The banking sector is used to capture rural surpluses for use in financing projects including rural industrialization.

The picture in the Central Asian republics is different. They became independent countries only in the 1990s and undertook several reforms simultaneously to ensure sovereignty and economic growth. Many adopted a 'big bang' approach similar to that in Eastern Europe where macroeconomic reforms dominated the early phase of transition (Rana, 1993). The first phase of transition was limited to liberalization of the economy and redistribution of the State-owned assets to the public. The second phase began in 1993 and involves creating financial institutions, developing skills and accumulating knowledge. The Kyrgyz Republic case study describes how rapid changes in property rights and liberalization of prices and foreign exchange are being implemented under the watchful eyes of donors. The creation of private enterprises and farms was secondary to the privatization of State-owned enterprises, and the banking sector is expected to play a role in the privatization strategy.

The rural sector is significantly affected because transition affects property rights and the allocation of resources through decollectivization and the changing patterns of land ownership rights. The choice of the transition path–gradual or big bang approach–is determined by initial conditions such as existing property rights, importance of agriculture and rural industries, inflation, and the philosophies of donors. Understanding the differences in transition paths and in initial conditions is important since it helps to anticipate the effects of the transition and the reform outcomes in rural areas.

The transition countries are grappling with several challenges in developing a market-based financial sector (Box III.2). Five interrelated problems pose major challenges in the transition countries. First, a part of the resource reallocation process can be effectively handled by the banking sector, but transition countries are characterized by weak and passive banking sectors with little capacity to assess credit risks and allocate resources. Therefore, there is a need to change attitudes towards the financial sector and learn about its role in market economies. The skill levels of the bankers need to be rapidly improved to function within a market environment.

Box III.2 Challenges in Developing the Financial Sector in Transition Countries

1. Strengthening the banking sector to improve efficiency
   - Reducing bureaucratic interference and overdues
   - Unclogging payment systems
   - Strengthening regulatory and supervisory systems
   - Developing legal systems that can enforce contracts and inculcate financial responsibility
   - Reducing corruption
   - Improving the skill level of staff to assess and manage risks

2. Reducing systemic problems in financial markets to increase competition
   - Reducing insider control of financial institutions
   - Developing capital markets
   - Reducing the political hold on institutions
   - Reducing barter transactions
   - Reducing barriers to entry for private banks and nonbanks

Source: Adapted from EBRD (1998).

Second, the financial infrastructure, such as regulatory and supervisory capacity, is very weak. Financial crises tend to occur when the financial sector expands rapidly into new activities, and the regulatory system cannot ensure transparency in operations, standardize auditing and accounting practices, and protect the rights of minority share holders and depositors. Banking crises have already occurred in countries, such as Russia, that liberalized their economies without developing their regulatory framework. Government intervention is needed to create a stronger regulatory structure.

The third problem for transition economies is that although they collected a vast amount of information on several aspects of their societies, much is now obsolete and not suited to market-based transactions. Little information is available to assess loan applications because it was not required for State-mandated credit allocations, and market and technical information to help make production and marketing decisions is limited. A major challenge is to develop public institutions, such as credit bureaus, that can facilitate the creation and dissemination of information that was not necessary prior to the 1990s.

Fourth, contract enforcement is difficult because the use of sanctions, such as loss of future benefits, is undermined during the transition process. The economy is so volatile that repeat transactions cannot be anticipated. Sanctions can work only when exchange relations are clearly defined, the level of uncertainty is low, and enforcement is easy. It has been challenging to develop institutions to enforce laws, to generate information for enforcement, and to encourage individuals and enterprises to demand the implementation of laws. In the absence of sanctions, trust can be used to consummate transactions but this requires building up of social systems that can facilitate the development of trust (Humphrey and Schmitz, 1998).

Finally, corruption, fraud, political interference, and implicit subsidies and guarantees in the transition economies are widespread and impede the development of an efficient banking sector.

Building strong financial institutions in transition economies is now seen as a much longer-term effort than first envisioned in the initial days following the collapse of State planning. The first phase of policy reform may turn out to be relatively easy compared to the second phase of institution building. The case study of the Kyrgyz Republic illustrates some of the problems. Financial institutions have portfolios dominated by nonperforming loans that need to be cleaned up and the institutions must be recapitalized. Managers and staff must develop new skills required for operating market-based financial intermediaries. Incentive systems must be designed to stimulate efficiency, and information systems must be created to give managers and loan officers timely information needed about institutional and clientele performance. The new and rehabilitated institutions need to be supported by a financial infrastructure that financial markets require to perform efficiently. New laws have been passed to support business transactions. In the area of finance, the new legislation expands the scope of types of property that can be subject to a security interest.

However, many legislative uncertainties remain that undermine lending against collateral. A detailed study of Romania, another transition economy, revealed a fragmented system of civil and commercial codes coupled with a large variety of ordinances and special laws on creating security interests that cause gaps in the types of loans that can be secured by movable property (Fleisig and Peña, 1998).

THE NEW EMPHASIS ON INFORMATION IN FINANCE

It is becoming clearer that poor nations differ from rich ones not just because of differences in capital, but because they also have less knowledge. Developing countries suffer from a knowledge gap in several areas, especially technology, and have incomplete knowledge about attributes, such as the creditworthiness of potential borrowers, referred to as information problems (World Bank, 1998b). Rural areas suffer from information disadvantages relative to urban areas, and the poor have more difficult access to information than the rich. Therefore, improving access to good information contributes to reducing income inequalities. Institutions are critically important in facilitating the flow of information essential for efficient markets; this view is well established in the public support for creating and disseminating new agricultural technologies. It is equally important in banking because of its public goods features. Improved processing of the economy's financial information is an appropriate government intervention in financial markets, and this is implicit in many recommendations proposed in the wake of the financial and economic crisis in Asia. Investing in improved information is a more promising way to encourage sustainable rural finance than the old paradigm policies to induce more lending in rural areas.

All financial transactions involve giving up funds now in return for a promise to be repaid in the future. Financial markets perform their economic function when they allocate scarce capital to the best projects, then monitor them to ensure that the funds are used appropriately (See Chapter II). Lenders need to evaluate the probability of getting repaid, which requires verifying information supplied by borrowers who have an incentive to exaggerate their ability and willingness to pay. Offering large amounts of collateral is one means that borrowers have to signal their intention to repay. Moreover, loan collateral helps resolve the contract enforcement problem in the event of default if the costs of realizing the collateral are reasonable.

Informal lenders often know and live in close proximity to their clients so they can more easily evaluate creditworthiness and monitor their performance. But formal institutions incur costs in collecting and analyzing data for loan appraisals, monitoring the use of funds, and enforcing contracts. Some financial institutions attempt to reduce transaction costs by using local sources of information to screen clients and by designing contracts that induce borrowers to respect them. For example, several Indonesian lenders use information obtained from third parties such as village headmen to screen borrowers. Joint liability groups require that members use their information about potential members in the process of group formation.

Information that is widely available about delinquent loans can lead to peer pressure for repayment.

The effective supervision and governance of financial institutions require many types of information. For example, bank supervisors require information to determine whether intermediaries are following established norms and are engaging in prudent behavior. Bank owners need information about the institution's performance and prospects, and bank managers must monitor the performance of loan officers. Loan officers, in turn, need information about prospective clients and timely reports on the repayment status of their borrowers. Members of joint liability group loans need to know the repayment status of other group members. Improved information often leads to better performance because incentives change. Better information helps regulators more readily identify problems, and helps managers to design and implement staff incentives for banks and cooperatives.

For efficient processing of information and design of contracts, financial institutions need supportive public policies to develop accounting and disclosure systems and to improve legal infrastructure. Empirical evidence shows that countries with legal systems that give high priority to secured creditors, rigorously enforce contracts, and set accounting standards that produce comprehensive financial statements, have better-developed financial intermediaries and enjoy faster growth (Caprio, 1998; World Bank, 1998b). Governments contribute to the performance of financial institutions by creating institutions that, because they are public goods, will not normally emerge spontaneously in the private sector. They include registries for recording asset transfers and financial transactions and credit reporting agencies (Fleisig, 1995). In addition, in rural areas they include land-titling projects to improve security of tenure and transferability of land, and land reform to give the poor greater access to land, which can be used as collateral for loans. Land reform can also destroy collateral, however, as occurred in the Philippines when uncertainties about the details of implementation in the 1980s prompted lenders for a time to accept only urban land as collateral.

Creating public institutions to support financial markets is especially urgent in transition economies because such institutions did not exist in centrally planned regimes in which the State allocated credit. On the one hand, the government must directly create, maintain, and support some public entities, such as a regulatory and supervisory system for bank and nonbank institutions. On the other hand, governments should support private sector entities to perform tasks for which they are more efficient, such as to accumulate credit histories, and maintain records on credit transactions and assets pledged as collateral.

The new information and communication technologies being created and adopted in developing countries present new opportunities and challenges. New technologies are making it easier and cheaper to acquire, manage, analyze, and transmit large volumes of data. Credit scoring models, for example, are being developed based on data for thousands of loans in order to predict poor credit risks. Smart cards are being designed so that a single card will carry a borrower's entire loan history. These cards can be used to withdraw funds against previously approved credit lines and to make loan payments. The financial institutions that are most successful in designing and adopting these techniques will be the most competitive. However, these new technologies are expensive, require large capital investments, and demand highly skilled personnel. State-owned financial institutions will likely have problems in justifying these expenditures. Likewise, small rural institutions will lag in being able to use them, and will have to find their market niche by specializing in technologies that utilize their superior knowledge of local environments and their personal relations with clients.

A STRATEGY TO BUILD RURAL FINANCIAL MARKETS

The previous sections summarized key concepts underlying the development of financial markets. This section presents a three-pronged framework for building rural financial markets in terms of 1) creating the policy environment, 2) building financial infrastructure, and 3) institutional development. Governments and donors need to evaluate these three areas as they set priorities for interventions and investments.

The key objective of the financial system was once narrowly defined as providing financial services at prices that reflect their cost (World Bank, 1989). In recent years, the emphasis has broadened, especially for microfinance, to consider the dual objectives of outreach and sustainability (Yaron, 1992). Outreach involves more than just number of clients served when the scarce use of public resources is considered. Generally speaking, a financial system meets more of society's objectives and merits the allocation of more scarce resources if it a) serves many clients, b) serves many poor clients, c) provides a large scope of services, d) costs the users as little as possible, e) provides services over a long period of time, and f) can be sustained with only a minimum of support from nonusers or taxpayers.[6] These should be the objectives of the policies and programs for rural financial markets.

Creating the Policy Environment

The urban bias of many economic and agricultural policies in developing countries contributed to the failure of old-paradigm agricultural credit projects and development banks. Many of these programs were introduced in environments that were hostile to creating healthy financial markets. Macroeconomic instability produced highly variable inflation rates. Repressed financial sector policies with interest rate ceilings prevented lenders from charging cost-recovery rates on loans. High reserve requirements discouraged deposit

---

[6] These criteria are a modification of those formulated in Navajas et al. (1998). Schreiner (1999) has proposed a broader framework for outreach in terms of six aspects: worth to users, cost to users, depth, breadth, length, and scope.

mobilization. Limits on bank branching and on creating new banks restrained competition among rural financial institutions. Cheap food policies, subsidized food imports, farm price controls, unfavorable agricultural terms of trade, and distorted foreign exchange rates contributed to this poor environment (FAO/GTZ, 1998; World Bank, 1998b).

Considerable progress has been made in many countries to improve macroeconomic policy, reduce uncertainty, correct the worst policy distortions, and improve farm profitability (See Chapter IV; further information is available in Rosegrant and Hazell, 1999). The process is far from finished, however, and many policies still discourage rural finance. As noted in the case studies, Thailand still imposes subsidized interest rates on Bank for Agriculture and Agricultural Cooperatives farm lending and restricts its ability to serve nonfarm clients in rural areas. India has a huge Integrated Rural Development Program that consumes vast public funds and discourages the emergence of unsubsidized institutions to serve poor clients. Low interest rates discourage innovation and competition. Thus, liberalization is a necessary first step if countries want to create a favorable environment in which financial markets can flourish. Portfolio restrictions must be carefully examined because they limit the lenders' ability to reduce risks through portfolio diversification.

Donors can specify general policy reforms as conditionalities for sector loans based on experiences of other countries; however, technical assistance is needed in many countries to diagnose specific local problems carefully and develop solutions. Moreover, policy changes involve stakeholders who need to participate in policy reforms (FAO/GTZ, 1998). Carefully crafted policies to attract stakeholder support may be as crucial to successful policy reform as are correct technical recommendations. The long and largely unsuccessful history of donor-sponsored agricultural credit and financial reform projects described in the Bangladesh case study, for example, provides ample evidence of how powerful groups can undermine the best technical solutions. Political economy issues may determine the appropriate sequencing of financial reforms but in ways that may be difficult to anticipate (Stiglitz, 1997).

Policy reforms are necessary to provide an environment conducive for creating financial markets in many countries. Some countries will be able to improve their financial systems greatly through system-wide reforms. In other cases, more direct proactive measures will be required to accelerate the process of building the financial infrastructure, as discussed in the next section.

Building Financial Infrastructure

Building financial infrastructure was largely overlooked in the old agricultural credit paradigm, but it has now emerged as one of the top priorities for improving rural finance. Frequently, it is more important than supporting a specific financial institution because improved infrastructure contributes to the entire financial sector, not just to institutions targeted for direct assistance. Information, legal, and regulatory systems represent parts of the infrastructure that directly affect financial transactions, while transportation and communications systems, particularly in rural areas, indirectly affect the costs and risk of finance.

Several problems have been identified in financial infrastructure. For example, many shortcomings in existing laws and regulations impede rural lending. It was discovered that titles registered by the land reform agencies in Bolivia and Peru were not registered in regular real estate registries; consequently, farm lenders could not accept them as loan collateral. Insecticide and fertilizer dealers in Bangladesh could not use inventories and accounts receivable as collateral for loans to extend more credit to their clients (Yaron, Benjamin, and Piprek, 1997).

Improving loan recovery is especially challenging. Bangladesh created special courts to handle rural loan defaults. Although political intervention undermines their effectiveness, they represent an institutional approach to a serious problem. Identifying specific reforms must be done on a country-by-country basis. Examples of potential importance are listed in Box III.3. The World Bank and the European Bank for

---

Box III.3 Changes in Infrastructure to Improve Finance

The following list gives examples of changes to improve finance:

- Title land and register it in a registry; lower the costs of registration and foreclosure.
- Reform legal registries and expand the scope for private operation.
- Reform the law of secured transactions; permit repossession and sale without extensive judicial intervention.
- Remove barriers to the operation of credit bureaus and use the ratings of credit bureaus in bank supervision and regulation.
- Permit witnesses to give legal standing to contracts signed by illiterates.
- Develop appropriate regulations for non-deposit-taking institutions.

Source: Adapted from Yaron, Benjamin, and Piprek (1997).

Reconstruction and Development are financing projects to implement such reforms, and the potential benefits through lower interest charges and increased supplies of funds are estimated to be huge (World Bank, 1998b).

Weak financial regulation and supervision were dramatically exposed in the financial and economic crisis in Asia, and have been identified as priority reforms in most developing countries for all segments of the financial system. Regulation is an increasingly important issue for NGOs engaged in microfinance (MFOs) (McGuire, Conroy, and Thapa, 1998). Deposit-taking institutions must be licensed in most countries, but the banking authorities have often chosen to ignore the small MFOs that take deposits from their own members. The potential problems have become more serious now that NGOs are mobilizing larger amounts of money and some, such as

ASA in Bangladesh, accept deposits from nonmembers. Many unanswered regulatory questions must be dealt with if rural finance is to evolve in a sustainable way. Crises can never be eliminated, but they can be mitigated through prudential regulations.

Some initial steps have been taken to conceptualize the types of regulatory approach that would be appropriate for MFOs (van Greuning, Gallardo, and Randhawa, 1999). Most Asian developing countries have not yet resolved important general regulatory policy issues, such as should credit cooperatives and MFOs be regulated and supervised by the same authorities that regulate commercial banks? What level of regulation is needed to assure safety but not stifle the creativity essential for expanding the financial frontier? What is the appropriate role for special apex organizations in supporting rural financial institutions? Then there are many technical issues to be resolved. What levels of reserves are prudent for agricultural lenders with portfolios concentrated in small geographic areas that specialize in financing activities subject to covariant income risk? What lender-of-last-resort arrangements are needed to protect rural financial intermediaries in the event of bank runs or temporary liquidity problems in times of drought and floods? What are the appropriate policies on reserves and capital and provisioning requirements for institutions that make largely uncollateralized loans?

Institutional Development

The third component of the three-pronged framework for developing rural financial markets is institutional development. The requirements for rural financial institutions (RFIs) to achieve high levels of outreach and sustainability have been identified as follows:

> "RFIs require appropriate governance, which entails clearly defined and limited roles and powers for government, donors, the central bank, and other agencies. Capable management with a high degree

of autonomy is also required, as are innovative and efficient operating procedures guided by a well-developed management information system" (Yaron, Benjamin, and Piprek, 1997, p. 99).

Institutions may not develop automatically just because the environment and financial infrastructure have improved. Institution building may be required to take advantage of the new emerging opportunities and markets (Krahnen and Schmidt, 1994). If financial services are to be broadly based, some groups, such as women, small farmers, and microentrepreneurs, may find that they are disadvantaged in responding to market opportunities (Fernando, 1994). Providing support to institutions that target these groups, particularly in their initial start-up phase, may yield high social returns provided that the subsidies are provided for specific institution-building purposes, and are transparent, time bound, and linked to performance. Ultimately, individual institutions need to experiment with alternatives in order to find the methods of operation that fit their objectives and capabilities.

Learning from Microfinance

Fortunately, much has been learned about institutional development in the last few years because of innovations that have been tested, especially by MFOs; thus some general principles and best practices are available for adaptation to local needs. These are discussed in detail in Chapter IV. Most of the strong MFOs have a strong mission and business plan explicitly oriented towards achieving high levels of efficiency by offering clients market-driven products. They have a clear goal of achieving institutional viability and self-sufficiency in a short period of time. Through experimentation, they have developed financial technologies and procedures that have resolved some of the high costs and risks associated with making small, short-term, uncollaterized loans to poor people. Many are new institutions that have had freedom to innovate and enjoyed strong donor support. Their successes provide lessons for rural finance. However, since many specialize in lending in urban or densely populated rural areas, there are limitations in the transferability of their experiences to rural environments.

Weak Financial Institutions: Close or Rehabilitate?

The process of building rural financial systems in Asia does not begin with a blank slate. Many countries created specialized agricultural development banks (SADBs) in the 1960s and 1970s with donor support. The SADBs share several characteristics (Pomareda, 1984; Gonzalez-Vega and Graham, 1995). They are largely State owned, serve only agricultural clients, specialize in lending with little attention to savings mobilization, and charge subsidized interest rates. SADBs are licensed and regulated with more attention often given to assuring compliance with lending targets than to safety and soundness. They are often subject to political intervention, so have limited ability to enforce loan contracts and seize collateral for nonpayment of loans. Many have been closed, some have been rehabilitated, and several exist with limited outreach and poorly performing portfolios.

Is it more cost effective to rehabilitate the SADBs or is it better to simply close them and start new institutions? Experience to date with rehabilitation has been checkered. Perhaps the most successful case in Asia is described in the Indonesia case study. The failing Bank Rakyat Indonesia was restructured into the highly profitable unit desa system. Other successful cases include Bank Pertanian Malaysia and the BAGRICOLA in the Dominican Republic (Adams, 1995). There have also been many failures, especially in Latin America where several SADBs were closed after repeated rescue attempts. The Agroprombank in the Kyrgyz Republic was closed because it was considered too costly to rehabilitate relative to the expected benefits. The agricultural development banks in Bangladesh, Nepal, and Pakistan continue to be among the region's poorest performing rural lenders in spite of repeated donor-funded rehabilitation projects.

The decision to close versus rehabilitate depends on the estimated benefits and cost of each alternative. Closing an institution could mean destroying assets that represent a sunk cost to society. It could also mean creating a new institution over a period of years if other institutions do not enter the market to fill the vacuum caused by the closure. Some SADBs may possess valuable information capital, human capital, and infrastructure. Information capital may exist in the form of knowledge about clients (credit histories and repayment records) and about the local environment that may be useful for a rehabilitated institution. Much of this information capital may also be embodied in human capital. The bank staff may have learned how to evaluate credit worthiness, but were not given the opportunity to use their skills, as occurred in the Dominican Republic (Gonzalez-Vega and Graham, 1995). Infrastructure in the form of a banking network and equipment may be salvageable, and there may be valuable goodwill among clients that would be lost with closing. Not all clients failed to repay their loans, and savers grew accustomed to using deposit services of SADBs located in areas unserved by other financial institutions.

The mere existence of these assets, however, does not automatically imply that rehabilitation is the preferred alternative. Several preconditions must be met before rehabilitation can have a reasonable chance of success (Adams, 1995; Gonzalez-Vega and Graham, 1995). These preconditions can be summarized as follows:

- Reasonably good environment in terms of macroeconomic stability, a minimum of financial repression, and a legal system that facilitates contract enforcement and swift conflict resolution.
- Dynamic agricultural sector with reasonably stable policies, remunerative farm policies, and well-developed rural support services.
- Past default problems due largely to government interference rather than staff incompetence or corruption.

- Broader mission for the institution to enable it to develop a diversified portfolio and include lending to nonfarm enterprises, deposit mobilization, transfer of remittances, and other services demanded by a rural clientele.
- Governmental commitment to a hands-off policy in the process of making and collecting loans.
- Creation of a board of directors chaired by a banking professional (frequently the Minister of Finance), with the majority of members representing the private banking sector, and authority granted to the board to set policies conducive to the institution's sustainability, safety, and soundness.
- Hiring a dynamic chief executive with banking experience, and giving that person the freedom to hire top management and dismiss existing bank staff not suited for a market-oriented banking mission.
- Compensation policies that will attract high-quality staff, and incentive packages designed to stimulate top performance of employees at all levels.
- Sufficient financial support to create a modern management information system and the adoption of a transparent accounting system designed to meet international standards.

Perhaps the most contentious and critical issues involved in rehabilitation are governance, recapitalization, and future sources of funds. To minimize the potential for political interference and strengthen the potential for effective governance, the government needs to transfer governance and control effectively to persons with strong banking experience and a private-sector orientation. At the same time, enough public resources have to be provided to clean up the existing nonperforming loan portfolio. The use of public resources and subsidies needs to be tied to explicit performance-based criteria to avoid subsidy dependence. If donor funding is to be used, it should be channeled into improving institutional capacity rather than for on-lending to targeted clients. The bulk of the future funds should come from savers. The behavior of the institution will change if its funds are mobilized from savers rather than donors or the government, and the savers will exercise some monitoring of the performance of the institution. To attract deposits, the institution will have to convince the public that it is a prudent lender, and this requires transparent operations, the use of international accounting standards, and audited financial statements. It will have to design savings instruments that are attractive to clients, and this process will contribute to making it more of a market-driven institution (Adams, 1995). Passing this market test is the first step on the road to sustainability.

IV DEVELOPING RURAL FINANCIAL MARKETS IN ASIA: WHAT HAS BEEN LEARNED?

Asian countries have employed a variety of policies in their efforts to expand formal finance in rural areas. The purpose of this chapter is to summarize how financial markets in rural Asia have evolved, and the lessons derived from both the good and the bad experiences in the region. The concepts discussed in the previous chapter are used to organize the analysis in this chapter. The next section begins with a summary of the views found in the first and second ADB studies of rural Asia. It then describes two Asian phenomena: the "East Asian Miracle" and the recent financial and economic crisis. This is followed by a discussion of the status of rural financial markets in the region today. The second section describes what has been learned from three of the more successful financial institutions in the region: the Bank for Agriculture and Agricultural Cooperatives (BAAC) in Thailand, the unit desa system of Bank Rakyat Indonesia (BRI), and the Grameen Bank (GB) in Bangladesh. They are discussed in more detail in the three case studies found in later chapters. The combination of successes and failures provides insights into the appropriate strategy to follow in the region as discussed in Chapter V.

MAJOR DEVELOPMENTS IN THE REGION: LEARNING FROM FAILURES

The studies of rural Asia conducted by the ADB in the 1960s and 1970s found heavy emphasis by most governments on creating institutions and programs to channel subsidized credit to farmers. Lessons learned about the problems of directed credit made little impact on the policies pursued by most Asian governments during the 1980s and 1990s. However, the failures in the region, along with some of its successes in microfinance, contributed to the emergence of the new paradigm, even though today many of the countries in Asia still pursue the old paradigm.

The Directed Agricultural Credit Paradigm in Rural Asia

The Perspective of the 1960s and 1970s

ADB made a survey of Asian agriculture in 1967/68 (ADB, 1969), which noted that following World War II many Asian countries had developed specialized agricultural lending institutions. Many were designed to support agricultural cooperatives that had a long history in several countries. For example, BAAC was formed in Thailand in 1966, and the Agricultural Development Bank in Viet Nam started the same year. In the early 1960s, the Agricultural Development Bank of Pakistan was created, the Republic of Korea merged its Agricultural Bank and cooperatives into the National Agricultural Cooperative Federation, and the People's Bank of Ceylon was created. In the Philippines, the Agricultural Credit Administration, the Development Bank of the Philippines, and the rural banks were developed during the 1960s. Most if not all of the share capital of these specialized institutions was provided by government grants or loans (Ong, 1969).

Direct lending to farmers by governments was also common in the 1960s. For example, the Provincial Food Bureau and the Provincial Supply Bureau in the PRC made short-term loans to farmers. Direct loans were made to farmers in Sri Lanka by the departments of Agrarian Services, Fisheries, and Land. In Thailand, various departments in the ministries of

Agriculture and Interior made loans to farmers and fishers (Ong, 1969).

A second rural Asian study by ADB in 1976/77 (ADB, 1978) reviewed the major developments that had occurred during the ten-year period following the first survey. It noted that many innovations and encouraging developments had occurred in financing agriculture. These included:

- A major expansion in the number of banking outlets in rural areas. Commercial banks in India had opened 5,000 new branches (largely as a result of nationalization of the banks). The Bank of Ceylon had set up 400 rural branches. In the Philippines, the Philippine National Bank had set up 100 branches, and over 500 rural banks had been established.
- Sharp increases in loan disbursements. Commercial banks increased agricultural lending in India by a factor of 32 from 1968 to 1974. Rural banks in the Philippines increased lending ten-fold during 1965 to 1975. In Sri Lanka, the People's Bank increased lending by a factor of almost 2.5 from 1969/70 to 1973/74.
- An expansion in the number of institutions making loans without collateral. Many were lending 100 percent of the cost of cultivation, and some were making long-term loans.
- Special programs had been introduced to increase food production by providing subsidized credit and inputs to farmers. The Bimas project began in Indonesia in 1967, and Masagana 99 started in the Philippines following the disastrous 1972 harvests.
- Governments encouraged or mandated existing financial institutions to increase agricultural lending by imposing credit quotas. They required rural bank branches to be opened in exchange for the authorization to open urban branches, and by creating credit guarantees.

In spite of these achievements, several problems were noted in the second survey:

- Loan recovery, which had plagued many earlier cooperative credit schemes, continued to be a serious problem (and later led to the collapse of both Bimas and Masagana 99).
- Interest rates charged to farmers were usually low, did not reflect the scarcity of credit, and often encouraged large farmers to preempt the scarce supplies.
- Medium- and long-term credit was limited, and the volume of agricultural credit actually fell in many countries relative to funds allocated to manufacturing.

Both the 1967/68 and 1976/77 studies were ambivalent in their conclusions about agricultural credit. The first study noted the difficulty of ascertaining the degree to which the demand for fertilizer and new seed associated with the new crop technologies was constrained by lack of credit (ADB, 1969, p. 41). The second study concluded, on the one hand, that governments in the region obviously did not utilize the powerful array of controls over State and private financial institutions "to encourage an adequate and proportionate flow of investment credits to the agricultural sector" (ADB, 1978, p. 94). On the other hand, the study noted that the new technology increased the demand for operating and investment credit, but warned that the small farmer credit programs in fashion were "generally unworkable in terms of actually serving the target group" (ibid., p. 258). Moreover, it argued that neither interest nor input subsidies, nor systems to control input use were likely to stimulate the use of credit or channel it in the right direction. It noted that the rapid expansion of credit institutions had exceeded either local demand or the capacity of institutions to supply and supervise credit (ibid., p. 261). This implied that the institutional issues associated with agricultural credit had not been resolved in spite of the many efforts undertaken since World War II to build rural institutions and to institutionalize the supply of agricultural credit.

Major Policies and Programs of the 1970s and 1980s

Notwithstanding the ambivalence implicit in these ADB studies, the decades of the 1970s and 1980s witnessed considerable efforts by policymakers to expand agricultural lending in most Asian countries. The approach used often during much of this period can be characterized as following a directed credit paradigm with the following characteristics:

- Interest rates for farm loans were subsidized and loans for small farmers were set at especially low rates.
- The source of funds for most programs was the government and donors. Local savings mobilization was largely ignored.
- The objective of government policy was to increase the supply of loans made to farmers with little attention given to institutional sustainability.
- Production packages were created for farmers in which credit was treated as an input like seeds and fertilizer.
- Credit was targeted for "productive purposes." Loans for consumption and rural nonfarm enterprises were ignored and, in some cases, prohibited.
- Many credit programs were aimed at small farmers and employed supervised credit through cooperatives as a means to ensure it was used properly.[1]
- Cooperatives were the primary credit channels in many countries, while commercial banks and agricultural development banks were more important in others.
- Transaction costs for lenders and borrowers were largely ignored.
- Some programs eventually broadened their target groups from small farmers to the rural poor.

---

[1] This approach emerged in response to the default and other problems encountered in early credit projects. Credit provided through cooperatives with strong extension support appeared to be promising in Brazil, Mexico, and India (FAO, 1964).

The Special Case of Directed Credit in East Asia

Studies during the 1970s and 1980s began to question the directed credit model as an appropriate strategy to speed growth and development. However, East Asia is often advanced as a special case in which directed credit and government intervention in financial markets made a more positive impact on economic growth than elsewhere. It is important to understand how the region's financial markets may have contributed both to its successes and to the financial and economic crisis in Asia that began in 1997. An analysis of the high-performing Asian economies led to the conclusion that good capital market fundamentals explained the contribution that capital markets made to efficient resource allocation in these countries. The rapid deepening of financial markets contributed to economic growth, but the record on directed credit was mixed. All East Asian economies provided generous credit to exporters with varying degrees of subsidy. The best success occurred in those countries with strong civil societies and professional public financial institutions such as in Japan, the Republic of Korea, Singapore, and Taipei,China (World Bank, 1993).

Five unique features have been proposed to explain the success of governmental interventions in East Asia's industrial growth (Stiglitz and Uy, 1996). First, national savings were promoted by creating postal savings and provident funds, restricting consumer credit, protecting banks against failures, employing mild financial restraints, and keeping public deficits low. Second, prudential regulations were employed to enhance the solvency of financial institutions. Third, financial institutions, including development finance institutions, were created and effectively utilized to augment resource flows to priority sectors. The successful institutions insisted on commercial standards and avoided political pressures to finance bad projects and poor incentives to screen and monitor projects. Fourth, the financial restraints slightly lowered interest rates and encouraged firms to invest. These also increased the franchise value of banks, which provided strong incentives for prudent banking. Finally, the results were more favorable than in many other developing countries because a large part of the directed credit went to private rather than public enterprises, credit allocation was usually based on objective performance criteria, credit was more common than outright subsides, total directed credit was relatively small compared with commercial credit, monitoring was more effective, and credit policy changes were made quickly when existing policies did not function properly.

The study left unanswered, however, the question of whether or not East Asia's successful experience could be replicated. The current crisis reveals that past financial policies may have contributed to rapid growth in Southeast Asia, but they also contributed to the currency and financial crisis that evolved into an economic and social crisis with potential repercussions reaching far beyond Asia.

Understanding the Financial and Economic Crisis in Asia

The rapidly growing literature on the Asian financial and economic crisis reports on competing assessments of its causes, reforms to be undertaken, and the need and methods for restarting the growth process. It is necessary to learn from these financial problems and proposed solutions in order to speculate about the implications for developing Asian rural financial markets.

The crisis was unexpected, as witnessed by the optimistic views about the region reported in a survey of Asia by the Asian Development Bank published in 1997 (ADB, 1997a) that was followed just a few months later by Thailand's currency devaluation. Analysts tend to agree that the seeds of the crisis were sown in the early 1990s with massive capital inflows that fueled a large increase in domestic bank lending, which drove investment in the region (e.g. Corsetti, Pesenti, and Roubini, 1998; Park and Song, 1998). Much of the investment was directed towards projects in the nontradable sector, especially speculative investments in stocks and other financial assets. In Thailand, specifically, this created a bubble in the real estate market financed partly by nonbank financial institutions. The region's spectacular export performance began to slow in 1996, and a growing number of firms suffered losses and were unable to meet their debt obligations. Several went bankrupt. The real estate bubble broke in Thailand in early 1997 and defaults in the financial and corporate sectors began to rise, sparking concerns among foreign and domestic creditors. The cost of offshore borrowing rose and countries began to finance a growing share of their current account deficits with short-term foreign currency loans. Thailand depleted its reserves trying to defend its fixed exchange rate and was forced to devalue. This contributed to financial panic among investors and led to contagious speculative attacks on other currencies. The massive inflow of capital into the region quickly turned into a massive outflow leading to a collapse in regional currencies.

The herd effect of foreign investors, contributing both to the boom and the bust, has been identified as one of the major causes of the crisis. However, analysts also argue that in retrospect, policy shortcomings in the region were partly to blame. A long list of structural distortions in the Asian financial and banking sectors was summarized as follows: "lax supervision and weak regulation; low capital adequacy ratios; lack of incentive-compatible deposit insurance schemes; insufficient expertise in regulatory institutions; distorted incentives for project selection and monitoring; outright corrupt lending practices; non-market criteria of credit allocation according to a model of relationship banking that emphasizes semi-monopolistic relations between banks and firms somehow downplaying price signals. All these factors contributed to the build-up of severe weaknesses in the undercapitalized financial system, whose most visible manifestation was eventually a growing share of non-performing loans" (Corsetti, Pesenti, and Roubini, 1998, p. 3).[2]

---

[2] The implications of this summary are somewhat at odds with the authors of Emerging Asia (ADB, 1997a, p. 120) who concluded that investment is subject to the market test in East Asia. Sachs (1997) also offered an early analysis of the potential threat of excessive lending driven by moral hazard incentives in Latin America, Central Europe, and Southeast Asia.

The IMF-supported response to the crisis employed a tightening of monetary policy and higher interest rates in an effort to restore investor confidence. Critics have argued that these policies contributed to a vicious circle: otherwise solvent companies could not pay the higher interest rates leading to higher levels of nonperforming loans and credit risk, exacerbating the recession, and causing a further contraction in the supply of credit (Corsetti, Pesenti, and Roubini, 1998; Stiglitz, 1998).

Many financial reforms have been recommended to correct these structural problems. They have been summarized as a) reducing the incentives for excessive borrowing, b) improving governance of the financial sector, and c) enhancing prudential regulation, especially for short-term capital flows (World Bank, 1998a). By mid-1998, the most seriously affected countries, Indonesia, Republic of Korea, Malaysia, Philippines, and Thailand, were planning or were already implementing financial reforms, including strengthening the supervisory and legal framework for banking operations; tightening capital adequacy requirements; strengthening accounting/auditing requirements; tightening bank disclosure, loan classification and provisioning requirements; tightening guidelines on loan exposure; and introducing a funded deposit insurance scheme (Kochkar, Loungani, and Stone, 1998). These changes have a great deal to do with information: improved information for financial institutions about the performance of clients, and improved information for regulators about the portfolios of financial institutions. Tighter regulations and better and more transparent information are expected to lead to more prudent behavior by financial institutions.

What are the implications of the crisis for the development of rural financial markets? First, as noted in the case studies, there is concern about the potential problems with rural loan recovery in Thailand and Indonesia because of a sharp rise in unemployment and fall in incomes. There is also concern about the supply of deposits and funds for rural lenders to make new loans, but the possible longer-term impact is more important.

The crisis has raised important issues about the fragility of financial systems associated with the globalization of capital markets and the appropriate ways to use financial markets for enhancing growth. One argument stresses that domestic financial reform should precede the opening of the capital account (Garnaut, 1998; Eichengreen and Mussa, 1998). This view implies accelerating the pace of banking reforms in countries like the PRC and India as they open their economies to more foreign investment. Demand will increase for more transparency in corporate and banking operations and greater attention to the governance of institutions in all countries. Although the rural financial system is largely outside the immediate concern of policymakers, efforts to strengthen financial systems will likely have spillover effects into rural banking.

There may be a desire in some countries to treat agricultural banking more like commercial banking. This would lead to a tightening of credit standards, more attention to credit risk, greater capital requirements, more rigorous credit appraisal, more realistic loan provisioning, better trained employees, and more professional management. These changes along with the cost of greater reporting requirements will drive up banking costs in the short run but will strengthen viability in the long run. The immediate reaction could be higher collateral requirements but, as the financial system becomes more professional, there should be greater potential to shift to cash-flow lending. There may be difficulties in designing an acceptable special regulatory framework for institutions licensed as specialized banks for the poor. Overall, these changes are consistent with the shifts in thinking that have occurred about the appropriate way to develop rural financial markets, as discussed in the next section.

Rural Finance in Asia in 1999

The analysis presented in the case studies reveals an obvious conclusion: adoption of the new paradigm is very uneven in Asia. Several countries in the region have adopted more of a market approach to rural finance than was the case in the 1960s and 1970s. Sadly, many countries have not done so, and they are paying the price in the form of poorly performing institutions that require large subsidies. Moreover, outreach is not increasing very rapidly; a large proportion of the rural population is still denied access to formal financial services. The new paradigm has been adopted more readily by some microfinance organizations (MFOs) than by traditional agricultural lenders.

The policies and institutions of Southeast Asian countries have generally evolved into more of a market-oriented approach than have other countries, and the results have been strikingly better. For example, Thailand has followed an approach to rural finance that emphasizes commercial banks and the government-owned BAAC. The private commercial banks were initially given quotas for agricultural lending that could be met by direct lending or by depositing funds in BAAC. The banks generally serve larger farmers and agribusinesses. BAAC has expanded, makes loans to both groups and individual farmers, serves most of the small and medium sized farms, and now reaches some 80 percent of the country's farmers. BAAC has slowly increased the share of savings in its total resources. Its interest rates are still somewhat subsidized and this negatively affects its sustainability. In aggregate, the agricultural credit to agricultural GDP ratio grew from about 0.06 in 1970 to nearly 0.70 by 1996. Most farmers now have access to the formal financial system, there is relatively little need for special credit programs for the poor, and the entire system is largely self-financed.

An important part of the Indonesian agricultural credit system involved the integrated Bimas project implemented through BRI from the late 1960s until it collapsed in the early 1980s. The major reforms undertaken by the BRI unit desa system in 1983/84 transformed it into one of the most dynamic rural financial institutions in the region. It serves millions of clients with nontargeted loans and mobilizes savings so successfully that surplus rural savings flow to urban areas to finance corporate lending. Both farm and nonfarm enterprises are served. Other rural financial institutions in Indonesia have been less successful, however, and appear not to have learned from the BRI example. The performance of many smaller provincial and local financial institutions is not as good as that of BRI. Many highly subsidized poverty-oriented projects have recently been created. They represent an unwise departure from the Government's drive to create sustainable rural finance, and may undermine some nonsubsidized financial institutions that follow a market-oriented approach.

The South Asian countries generally have been less successful than Southeast Asian countries in developing viable rural financial systems in spite of the huge amount of resources spent on the task. Bangladesh, Pakistan, and Nepal have emphasized targeted lending by specialized agricultural development banks (SADBs) to individual farmers and cooperatives. Funds have largely come from the government and donors. Loan recovery rates are low, and in all three countries, financial institutions are highly subsidized. The top-down approach used in rural cooperative development also has serious problems in these countries.

India nationalized its banks and implemented a massive expansion of public and private bank branches and cooperatives in rural areas, and created specialized regional rural banks to reach the rural poor, small farmers, landless workers, and small entrepreneurs. The government still owns 80 percent of the banking industry, and the cooperatives are significantly controlled by the states. The National Bank for Agriculture and Rural Development (NABARD) is the apex institution responsible for agricultural credit policy and refinancing rural lending. The Integrated Rural Development Program (IRDP) was created in 1978 for poverty alleviation. It provides subsidized loans and cash subsidies to the poor. Loan recovery is a serious problem for banks and cooperatives, and the loan *melas* of the 1980s (see Chapter VIII) and the loan waiver of 1991 represent political abuses of the banking sector that damaged credit discipline. Interest rates on loans were largely deregulated in 1996, but many financial institutions have not used this flexibility to improve their sustainability. The rural financial system has expanded outreach; however, it provides poor quality service and is highly subsidized. The country is trying to move towards more of a market-oriented system, but progress is slow because the strong tradition of mandated credit is proving difficult to change.

The formal financial system in Bangladesh is under severe stress. The nationalized commercial banks, agricultural development banks, and even many of the new private commercial banks face huge loan recovery problems, as do the agricultural cooperatives. The central bank sets quotas for agricultural lending and rediscounts rural loans. Surprisingly, a robust microfinance movement has emerged, which includes the specialized Grameen Bank and hundreds of NGOs that lend to the poor. These microlenders have achieved significant breadth and depth of outreach, although most are highly dependent on subsidies. Fortunately, most have avoided the bad-debt syndrome that plagues the banks. The combination of bank, cooperative, and microfinance lending amounted to about 9 percent of agricultural GDP in 1993/94, which was higher than a decade earlier. The future of rural finance is unclear. The MFOs have been freer than banks to adopt a market-oriented approach, but both the agricultural lenders and microlenders fail to cover fully their costs and risks of lending.

The transition economies, represented by the PRC and the Kyrgyz Republic in this study, face the major challenge of building a market-oriented financial system. The PRC has gone through three phases of financial reforms since 1979. The rural sector is now served by a state bank, a policy bank, rural credit cooperatives (RCCs) and rural credit foundations (RCFs). The financial system has been successful in mobilizing a large amount of savings from rural households. The RCCs are most important in mobilizing these savings and they channel a significant share of these resources into loans to township and village enterprises (TVEs). The unregulated RCFs emerged in the 1990s in response to the demand for financial services by households and collectives. They are more important in lending to households than to TVEs and collectives. Lending quotas and interest rate ceilings have been relaxed for commercial banks but, because of high costs and loan defaults, there are serious doubts about the sustainability of most rural financial institutions. Loan recovery is a serious problem for most institutions and jeopardizes sustainability. Information is incomplete about rural access to the formal financial system and the viability of the system.

The financial system in the Kyrgyz Republic is highly unstable and the banks, including the two that service rural areas, have serious problems with nonperforming loans. Interest rates have usually been negative in real terms and subsidized farm loans are provided through local government budgets. There is little information about the newly created Kyrgyz Agricultural Finance Corporation or the savings and settlement companies that are designed to mobilize savings and provide payment services. Likewise, several donor-assisted microfinance schemes have recently been started in rural areas, but there is little information about their performance. The entire system is weak and most institutions have little capacity to make good loans and recover them. The weaknesses of the financial system constrain the emergence of a vibrant agricultural sector.

To summarize, this survey of rural Asia has revealed a surprisingly large number of countries that have made relatively little progress in adopting the new paradigm in their rural financial policies. Although there are important exceptions, the primary problems today are similar to those two decades ago:

- Interest rates are often too low to cover the costs and risks of lending. Some MFOs have adjusted their rates high enough to cover most costs, but regulations and political pressures have kept rates low for many agricultural lenders.
- Countries have resisted adopting more of a market approach to rural finance. Targeted programs, subsidized refinance funds, and restrictions on clientele served still exist, although they are somewhat less repressive than in past years. The sustainability of financial institutions continues to be a secondary objective.

- Many rural financial institutions are weak and exist only because of subsidies. Nonperforming loans are a serious problem and sap their vitality.
- Savings mobilization is still relatively neglected in spite of the earlier successes of rural cooperatives in Japan, Republic of Korea, and Taipei,China.
- Policymakers continue to be largely preoccupied with the problems of agriculture and overlook the broader demand for financial services by the rural nonfarm economy.
- Most rural finance institutions are ill-equipped to make long-term loans and to utilize new information and communication technologies characteristic of modern banking.

LEARNING FROM SUCCESS: THREE FLAGSHIP INSTITUTIONS

The authors of the ADB studies in 1967/68 and 1976/77 faced a serious problem. They could document the many failings of agricultural credit projects and identify a few promising trends (e.g., number of banking outlets, increases in disbursements), but they had few successes to enable them to evaluate what is possible with a different approach. Fortunately, today there are several successful Asian institutions that illustrate the possibilities, as discussed in the following sections.

What are the Characteristics and Performance Indicators of Successful Rural Financial Institutions?

Three Asian institutions have been studied extensively because their performance has been far superior to that of most rural financial institutions in the developing world. These flagship institutions are BAAC in Thailand, the BRI unit desa system in Indonesia (BRI-UD), and the Grameen Bank (GB) in Bangladesh.

Comparative information about them is presented in Table IV.1
and more details are provided in the country case studies.

Table IV.1:   Selected Characteristics and Performance Measures of
BAAC, BRI-UD, and the Grameen Bank

Item	BAAC	BRI-UD	GB
Year established/reorganized	1966	1983/84	1983
Clientele	Farmers, cooperatives, farmers' associations	Rural low-and middle-income households	Rural poor
Financial services	Loans and savings deposits	Loans and savings deposits	Loans and compulsory savings
Lending technology	Group and individual	Individual	Group
Approximate number of loans outstanding	3.1 million	2.3 million	2.1 million
Volume of loans outstanding	$3.8 billion (non-cooperative loans)[a]	$1.2 billion	$289 million
Average outstanding loan	$1,285	$567	$142
Average outstanding loan as percent of GDP per capita	42[b]	54	64
Average annual volume of savings	$2.8 billion	$2.6 billion	$133 million
Average annual savings as percent of average annual outstanding loans	66.5	199.0	45.6
Number of savers	4.4 million[c]	14.5 million	2.1 million
Approximate nominal effective annual interest rate	8.3 to 15.5	32.7	20
Interest rate spread	1995: 4.1	1994: 21.7	1995: 8.0
Total operating costs as percent of annual average outstanding loans	1995: 3.5	1994: 13.5	1995: 10.6
Return on assets	1995: 0.55	1994: 4.8	1995: 0.14
Percentage of outstanding loans in arrears	8.3	6.5	3.6
Subsidy dependence index	1995: 35.4[b]	1995: negative[d]	1996: positive[e]

Source: Adapted from Yaron, Benjamin, and Piprek (1997) except where noted.

[a] BAAC reported total loans outstanding in 1996 of baht 177 billion (about $6.9 billion).

[b] Reported by Muraki, Webster, and Yaron (1998b). According to their estimates, in 1995 BAAC would have had to increase its average yield on loan portfolio from 11.0 to 14.89 percent (i.e., 35.4 percent) to be free of subsidies.

[c] Reported by Fitchett (1997).

[d] Charitoneko, Patten, and Yaron (1998) reported that the BRI unit desas were so profitable in 1996 that they could have reduced their yield on loan portfolio from 31.6 to 16.3 percent and still have remained subsidy independent.

[e] Reported by Morduch (1998b). According to his calculations, the GB would have to increase its nominal interest rate on general loans from 20 to 33 percent to become free of subsidies.

The data in Table IV.1 present a comparative analysis of institutional performance using the two criteria increasingly accepted as the appropriate framework for analysis: outreach and self-sustainability (Christen et al., 1995; Yaron, Benjamin and Piprek, 1997). This framework does not attempt to assess impact on clients (as was advocated in the old paradigm), but rather focuses on the performance of the financial institution. The implicit assumption is that clients will continue to use the organization if it provides them with useful services that make a positive impact on their lives.[3]

Outreach refers to the increased degree of market coverage for low-income groups previously without access to formal financial services. It includes both a horizontal dimension (breadth of outreach or number of clients served) and a vertical dimension (depth or level of poverty of clients). In addition, the types and variety of financial services offered are also considered. Sustainability refers to the ability of a financial institution to supply financial services on a continuous cost-covering basis without external subsidies. A sustainable institution must cover its costs including operating expenses, loan and inflationary losses, and the cost of funds without external subsidies. It must make a profit to compensate owners, to accumulate reserves against future losses, and to fund new investments. Subsidy dependence is the inverse of sustainability, and the calculation of a subsidy dependence index (SDI) has been effectively used to evaluate the degree of subsidization received by a financial organization (Yaron, 1992).

Sustainability is a desirable objective for financial institutions for at least two reasons: first, the temporary access to loans for a targeted clientele may produce some benefits, but creating a long-term sustainable financial relationship is more valuable because it provides clients with the opportunity for future benefits. Moreover, a sustainable institution benefits more

---

[3] The case studies discuss other indicators of the performance of the financial system, such as trends in the volume and interest rates charged for informal loans. Studies of other impact measures are also cited.

clients than one that begins with a flourish but collapses in a few years. Second, a sustainable institution is generally free of the whims and budgetary constraints of the government and donors. This helps borrowers develop positive expectations for long-term access to services if they observe the terms of their loan contracts. It also helps the institutions grow beyond the limits permitted by the subsidies provided, and helps shield them from political intrusions. Many MFOs are striving to achieve operational sustainability by covering their operational costs exclusively through interest income. In addition, several others are attempting to cover loan and inflationary losses without external subsidies.

Concerns have been raised regarding possible trade-offs between outreach and sustainability (e.g. Hulme and Mosley, 1996). Institutions that strive for self-sustainability may try to reduce costs through making larger repeat loans to existing clients rather than making additional small loans to new poor clients. Conversely, realizing economies of scale through achieving a wider outreach may contribute to sustainability since costs per unit lent decline as loan volume rises. Therefore, achieving greater breadth of outreach may improve sustainability, while reaching greater depth of outreach may detract from sustainability if the costs and risks of lending cannot be covered by interest income.

The three financial institutions have slightly different objectives (Table IV.1). BAAC was created in 1966 with a specific mandate to serve agriculture and only recently began to serve nonfarm enterprises. BRI-UD was reorganized in 1983/84 following the collapse of Bimas and it took on the objective of serving rural low- and middle-income households. Its loan portfolio has been dominated by loans for trading and other nonfarm activities. Grameen started as an NGO program in 1976 and became a specialized bank for the poor in 1983. Almost 90 percent of its current clients are women, and many of them borrow for farm-related and nonfarm activities. Therefore, BAAC is largely an agricultural lender, GB is a specialized MFO, while BRI-UD fits between the two orientations. BAAC and BRI-UD are more active than GB in savings mobilization.

GB largely makes group loans, BRI-UD makes only individual loans, and BAAC uses both types of technology.

All three institutions have millions of clients with loans, but BAAC has been relatively the most successful as it reaches over 80 percent of the country's farm families. It has a larger loan portfolio because of its larger average loan size. The frequent method for evaluating depth of outreach (i.e. poverty level of clients) is to compare average loan size with the country's GDP per capita. In that comparison, BAAC also performs well in reaching the poor.

Two performance criteria sharply differentiate the three institutions. The first is savings mobilization. The total amounts of savings for BAAC and BRI-UD are roughly equal, but the number of savers is much larger in BRI-UD. Moreover, the total savings in BRI-UD far exceed its loan balances, while BAAC and GB rely on other sources of funds for a significant share of their total lending. Unlike the other two, Grameen does not actively promote voluntary savings.

Sustainability is the second major difference among the three. BAAC employs a policy of low interest rates, and as a result its interest rate spread is the smallest. Although it is highly efficient, as shown by its 3.5 percent operating costs, its profits and return on assets are low. It has some problems with loan arrears, especially for loans made to cooperatives and farmers' associations. Considering the various types of subsidies received, it would have to raise the average yield on loans from 11 to almost 15 percent to become free of subsidies. The GB has an even more serious problem because, to be free of subsidy, it would have to raise its nominal interest rate on general loans from 20 to 33 percent.

BRI-UD is unique. It charges the highest interest rates and earns the highest rate spread of the three, so it can easily cover its higher operating costs. In fact, it was so profitable in 1995 that it could have reduced its yield on loan portfolio from 31.6 to 16.3 percent and still remained free of subsidy. Given these estimates, BAAC would need to charge roughly a 15 percent nominal rate for its loans, BRI-UD almost 16 percent, and GB about 33 percent. However, these values vary from year to year depending on the amount of subsidies received, and it would be necessary to evaluate carefully loan loss provisions, profits needed for future investment and growth, and several other factors before determining optimum interest rates. Simply by considering the differences in loan sizes, it should be expected that BAAC would reach self-sufficiency with lower interest rates, while the GB would need to charge the highest rates of the three.

What Factors Determine the Success of Rural Financial Institutions?

The experience of these three institutions along with analyses of financial institutions in other countries reveals crucial factors that influence the ability of financial institutions to achieve outreach and self-sustainability. The three-pronged framework for developing financial markets, described in Chapter III, is used as the way to organize the ideas presented here.

Policy Environment

The past urban bias of many economic policies in Asian countries has been reduced so prospects have improved for agricultural firms to be profitable. Profitable clients make better customers for financial institutions. However, other policy issues that influence the prospects for developing sound rural financial markets must be addressed in many Asian countries.

i. Interest Rates

Interest rates for farm loans are controlled in some countries and, in others, financial institutions are reluctant to raise rates even when they have been deregulated. To reduce subsidy dependence, financial institutions must charge rates high enough to earn interest spreads that will cover operating costs and losses. Interest rates must be positive in real terms to compensate savers for supplying resources for lending, and enough profits must be realized to provide owners with a reasonable return on their capital and resources to generate reserves and reinvest for future growth. The financial institutions must be free to price their services according to the costs and risks of the clients served. Countries that control interest rates at low levels for the benefit of certain sectors or groups of clients destroy the possibility of institutions covering their costs. The low-interest-rate policies of BAAC and GB, and many MFOs, are well intentioned to assist their borrowers, but the cost for the institutions is that they cannot become completely self-sufficient. They have to rely on governments and donors to provide subsidies continuously. This introduces uncertainties and the possibility of politically motivated terms and conditions attached to such support. BRI-UD is able to avoid these problems because it determines the structure of its interest rates.

The second problem noted in the case studies is that institutions that operate on market principles face competition from subsidized institutions. So far this problem has not seriously affected these institutions but it is becoming more serious today in Indonesia. The Indonesian Government, the World Bank, and the UNDP are pumping subsidized credit into villages as part of projects designed to alleviate economic and social problems caused by the current crisis. BRI-UD may not be seriously affected; however this well-intentioned effort may contribute to the failure of some rural banks and other local financial institutions. It may also undermine the credit culture: the soft conditions and weak enforcement procedures associated with these special projects may lead borrowers to think of loans as grants. It is tempting for governments to channel emergency assistance through existing networks of financial institutions, but it can have a corrupting influence and damage institutional viability.

The freedom to set interest rates is often linked to the freedom to select clients. Subsidized credit projects usually carry restrictions about the target group to be served. This is a problem for the policy loans made by BAAC. The more narrowly specified the target group (e.g. small rice farmers), the greater is the chance that the lender will end up with a risky, undiversified portfolio. Moreover, the greater the subsidy, the greater the potential for political intrusion over credit allocation, as demonstrated in the case of the Indian loan melas.

ii. Client Selection

With the exception of the special government projects administered by BAAC and the restrictions placed on the nonfarm enterprises it can serve,[4] these three flagship institutions select their own clients. Financial institutions must be able to design and market financial services that match the demands of their potential clients. They must avoid targeted programs that constrain them to serve a specific group or type of client. Such regulations or mandates inhibit them from diversifying their portfolios as a protection against systemic risks.

Clients should self-select themselves to use the products offered by specific institutions rather than being targeted by a specific program. This flexibility creates a banking relationship in which the clients realize that financial services are offered to them, not because of mandates, but because the institutions perceive them as valued clients. The institutions may choose to market certain products to specific types of clientele expected to be most interested in them. For example, the GB has increasingly shifted its membership to women because they were found to be better suited than men for attending the weekly meetings necessary for membership. Likewise, some MFOs require clients to operate a business for several months before seeking a loan as a way to avoid the high failure rate of new business start-ups.

---

[4] In early 1999, legislation was passed in Thailand that gave BAAC broader authority to make rural nonfarm loans.

Financial Infrastructure

i. Legal and Regulatory Framework

The three flagship financial institutions operate under formal legal charters and are subject to regulations. This gives them an important advantage because it permits them to legally take deposits. The regulations may be different from those applicable to commercial banks to account for the special nature of their loan contracts and the absence of physical collateral to back the loans. Although the capacity and skills of the regulatory and supervisory authorities have been questioned in all three countries, especially during the financial crisis in Thailand and Indonesia, the safety and soundness of these institutions has thus far been assured. Of course, this is due in part to the backing they get from their governments and donors. The financial and economic crisis in Asia revealed that strengthening the regulatory framework is a requirement in all three countries in order to support the development of strong financial institutions.

One of the important lessons of the Bangladesh microfinance experiences is that it is possible to avoid temporarily some of the problems that affect the commercial banking system, such as complicated and expensive legal procedures to collect loans. Contract enforcement for micro and small loans requires securing payment without resorting to the legal system. As long as clients are motivated to repay by peer pressure and a desire to access a further loan, financial transactions can occur in the absence of a good, inexpensive legal framework. However, problems may develop when the Bangladesh MFOs make larger individual loans and more traditional forms of contract enforcement are required. The more the MFOs begin to act like traditional banks, the more they will share the same problems.

ii. Information Systems

No systematic analysis has been done about the information systems used in these three countries. Grameen has a centralized system in which all accounts are recorded. It was reported that this system saved it from the problems encountered by many other MFOs whose records were swept away in a recent flood. Land titling projects are underway in Thailand. They should make it easier and cheaper to access information about the legal status of land offered as collateral, and this will reduce transaction costs for lenders.

As the financial markets become more sophisticated and competitive, efficient systems will be required to supply information about the indebtedness and repayment history of borrowers. A lender must have ready access to information to determine if a loan applicant has outstanding loans elsewhere. This information must be accurate and current. Regulated institutions often have to provide the names of delinquent borrowers such that one institution knows a borrower's status with another institution. However, this information is usually not available from nonregulated institutions. Some countries in the region have a special problem in simply identifying people because there are no national identity cards.

Institutional Development

The three flagship institutions have benefited from a reasonably good policy environment and financial infrastructure, but an important part of their success is due to the careful process of institutional development that each has undertaken. This includes the design of the institution, management and governance, incentive systems, human capital development, and a variety of other factors.

i. The Design of Products and Services

Financial institutions must design specific products and services with two objectives in mind. The first is expected demand from perspective clients given the products supplied by other formal and informal sources. The second is the ability of the institution to cover the costs of offering the product or service, either as a single transaction or over the life of a long-term relationship with a client. It may be impossible, for example, for a financial institution to offer competitively very small, emergency loans normally supplied by friends, relatives, neighbors, or moneylenders. BAAC and GB, as well as many MFOs, have demonstrated that it is possible to successfully design products and technologies to make short-term working capital loans without using the formal collateral normally required by formal lenders. A few are experimenting with longer-term housing loans.

An important characteristic of these three institutions is that they have used market research, test marketing, and pilot projects to test and adapt their products to meet the demands of clients. For example, the case studies describe the efforts that BRI-UD and BAAC have made to develop attractive savings products that contributed to their growth in savings. These organizations are also very liberal about loan use. Unlike targeted credit projects, they lend for a variety of purposes and recognize that clients are usually the best judge of how to use loans. However, they demand repayment regardless of whatever success or failure the borrower experienced in investing loan proceeds.

ii. Loan Recovery and Long-Term Relations

The design of products and services is related to loan recovery, which often determines the difference between success and failure of financial institutions. Borrowers with good repayment records cannot be expected to pay interest rates high enough to cover large loan losses. These three institutions report arrears of less than 10 percent and their actual loss rate is much lower. Good repayment occurs for several reasons. First, the institutions increase the borrowers' ability to repay by making mostly small loans and by setting repayment schedules that are consistent with the borrowers' cash flow and repayment capacity. The GB uses a weekly repayment schedule while BRI-UD requires monthly payments. A schedule of frequent payments keeps the size of each payment small and provides the institution with the opportunity to keep in regular contact with clients. As competition rises, products and technologies need to change. The loss of customers may be a sign of poor service. For example, the GB and other MFOs in Bangladesh have recently experienced high drop-out rates, and one explanation may be the excessively rigid loan products, repayment schedules, and savings requirements (Wright, 1999).

Second, the institutions stimulate borrower willingness to pay in two ways. Joint-liability group lenders expect that peer pressure among the group members will contribute to repayment. An even more important factor is that the institutions promote the image of seeking a long-term business relationship with the client. Therefore, the expectation of a future loan with superior terms and conditions acts as an important inducement for repayment. In addition, BRI-UD uses the positive incentive of interest rebates as a stimulus for on-time payments, while BAAC imposes penalties for late payments.

Another factor affecting repayment is timely information about clients. All three institutions have good internal information systems. Loan officers know immediately when loans become overdue so they can follow up with their clients, analyze problems, and arrange for repayment. Loan payments and savings deposits are made weekly by GB clients in a transparent way in open meetings such that everyone immediately knows if someone is late in paying. This process places great social pressure on delinquent borrowers.

iii. Management and Governance

Managing large institutions with thousands of staff and hundreds of outlets is a huge task in countries where communication infrastructure is lacking. These three institutions have the reputation of being professionally managed and have achieved a high degree of efficiency in their operations. The management of these institutions has considerable autonomy in day-to-day operations. The founders of BRI-UD and GB are well known for their vision and commitment, and they have managed to instill it in their subordinates. The Government of Thailand is given high marks for choosing good managers for

BAAC. The attributes of good management and efficiency rather than political expediency were demanded by the governance system. The presence of foreign advisors who argued for strong institutional performance may have been an important protection for BRI-UD against political pressures.

iv. Staff Incentive Systems

Performance-based staff incentive systems are found in most successful institutions. The BRI-UD system was designed on the specific concept of profit and loss centers, which provides a framework for performance-based remuneration. Both BRI-UD and BAAC stimulate high levels of staff efficiency through formal staff incentives tied to bonus payments. Bonuses are paid either on institutional performance or the efficiency of the individual employees in making loans and mobilizing savings. They have also paid base salaries that are higher than some equivalent jobs in the public or private sector. Each loan officer serves a large number of clients and manages a large portfolio as a result of these incentives. GB has operated under more difficult constraints because of the negative example of the personnel policies of the bureaucratic State-owned banks. Group spirit and social commitment play a relatively larger role in affecting staff performance. In the difficult flood period, the GB first aided its employees to enable them to service their clients, and it offered special compensation and vacation time for those working under difficult circumstances.

v. Human Capital Development

The recruitment and hiring policies of these three institutions are different. BAAC and GB have higher educational requirements for potential loan officers, while BRI-UD hires staff with lower education levels, but who know the local environment in which they are assigned. All three have used intensive training programs for new employees to instill institutional mission and pride and to teach specific procedures and skills. BAAC has an ADB technical assistance project to improve its operations and staff training. The demands on its staff will rise with the recent authorization to expand lending to new clients in nonfarm enterprises and to increase loan sizes for some of its existing farm clients. The new staff of BRI/UD and BAAC are assigned as trainees or apprentices so they can be evaluated before being hired as regular staff. Loan officers in BRI-UD earn higher levels of loan approval authority as they gain more experience. Decentralization of decisionmaking is possible because of the large investments made in human capital development.

V DEVELOPING RURAL FINANCIAL MARKETS IN ASIA: WHAT SHOULD BE DONE?

This chapter summarizes the key findings of this study and identifies priority actions to be taken to strengthen rural financial markets. The first section summarizes the major conclusions of the research. The second section discusses the problems in implementing the new paradigm in Asia. These two sections draw heavily from the previous chapter and the case studies presented in Part B. The third section outlines the key recommendations. The fourth section discusses special issues for donors, and the last section presents some final thoughts on the region's challenges in entering the twenty-first century.

MAJOR CONCLUSIONS

The Rural Economy, the Green Revolution, and Rural Financial Markets

Although it is difficult to measure impact precisely, a major conclusion of this study is that robust rural financial markets are correlated with rapid agricultural growth in Asia. The PRC is the only country in the region that has experienced rapid agricultural growth without the benefit of a strong market-oriented rural financial system. No country in the region has developed a strong rural financial system without having a progressive agricultural sector. Moreover, rural financial institutions are part of the overall financial system; it is logical that no strong rural financial institutions exist in a country with a weak financial sector.

The financial sector can respond to opportunities created by rapid economic growth, but cannot accelerate the growth process in the face of an unfavorable economic environment. Agricultural credit, for example, can facilitate economic transactions, enable borrowers to adopt technology, make investments, smooth consumption expenditures, and ameliorate risks. However, credit cannot compensate for unprofitable production activities. It cannot compensate for missing roads, bridges, and communications. It cannot compensate for bad seed, missing input supplies, inefficient marketing systems, and poor transportation. These fundamental economic and agricultural bottlenecks must be addressed before more loans can make a significant impact. Moreover, merely granting loans to the poor is unlikely to lift them single-handedly out of poverty.

Rural financial markets consist of formal, semiformal, and informal financial arrangements. Banks, cooperatives, moneylenders, friends, and relatives, and commodity traders are all part of the financial system. Informal loans are often used for short-term emergency and consumption purposes, but they also finance production and marketing activities. Formal loans are more likely to be used for large-scale investments and major working capital expenses. Both informal and formal finance play a role in financial markets, and firms and households often use both sources because of their unique characteristics.

Experience has shown that the massive amount of directed credit channeled to agriculture to support the green revolution did not have the desired impact. First, it did not contribute significantly to the adoption of technology beyond what would have occurred without it. Farmers convinced of the merits of the new technology used self-finance and informal financial sources in the absence of formal credit supplies. The destructive effects of the directed credit strategy on formal financial institutions overshadowed any positive impact. Second, there is little evidence to demonstrate that expanded formal finance made a significant impact on the importance of informal finance or on its terms and conditions. Where informal finance has been historically important, it continues to finance many consumption and emergency loans for rural households.

Intervention by the State in Rural Financial Markets

The governments in all Asian countries have intervened in their rural financial markets to a greater or lesser degree during the past three decades. Often that intervention has been greater for agriculture than for other sectors. Directed agricultural credit programs with heavily subsidized rates were the norm in the 1970s and 1980s and donors contributed heavily to them. The primary governmental interventions have included interest rate regulations, lending quotas, directed and subsidized credit projects, special refinance facilities for agricultural lending, and funding specialized agricultural development banks. Agricultural loan forgiveness and write-offs have been frequent, financial institutions have been created and rehabilitated with government subsidies, and guarantee funds have been designed and capitalized. Whereas 25 years ago the rationale for intervention was to stimulate the adoption of green revolution technologies, especially by small farmers, today the rationale is more frequently the social objective of making small loans to the poor to alleviate poverty.

The high costs and risks of providing financial services in rural areas explains some of the problems encountered by rural financial institutions, but poor governmental policies and investments also play a role. Many governments engaged in directed agricultural credit policies that in retrospect proved to be damaging to rural financial markets. At the same time, they often failed to do what governments should do. There were three major problems with this approach:

- First, too little attention was paid to creating a favorable policy environment in which healthy financial markets could grow and develop.
- Second, a suitable financial infrastructure was not created. Most importantly, a strong prudential regulatory and

supervisory framework was not created to protect the financial system. This became clear in the recent economic and financial crisis in Asia. Moreover, political involvement in financial markets, such as has occurred in Bangladesh, India, and Indonesia, prevented the effective enforcement of existing regulations.

- Third, too little attention was paid to institution building. The governments and donors channeled too many resources through financial institutions into agricultural lending and not enough into financial institutions to build up capacity for efficient financial intermediation.

Significant financial liberalization was not undertaken in most Asian countries until the 1990s, even though many negative effects of financial repression and subsidized directed credit were identified well before then. Even today, many countries continue to employ the outdated directed credit paradigm for agriculture and resist the lessons of microfinance.

Major Shortcomings of Asian Rural Financial Markets

The major shortcomings of Asian rural financial markets can be briefly summarized as follows:

- Most countries have resisted adopting a market-based approach to rural finance. This is especially true for Bangladesh, the PRC, and the Kyrgyz Republic in our six-country sample. Financial policies are somewhat less repressive than in past years in most countries, but the sustainability of financial institutions is usually a secondary objective compared with the goal of increasing disbursements.
- Regulations and political pressure prevent rural financial institutions from setting loan interest rates high enough to cover the costs and risks of lending. Many MFOs have set more realistic interest rates.

- Many financial institutions, especially the State-owned commercial and agricultural development banks, are weak due to their large portfolio of nonperforming loans, and exist only because of subsidies.
- Rural savings mobilization is still neglected, and most formal institutions that serve agriculture and the MFOs that serve the poor rely on government or donor funding.
- Policymakers have been more concerned about financing agriculture than about meeting the financial demands of rural nonfarm enterprises.
- Because of their many problems, most rural financial institutions are ill-equipped to make long-term loans, and to use the explosion in new information and communication technologies. As a result, Asian agriculture will be at a disadvantage in competing in global markets in the twenty-first century compared with other countries with more modern financial institutions.

Asian Success Stories

In spite of this overall negative picture, there are a few examples of successful rural financial institutions in Asia. These flagship institutions either avoided the directed agricultural credit syndrome or recovered after it was discontinued. They have made good progress in expanding outreach to marginal clientele groups and improving financial sustainability. BAAC in Thailand is unique in its portfolio largely composed of agricultural loans with an increasing share being medium and long term. It has achieved extraordinary outreach by serving most of the country's farm households, and reaching well down in the poverty profile with its services. It could become entirely free of subsidies by raising its portfolio yield by only three to four percentage points. The BRI unit desas in Indonesia are famous for turning their loss-making agricultural lending into highly profitable operations that specialize in small loans in rural areas for farm and nonfarm activities. They have generated large profits that subsidize other bank operations. The Grameen Bank in Bangladesh is well known for its large outreach, especially to poor women, but its chief handicap is that it is still overly dependent on subsidies.

These successful rural financial institutions and the best MFOs have several similarities. They include effective methods to reduce the information and transaction costs of lending, incentives to induce staff to engage in behavior conducive to the health of the organization, and considerable autonomy to develop programs, design products, and set policies. The best MFOs use subsidies to strengthen their institutions and expand operations rather than create dependency on them. They develop valuable long-term financial relationships with clients, who strive to protect personal reputations by fulfilling credit contracts to maintain access to future financial services. This implicit contract for future services and the technology used to make and collect loans contribute to achieving good loan recovery. Grameen and BAAC use joint liability group lending as a collateral substitute for poor households, while the BRI unit desas and several other Indonesian programs successfully use individual lending to reach the poor.

The successful institutions provide important lessons for rural finance. First, institutional development requires a long-term commitment: strong institutions are not created overnight. Second, good institutional design is important, but the policy environment and financial infrastructure are also important. If they are not supportive, at least they must be benign. Third, women, landless, the poor, and other marginal clientele can be effectively served if the correct products, instruments, and technologies are used. Fourth, a large outreach can complement the objective of reaching sustainability, but reaching low levels of poverty may detract from financial sustainability. Fifth, microfinance is not a panacea. It often serves women better than men, is most cost-effective in densely populated areas, and works best with small short-term loans repaid in frequent small installments. Therefore, rural financial institutions cannot easily meet their objectives by simply mimicking microfinance.

PROBLEMS IN IMPLEMENTING THE NEW PARADIGM

The Asian region faces several problems in adopting the new financial market paradigm, as do many developing countries elsewhere. These problems include some special regional issues and uncertainties resulting from the financial and economic crisis.

Special Asian Problems

Although Asia has a few flagship financial institutions, it also has many poor ones. For example, in Asia there are more MFOs serving large numbers of clients than in other regions, but Asia lags behind Latin America in the commercialization of microfinance. Except for Indonesia, few Asian MFOs are evolving into some type of regulated institution, and there is little evidence of commercial banks entering rural finance or microfinance with a commercial orientation.

The slow spread of commercial rural financial activities can be attributed to three sets of problems. First, government and institutional policies inhibit market-oriented operations to a greater degree than in many developing countries elsewhere. For example, interest rate regulations prevent charging the rates needed to cover the high transaction costs and risks of serving poor clients and rural areas with small loan and deposit services. Rigid personnel policies discourage the use of bonuses and other incentives to spur high levels of efficiency from the management and staff of financial institutions. Second, some influential Asian leaders resist adopting the new paradigm and advocating a clear institutional mission to develop strong market-driven financial services. Instead, their mission is to channel loans to the poor and their views, such as the poor having a right to credit, mix social objectives with good banking policies. Their underestimation of the importance of deposit mobilization and other financial services, coupled with a view that the poor cannot pay high interest rates, discourages the emergence of true market-oriented financial intermediaries. Therefore, many Asian MFOs do not have a clear mission of achieving high levels of efficiency and becoming subsidy free within a short period of time. Ready access to subsidized government and donor funds without clear performance expectations contributes to this problem.

Third, there are six sets of circumstances within Asia that pose special challenges for providing financial services in rural areas, especially for the poor. Financial organizations successful elsewhere under quite different circumstances offer only limited guidance on ways to tackle these difficult challenges:

- First, many transition economies in the region have nascent financial systems that are weak and underdeveloped. The uneven pace of economic reform suggests that the old State-planning mentality is still alive and well in some countries.
- Second, there are several conflict-affected countries. The temptation for policymakers in these countries is to distort the financial system by attempting to meet emergency needs and create employment for uprooted people through the rapid disbursement of loans. This weakens the financial institutions and prevents them from appropriately screening clients and establishing long-term banking relationships based on good performance.
- Third, the region has several disaster-prone areas, such as the lowlands of Bangladesh, subject to regular flooding, drought, and other natural disasters. These regions are difficult to serve at best and, unfortunately, most financial institutions including the MFOs are not well designed to cope with large systemic risks.
- Fourth, there are remote areas with especially poor transportation and communication, such as in Nepal and parts of the PRC, which will always be expensive to serve by even the most efficient institutions.
- Fifth, the region includes countries with influential religious communities that regard high interest rates

as immoral; therefore, interest rates and fees must be disguised so the true cost of borrowing is not transparent.

- Finally, the very large countries, India and the PRC, have unique problems. They face enormous difficulties in developing an efficient rural financial system involving multiple institutional forms with thousands of banking outlets to serve millions of clients with differing languages and cultures spread over an enormous landscape.

The Financial Crisis and Beyond

The financial and economic crisis in Asia has introduced tremendous uncertainty into the world economy. Its spread to Russia and Brazil is a cause of concern for investors, and the desirability of liberalized international capital markets is being seriously questioned. Investors suffer from a herd mentality: investment funds are being withdrawn from developing countries not exposed to the same problems as were Indonesia, Republic of Korea, Malaysia, and Thailand. Leaders in the region question the wisdom of free capital flows and Malaysia recently introduced new restrictions. Some of the questions being asked about the world economy include: Will the $500 billion that Japan pledged to bail out its ailing banks be sufficient to restore the country to its role as economic locomotive for the region? Will the financial support given to Russia by the international community stem the contagion effect in Central Asia? Will greater social and political unrest break out in Indonesia? Will the PRC devalue its currency and, if so, what will be the impact on other Asian countries? Will other countries in the region reverse their economic and financial reforms and re-impose greater regulations on capital and financial markets? Will the US and Europe maintain economic growth and a strong demand for imports from developing Asian countries?

In one way or another, the crisis in all four of the most seriously affected Asian countries involves financial sector problems: reforms without adequate regulation to protect financial institutions, short-term over-borrowing in foreign currencies, speculative investments fueled by low interest rates, and implicit entitlements to a government bail out for banks if priority loans fail. These problems occurred because of liberalization combined with political changes that increased the power of special private interest groups relative to macroeconomic technocrats. These cases point to liberalization gone awry, and the countries are now implementing reforms to prevent a repeat of the crisis.

The implications for future financial policies in Asia are unclear. The current problems could trigger a political backlash and increase pressures for returning to more restrictive economic and financial regimes. The economic impact so far appears to be less serious for rural Asia, but a fundamental change in financial policies could spill over into rural financial systems. If the leaders in the region reverse their financial reforms, opportunities for governments and donors to implement financial reform projects may be prejudiced. A serious immediate problem is that the subsidized credit programs being implemented in the wake of the crisis threaten to undermine the viability of financial institutions trying to adopt market-based principles. The concern of donors to respond quickly to the social problems created by the crisis may distract them from the longer-term problems of creating strong rural financial markets.

RECOMMENDATIONS

The wide range of circumstances found in Asia today and the different problems found in rural financial markets mean that no single set of recommendations can be made that will be universally applicable. The following recommendations must be evaluated with respect to each particular situation. Some are immediately applicable while others may have to be delayed until conditions are more favorable.

Creating an Appropriate Policy Environment

Interest Rate Reforms

Most Asian countries need to relax interest rate controls to allow rural financial institutions to set rates consistent with costs and risks. Interest rate liberalization should be undertaken as quickly as macroeconomic, exchange rate, and other considerations permit. Where interest rates have been liberalized, financial institutions need to respond by adjusting their rates to more realistic levels. Governments and donors should charge market interest rates for funds provided to MFOs that do not yet mobilize voluntary deposits so that these MFOs have incentives to seek greater efficiency and self-sufficiency.

Loan Targeting and Institutional Support

Funds provided to rural financial institutions and MFOs should be in the form of general liquidity support rather than targeted for specific clientele. If these funds are subsidized, the subsidies should be used for institutional development rather than passed on to borrowers as interest subsidies. Specific performance-based criteria should be established for receiving such financial support.

Emergency Loans

Financial institutions are poor channels through which to allocate subsidized emergency loans designed to alleviate social and economic crises following natural disasters, conflict situations, and financial and economic crises. These funds are usually intended for rapid disbursement without careful attention to client selection, credit worthiness, and recovery enforcement procedures. Emergency assistance should be channeled through institutions other than banks and MFOs. Financial institutions that participate in such programs risk contaminating their regular portfolios with borrowers who do not understand the difference between the obligation to repay regular loans and the greater forbearance implicit in emergency loans.

Institutional Autonomy and Political Interference

Financial institutions must be given the autonomy to pursue sound banking practices. Loan melas, loan forgiveness programs, and other types of political interference damage financial institutions and create unhealthy expectations by clientele. Countries that desire strong financial systems must find ways to shield rural financial institutions from well-intended but detrimental political interference.

Building Financial Infrastructure

In countries where the policy environment for rural financial markets is improving, projects to build public institutions that reduce the cost of financial intermediation will generate high returns because they benefit all financial agents.

Legal and Regulatory Systems

Prudential regulations and supervisory systems need to be strengthened in most countries. Supervision of rural financial institutions must shift from verifying whether disbursement targets and specified loan terms and conditions are met, to ensuring the use of practices that lead to institutional safety and soundness. Emergency procedures must be developed to support rural financial institutions in times of massive systemic shocks such as drought and floods. The gaps in and inefficiencies of legal and judicial systems must be reduced such that contract enforcement is less costly and time consuming, and moveable property can be more easily used as collateral for loans.

Information Systems

All countries need to review the information systems that support their financial systems. Institutional changes and innovations that reduce the costs of acquiring and using information lower lending costs for all financial institutions and help drive down interest rates. Land titling, credit reporting systems, and collateral registries contribute to the stock of public information used by financial institutions. Some information systems have public goods attributes; therefore, they are an appropriate government investment. Special attention is needed for personal identification systems. A good credit record is an asset, but it needs to be portable to have maximum value. Computerized identification cards may eventually become inexpensive enough for the credit histories of borrowers to be stored on them. This would enable individuals to carry their credit histories to new locations and more rapidly gain access to financial services from new institutions.

Institutional Development

The best rural financial institutions have spent great effort in building their institutional capacity. Some, such as the Grameen Bank, have successfully tapped donors to help finance these investments. More importantly, institutional development represents a commitment by owners and managers to establish high-quality, efficient, and sustainable services in which farm and nonfarm entrepreneurs are treated as valuable clients. This philosophy is absent in many rural Asian financial institutions, however, and requires a fundamental change in attitudes, beginning with the managers and carried down to the lowest-level loan officer and teller.

Financial institutions interested in serving clients know their products and services must be designed to meet demands. Too frequently, Asian institutions fail to consider client preferences; market research and test marketing must become an integral part of an institution's operations. Greater attention to client preferences and more flexible financial products will be reflected in better loan recovery because clients will want to preserve their reputations and maintain access to services in future.

Many Asian financial institutions need greater autonomy to adapt to the new market-oriented paradigm and to develop staff incentives with sufficient flexibility to reward outstanding performance and productivity. Simultaneously, the skill levels of staff in most institutions must be greatly improved to decentralize decision-making processes. Greater decentralization will speed operations and reduce transaction costs for clients. The standardized financial products currently offered by MFOs will need to be more flexible when offered by rural financial institutions and their use will require greater staff skills.

Two Special Challenges for Institutional Development

Building a strong rural financial system in any country requires assessing the status of existing institutions. Existing poorly performing institutions need to be dealt with in some countries; in some, MFOs might be upgraded to serve a wider rural clientele.

Rehabilitating Failing Institutions

Several Asian countries have failing agricultural development banks, cooperatives, and credit unions with an infrastructure of offices and personnel. Closing them will be the most rational solution in many cases, as discussed in Chapter III. However, the BRI experience following the termination of Bimas and several recent credit union rehabilitation projects in Latin America suggest that under certain circumstances these resources, which represent a sunk cost to society, may be salvaged and transformed into viable institutions. The minimum necessary conditions for rehabilitation include a political consensus for fundamental reforms, a firm commitment to recruit independent directors and hire professional bankers as managers, the flexibility to replace staff whose views are inconsistent with the new mission, and the freedom to develop and price new products and services. These conditions are often not met because of vested interests in the existing institutions. But when they are met, technical assistance may be useful for disposing of nonperforming assets, developing new products, creating management information and staff incentive systems, and training staff in modern banking practices. Grants and loans may complement local resources to upgrade facilities and equipment, and augment loan capital.

Upgrading MFOs and Supporting Apex Institutions

Assisting governments to upgrade existing MFOs may be an effective way to expand the financial frontier and serve a broader rural clientele even though there are major challenges in this strategy. First, there are important regulatory and supervisory problems to resolve, especially when MFOs begin large-scale savings mobilization. Second, some MFOs may effectively use small amounts of financial assistance without becoming subsidy dependent and swamping their limited capacity. The problem is that the amount of such funding will usually be relatively small and small-scale efforts may be too costly for most donors to manage. Providing appropriate supervision of these projects is expensive. For example, CGAP decided to make only five grants to organizations in 1998 so that it could monitor the recipients properly.

Third, channeling funds through apex institutions is sometimes viewed as an attractive method to transfer larger amounts of money and the responsibility of screening and monitoring individual MFOs to another intermediary. Apex institutions are discussed in the Banagladesh and India case studies. The positive perceptions about the operations of the Palli Karma–Sahayak Foundation (PKSF) in Bangladesh provide encouragement for this approach. The relatively poor performance of apex organizations in India, however, provides evidence that they are not automatically successful. Several conditions are necessary for success: the rationale to justify an apex requires that several candidate MFOs already exist to be screened and monitored; the country must have skilled personnel to carefully evaluate MFOs, determine those to be funded, and develop appropriate performance expectations for receiving funds; the apex must have sufficiently strong leadership to withstand pressures to disburse to MFOs that do not meet minimum standards; and the environment for financial institutions must be conducive for MFOs to transform successfully into self-sufficient financial institutions in a relatively short time horizon by receiving limited amounts of resources. Relatively few countries in the world meet these conditions as Bangladesh did when PKSF was created. Even so, PKSF has received donor support for strengthening its operations.

MAJOR ISSUES FOR DONORS

Donors can observe and learn from the various country experiences they support. These experiences need to be shared and evaluated internally, then communicated to field personnel and local institutions. Dissemination of information to local policymakers will contribute to better policymaking, and dissemination to local practitioners will speed adoption. USAID and CGAP are becoming important sources of best-practice information, and ADB could assume a more ambitious role in Asia. Systematic linkages and exchanges between the ADB and, for example, the Philippines Coalition for Microfinance Standards and Cashpor Inc., could stimulate discussions about the new paradigm and build a regional consensus for better financial policies. Likewise, familiarity tours for policymakers and practitioners to study flagship institutions would provide opportunities to view how organizations in the region successfully improve outreach and sustainability.

In the design of projects, donors must select situations favorable to success and avoid those that are not. For example, the PRC is firmly committed to a heavy governmental role in controlling its rural financial system. Attempts to develop a market-oriented financial institution today would be doomed to failure under these conditions. Moreover, there are impoverished and conflict-affected countries where poor households would benefit from emergency financial assistance, but not in the form of so-called loans through financial institutions that are not allowed to choose clients and enforce financial contracts. There are also countries in which rigid financial regulations, especially interest rate controls, make it impossible to offer financial products at prices that cover costs and risks of serving rural clients.

When conditions are unfavorable, donor assistance should have two objectives. First, use structural-adjustment projects to support policy changes needed to create better conditions for market-based financial markets. Second, seek other opportunities for project assistance to benefit the intended recipients, but in ways that will not damage whatever credible financial institutions may exist. Compensating for the reported decline in public sector investments in rural infrastructure in several countries may offer one such opportunity. Projects to improve and disseminate technology and to assist with business development may be another. Improvements in infrastructure and the profitability of farm and nonfarm rural enterprises indirectly create the conditions required for financial markets to emerge at a later date.

FINANCIAL MARKETS FOR THE TWENTY-FIRST CENTURY: IS ASIA READY?

The financial dualism that exists in financial markets appears to be increasing in many Asian countries. First, urban financial markets are modernizing faster than are their rural counterparts. Second, large farmers, plantations, agribusinesses, and rural industries obtain financial services from modern urban financial institutions, while most small farmers, landless workers, and small rural nonfarm enterprises must rely on their savings and informal finance. In countries where microfinance is expanding, some micro firms and poor rural households can access NGO loans. This segmentation creates a "missing middle" in which small and medium farmers and nonfarm firms fall between the two sources of supply: they are not well served by either larger financial institutions or microfinance.

The rural financial markets in most of Asia are poorly prepared to enter the next century. Many institutions are weak and are dependent on government and donor funding. They lack technical competence to evaluate credit risks, the financial infrastructure is not supportive, and governmental policies are often more destructive than supportive. New information and communication technologies are revolutionizing financial instruments and financial management strategies, but most Asian rural financial institutions are worlds away from these innovations. Therefore, a second dimension of financial dualism is arising, which might be called a "digital divide" because it separates those using modern computers and communication technologies from those that do not. It is possible to leap-frog over old technologies as is occurring with the Grameen Bank cellular phone franchise in Bangladesh. This requires supportive policies by governments that are often poorly equipped to deal with these challenges.

Asian countries with weak financial markets will suffer in the worldwide competition for markets compared with other developing countries with better rural financial systems. The opportunities for rapid improvement, however, exist in Asia. The region's advanced flagship financial institutions can serve as models for other institutions. Moreover, several countries have highly trained personnel who could create new financial technologies and manage institutions if they were given the opportunity, flexibility, and financial support by governments in the region. The roles of government are to create a favorable environment, invest in supportive infrastructure, and build institutions; recognize the role that the private sector can play in financial markets; and avoid negative policies that undermine institutional viability, such as trying to solve social problems by channeling subsidized loans through financial institutions.

Asia has the potential to build strong market-oriented rural financial systems. However, so far most countries have lacked the vision and will to make the necessary changes. The status quo benefits the rural elite but is prejudiced against the poor.

VI INTRODUCTION TO THE CASE STUDIES

OBJECTIVE OF THE STUDY

The general objective of this study was to analyze developments in the provision and use of financial services in rural Asia since the 1970s. In view of the large number of Asian economies, we used the country-case-study method and focused on three main features in each case: analysis of the general financial-sector strategy of the country, and specific policies implemented regarding rural financial markets to determine how they affect the framework within which the country's rural financial system operates; the evolution and trends in the structure, conduct, and performance of the rural financial markets; and analysis of information, where available, at the levels of both the financial institutions and rural firms and households, on the impact of rural financial development. Following the analyses, recommendations are made about the changes in policies, financial infrastructure, and institutional development needed to promote the establishment of rural financial markets that are consistent with sustainable development.

Chapters II and III presented a summary of the conceptual evolution that has occurred since the 1970s regarding rural financial markets. These chapters reviewed the basic functions of financial markets, identified the major participants in those markets, described the paradigm shift that is occurring in approaches to financial market development, summarized some of the recent developments in microfinance, and presented a three-pronged framework to use in evaluating the needs and constraints of the rural financial system. The same general outline is followed for each of the six case studies presented here. However, each case is based almost exclusively on available literature, the extent of which varies considerably from country to country; the content and level of detail provided for each case varies correspondingly.

SELECTION OF CASE-STUDY COUNTRIES

The rural economy of Asia is huge, heterogeneous, and defies easy categorization and analysis. On the one hand, Asia is home for some of the most dynamic and successful agribusinesses in the world, that satisfy domestic food demands and penetrate competitive foreign markets. On the other hand, it is home for millions of poor people who are only slightly better off than their ancestors. Prior to the financial and economic crisis that began in 1997, the region had some of the fastest-growing economies in the world but also some with poor economic performance. Moreover, some of the transition and conflict-affected countries in the region have even experienced negative growth rates. The rural financial markets in a few countries are served by strong financial institutions that provide sophisticated services on market terms, while others are dominated by weak and subsidized institutions and NGOs that are dependent on donors and whose sole function is to dispense credit.

An analysis of rural financial markets in Asia must attempt to account for this heterogeneity. Since it was impossible in this study to cover all economies in the region, the decision was made to select cases that reflect the broad range of circumstances and approaches to financial market development found in the region. Each of the six countries selected represents a particular kind of scenario.

Bangladesh and India were chosen to represent South Asia. Typical of this region, they are poor, densely populated, and the State has intervened heavily in their financial sectors.

Bangladesh has received massive amounts of donor support to develop the world's most comprehensive NGO-based system of lending to the poor. India, however, has aggressively imposed quotas and mandates on commercial banks in attempts to force them to expand the financial frontier into rural areas, and has established a vast network of regional rural banks and cooperatives.

The Kyrgyz Republic and the PRC represent Central Asia. Both are in transition from centrally planned to market economies. The PRC began to liberalize its rural economy as early as the late 1970s while the Kyrgyz Republic did not begin until a decade later. The PRC is an old country that is modernizing old institutions while the Kyrgyz Republic is new and has to build many institutions from scratch. The former is a huge, heavily populated country while the latter is comparatively small in size and population. The PRC has been among the world's leaders in agricultural growth in recent years while the Kyrgyz Republic has experienced negative growth. Both countries have made little progress in developing strong market-oriented financial institutions for rural areas.

Indonesia and Thailand in Southeast Asia represent rapid-growth economies that were severely impacted by the financial and economic crisis in the region that began in 1997. Both are experiencing a decline in average farm sizes but have dynamic agribusinesses, especially Thailand. Both countries are known worldwide for having developed rural financial institutions that today serve millions of clients with a minimum of subsidies.

COMPARATIVE ANALYSIS

Economic Growth

The six countries have widely different income levels (Table VI.1). In 1996, Thailand, the richest country, had a per capita GDP ($1,956 in 1987 dollars) almost ten times that of the poorest country, Bangladesh ($212). India's level ($464) was roughly

double that of Bangladesh. Estimates for the Kyrgyz Republic
have been quite volatile and were reported to be $555 in 1995
dollars, while the PRC was about the same level but in 1987 dollars
($515). Indonesia's GDP per capita ($748) was about 50 percent
higher than the PRC but less than half that of Thailand.

Real GDP per capita growth rates for Bangladesh and India
have been under 4 percent per year since 1967, while the rates
for Indonesia and Thailand have been in the 4 to 7 percent range.
The PRC's growth rate has been higher than 8 percent since 1980.
The Kyrgyz Republic is the exceptional case, reporting an annual
negative growth rate of 12 percent in the 1990s.

Table VI.1: GDP and GDP Per Capita Growth Rates

Item	Bangladesh	India	Kyrgyz Republic	PRC	Indonesia	Thailand
Per Capita 1996 GDP (constant 1987 $)	212	464	555[a]	515	748	1,956
Annual Growth Rates (%) of Per Capita GDP (constant 1987 $)						
1967–1980	-0.50	1.34		5.18	4.98	4.32
1980–1989	2.02	3.61		8.25	4.05	5.58
1989–1995	2.74	3.39		9.59	6.28	7.76
1980–1995	2.31	3.52	-12.0[b]	8.79	4.93	6.45

[a] In 1996 dollars.
[b] Real GDP annual growth rate.

Sources: ADB (1997c); World Bank (1998c).

Land, Population, and Agriculture

The enormous differences in the size and population of
these six countries can be seen in the data in Table VI.2. The
PRC has about 9.6 million square kilometers (km^2). India is
approximately one third that size, Indonesia one fifth, Thailand
one twentieth, and the Kyrgyz Republic and Bangladesh only
about one fiftieth. Their respective population densities give a
quite different perspective. Bangladesh is in a category all its

Table VI.2: Land, Population, and Agriculture

Item	Bangladesh	India	Kyrgyz Republic	PRC	Indonesia	Thailand
Total Area (km²'000)	144.0	3,287.6	198.5	9,561.0	1,904.6	513.1
Population (1997) (millions)	125.6	955.2	4.7	1,230.0	199.9	60.6
Annual Population Growth Rate (%)						
(1993–1997)	1.9	2.0	0.9	1.1	1.6	1.1
(1993–2010)[a]	1.7	1.5		0.8	1.3	0.7
Population Density (persons/km², 1997)	872	291	23	128	105	118
Rural Population as Percent of Total Population						
1975	90.7	78.7	62.1	82.7	80.6	84.9
1985	86.6	75.7	61.8	77.5	73.9	82.1
1995	81.1	72.8	60.8	68.9	63.7	79.6
Share of Agricultural Labor in Total Labor Force (%)						
1966	85.16	73.73		80.25	69.70	81.37
1975	78.01	71.08		76.26	62.08	75.37
1985	68.90	66.74		73.24	56.46	67.48
1995	60.56	61.87		69.54	51.78	60.32
Cropped Area per Capita (ha, 1994)	0.08	0.18	0.32	0.08	0.16	0.36

[a] *Source:* Projections of the International Food Policy Research Institute, Washington DC.

Sources: ADB (1997c); Rosegrant and Hazell (1999).

own with nearly 900 people per km² in 1997; India is second with about one third that density. The PRC, Indonesia, and Thailand have just over 100 people per km², while the Kyrgyz Republic has only 23. In addition, there are considerable differences in population density within the countries.

Annual population growth rates are still about 2.0 percent for Bangladesh and India, which is consistent with their low income levels. The PRC, Kyrgyz Republic, and Thailand are at about 1 percent, while Indonesia is 1.6 percent.

Countries and regions within countries with very high population densities offer the potential to create highly concentrated financial programs that can provide small loans and deposit services to a large number of poor clients in a relatively small area. The entire country of Bangladesh fits this situation. Programs operating in sparsely populated areas, however, face a difficulty in achieving high levels of bank staff productivity. Even though the PRC has a huge population, this country is implementing lending programs for the poor in relatively sparsely populated areas.

The differences in land quality among the six countries are reflected in the amount of cropped area available per capita. These estimates place Bangladesh, the poorest of the six, and the PRC in the same category of having only 0.08 hectares (ha) per capita. India and Indonesia are somewhat better off with roughly twice as much land per capita. The Kyrgyz Republic and Thailand are the two relatively land-abundant countries with over 0.30 ha per capita. The share of agricultural labor in the total labor force is declining in all six countries. It is surprising, however, that with the relatively high per capita income in Thailand, that country still has about 60 percent of its population employed in agriculture, which is about equal to the level in Bangladesh, the poorest country.

The reported growth rates in agricultural productivity reflect general perceptions about these countries (Table VI.3). Bangladesh's agricultural growth rates are low and were lower in the 1990s than in the previous decade. Indonesia and India have had fairly strong agricultural annual growth rates of about 3 percent. Thailand is intermediate with 3.6 percent growth while the PRC has the highest rate, close to 5 percent. With the exception of Bangladesh and the Kyrgyz Republic, the rate of agricultural growth has surpassed population growth rates, thereby providing room for improvement in per capita food consumption.

The sources of agricultural productivity growth reveal fairly consistent patterns since 1961. The PRC has had consistently high growth rates in both labor and land productivity, as has Indonesia. India has had a slightly slower productivity growth than Indonesia in both indicators. Thailand's performance has been poorer than these three cases but has been somewhat better than Bangladesh in labor productivity growth. The relatively poor performance of Bangladesh implies that it has been especially difficult for that country to improve rural incomes and food availability per capita.

Table VI.3: Growth in Agricultural Productivity

Item	Bangladesh	India	Kyrgyz Republic	PRC	Indonesia	Thailand
Average Annual Growth Rate of Agriculture (%)[a]						
1980–1990	2.7	3.1		5.9	3.4	4.0
1990–1996	1.2	3.1	-4.6	4.9	2.8	3.6
Annual Growth Rates in Labor Force in Agriculture (%)						
1961–1969	1.02	1.19		4.04	0.79	2.08
1970–1979	1.11	1.41		0.77	0.60	1.97
1980–1989	1.79	1.54		0.65	0.83	1.39
1990–1993	2.06	1.14		-0.08	0.40	0.42
Annual Growth Rates in Labor Productivity per Worker in Agriculture (%) (dollars/worker)						
1961–1969	0.37	1.37		1.48	2.51	1.91
1970–1979	1.29	2.62		2.90	2.32	0.69
1980–1989	0.21	1.62		5.39	1.92	1.44
1990–1993	0.57	1.74		2.66	2.33	1.50
Annual Growth Rates in Land Productivity in Agriculture (%) (dollars/ha)						
1961–1969	1.39	2.78		3.40	3.95	1.56
1970–1979	1.50	3.60		1.61	2.06	1.14
1980–1989	2.86	3.03		5.62	3.96	2.07
1990–1993	1.73	3.04		3.43	3.48	1.56

[a] World Bank (1998c).

Sources: FAOSTAT. Agricultural Production Indices, 3 November 1998; Land-Use Domain, 22 May 1998; Population Domain, 24 August 1998. Available: http://faostat.fao.org. See also Rosegrant and Hazell (1999).

Structural Transformation

The evolution in the GDP share of the major sectors of the economy has followed the classic pattern of structural transformation (Table VI.4). The agricultural share has declined in all countries over the 22-year period from 1975. With the exception of the Kyrgyz Republic, there is an inverse relationship between the share of agriculture in GDP and per capita GDP.

Table VI.4: Share of Major Sectors in GDP
(percent)

	Agriculture			All Industry			Services		
	1975	1985	1997[b]	1975	1985	1997[b]	1975	1985	1997[b]
Bangladesh	59.1	41.8	29.3	11.1	16.0	17.5	29.8	42.3	53.2
India	40.5	33.0	27.0	23.7	28.2	30.0	35.8	38.8	43.0
Kyrgyz Republic			46.5			21.4			32.1
China, People's Rep. of	34.0[a]	28.4	20.2		43.1	49.0		28.5	30.8
Indonesia	31.7	23.2	16.1	33.8	35.8	43.9	34.6	40.9	40.1
Thailand	26.9	15.8	11.2	25.8	31.8	39.8	47.3	52.3	48.9

[a] World Bank (1997a) for the PRC for 1970.
[b] ADB (*Available: http://www.adb.org*) for 1997 data.
Source: ADB (1997c).

The 11 percent agricultural share for Thailand is especially low considering that 60 percent of the population is still employed in agriculture, suggesting a potentially large emerging gap in incomes between rural and urban areas. However, as discussed in the case study, this gap has been reduced through nonfarm income earned by farmers. The patterns are not so consistent for industry and services across the six countries. The PRC has a larger share of GDP in industry than implied by its per capita GDP, while Thailand has a relatively lower share. Likewise, the size of the service sector in India, and especially Bangladesh, is higher than expected from their per capita incomes.

Financial Deepening

Financial deepening refers to the growth of the financial sector relative to the rest of the economy. As the economy modernizes, financial deepening occurs because the financial sector must accommodate the demands of a more productive and sophisticated production sector. A popular measure of financial deepening of the banking sector is the ratio of M_2 to GDP where M_2 refers to the sum of money in circulation plus near money such as savings accounts. This ratio is reported for the six countries in Table VI.5.

Table VI.5: M_2/GDP

Year	Bangladesh	India	Kyrgyz Republic	PRC	Indonesia	Thailand
1975	0.11				0.16	0.34
1980	0.19	0.46		0.37	0.17	0.38
1985	0.26	0.51		0.54	0.24	0.56
1990	0.30	0.56		0.79	0.40	0.70
1996	0.35	0.55	0.16	1.12	0.55	0.80

Sources: ADB (1997c).

All the case-study countries showed significant increases in financial deepening of the banking sector during the past two decades. The rates of change have been quite different, however. The PRC reported a sharp increase in savings in the 1990s; its M_2/GDP ratio surpassed 1.0 in 1996. Thailand's M_2/GDP ratio more than doubled from 0.34 to 0.80 in the same period. India and Indonesia were at the same level of 0.55 in 1996, but India started from a higher base and has grown more slowly. Bangladesh recorded a low ratio, 0.35, while the Kyrgyz Republic was even lower at 0.16, indicating the limited role that the financial sector plays in that transition economy.

These data provide insights into the role of the financial systems in these countries. Evidently banking is relatively more important in the PRC and Thailand than in the other countries. In the former case, savings have grown enormously due to rapid income growth and the absence of consumption and private investment alternatives. In Bangladesh and the Kyrgyz Republic, a large amount of money circulates outside the banking system. Some savings are mobilized by NGOs in Bangladesh, but they are not reported in bank statistics. Inefficiencies in banking and restrictions on interest paid on savings are additional explanations for the low levels of financial deepening observed in some countries.

VII Rural Financial Market Development in Bangladesh: Failing Banks, Thriving Microfinance

OVERVIEW OF THE FINANCIAL SYSTEM

Bangladesh is the poorest of the six case-study countries selected for this research. Per capita GDP in 1996 was estimated to be only $212 in 1987 US dollars. With its huge population of 126 million and relatively small land area, there is an average of 870 persons per square kilometer. The country lacks raw materials but has productive croplands. It is subject to periodic floods including a severe one that devastated the country in 1998.

In spite of its serious problems, the country has made notable progress in several areas (Quibria, 1997). Food production has increased by 3 percent per annum since the 1980s and the country is on the verge of food self-sufficiency, albeit at a low level of consumption. Considerable hunger and malnutrition still exists. With the widespread adoption of family planning practices, fertility has fallen and the annual population growth rate is just under 2 percent per annum. Poverty is serious but the incidence is reported to have declined from over 70 percent of the total population in the early 1980s to less than 50 percent by the early 1990s. This decline was attributed to broad-based growth that occurred through improved agricultural technology, labor-intensive industrialization, and rapid growth of the informal service sector. The country has achieved a degree of macroeconomic stability and has enjoyed a very low inflation rate, about 5 percent per annum, in the 1990s.

Bangladesh faces many serious problems, including relatively low savings and investment rates, and low levels of efficiency of the public sector. The commercial banking sector is inefficient, and its performance has worsened in recent years in several major dimensions. There are serious weaknesses in the regulatory framework and the legal and judiciary system to support the financial system.

The formal financial system today is comprised of the central bank (Bangladesh Bank - BB), four nationalized commercial banks (Sonali, Janata, Agrani, and Rupali - NCBs), 18 private commercial banks, 12 foreign commercial banks, and 4 nationalized specialized banks. Two of the four specialized development finance institutions (DFIs) serve agriculture: the Bangladesh Krishi Bank (BKB), and the *Rajshaki Krishi Unnayan* (RAKUB). In addition, two cooperative networks serve the rural sector. The traditional cooperatives are under the Registrar of Cooperative Societies financed by the Bangladesh Sambaya Bank Ltd. (BSBL). The two-tier Comilla type cooperatives are under the Bangladesh Rural Development Board (BRDB) and are financed by Sonali Bank (World Bank, 1996a; Hossain and Rashid, 1997; Wade et al., 1998).

The problems of the banking system originated several decades ago. The Pakistan Government of the 1950s and 1960s used financial institutions as a cheap source of credit for priority sectors including exports and industrialization. Beginning in the 1960s, loans were made to strengthen the Bengali entrepreneurial class. But at the time of Bangladesh Independence in 1971, the Bengalis owned only 23 percent of the fixed assets in the industrial sector (Sobhan, 1991). Controls over interest rates, selective credit allocation programs, complex rules and regulations for money and capital markets, and overvalued exchange rates were all part of a repressive financial system that Bangladesh inherited. The problem worsened in 1972 when the new Government nationalized the financial institutions and heavy industries and created three specialized banks. Much of the lending from 1972 to 1975 by the DFIs was directed at building up the public sector. Two of the NCBs (Pubali and Uttara) were denationalized in 1984. Several private banks were licensed in the 1980s and 1990s.

State intervention in the banking sector during the last two decades has included interest rate controls, targets for commercial bank lending to priority activities, and rules regarding the opening of new branches. Many nationalized industries have incurred heavy losses and, under instruction of the Government, the NCBs have provided loans to keep them alive. Loans were scarce after the priority sectors were accommodated and interest rates were negative in real terms. Thus, private sector demand has been rationed among the economically and politically powerful. This has contributed to inefficiency in investment and the nonpayment of loans. The NCBs had to be recapitalized in the late 1980s and early 1990s to keep them solvent (Hossain and Rashid, 1997).

After 1975, the principal donors to Bangladesh promoted the idea of curbing the public sector and channeling resources to the private sector. Sizeable lines of credit were extended to the private sector through the two industrial DFIs, the Bangladesh Shilpa Bank (BSB) and the *Bangladesh Shilpa Rin Sanstha*. Donor lending accelerated in the late 1970s, and the DFIs began to channel credits rather indiscriminately, without careful scrutiny of borrowers' entrepreneurial experience, collateral position, or the market worth of the projects. To obtain new credit lines, the DFIs sped disbursements to the point where loan portfolios became seriously compromised. Apparently, the donors did not conduct in-depth evaluations of DFI performance during this period (Sobhan, 1991).

The country's aid-based development strategy is alleged to contribute to the bad-debt problem. Businesses do not pay their debts because they know that sooner or later the aid givers will refinance the banking system and past loans will be written off. The notion that debts do not have to be paid affects most classes of people to the detriment of the country (Novak, 1993, cited in Hossain and Rashid, 1997).

In the early 1980s, the magnitude of the repayment problems became clearer, studies and audits were conducted, and agreements were signed with donors regarding collection efforts. The donors suspended disbursements and withheld new loans pending the outcome. Attempts were made to improve collections but by 30 June 1990, accumulated overdues reached taka (Tk) 10.5 billion compared with Tk8.5 billion disbursed; thus, the default rate was 123 percent of disbursement for the two DFIs (Sobhan, 1991). After five years of collection efforts, there was little evidence of improvement, but there were negative consequences for industrial investment and output. Moreover, the experience with these two DFIs established the culture of default that spread into the rest of the economy.

During the late 1980s and in the 1990s, several attempts were made to implement financial sector reforms, often with the encouragement and technical support of the donor community. The accomplishments include: significant deregulation of interest rates, decline in the role of directed credit, recapitalization of and greater freedom for the NCBs, introduction of loan provisioning to make loan recovery problems more transparent, licensing of several private and foreign banks, commitment to privatize Rupali Bank, and the initiation of commercial transactions for one DFI (Rana, 1997).

Many initiatives have been taken in attempts to deal with the loan recovery problem. For example, the 1986 loan recovery program included prosecution of willful defaulters, prohibitions against defaulters holding public offices or bank directorships, limitations on access to new loans, and denial of import licenses to industrial loan defaulters. An interest amnesty program was introduced in 1986 to induce payments on agricultural loans. A Financial Loan Courts Act was passed to establish loan courts at the district level, to close legal loopholes, and to allow the prosecution of defaulters. The Government has attempted to shame defaulters by publishing lists of the most egregious offenders (Hossain and Rashid, 1997). A Credit Information Bureau was established in the Bangladesh Bank to record the performance of borrowers, and a Large Loan Review Cell was set up to review all newly sanctioned bank loans over Tk1 crore (Tk10 million).

The results of these reform measures have been mixed. As a result of deregulation, real lending and deposit rates have risen. There is some evidence of greater competition but also of collusive pricing by the private banks. Political interference continues to be great. For example, a decision by the outgoing Government on the eve of the national election on 15 February 1996, permitted blanket rescheduling of all bank loans on the basis of a 10 percent down payment. This political action once again undermined the credibility of policymakers in their attempt to restore discipline, and apparently permitted influential defaulters to contest the parliamentary elections (Sobhan, 1997). These problems have contributed to the emergence of a bad-debt culture.

Recent data reveal that the banking system is unsound and that there has been little improvement. The problems are especially serious for the specialized banks. Classified loans in the NCBs rose from 32 to 37 percent from 1994 to 1997, while they fell from 44 to 31 percent in the private domestic banks. Moreover, these high levels understate the nonperforming loan problem when measured by more rigorous international standards (Wade et al., 1998). There is a low probability that many of these loans will be paid. Assuming an 80 percent loss rate, the expected loan losses are roughly estimated to be 6 percent of the country's GDP. The domestic banks are deficient in loan loss provisions and are effectively insolvent in spite of substantial recapitalization by the Government in the early 1990s in an amount of about 5 percent of GDP. The steady growth in deposits, however, has provided sufficient liquidity for the domestic banks.

The persistence of the banking problem is attributed to a lack of political will to deal with the root causes. The Government has been deterred by the perceived strength of the major defaulters, and the fear of possible bank runs if weak banks are closed. Prudential regulations concerning loan classification, provisioning requirements, and capital adequacy are now close to international standards but the key problem is weak and inadequate enforcement. The NCBs are subject to priorities set by the Government that may differ from prudential concerns. The Bangladesh Bank is weakened by strong and militant unions that interfere in personnel, recruitment, and promotion decisions. The deposit insurance scheme is grossly underfunded compared with its legal liabilities. The commercial banks suffer from weak corporate governance, and the concentration of nonperforming loans in relatively few borrowers is indicative of an imprudent credit policy. The private banks are reported to be hampered by insider lending, fraud, and negligence (Wade et al., 1998).

APPROACH TO RURAL AND AGRICULTURAL FINANCE

The provision of financial services in the rural economy in Bangladesh has been subject to similar types of State and political intervention with similar disastrous results. The surprising feature of Bangladesh, however, is that a strong NGO financial system has emerged in spite of the bad-debt culture that has also infected agricultural lending. To understand developments affecting rural areas, it is necessary to analyze banks and cooperatives, the Grameen Bank (GB), and financial NGOs. The problem is that there is no easy way to aggregate the data for these three groups of institutions. Although the GB and many NGOs are considered to be rural institutions, they often operate in small towns and peri-urban areas, serving clients whose activities (e.g. trading) would not be considered agricultural in some economic classifications. Therefore, when statistics on agricultural loans are presented, they refer to banks and cooperatives only, and they underestimate total lending because of the important role of the GB and the NGOs. Yet it is incorrect to classify all GB and NGO lending and deposit mobilization as agricultural.

The NCBs and the agricultural DFIs have been subject to several measures designed to push financial services, especially loans, into rural areas. First, from 1978 to 1981, the banks were required to open two new rural branches for each new urban branch. As a result, about two thirds of the NCB branches, over half the denationalized bank branches, and 90 percent of the DFI branches are now in rural areas (Hassan, 1997). This branch expansion has contributed to the large commercial bank share of rural loans and deposits. Second, the Agricultural Credit Department (ACD) of the BB has set agricultural loan targets for banks. There have been few effective sanctions for not reaching the targets, such that between 1981/82 and 1994/95 the actual lending ranged from a low of 45 percent to a high of 100 percent of the target. Agricultural credit as a proportion of total credit rose from 20 percent in 1981/82 to a high of 34 percent in 1984/85, then gradually fell until it reached 22 percent in 1994/95 (Khalily, Huda, and Lalorukh, 1997). Third, lending rates have been controlled, and banks have been encouraged to make agricultural loans that the BB would refinance at a subsidized rate. The refinance subsidy was terminated for the NCBs in 1991 but was continued for the DFIs.

Five interest exemption programs were implemented during 1982–1991. Depending on the years, the basic objectives were either to ease the loan burden of the borrowers or to encourage them to repay overdue loans. The 1984 and 1985 programs provided for interest exemptions and loan rescheduling without penalty interest for borrowers affected by natural calamities. The 1985 program exempted interest only for cyclone-affected borrowers. The 1986 and 1987 interest exemption programs aimed at improving the recovery rate and were applicable countrywide to crop loans up to Tk10,000 (including principal, interest, and service charges).[1] The 1991 program was part of the Government's election promise. It provided for exemption of principal, interest, and overdue interest penalties up to Tk5,000.

---

[1] In this period, $1 = Tk30 approximately.

A study of agricultural loan recovery concluded that the 1991 program did increase loan repayment but at a huge cost. It not only contributed to revenue loss but also to capital loss for the banks. The exempted principal meant that the banks had to compensate depositors out of their capital and/or profits. The total cost of the 1991 program for the NCBs and DFIs was estimated at Tk350 million. The frequency of these programs has contributed to borrower expectations about future interest exemptions, and is believed to have contributed to low and declining recovery rates for agricultural loans (Khalily and Meyer, 1993).

Loan recovery was also found to be negatively affected by political elections. The Government is not likely to pursue loan recovery vigorously during an election period because of the negative effect it may have on voters. Moreover, local officials intervene during elections to influence who can most easily get loans, and which borrowers can avoid pressure from bank officials to collect overdue loans (Khalily and Meyer, 1993).

THE EVOLUTION AND CURRENT STATUS OF KEY RURAL FINANCIAL INSTITUTIONS

The evolution of agricultural lending is indicated in Table VII.1. Total disbursements to agriculture represented almost 7 percent of agricultural GDP in 1983/84, then fell in absolute and relative terms thereafter until 1990/91, when they represented less than 2 percent of agricultural GDP. They rose steadily in the 1990s and represented 3.6 and 3.8 percent of GDP in 1995/96 and 1996/97, respectively. The largest single source of funds has been the DFIs of BKB and RAKUB that together represented half to two thirds of total loans. The commercial banks have represented about one third, and cooperatives 1 to 10 percent depending on the year. About half the total disbursements have been for crop loans.

Table VII.1:   Agricultural GDP and Loans Granted, 1983/84 to 1996/97
(taka crores[a] at current prices)

Year	Agricultural GDP	Loans by Organization				Loans by Type				Total Ag. credit as % of Ag. GDP
		NCB[b]	BKB/RAKUB[c]	BRDB COOP[d]	BSBL COOP[e]	Crop	Term credit[f]	Other[g]	Total	
1983/84	14,840.3	324.1	592.4	66.8	22.0	635.9	278.7	80.8	1,005.3	6.77
1984/85	16,997.0	386.2	614.7	123.6	28.3	564.8	421.1	145.9	1,152.8	6.78
1985/86	18,838.2	156.7	365.1	96.0	14.0	275.6	192.8	168.8	631.8	3.35
1986/87	21,976.1	134.1	441.9	74.2	17.1	312.5	129.8	148.0	667.3[h]	3.04
1987/88	23,162.3	177.5	379.2	85.6	14.0	383.1	130.3	142.9	656.3	2.83
1988/89	24,539.2	240.9	487.0	62.3	17.7	340.0	186.7	171.0	807.6[h]	3.29
1989/90	27,179.0	207.0	423.0	54.8	1.9	359.8	156.9	170.1	686.8	2.53
1990/91	30,059.6	182.2	361.2	49.9	2.3	302.5	139.7	153.4	595.6	1.98
1991/92	31,243.8	270.7	503.5	17.4	3.1	346.4	260.4	187.8	794.6	2.54
1992/93	28,884.2	262.7	563.9	11.9	3.4	388.5	247.2	197.2	841.9	2.91
1993/94	30,589.0	345.3	742.3	12.0	1.2	515.1	392.4	193.3	1,100.8	3.59
1994/95	36,137.0	457.1	958.1	73.2	1.9	696.7			1,490.6	4.12
1995/96	38,990.0	437.8	951.0	91.0					1,479.8	3.80
1996/97	41,831.0	446.6	958.1	110.7					1,515.4	3.62

a One crore = Tk10 million.
b Nationalized Commercial Banks.
c BKB is the Bangladesh Krishi Bank; RAKUB is the Rajshaki Krishi Unnayan.
d BSBL is the Bangladesh Sambaya Bank Ltd.
e BRDB is the Bangladesh Rural Development Board.
f Includes agricultural term credit as well as financing for marketing, transportation, and agro-industries.
g Includes loans for fisheries, tea production, and cold storage facilities for agricultural products.
h Includes some loans for which breakdown is not available.

Source: World Bank (1996a). Updated with data from the Bangladesh Bank.

The aggregate data suggest that member-based institutions (GB and the NGOs) advanced Tk1,660 crore[2] in 1993/94, while the banks and cooperatives disbursed about Tk1,100 crore as agricultural credit and another Tk11 crore in poverty alleviation programs. If all these funds went into agriculture, then the ratio of total agricultural credit to agricultural GDP would have reached about 9 percent, surpassing the 1983/84 levels. Obviously, the growth in disbursements in recent years has been due to the microfinance organizations (MFOs).

Participants

The formal banking sector is composed of the NCBs, the DFIs, and agricultural cooperatives. As described above, they have played the predominant role in agricultural lending, but in recent years their role has declined in relative importance in financing the rural sector. They make loans largely to individual farmers and focus on crop lending; they do not serve the wider demands for rural finance. An important development has been the emergence of member-based institutions that include the GB and hundreds of MFOs that make loans, often to groups of borrowers. The most important of these institutions are described here, beginning with the GB. Most MFOs in Bangladesh, unlike those in many developing countries, are rural oriented. The expansion into urban areas has been recent (Chowdhury, 1998).

The concept of the GB had its origin in 1976 when its founder, Professor Muhammad Yunus, began making working capital loans to poor people in rural villages. Initially, he worked with local banks that provided the funds, but in October 1983, the GB was chartered as a specialized bank for the poor. He adopted the idea of joint-liability group lending, that had been used without great success in other countries for small farm

---

[2] One crore = Tk10 million. At the official exchange rate in February 1996 of $1 = Tk41.00, a crore was equal to $243,900.

lending programs, and made it work in Bangladesh. Over time, the clients have increasingly been poor women. Individuals organize themselves into borrowing groups of five persons, usually of the same gender, and elect a chairperson who is responsible for group discipline. Membership is limited to people who own less than one-half acre of land, are not members of the same household, have similar economic resources, and live in the same village. The similarity of residence and economic background contributes to the effective functioning of the groups (Khandker, Khalily, and Khan, 1996).

The groups meet weekly, at which time each member makes an obligatory small savings deposit (Tk1 per week). Initially two members are given credit and are observed for one or two months. If they repay regularly in weekly installments, the next two members are granted loans. The leader is usually last to get a loan. The loans tend to be small, Tk2,000–5,000 ($48–120) up to a maximum of Tk10,000 ($250). They are given to individuals in the group, but peer pressure is created because if any member defaults, the entire group becomes ineligible to receive additional loans. This feature has been identified as key to good repayment, but loan repayment behavior is increasingly recognized as being more complex than simply using joint liability as a collateral substitute. For example, the Grameen staff attend the meetings of the Grameen centers, which are comprised of five to eight borrowing groups that meet weekly, and monitor loan use. The credit transactions are openly conducted at these center meetings such that everyone sees who borrows and who repays.

In addition to the weekly savings, each member is required to contribute 5 percent of each loan received to a group fund managed by the group. Each borrower is also required to contribute 25 percent of the total interest due on the loan principal to an emergency fund that the GB manages for use as insurance against potential default due to death, disability, or other misfortune. This fund is also used to provide life and accident insurance, to repay bad debts, and to undertake activities to improve the members' health, skills, and education and investment opportunities. Members also develop a stake in the organization by being required to buy an equity share of Tk100.

The GB has targeted women as clients because they are poorer than men, have been overlooked in other development projects, have been found to be better credit risks, and are better at following program rules. The bank has a comprehensive social development program outlined in 16 decisions that members must follow.

Six types of loans were granted by the GB in 1992. General loans (82 percent of total volume) are provided for one year at a nominal interest rate of 20 percent. Collective loans (0.2 percent) are made to centers for joint ventures, but they are declining in total share because of poor repayment. House-building loans (8.8 percent) require weekly payments over ten years and are charged an 8 percent nominal interest rate. Technology loans (9.4 percent) fund larger projects and are made for larger amounts of money. Several categories of general loans were added in 1992. They included short-term seasonal loans, special loans, food storage loans, and capital recovery and destitute loans in areas where floods destroyed assets used for income generation (Khandker, Khalily, and Khan, 1996).

One of the outcomes of the poor quality of public services in Bangladesh has been the emergence of thousands of NGOs. It is estimated there may be as many as 1,000 that are MFOs. All provide loans, some mobilize savings, and many provide nonfinancial services, such as training, consciousness raising and skills development. Most use the group lending technology popularized by the GB, but some work with much larger groups. The majority are small, serving only a few hundred persons, while others are huge. For example, the Bangladesh Rural Advancement Committee (BRAC) served more than 15 percent of the country's 82,000 villages in December 1994. It had many programs and commercial enterprises, and its rural development and rural credit project contained credit components that covered 13,224 villages with 196 branches (Khandker and Khalily, 1996).

The ten largest MFOs in the country in terms of loans outstanding are listed in Table VII.2. The total membership of

Table VII.2: Top Ten Financial NGOs: Members, Disbursements, Loans Outstanding and Staff, December 1997

Rank (1)	Name of NGO (2)	Inception year of credit program (3)	Total members (4)	Net savings (Tk"000) (5)	Loans (Tk'000)		Total staff (8)	Savings-ratio 5/7 (9)
					Disbursements during 1997 (6)	Outstanding December 1997 (7)		
1	BRAC	1974	2,011,417	1,750,000	6,880,000	3,686,000	20,433	0.47
2	PROSHIKA	1976	1,231,883	10,583	2,421,450	2,090,710	3,197	0.01
3	ASA	1991	805,631	721,914	2,967,199	1,566,966	4,787	0.46
4	SWANIRVAR Bangladesh	1979	682,350	138,285	86,300	321,500	2,319	0.43
5	RDRS-Bangladesh	1991	274,275	84,257	345,731	264,152	1,611	0.32
6	Thengamara Mohila Sabuj Sangha (TMSS)	1987	268,200	53,155	267,856	146,985	952	0.36
7	Society for Social Service (SSS)	1991	60,577	50,584	231,479	128,099	481	0.39
8	Bangladesh Extension Education Services (BEES)	1988	38,230	25,283	99,121	92,354	440	0.27
9	CODEC	1985	29,155	-	88,511	83,261	526	-
10	Buro, Tangail	1990	45,003	26,677	119,565	65,960	424	0.40

Source: Credit and Development Forum (1997).

BRAC is listed at over 2 million, but it is not clear what proportion of the members receive loans in any one year. PROSHIKA also offers many nonfinancial services and it is also not clear how many of the 1.2 million clients receive loans. ASA is one of the most interesting MFOs, and it may be the most dynamic MFO in the country today. It started in the 1980s by providing many services, but found they were not highly valued by its members, so it switched in the 1990s to providing financial services only. It is now aggressively mobilizing savings, and has added an individual loan product for clients who either outgrow group lending or are never attracted to it.

Outreach

It is difficult to assess the total outreach of the formal financial system and the MFOs into rural areas. The World Bank (1996a) used a number of assumptions to arrive at the estimate that the banking system may have reached about 5 percent of the country's 16 million rural households in fiscal year 1994. It was further assumed that GB and the MFOs might have served about 4.9 million clients that year for a coverage of over 25 percent of the households (Table VII.3). If those numbers are roughly correct and if one household is served by only one institution, then over 30 percent of total households received commercial bank or MFO loans in that year.

The GB has been quite successful in several performance measures. Total annual disbursements rose from Tk54.8 crore in 1986 to Tk265.6 crore in 1990 and Tk1,525.1 crore in 1994. It had a membership of 1.9 million by 1994 of which 94 percent were women (Khandker, Khalily, and Khan, 1996). By 1996, it had 2.1 million members, reached about half of all villages in the country, had a network of 112 area officers and 1,056 village branches, and had Tk11,798 million ($289 million) in outstanding loans. The average outstanding loan was Tk5,708 ($142) or about 64 percent of GDP per capita. Savings represented almost half of loan volume at Tk5,366

Table VII.3: Major Microcredit Programs: Annual Disbursements During
1990–1995 (Tk million) and Number of Borrowers ('000) in 1994/95

Programs	1990/91	1991/92	1992/93	1993/94	1994/95	Borrowers
Formal Sector						
Grameen Bank	2,642	5,200	10,622	13,912	15,000	1,861
BRDB	205	352	688	878	1,647	521
Commercial banks	53	43	52	80	104	
NGOs						
PROSHIKA	121	127	224	303	423	417
Small PKSF partners	-	44	198	399	675	290
SWANIRVAR	45	44	62	109	132	598
NGO Subtotal	606	1,015	1,790	3,066	4,451	2,397
Grand Total	3,506	6,610	13,152	17,936	21,172	4,779
Total ($ million)	98	173	336	448	520	-

Source: Nagarajan and Gonzalez-Vega (1998b); original in World Bank (1996a).

million ($133 million) with an average savings account of
Tk2,605 ($65) (Yaron, Benjamin, and Piprek, 1997).

The next two largest MFOs were BRAC, serving 700,000
borrowers, and ASA with almost 400,000 (Table VII.3). BRAC
disbursed just over Tk2 billion in 1994/95 and ASA just over
Tk1 billion. PROSHIKA and SWANIRVAR are next in number
of clients served, but they disburse relatively smaller amounts
of funds per client. A large number of smaller MFOs together
disbursed 15 percent of total disbursements in 1994/95.

Data were reported to the Credit and Development
Forum by 380 NGOs as of December 1997 (Credit and
Development Forum, 1997). These NGOs reported a total
membership of over 6.7 million persons, of which 81 percent
were female. Just over 4.2 million were reported as borrowers
with total disbursements during the year of Tk15 billion. There
are many small NGOs that make loans, but they represent a
small share of the total market. The top 20 NGOs had 86 percent
of the members and 95 percent of the value of the loans
outstanding.

As noted above, the amount of credit now going into
agriculture as a share of GDP may be approximately equal to
that in the early 1980s. The mix of borrowers is likely to be

quite different, however, because of the efforts made by the MFOs and the GB to reach the poor. The uses of borrowed funds may also be quite different because many of the credit lines provided by banks and cooperatives were directed toward tubewells and other targeted inputs designed to stimulate agricultural production. Many MFOs, however, are more flexible regarding loan purpose, and the most important criterion is that the borrower repay the loan rather than use it for some specific purpose. Flexibility in loan use makes MFO loans more attractive to the borrowers.

There are relatively few studies to determine who is borrowing, for what purpose, and how far down the poverty profile the commercial banks, cooperatives, and MFOs reach. A small World Bank survey revealed that 44 percent of households had borrowed in the past two years. Of these, 56 percent borrowed from informal sources, 44 percent from the banks or cooperatives, and 10 percent from GB or the MFOs. There was little overlap reported in borrowing. Only 8 percent reported borrowing from both informal sources and banks, and 1.7 percent from informal sources and GB or an MFO. These results may not be fully representative because this sample was drawn from geographic areas close to bank branches (World Bank, 1996a). Moreover, anthropological studies tend to show rich patterns of financial behavior, in which persons borrow from informal sources in anticipation of getting an MFO loan or to pay an MFO loan installment (e.g. Rahman, 1999; Todd, 1997).

Sustainability

The most important factor affecting the sustainability of financial institutions in Bangladesh is loan recovery. The IMF estimated that about a quarter of total overdue loans were attributable to the agricultural sector (Wade et al., 1998). The evolution in agricultural loan recovery is shown in Table VII.4. The recovery rate fell from over 40 percent in 1983/84 to a low of 13.7 percent in 1990/91. Then it slowly rose but by the mid-1990s recovery was still only half that 12 to 13 years earlier. The total loans outstanding in 1996/97 amounted to Tk8,256 crore (about $2 billion) compared with the annual disbursement that year of Tk1,517 crore (about $370 million). In most years, the actual disbursements have been less than the targeted amounts set by the BB.

Agricultural loan recovery data for 1994/95 are presented in Table VII.5 by type of intermediary. The highest recovery rate for loans due in that year was achieved by DFIs at 65 percent. NCBs were second at 37 percent and cooperatives were third at 33 percent. Overall loan recovery for current loans increased from 50 percent in 1993/94 to 56 percent in 1994/95, but the percentage of total recovery fell from about 9.5 to 7.8 percent. Moreover, there were fairly large differences among the institutions within each category. Analysis of loan recovery data revealed that some banks did a better job of collecting loans made through their own financial programs than through the collaborative schemes designed by donors for poverty alleviation (World Bank, 1996a). Recovery rates were also expected to be poorer for larger farmers, and there was little evidence that weather risk explained differences in loan recovery between 1991 and 1994.

In contrast with this negative recovery experience, the GB disbursements for general crop loans, which were about 25 percent of its portfolio in 1994, had a loan recovery rate of 99 percent. Likewise, data reported for two NGOs that lend to agriculture showed good recovery. The problem, therefore, is that public ownership has made the formal institutions vulnerable to political interference. Pressures to disburse, noneconomic considerations in loan approvals, and political forgiveness contribute to poor portfolios (World Bank, 1996a). So far, the GB and the major MFOs have avoided the worst of these problems. Anecdotal evidence suggests that during periods of loan waivers, they have had to work energetically to convince their borrowers that the waivers did not apply to their loans.

Total loan recovery has been regularly reported by the GB to be 98 or 99 percent. However, these numbers are based on the amount overdue as a fraction of loans due. Morduch

Table VII.4: Agricultural Credit Disbursement and Recoveries, 1983/84 to 1996/97
(taka crores at current price)

Year	Program target	Disbursement	Falling due and overdue	Recovery	Percentage of recovery	Overdue	Outstanding
1983/84	1,115.0	1,005.3	1,238.2	517.6	41.8	755.7	2,077.4
1984/85	1,150.0	1,152.8	1,515.0	583.9	38.5	1,158.9	3,034.2
1985/86	1,276.5	631.7	2,375.2	607.2	25.6	1,778.8	3,514.3
1986/87	1,075.0	667.3	2,683.5	1,107.6	41.3	1,576.0	3,294.4
1987/88	1,050.0	656.3	2,528.2	595.8	23.6	1,932.4	3,863.5
1988/89	1,250.0	807.6	3,044.7	578.0	19.0	2,355.7	4,711.7
1989/90	1,350.0	686.8	3,986.3	701.9	17.6	3,284.3	5,381.3
1990/91	1,310.0	595.6	4,556.7	625.3	13.7	3,933.8	5,703.5
1991/92	1,322.1	794.6	4,170.2	662.1	15.9	3,572.3	5,369.6
1992/93	1,474.4	841.9	4,719.9	869.2	18.4	3,854.4	5,692.8
1993/94	1,643.1	1,100.8	5,141.2	979.1	19.0	4,203.7	6,222.0
1994/95	1,963.0	1,490.4	5,613.3	1,124.1	20.0	4,490.5	7,045.2
1995/96	2,442.0	1,481.6	6,193.5	1,273.1	20.6	4,920.4	7,769.1
1996/97	2,196.8	1,517.3	6,900.7	1,594.3	23.1	5,312.8	8,256.2

Source: World Bank (1996a). Updated with data from the Bangladesh Bank.

Table VII.5: Status of Agricultural Loan Recoveries from 1 July 1994 to 30 June 1995*

(taka crores at current prices)

Name of bank/ organization (1)	Amount of loans overdue from previous years (2)	Recovery from loans overdue from previous years (3)	Percentage of recovery of overdue loans (4)	Amount of loans due in the current year (5)	Recovery from loans due in the current year (6)	Percentage of recovery of current loans (7)	Total recoverable loans (2+5) (8)	Total loans recovered (3+6) (9)	Percentage of recovery (10)
Nationalized Commercial Banks									
Sonali	595.23	59.01	9.91	149.35	60.89	40.77	744.58	119.90	16.10
Janata	239.73	42.48	17.72	102.80	40.44	39.34	342.53	82.92	24.21
Agrani	141.93	43.36	30.55	94.42	30.00	31.77	236.35	73.36	31.04
Rupali	65.19	7.86	12.06	13.72	2.91	21.21	78.91	10.77	13.65
Subtotal	1,042.08	152.71	19.65	360.29	134.24	37.26	1,402.37	286.95	20.46
Development Banks									
BKB	1,562.53	106.17	6.79	642.16	488.17	76.00	2,204.69	594.34	26.96
RAKUB	752.68	58.49	7.77	300.44	120.34	40.05	1,053.12	178.83	16.98
Subtotal	2,315.21	164.66	7.11	942.60	608.51	64.56	3,257.81	773.17	23.73
Cooperatives									
BRDB	651.73	8.23	1.26	81.74	26.87	32.87	733.47	35.10	4.79
BSBL	179.43	1.26	0.70	1.10	0.29	26.36	180.53	1.55	0.86
Subtotal	831.16	9.49	1.14	82.84	27.16	32.79	914.00	36.65	4.01
Grand Total	4,188.45	326.86	7.80	1,385.73	769.91	55.56	5,574.18	1,096.77	19.68
Summary FY: 1993/94	3,921.03	370.80	9.46	1,220.83	608.32	49.83	5,141.96	979.12	19.04

* Provisional data for FY 1995.
Source: World Bank (1996a).

(1998b) estimated that 7.76 percent of loans were not repaid after more than one year, and 5.87 percent were not repaid after more than two years. These estimates refer to all loans made from 1985 to 1997. Moreover, there was a declining trend in loan repayment at the end of the period.

Matin (1998) studied the GB repayment problem in a case study of four villages in Madhupur. He discovered that the on-time repayment rates in 1995 were only 47 percent. Surprisingly, none of the borrowers interviewed thought poor repayment would adversely affect their chances of getting future Grameen loans. The GB had introduced seasonal and housing loans in the area as well as standard general loans. Rising levels of indebtedness was one factor explaining the rise in loan recovery problems.

Sustainability of the GB has been directly measured. Many NGOs in Bangladesh are dependent on foreign funds, and Grameen has received many domestic subsidies and foreign grants and soft loans. Recently, Government-guaranteed bonds have become a larger share of its total resources. The bank reported profits of $1.5 million during 1995/96, but this was attributed to a variety of direct grants and implicit subsidies. By imputing values for all these subsidies, Morduch (1998b) estimated that the GB would need to raise its nominal rate on general loans from 20 to 33 percent per year to become free of subsidies. There are legitimate questions about the ability of borrowers to absorb such a large increase. These results suggest that the GB will have to continue to rely on subsidies for its survival, and this raises questions about its ability to become completely self-sufficient as has occurred with some MFOs in Latin America.

Information on the sustainability of the NGOs is limited. Part of the problem is that many provide nonfinancial services to their members; a complete analysis would require that their financial operations be accounted for separately. CDF statistics (Credit and Development Forum, 1997) for 1997 for the 380 NGOs showed that foreign donations were the source of over 30 percent of their total revolving loan funds. Just over 16 percent was lent by the apex organization, Palli Karma-Sahayak

Foundation, a similar amount was mobilized from savers, and just less than 14 percent came from bank loans. Service charges, own funds, and other sources represented the balance.

The second most important issue affecting the sustainability of financial institutions after loan repayment is net income. Bangladesh has made some progress in deregulating interest rates for NCBs and DFIs, enabling them to move within a band set by the central bank. The problem is that with loan recovery so low, interest rates cannot be raised high enough to cover losses. This makes loan recovery the major problem for banks.

The sustainability issue is more complicated for the GB and the MFOs. Their reliance on subsidies helps keep interest rates low relative to their costs. However, there is considerable resistance to the concept of charging poor clients rates that are high enough to cover the full costs and risks of serving them. Moreover, if the estimate that the GB must raise its rates from 20 to 33 percent is indicative of the MFO sector, then raising the rates by this magnitude may reduce the demand for loans. The microlenders, therefore, must continuously evaluate the efficiency of their operations, the types of products and services offered, and the demands of existing and future clients.

DEPOSIT MOBILIZATION

NCBs have been the most aggressive financial institutions in mobilizing savings while the DFIs have largely lent funds provided by the BB. Unfortunately, the most recent analysis is for 1973–1984. In 1973, the NCBs held 90 percent of total bank deposits. By 1984, their share had fallen to 70 percent while the share of the DFIs had risen from 2.0 to 5.5 percent. Private and foreign banks held the balance. The expansion of bank branches into rural areas made a significant impact because the share of rural deposits in total deposits rose from 9 percent in 1976 to 17 percent in 1984. About half of the rural accounts in 1983 and 1984 were Tk5,000 or less (Khalily, Meyer, and Hushak, 1987).

District-level deposit data were studied for 1983 and 1984, and it was found that the number of bank branches and interest rates paid on deposits had a significant impact on the volume of district deposits (Khalily and Meyer, 1992). Total rural deposits grew rapidly during this period with the expansion of rural bank branches, in spite of notoriously poor quality service and the lack of significant marketing of savings products.

Most MFOs are not nearly as aggressive in providing savings services to their clients as they are in making loans, as noted in the savings-to-loan ratios reported in Table VII.2. BRAC and ASA are best in mobilizing savings, which now are close to half their total loan volume. The sources of funds for these MFOs are shown in Table VII.6. Foreign donations are still the major source of funding for BRAC and PROSHIKA, but some of these funds are designated for expansion purposes and for nonfinancial services. ASA has been more aggressive in mobilizing deposits, and savings now represent more than a third of its total funds. The 380 NGOs reported to CDF that total member savings represented just 16 percent of their revolving loan funds, and the top 20 held 90 percent of those savings.

Most MFOs undervalue savings services for poor households and they have not been aggressive in creating attractive products for voluntary savings. The GB members have perceived their obligatory savings to be an additional cost of borrowing. Lack of access in times of emergency reduces the value of these savings as a means for the poor to manage emergencies, and reduces the value of the MFOs to assist the poor to escape poverty (Hulme and Mosley, 1996).

The success of ASA has promoted some MFOs to pay more attention to the demand by the poor for financial services other than loans. A particularly interesting approach is being tested by SafeSave, a cooperative organized by Stuart Rutherford, in collecting savings on a daily basis from urban slum dwellers in Dhaka. It began operations in August 1996 and by 31 October 1998 had mobilized over Tk2 million (approximately $45,000) in savings. It also uses borrowed funds and had over Tk3 million ($65,000) in outstanding loans made

Table VII.6: Top Ten Bangladesh Financial NGOs: Sources of Funds

Rank	Name of NGO	Member savings	PKSF	Local bank	Foreign donations	Service charges	Own funds	Others
1	BRAC	17.5	10.3	2.9	50.7	13.8	0.0	4.9
2	PROSHIKA	6.5	20.2	1.1	43.6	23.9	0.0	4.7
3	ASA	38.2	22.6	0.0	24.3	12.6	2.4	0.0
4	SWANIRVAR Bangladesh	0.0	0.1	99.9	0.0	0.0	0.0	0.0
5	RDRS-Bangladesh	0.0	15.7	0.0	0.0	30.8	53.5	0.0
6	Thengamara Mohila Sabuj Sangha (TMSS)	19.9	69.9	0.0	0.0	10.2	0.0	0.0
7	Society for Social Service (SSS)	24.4	45.6	0.0	1.3	23.5	0.0	5.3
8	Bangladesh Extension Education Services (BEES)	21.8	0.0	0.8	38.6	20.0	6.7	12.1
9	CODEC	19.5	0.0	0.0	60.7	4.6	7.2	7.9
10	Buro, Tangail	28.3	0.0	0.0	45.6	20.3	0.0	5.7

Sources (percent)

Source: Credit and Development Forum (1997).

to the savers. Surprisingly, saving and repayment patterns were little affected by the July 1998 flood. The organization aims to be innovative in the design of savings instruments and to train other organizations in the approach. One replication has 100,000 clients in 50 urban branches (SafeSave, 1998).

MICROFINANCE

Most of the financial services provided by the GB and MFOs can be classified as microfinance, in contrast to most of the loans made by NCBs and DFIs. It is interesting to note how well the GB and MFOs have performed in expanding outreach and recovering loans compared with the dismal performance of the NCBs and DFIs.

An important feature of the microfinance sector in Bangladesh is the large apex organization established in 1990, the Palli Karma-Sahayak Foundation (PKSF). It has the dual objective of making loans to large NGOs, and building the capacity of small NGOs as well as lending to them. It operates with funds obtained from the Government and donors. It receives requests from MFOs for loans for on-lending to their clients, reviews them, decides which to fund, monitors the loans, and provides some technical assistance to the MFOs. By early 1998, it was providing funding for 154 partner organizations (Table VII.7). In 1996/97, it disbursed Tk1.6 billion. The total disbursements for its MFO partners during 1990–1998 amounted to Tk3.4 billion compared with an annual disbursement of Tk15 billion made by GB in 1994/95 (Table VII.3).

PKSF enjoys a great deal of autonomy. It has a 25-member governing body, about half of whom consist of private sector members, including leading personalities and social workers of international reputation. Policies and daily operations including loan approvals are the responsibility of a seven-member Governing Board. The Board has full autonomy over staff compensation, and salary levels are higher

Table VII.7: Number of Partner Organizations and Volume of Loans Disbursed by PKSF, 1990–1997

Year	Annual number of new partners	Total number of partners	Annual rate of growth of partners	Amount disbursed (Tk million)	Amount recovered (Tk million)	Average amount disbursed[a] (Tk million)
1990/91	23	23	-	3	-	0.13
1991/92	27	50	11	27	1	0.53
1992/93	31	81	62	113	10	1.39
1993/94	18	99	22	185	40	1.87
1994/95	15	114	15	302	110	2.65
1995/96	12	126	11	470	197	3.73
1996/97	22	148	18	1,620	129	10.95
Jul. 97– March 98	14	154	4	1,473	291	9.56

[a] Amount per organization based on the cumulative number of active partner organizations at that time and the volume disbursed that year.

Source: Nagarajan and Gonzalez-Vega (1998b).

than those paid by the Government and the large NGOs. PKSF encourages its partner organizations to fully recover recurring costs from interest income. It lends at nominal annual rates ranging from 3 to 4.5 percent and requires a minimum on-lending nominal rate to final borrowers of 16 percent (ADB, 1997a; Nagarajan and Gonzalez-Vega, 1998b).

Although there is considerable enthusiasm in many Asian countries for creating apex institutions, it seems that Bangladesh is one of the few countries that meets the necessary conditions for reasonable success. These conditions are described in Box VII.1.

The MFOs generally are not well linked to banks although they use bank branches for their financial operations. Before becoming a specialized bank for the poor, Grameen operated as an NGO that screened and organized borrowers, and introduced them to banks. It was hoped that by incurring these costs the banks would then develop banking relations with the borrowers without further Grameen involvement. Since that rarely happened, the Grameen program was converted into a bank. As noted in the CDF statistics, the 380 NGOs reported borrowing only 14 percent of their revolving loans from a bank. Among the large NGOs, for some time there was only one example reported in which an NGO successfully borrowed from a bank. This was a loan from Agrani Bank (an NCB) to ASA. It came about because of strong donor pressure, and the bank required ASA to provide its headquarters building as collateral. Because of this collateral requirement, a second loan was not requested after the first was repaid.

An important issue in the microfinance community around the world and in Bangladesh in particular, has been the impact of being a member of an MFO and receiving a loan. This issue would not be as significant a question if MFOs were commercially self-sufficient organizations. However, since some MFOs cannot or do not want to become independent from government and donor grants and loans, a logical question is whether the subsidies provided to them make a positive impact on their borrower-members. Impact analysis in this

Box VII.1 The Palli Karma-Sahayak Foundation (PKSF) in Bangladesh

PKSF is owned by the Government of Bangladesh but has complete autonomy. It functions in a densely populated country, which has an established microfinance market with several big MFOs. Some have been serving a large clientele for over two decades with proven technologies. Several small NGOs also exist. It is reported that about 300 to 350 potentially sustainable MFOs exist among the specialized MFOs currently operating in the country. Several big NGOs such as ASA, BRAC, Grameen Bank and PROSHIKA also function as apexes to help develop MFOs and link them with PKSF. It is in this environment that PKSF plays a role as an intermediary and capacity builder of MFOs. Some donor projects also work to upgrade the MFOs.

A strong board, composed of distinguished leaders in the field of microfinance, heads PKSF. It applies clear and strict criteria in the selection of partners for funding. The financial intermediary role is the primary function, while some capacity building is carried out in collaboration with the existing big NGOs. It has recorded profits since 1997 and is expected to be financially sustainable by 2002.

As of March 1998, PKSF served 154 MFOs of which about 20 have more than 50,000 clients each. The loan recovery rate from MFOs has been around 98 percent and loan recovery by partner MFOs from their clients has been around 99 percent.

There are some concerns about PKSF. The implicit use of Grameen technology as a base to screen applicants may restrict entry by some innovative MFOs that follow alternative technologies. Also, the provision of a uniform loan size for first-time borrowers may have to be altered to suit the demand and repayment capacity of the MFOs. Not withstanding these concerns, PKSF is a comparatively successful domestic apex organization. It has been recommended as a role model for apex organizations in other developing countries. The following favorable conditions explain PKSF's success.

(continued next page)

Box VII.1 (continued)

- PKSF operates in a large, advanced microfinance market, where several leading MFOs have developed and adapted effective lending technologies and are directly involved in disseminating them.
- It has access to abundant funding, most of which is invested rather than granted as loans to MFOs. This asset structure curbs disbursement pressures and generates income to cover costs.
- PKSF has access to a large pool of cheap, well-educated human resources appropriate for its labor-intensive operations.
- PKSF has operated in an environment characterized by a supportive but not interventionist Government. This, combined with the exceptional standing of its board members, has guaranteed independence from political pressures despite Government ownership. This has helped PKSF to fend off disbursement pressures.
- The leaders of the organization have been primarily concerned with its sustainability and, consequently, with the sustainability of its MFO clients.

Source: Abstracted from Nagarajan and Gonzales-Vega (1998b).

situation is recognized as being extremely complex. One of the most comprehensive and sophisticated impact studies conducted to date was the World Bank's attempt to measure several dimensions of impact on members of the GB and other MFOs. One study concluded that borrowing had a positive impact on household expenditures, nonland assets held by women, male and female labor supply, and schooling of children. Credit supplied to women had more impact than credit provided to men (Pitt and Khandker, 1998). But in a later study of the same data using a different approach,

Morduch (1998a) found little difference in consumption between members and the control group, and that children of members were not more likely to go to school. This study found, however, that members had less variability in consumption and labor supply across seasons; thus, membership may do more to reduce vulnerability than to reduce poverty.

A number of impact studies have attempted to demonstrate that women have or have not become empowered by membership and borrowing (e.g. Amin, Becker, and Bayes, 1998). The most recent is an in-depth anthropological study of Grameen Bank borrowers in one village (Rahman, 1999). The author observed some negative features of peer pressure. For example, if one member is delinquent in making a loan payment, all members are detained beyond the normal ending time of their weekly center meetings. Due to this delay, women have been beaten because they did not return home in time to prepare regular meals. Such incidents demonstrate the difficulty in using credit as a tool to change complex, traditional social patterns.

INFORMAL FINANCE

Informal finance has not been as well studied in Bangladesh as in some other Asian countries, but a few key studies suggest patterns similar to those found elsewhere (Rutherford, 1996). Islam, Von Pischke, and de Waard (1995) summarized the results of 16 industry case studies. None of the industries were specifically linked to or located in rural areas. The results were similar to those typically found in small industry studies. The initial capital for the businesses came from owners' savings and loans from friends and relatives. Retained earnings were the major source of funds for expansion. Working capital was frequently obtained through trade channels in the form of raw materials and supplies obtained on credit, and advances received from clients.

The total magnitude of informal lending is hard to estimate. Ghate (1992) reported on surveys suggesting that about one third of borrowings came from informal sources, and two thirds from formal. Some 8 percent of households reported formal loans versus 36 percent for informal. There was no information to judge the representativeness of these data.

Anthropological studies in the mid-1980s described a large number of different types of informal loans in rural areas (Maloney and Ahmed, 1988). Ghate (1992) summarized several Bangladesh case studies conducted in 1988 as part of a regional ADB study. He found that the main types of informal loans were (i) *dadon* or forward sales of crops to finance crop production; (ii) trade credit extended on a profit-sharing basis or against tied sales or purchases; (iii) small loans for consumption or for petty trading and processing; and (iv) larger and longer-term loans for both consumption and production collateralized by usufructuary land mortgages.

The Islamic prohibition of interest had four consequences: a large proportion of *dadon*, in which the price discounts and forward sales substitute for interest; a high frequency of profit sharing in lieu of interest; an extremely high share of interest-free credit; and frequency of usufructuary land mortgages. Maloney and Ahmed (1988) reported that 57 percent of informal loans carried no explicit interest. These loans were often made by relatives, friends, neighbors, and patrons, and were mostly small loans for subsistence. When interest was charged, the nominal interest rates varied widely between 2 and 10 percent per month. People who borrowed from moneylenders usually paid 5 to 10 percent per month. Women who lent to each other charged 10 to 20 percent per month. Rates of 5 to 10 percent per month were not viewed as too high considering the cost and trouble for the lender to make small short-term loans.

One case study of noninterest transaction costs for formal bank loans in Bangladesh found a range in nominal interest rates of 245 percent for small loans to 58 percent for large loans (Ahmed, 1989). These costs include travel costs, the value of time lost, bribes, and other incidentals. Such high transaction costs help explain why some borrowers choose informal loans with higher interest rates but lower transaction costs rather than formal loans with lower interest rates.

Anthropological accounts (e.g. Todd, 1997) refer to microfinance borrowers using loan proceeds to pay off informal loans, and women borrowing informally to pay their MFO loan installments. Sinha and Matin (1998) investigated credit transactions in one northern village and found that most borrowers from the GB and other MFOs active in the area also borrowed from informal sources. Informal loans enabled some borrowers to invest more rapidly than permitted by the rigid lending technology of the formal lenders. For others, however, the informal loans helped smooth consumption and pay formal loans, and some were on a spiraling debt cycle. These accounts suggest that poor people in Bangladesh use a variety of loan sources to manage their household accounts. This pattern is consistent with the findings of detailed household studies in most developing countries.

FINANCIAL CRISIS AND NATURAL DISASTERS

Bangladesh was largely unaffected by the financial and economic crisis in Asia. The country has not attracted much private foreign capital, has not experienced rapid economic growth, and did not suffer from a highly overvalued exchange rate, as did Indonesia, Thailand, and other countries in the region. Bangladesh may suffer problems in the future, however, due to increased competition in export markets from other countries that were forced to devalue. This problem could worsen if China also devalues its currency.

The most recent serious shock that Bangladesh has faced was the severe flooding that started in July 1998 and continued into September. An important question concerns how the financial sector was affected, and what needs to be done to safeguard financial systems that face such natural disasters.

Some reports suggested that this flood was much larger than others in recent years. The GB reported that 71 percent of its branches and 52 percent of its members were affected (Barua, 1998). CARE Bangladesh reported that 24 of its partner NGOs in urban and peri-urban Dhaka had over 100,000 affected households (CARE Bangladesh, 1998). The GB did not provide information on loan recovery, but there were immediate reports that its liquidity problems might require donor assistance. CARE reported serious cash-flow problems for the 24 NGOs. For June–September, total cash inflows (savings plus loan payments) were 22 percent below projected levels. Only 57 percent of clients maintained on-time payments after the flood, and only 48 percent continued to make regular savings deposits. This shortfall forced the NGOs to suspend paying staff salaries, rent and other recurrent expenses, employing new staff, and disbursing new loans. A plan was developed to mobilize additional donor resources in order that emergency loans could be made to current members of the NGOs.

The effects of this natural disaster prompt two questions. First, what mechanisms need to be designed to support financial institutions in these kinds of crises? Second, what is the appropriate role of the MFOs in responding to the needs of their members? The answers will vary from one situation to another, but two answers seem to be obvious. The first is that any financial institution that is subject to periodic shocks, such as floods in Bangladesh, must anticipate the problem and design methods to assure its survival. The problem with NGOs is that they have no owners who can be expected to inject more capital to restore liquidity, nor do they have access to central bank emergency funds. NGOs should hold extraordinarily high reserves as precautionary balances, but in practice most are undercapitalized and hold few reserves. Second, analysis of previous natural disasters provides lessons for disaster-prone countries (Nagarajan, 1998). The affected MFOs should not write-off existing loans as this may jeopardize their future viability and set a bad precedent for borrowers. Any special relief activities should be short term and channeled through separate disaster-management windows to distinguish the relief from regular MFO operations. Longer-term strategies include portfolio diversification by increasing the range of type and location of clients and type of enterprises funded.

CURRENT POTENTIAL AND CONSTRAINTS FOR RURAL FINANCE

Bangladesh has had an unfortunate history with its financial system ever since Independence. The original strategy to use State-directed credit to build an entrepreneurial class has evolved into a financial system undermined by politics. Bad debts strangle the system and there are few signs that the problem will be solved in the near future. Initially, donor projects contributed to the problem, and subsequent donor activities have been unsuccessful in resolving it. The country has become addicted to foreign aid for bailouts of its financial system.

The policies designed to push financial services into rural areas had the positive effect of expanding the rural network of NCB and DFI branches, and contributed to the growth of rural bank deposits. This branch network is used to channel subsidized loans to farmers. Unfortunately, the rural financial system became infected with the same bad-debt disease that affects the urban bank branches. A huge NGO system has emerged because of the failure of the public sector to supply basic services. The GB and the financial NGOs have surpassed the banks in making loans, a large portion of which go to rural areas. Surprisingly, they have avoided serious default problems in their programs of lending to the poor. They have succeeded in developing systems to deliver highly standardized small loans to poor people. They have been more successful at serving female clients than male. The chief weakness is that many MFOs are highly dependent on Government and donor funding; therefore, they are not self-sustaining in spite of good loan recovery. Many also lag behind MFOs in other parts of the world in creating more individualized products to meet the heterogeneous needs of the poor for financial services.

The inescapable conclusion is that the rural financial system in Bangladesh is fragile. A gap has emerged between the rural market segments served by the banks and those served by the NGOs (McGregor, 1994). The formal financial institutions are saddled with bad debts with few signs of improvement in spite of vast amounts of donor assistance. The GB and MFOs have stepped in to substitute for the poorly performing banks, but they are highly dependent on Government and foreign funding. Although some 25 to 30 percent of rural residents may currently have access to formal loans, future access is uncertain because many financial institutions are not self-sufficient. Moreover, even the financial NGOs cannot meet all the demands for financial services of the poor because of insufficient total supplies, program requirements that discourage some of the poor from participating, and high dropout rates (Evans et al., 1999). Even if outreach increases, many of the problems of the rural poor cannot be solved by financial services alone (Khandker, 1998). Important reforms are required before the country can be assured of an efficient and sustainable rural financial system.

Creating the Policy Environment

Political intrusion is currently the single biggest obstacle to the development of a sound market-based financial system in Bangladesh. Resolving this problem must be the top financial policy priority. Donors have funded one project after another over the past two decades with the expectation that each time the Government would seriously commit itself to reforms. But each improvement made in the system seemed to reveal a new problem. For example, at one time privatization of NCBs and licensing of new banks was expected to make a major improvement. But, as noted above, the loan recovery problems of private banks are almost as serious as those of State-owned banks. Donors can make little impact on the formal financial system until politics are excluded from financial transactions.

It is time for donors to stop providing financial assistance to the banking system until that happens.

The second key policy issue concerns interest rates. Because of political pressure and social resistance, the country has resisted charging the level of rates needed to cover the costs and risks of financial operations. The financial institutions need greater freedom to price their products and services. Subsidies to MFOs, unless they are limited to capacity building, retard the process of achieving sustainability and discourage competition.

Creating and Strengthening the Financial Infrastructure

The most important financial infrastructure issue is the current status and future needs of the system of prudential regulations and supervision for financial institutions. At the top end of the financial system, many reforms have been made in the past two decades concerning the regulatory framework and the legal system to support financial transactions. An obvious problem is that the regulatory role of the Bangladesh Bank is undercut by political intervention, such that the technical merits of these recent reforms have not been tested. In spite of the special debt courts, legal enforcement can drag on for years due to undisciplined procedural wrangles, politics favoring debtors, and lack of execution capacity (Lee and Meagher, 1999). It is unclear exactly what reforms remain to be undertaken. The GB has a special charter from the BB, but in practice it operates relatively independently of the Government (Carpenter, 1997). It has accessed huge amounts of foreign funds so its survival has not been threatened, and there has been little reason for the regulatory authorities to exercise an active supervisory role. It is not clear how appropriate the terms of the charter and regulatory relationship will be, or how well the BB will effectively exercise its role as the GB becomes less dependent on donor funds and mobilizes more savings.

Since many MFOs have received financial support from foreign sources and savings mobilization is relatively underdeveloped, there has been little pressure to regulate them. Now that some are mobilizing more voluntary savings, the regulatory issue is becoming more important. As long as the MFOs avoid being infected by the bad-debt disease, the savings mobilized from the poor may not be at great risk. Recent information about higher delinquency rates than expected in the GB is unsettling, however, and may portend problems for other MFOs as well. Donors have a huge stake in the NGOs that they have created and nurtured. Now their responsibility is to take the next step by helping to create an appropriate regulatory system to protect these organizations, but not strangle them with excessive rules and regulations.

There are various ways in which MFOs may evolve as they strive for sustainability. Different forms of regulation will be required for different situations. Some of the largest and better organized may become licensed banks for the poor under charters similar to GB.[3] This would give them the opportunity to legally mobilize deposits from the public. Others may find the charter requirements too onerous and may become specialized lenders of funds provided to them by banks and the PKSF. As part of their relationship with banks, some may mobilize savings and deposit them in banks. Some NGOs may continue to be largely self-regulated while a third party could be licensed to regulate others.

A Credit Information Bureau has been created, but it is located in the Bangladesh Bank, so it may not have as much independence as would be ideal. It is reported that it covers only the largest transactions, and the perfection of liens in the various registries is subject to delays of three weeks to a month (Lee and Meagher, 1999). In the mid-1980s, the Agricultural Credit Department of the Bangladesh Bank was swamped as

---

[3] Eight new private licenses were issued for eight new private banks in 1999. BRAC received one of these licenses but it is unclear what market niche it will try to serve relative to its current clients as an NGO.

a result of collecting information from all rural branches to inform the Government and donors about disbursements and recoveries for hundreds of different credit lines. This problem distracted the banks from collecting information needed to improve management. The situation highlighted the importance of good information systems for efficient bank regulation and supervision.

Institutional Development

Several technical assistance projects have been implemented over the past two decades to strengthen the NCBs and DFIs. The changes these projects nurtured have been undermined by lack of enforcement. There is little reason to do anything further with the banks, however, until the political intrusion question is resolved. Moreover, at one time the system of targeted agricultural credit was so highly structured, there was little opportunity for loan officers to exercise judgement in making loan decisions. Likewise, the staff of the GB and other MFOs that use group lending have been given relatively little discretion in selecting clients and determining loan amounts and conditions. Their skills will need to be significantly upgraded as loan sizes rise and more attention is required to evaluate borrower creditworthiness and debt repayment capacity.

The formal banking institutions, GB, and the large MFOs have hundreds of outlets, and have developed information systems to monitor operations, savings accounts, loan disbursements, and repayments. Information is not available to evaluate how efficient these internal systems are in collecting and managing information, and the extent to which inefficiencies contribute to loan recovery problems. At one time the accounting systems of the banks were admittedly quite inadequate. Presumably they have improved, but the problem may now be with small NGOs that began their operations by providing nonfinancial services and are now involved in lending. Donor projects aim to resolve these problems but it is unclear how far they have progressed.

The recent floods underscore the risks of agricultural lending in a country regularly subject to natural disasters. Since they occur with such frequency in Bangladesh, financial institutions should be prepared to deal with them. If they are not, it represents a failure in their management and the Government and donors that support them. More attention is needed to devise appropriate levels of reserves and speedy access to emergency funds for MFOs that by design have few capital reserves. Donors need to give as much attention to helping MFOs develop long-term risk management strategies as they do to providing funds for on-lending to clients. They need to assist the NGOs to develop prudent savings mobilization strategies so they can eventually become financially self-sufficient.

There are suggestions that the MFOs in Bangladesh are approaching a critical point in their approach to serving clients. The GB and the large MFOs have successfully lent to millions of poor people. By offering only a few highly standardized loan products and utilizing a simple system of obligatory savings collection, they have reduced internal accounting and control problems. But this simplicity comes at a cost: clients have to adapt to the services offered rather than the MFOs tailoring their services to client preferences. This inflexibility may contribute to the high rates of client drop-outs, which reach 10 to 15 percent per year in the GB and BRAC. Drop-outs cost the MFOs money because, to maintain credit volumes, they must be replaced by new clients who have to be oriented and trained.

One solution is to introduce more flexibility in the financial services offered (Wright, 1999). ASA and Buro Tangail are already doing so in their programs. The problem is that flexibility implies more complicated tasks for credit officers and more sophisticated systems for financial controls. Cash flows will become more complex to plan, predict, and manage for the MFOs. Costs may rise, but most MFOs are already having difficulty in covering costs with revenues. It may be difficult for some clients to pay the higher cost of more individualized products.

A more general issue concerns the ability of MFOs to expand their scale of operations, serve more male clients, extend larger and longer term loans, and lend to farmers engaged in larger-scale, more seasonal crop and livestock operations. This involves upscaling, that is making larger more complex loans in which the earnings from the enterprise or activity financed are more important than other sources of household income in determining repayment. If the MFOs become successful in upscaling, it would represent an important breakthrough because it would show that their products, services, and lending technologies are robust enough to serve not just the poor, but also the market segments traditionally served by the NCB and DFIs. This would be a truly remarkable breakthrough in banking in Bangladesh.

VIII Rural Financial Market Development in India: Large Institutions, Poor Performance

OVERVIEW OF THE FINANCIAL SYSTEM

The current formal financial institutions in India are the result of evolution and constant Government intervention over the past three decades. After the famine of the 1960s, financial sector policies were based on the premise that constrained access to credit would impede the adoption of green-revolution technologies and delay attainment of food self-sufficiency. Poverty alleviation has been a major political objective since the late 1970s and expansion of formal finance to serve the poor has been perceived as an important strategy to achieve it. Therefore, the Government has intervened heavily in the banking sector with policies for bank branching, mandatory quotas and below-market interest rates for loans to the priority sector, frequent waivers on loan principal and/or interest, and recapitalization and refinancing of loss-making institutions. The infamous loan *melas*[1] in the 1980s, in which large volumes of

---

[1] Loan *melas* were loan festivals during which many subsidized loans were made by the nationalized banks to the weaker sectors. A government official was present during these festivals. Since the banks were required to make a large number of loans in a short period, the borrowers were not screened for their credit worthiness. These *melas* were discontinued three years after their introduction in the early 1980s when the then Minister of Finance left office.

funds were imprudently issued as subsidized loans to the supposedly weaker segments of society, and loan waivers offered until 1991, were classic examples of abuse of the banking sector for political purposes, especially at the time of elections.

The policies for branch banking, on the one hand, may have contributed to the expansion of commercial banks into rural areas and to their lending to the rural population. The average population covered by a bank branch declined from 65,000 in 1969 to 15,000 in 1998. More than half the branches of formal institutions, which include 27 nationalized commercial banks; 35 domestic, private commercial banks; and 29 foreign commercial banks; branches of several agricultural, urban, and land-development cooperatives; and 196 regional rural banks (RRBs) are now located in rural areas. The RRBs are a hybrid form between commercial banks and cooperatives. They were established in 1975 as a subsidiary of the public-sector commercial banks to service the rural poor, small and marginal farmers, rural artisans, landless workers, and small entrepreneurs.

Other policies such as directed credit, loan waivers, subsidies, and the bailing out of nonperforming institutions, on the other hand, have contributed to a breakdown in borrower discipline and a weakened financial sector. The percentage of nonperforming loans to total loans made by commercial banks in 1996 was about 20 for India compared with only 10 for Indonesia and 7.7 for Thailand (Claessens and Glaessner, 1998). In India, this percentage declined in 1998 to 8.2 but loan recovery rates for the majority of formal financial institutions still remain very low, averaging about 60 percent (Talwar, 1999). The performance of loans made to the priority sector under the directed credit program has been especially dismal. The cumulative losses due to nonperforming loans made to the priority sector and to small and State-owned industries amounted in 1994 to about 2 percent of the total loss rate of 8.5 percent of the banks' assets (Nayak, 1995).

In the 1990s, the country embarked on a paradigm shift in its approach to the financial sector but the political hold on the banking sector is still significant.[2] There were efforts beginning in 1992 to liberalize the financial sector and strengthen it by re-orientating banks and other financial institutions toward a market-based financial system by increasing competition and improving the quality of financial services (Box VIII.1). The reforms have been partly successful in converting some public-sector development finance institutions into profit-oriented companies, in easing the entry of foreign and private banks, and in granting some functional autonomy to banks (Bhandari, 1997).

As of mid-1996, the country's banking regulatory framework was considered satisfactory and improving, while supervisory quality and transparency were rated as fair and improving (Claessens and Glaessner, 1998).[3] New supervisory initiatives to improve efficiency, such as an offsite monitoring and surveillance system, have been introduced to supplement periodical onsite inspections of financial institutions (Talwar, 1999). However, the effects of the reforms have yet to be realized in several other dimensions. A composite score for banking sector performance based on asset quality, management, capital adequacy, earnings, liquidity, operating environment, and transparency–on a scale in which the lower the score, the better the performance[4] –was estimated to be around 5.8 for the Indian banking sector compared to 4.6 for Indonesia and 5.2 for Thailand. While the scale for commitment to opening the banking sector in India was calculated at 2.7, the scale for actual implementation was only 2.25, indicating a gap between policies and implementation. These scores were closer to each other

---

[2] The financial sector reforms were part of several reforms implemented in India beginning in1992, to address the severe macroeconomic crisis that led to the fall of foreign exchange reserves, and a degradation in India's credit rating that led to the decline of foreign lending to the country (Chandavarkar, 1998).

[3] A five-point scale based on a qualitative assessment was used for the rating. The scale is calibrated as very good, good, satisfactory, fair, and weak.

[4] Percentage weightings for calculation of overall score were 25 for asset quality, 20 for management, 15 for earnings, 5 for liquidity, 15 for operating environment, and 5 for transparency.

**Box VIII.1 Selected Features of Financial Sector
Reforms in India**

1. **Competition**: Encouraged by allowing entry of foreign and
   some domestic private banks, by permitting urban
   cooperatives to provide agricultural finance, and by
   introducing local area banks and specialized, agricultural
   development financial institutions in rural areas.

2. **Mandatory quotas to priority sector**: The definition of
   priority sector has been expanded to include small business
   and transport operators in the rural areas. In addition,
   the quota for the previous components of the priority sector
   such as small and marginal farmers, artisans, cottage
   industries, and weaker sections including women and
   lower caste people was lowered to 10 percent of the total
   credit made by banks compared with 28 percent until 1992.

3. **Prudential norms**: Introduced into commercial banks in
   1992/93, into regional rural banks (RRBs) in 1995/96, and
   into cooperatives in 1996/97.

4. **Interest rates**: Deposit and lending rates were completely
   deregulated for cooperatives in October 1994 and for RRBs
   in August 1996. Lending rates for commercial banks are
   still regulated up to Rs200,000 ($4,700), but deregulated
   above that limit.

---

for Indonesia and Thailand. The total volume of credit from
the banking system was about 23.9 percent of GDP in 1995,
the least among several Asian countries, and the ratio of M_2
(money in circulation through the banks) to GDP was about
50 percent, indicating a low level of financial deepening.

Governmental influence in the financial sector is still
substantial. The Government owns about 80 percent of the
banking industry (Bhandari, 1997) and the cooperatives are also
significantly controlled by the states under the Cooperative
Societies Act. The financial system is overstaffed with employees
who oppose computerization that would close the information

gap and lower transaction costs. The legal structure is ineffective in withstanding political pressures and cannot handle the vast load of lawsuits, thereby making contract enforcement difficult (Chadavarkar, 1998). The slow pace of half-hearted reforms has made several analysts suspicious of the country's ability to create a financial sector suitable for a sophisticated market economy in the near future.

The overall structure, conduct, and performance of the financial system has a profound impact on the rural sector that constitutes about three quarters of the country and employs about two thirds of the total working population in agriculture and allied activities. A considerable decline has occurred in rural poverty in the past two decades, from 56.4 percent in 1973/74 to 37.3 percent in 1993/94. The decline was more significant during 1977–1988 (2.5 percent per year) than during 1988–1994 (1.1 percent per year). This decline was attributed to the spread of the green revolution to poorer parts of the country, the increased allocation of financial and nonfinancial resources for poverty alleviation, and the improvements made in the public food distribution system. However, the actual number of people below the poverty line and the income inequality in rural areas have increased significantly in the past two decades (Rao, 1998). The increase in rural poverty has become a major concern for the Government, leading to the formulation of several policies for poverty alleviation.

APPROACH TO RURAL AND AGRICULTURAL FINANCE

Rural finance is considered to be a major program that appeals to the rural poor. As a result, a supply-leading approach has been employed for rural and agricultural finance to cater to the rural population, which is a major vote bank for the political parties. Indeed, the majority of the governmental interventions described above were done with the rural sector as the primary focus. The interventions may have lacked economic rationale but were loaded with short-term political objectives.

In addition to direct interventions in rural banking, the Government launched a major poverty alleviation program, the Integrated Rural Development Program (IRDP), in 1978. Loans are made through the banking system at subsidized rates to the rural poor whose household income is below Indian rupees (Rs) 11,000 ($305) per year. Besides the loan, a cash subsidy is paid to borrowers and is set at 25 percent of the total cost for projects financed for small farmers, 33 percent for projects for agricultural laborers, and 50 percent for lower-caste persons. The cash subsidies are provided at the time the loan is disbursed. There are special quotas for lower-caste persons, physically handicapped, women, freed bonded laborers and the poor who adopt family planning. Loans made by commercial banks are subject to a nominal interest rate ceiling of 12 percent per annum and the loans are made for a maximum of three years. As of 1996/97, the maximum loan under the program has been Rs25,000 ($690) with an average loan size of about Rs8,150 ($230). Since the average per capita income in India is estimated at about Rs13,000 ($365) and the poverty line is drawn at a per capita annual income of Rs11,000 ($310), one can argue that the program is targeted at the poor.

There has been a reduction in farm sizes and diversification of farm households into small and microenterprise activities since the 1980s. It has been estimated that there exists a demand for $8 billion per annum in microloans from 60 million rural poor households, but the formal sector serves only 20 percent of the demand (Anon., 1998b, 1998d). Microfinance programs are now considered essential for providing working capital and financing nonfarm activities. Microfinance has been attempted on a large scale since the early 1990s. The importance of self-help groups (SHGs) was also recognized in the late 1980s, and in 1992 a pilot linkage program was initiated under the directive of the Government to link SHGs with banks either directly or through NGOs as guarantors or intermediaries. The Government intends to link 200,000 SHGs with banks by 2002. In addition, Citibank launched an $800,000 microcredit scheme in 1998 to provide microloans through NGOs (Anon., 1998c).

The commercial banks have introduced several innovative schemes to finance the rural sector. They include the green-card scheme that allows established farmer clients to access credit on demand without lengthy paperwork, agricultural overdraft schemes that provide credit throughout the year for farming, and installment schemes for the purchase of machinery and equipment for small businesses (Rao, 1995).

THE EVOLUTION AND CURRENT STATUS OF KEY RURAL FINANCIAL INSTITUTIONS

Participants

As of June 1998, the country had 32,662 rural and semi-urban branches of commercial banks, a cooperative network with 92,682 primary agricultural credit societies (PACS), over 2,000 branches of land development banks that primarily provide term loans for the purchase of land and land improvements, and about 14,136 branches of RRBs. The average population per rural bank branch ranges between 17,000 and 21,000 persons (Sankaranarayanan, 1998). In addition, urban cooperatives are also allowed to operate in rural areas.

The Reserve Bank of India (RBI) is responsible for broad financial sector policies and is the general regulatory authority for commercial banks and urban credit cooperatives. The National Bank for Agriculture and Rural Development (NABARD), formed in 1982, is an apex refinancing institution for the cooperatives, RRBs, and the commercial banks engaged in rural lending. NABARD is also mandated to coordinate, supervise, and build the capacity of rural financial institutions such as the RRBs and PACS. The Deposit Insurance and Credit Guarantee Corporation insures small depositors and guarantees the rural loans made by the formal institutions. The National Cooperative Development Corporation promotes the cooperative sector and provides loans and subsidies to cooperatives to improve their performance.

The results from the All India Rural Credit Survey in 1954 helped form the basis for rural credit policy in independent India. The cooperatives, first initiated in 1904, were intended to be the major source of rural finance in the 1950s and early 1960s. In the early 1960s, however, the cooperative sector was considered to be inadequate to meet the demand, especially with the advent of the green revolution.

During 1950–1969, the role of privately-owned commercial banks in rural finance was minimal and indirect; they only financed agro-processing firms and purchased bonds floated by the land development banks. The share of agricultural loans in total lending by commercial banks ranged from 2.0 to 2.2 percent and most of their loans were made to plantations. There were few commercial bank branches in rural areas despite the RBI directive in 1954 that they open at least one branch in unbanked rural and semirural areas for every branch opened in previously banked areas. Therefore, 14 major commercial banks were nationalized in 1969 with the ostensible intention of improving services, especially in rural areas. The hidden political agenda, however, was to win the favor of the rural masses for the ruling party.

After nationalization, the share of bank loans in rural areas increased from 2.2 percent in 1968 to about 10 percent by 1976. Nearly 64 percent of the 5,375 new commercial bank branches that opened during the first three years after nationalization were located in previously unbanked areas. The population covered per rural bank branch declined from 65,000 in 1969 to 37,000 by 1972 (Jha, 1988). To further increase outreach into rural areas, RRBs were introduced in late 1975. By 1979, the number of bank branches increased three fold from 1969 levels and the population per rural bank branch in most parts of the country declined from 37,000 in 1972 to 18,000. Access was still considered to be low, so seven more commercial banks were nationalized in 1980. As a result, more than half of all bank branches were located in rural areas and the population served per rural bank branch declined to 15,000 (AFC, 1988).

Bank nationalization was also coupled with the introduction of the lead bank scheme in which all districts were allocated to the nationalized banks and a few private banks to initiate and lead development in each area. The lead bank was also responsible for priority-sector lending, and collaboration with extension agencies and other banks in the area to formulate a comprehensive local development plan. Agriculture and cottage industries were considered to be the priority sectors and banks were required to make a minimum of 30 percent of their total loans to these sectors.

Differential rates of interest were introduced in early 1972, with the result that public banks faced a ceiling of a 4 percent nominal rate per annum for loans made to the population identified as weak in the rural society. The banks were required to allocate one percent of the total loans made to the priority sector at this rate. In 1978, the RBI directed the commercial banks and the RRBs to charge a uniform nominal interest rate of 9 percent per annum on loans to the priority sector irrespective of loan size. The RBI also mandated that commercial banks should not insist on down payments for loans made to small rural borrowers.

New problems arose due to the rapid branch expansion because of inadequate numbers of trained staff. Therefore, in 1986, several bank branches were consolidated to improve efficiency and quality of services. Commercial banks were authorized to open new rural branches only if they were underbanked by RRBs, and a minimum distance of 10 kilometers had to be maintained between bank branches. The commercial banks were also advised to set up satellite or mobile units where the volume of business and logistics would not permit a regular bank branch. As a result, branch expansion slowed down. By 1986, the total number of nationalized banks, private banks, and RRBs was about 53,265, an increase of only about 23,000 from 1979. About 56 percent were located in rural areas and the population served per rural bank branch in 1986 ranged from 17,000 to 21,000 in remote rural areas. Access to rural, formal financial institutions had improved and a 1986 survey reported that only 2.9 percent of a randomly surveyed rural sample in several states did not borrow from any formal source due to the lack of a bank branch (AFC, 1988).

The expansion of bank branches was not a random process. An analysis of data from 85 randomly drawn districts in 13 states for 1960/61 to 1980/81 revealed that the banks responded to the opportunities created by the green revolution. Branches tended to be located in villages with high irrigation potential, where the rainy season was longer, and in areas favorable to green-revolution technologies. Branch growth was lower in areas where the incidence of floods and drought was high and where the green-revolution technology was less applicable due to lack of water control (Binswanger, Khandker, and Rosenzwieg, 1993). Estimates of the effect of bank expansion on agricultural investment and output indicated that a 10 percent increase in the number of commercial bank branches increased investment in animals and pumpsets by 4 to 8 percent. The corresponding increase in tractor investment was 1.4 percent.[5] The expansion in bank outlets had a direct impact on crop output with an elasticity of only 0.02, but a larger effect was observed on the demand for fertilizer, which increased by 23 percent. It was concluded that banks tend to spur increase in output through increases in fertilizer use.

Outreach

More than 72 percent of the total 64,547 bank branches were located in rural and semi-urban areas by 1998 (Table VIII.1). The population per bank branch was then about 17,000 to 21,000 per rural branch. But the impressive expansion in bank branches was not matched by outreach, measured in terms of volume of loans made, depth of outreach as numbers of poor people served, and length of outreach reflected by the volume of short- and long-term loans made.

---

[5] For comparison, a 10 percent increase in investment in electrification increased investments in animals by 7 percent and pumpsets by 4 percent.

Table VIII.1:   Commercial and Regional Rural Bank
Branches by Region, 1979–1998

Year	Rural	Semi-urban	Urban	Metropolitan	Total branches (number)	Pop./bank branch ('000)
1979	49.7				30,201	18
1985	55.4	20.1	14.1	10.0	51,976	15
1986	55.8	19.8	13.5	10.9	53,265	14
1990	58.1	18.9	12.8	10.2	59,388	12
1992	58.3	18.7	12.9	10.1	60,528	11
1994	57.3	19.0	13.4	10.3	61,742	14
1995	56.1	19.8	13.7	10.4	62,346	14
1997	51.3	21.6	14.9	12.2	64,116	15
June 1998	50.9	21.6	15.1	12.3	64,547	15

Source: Reserve Bank of India (1998).

Despite these efforts to expand banking services into rural areas, and while the absolute volume of agricultural loans made by the major financial institutions grew from Rs89.8 billion in 1982 to Rs419.1 billion in 1996 (close to a four-fold increase in 15 years), there has been a decline in real values (Table VIII.2).[6] The ratio of agricultural credit to agricultural GDP increased only marginally from 0.159 in 1982 to 0.195 in 1989 and started to decline thereafter. There was a 15 percent decline in the real volume of credit to the agricultural sector in 1996 compared with that in 1982.

The commercial banks currently account for about two thirds of the formal sector loans made to agriculture. Nonetheless, cooperatives are still very important in rural India. The commercial bank share in term credit from all rural formal financial institutions has increased, while the share of cooperatives in short-term credit has been roughly consistent (Table VIII.3). Commercial bank lending for long-term purposes declined during 1991–1995, in part due to the Agricultural Debt Relief scheme of 1989/90 that required commercial banks to

---

[6]   The exchange rate in 1996 was 1$ = Rs35.5.

Table VIII.2: Agricultural Loans Made by Major Rural Financial Institutions, Agricultural GDP, and Ratio of Agricultural Credit to Agricultural GDP, 1982–1997

Year	Cooperatives (Rs Billion)[a]	Commercial banks (Rs Billion)[b]	Regional rural banks (Rs Billion)[c]	Total agricultural credit (Rs Billion)	Agricultural GDP (Rs Billion)	Ag. Credit/ Ag. GDP
1982	31.1	53.7	5.0	89.8	561.5	0.159
1985	43.2	90.7	5.0	138.9	772.2	0.181
1988	62.4	141.3	5.0	208.7	1140.7	0.183
1989	73.9	169.2	5.0	248.1	1270.5	0.195
1990	68.8	171.9	5.3	246.1	1480.0	0.166
1991	75.4	186.7	6.0	268.1	1727.7	0.155
1993	101.9	212.1	9.7	323.8	2237.0	0.145
1994	94.1	239.8	10.8	344.7	2590.6	0.133
1995	104.8	242.1	13.8	360.7	2765.8	0.130
1996	124.8	275.1	19.2	419.1	3101.4	0.135

[a] Loans from primary agricultural cooperative societies only.

[b] Loans made by commercial banks in the priority sector category.

[c] Data not available before 1990. A volume of Rs5 billion is assumed, which is the average volume of loans made by RRBs during 1980–1990.

Source: Reserve Bank of India Bulletins, various years; NABARD annual reports, various years. Data on agricultural GDP from the Asian Development Bank.

waive principal and interest due for term loans. Commercial banks perceived term loans as being risky and thus contributed to a decline in term lending from 62 percent in 1990/91 to 55 percent in 1994/95. After 1996, an increase occurred in the share of commercial banks' short and term lending, while a decline occurred for cooperatives and RRBs, perhaps because several RRBs are not functioning and the cooperatives are riddled with overdues. The share of the RRBs in total loans has been small for both short- and long-term lending.

The growth rate for short-term credit from the cooperatives has remained constant at a little over 10 percent during 1978–1985 and 1986–1995; however, long-term disbursements have declined (Table VIII.4). The growth rates for both short- and long-term lending declined for commercial banks. In general, there was a slowdown in disbursements for both short and term loans from all three types of rural financial institutions from 1973–1985 to 1986–1995.

A total of Rs5 billion was disbursed in 1996/97 under the IRDP program, and a total of Rs53.6 billion has been disbursed since 1985 (Table VIII.5). With the reported average loan size of about Rs8,500, this program appears to reach poor people. It is estimated to have reached about 51 million people since its inception in the early 1980s, but this is only one sixth of the total of 300 million people estimated to be under the poverty line in rural areas. The largest share of these loans was made by the RRBs, closely followed by the commercial banks.

Sustainability

A financial institution is considered to be sustainable if it can cover all risks and transaction costs, loan losses, and cost of capital through interest and other earnings without external subsidies. Based on these criteria, none of the rural, formal financial institutions in India can be considered sustainable. Most of the institutions are plagued with huge arrears and incur high transaction costs in providing financial services. Loan losses and transaction costs are invariably higher than earnings,

Table VIII.3:   Percentage Share of Formal Financial Institutions in Short-Term and Long-Term Agricultural Loan Outstandings

	1983/84	1990/91	1992/93	1993/94	1994/95	1995/96	1996/97	1997/98
Short term								
Commercial banks	28	36	24	26	34	38	41	42
Cooperatives	69	61	71	69	60	57	55	55
RRBs	4	2	5	5	6	5	4	3
Long term								
Commercial banks	52	62	49	49	55	65	70	71
Cooperatives	41	33	43	44	39	29	25	24
RRBs	7	5	7	7	6	6	5	5

Source: World Bank (1998d); Government of India (1998); NABARD annual reports, 1993/94 and 1996/97.

Table VIII.4:   Growth in Short- and Long-Term Agricultural Loan Disbursements, by Type of Institution

	Growth rates in annual disbursements (percent)			
	1973–1985		1986–1995	
Items	Short term	Long term	Short term	Long term
Cooperatives	10.8	12.0	10.6	10.4
Commercial banks	19.1	22.4	10.6	7.5
Regional rural banks	14.8	18.0	12.9	3.7
Total	13.0	17.5	10.7	8.4

Source: World Bank (1998d).

Table VIII.5: IRDP Loan Disbursement by Type of Institution,
Refinanced by NABARD, 1985–1997
(Rs Million)

Years	Land development banks	Commercial banks	RRBs	Cooperatives	Total
1985–1989					12,316
1990/91	120	3,090	2,340	470	6,020
1991/92	140	3,420	2,220	690	6,470
1992/93	180	3,510	2,100	700	6,490
1993/94	160	3,300	2,360	800	6,620
1994/95	160	2,940	2,380	720	6,200
1995/96	170	1,640	2,080	720	4,610
1996/97	160	1,350	2,780	840	5,130

Source: NABARD, annual reports, various years.

such that they require constant refinancing and recapitalization by the apex institutions.

The most serious problem is poor loan recovery. The loan recovery rates measured as a percentage of loans collected to total amount due was 50 to 60 percent throughout the 1980s to the mid-1990s (Table VIII.6).[7] The recovery performance nonetheless varied by location: several southern states recovered over three fourths of the loans made, while several northeastern and northern states did not recover even half the loans made in rural areas (NABARD, 1998). Banks now report an upward trend in loan recoveries due to greater freedom in collecting loan dues and an improved legal framework to help foreclose collateral (Bhandari, 1997). Nonetheless, the recovery rates are still less than 60 percent. If this trend continues, bank capital will erode, resulting in bankruptcies or the requirement for more recapitalization from apex organizations.

---

[7] Loan recovery is calculated as the ratio of principal and interest collections during the period to the sum of amount falling due during the period and overdues from prior periods. However, lumping the old loans with new loans creates a problem in that it cannot be clearly discerned whether new loans are performing better than the old loans.

Table VIII.6: Percentages of Loans Recovered by Major, Rural, Formal
Financial Institutions, 1982–1996[a]

Years	Primary agricultural credit societies	Primary land development banks	Regional rural banks	Commercial banks
1982/83	60	52	52	55
1986/87	60	59	50	57
1989/90[b]	51	28	33	49
1992/93	53	52	41	56
1995/96		61	56	

[a] Recovery refers to total principal and interest amount recovered relative to old and new loans
that were due on that date.

[b] 1990: Worst drought year; loans written off.

Sources: Sankaranarayanan (1998); NABARD Annual Report, 1996/97.

Many rural financial institutions report losses. Only one fourth of the RRBs are profitable compared with two thirds of the cooperatives (Table VIII.7). The percentage of institutions making profits did not significantly improve from 1980/81 to 1996/97. The RRBs have incurred huge losses due to high transaction costs and low loan recoveries (Bhandari, 1997). Of the 196 RRBs, 172 reported losses in 1993 and have eroded their reserves, equity, and deposits. Based on the recommendation of the Narasimhan Committee, 49 of the profit-making RRBs were chosen for restructuring in 1996 and another 50 were chosen in 1998. However, the policy for loss-making RRBs is not clear. They will continue to drain resources if they are not immediately restructured, privatized, or closed down.

Table VIII.7: Percentage of Major Rural Financial Institutions
Reporting Profits

Institutions	1980/81	1985/86	1990/91	1992/93	1995/96	1997/98
RRBs		24	22	12	22	22
PACS	59	54	56	55	61	
Land development banks	46	40	42	39	51	63

Source: NABARD (1998).

Surprisingly, little is reported regarding the use of credit guarantees by financial institutions to recoup losses. The low premiums and high loan-loss coverage may offer incentives for institutions to be lax in their recovery process. However, the high transaction costs involved in collecting on the guarantees may have resulted in little use of guarantee funds. Furthermore, there may be constraints in accessing refinance for those collecting their guarantees. The situation may indicate the redundancy of the guarantee program due in part to improper implementation and incentives.

Repayment problems have become pervasive and are the result of eroding discipline among borrowers. A 1993 survey of 600 rural households showed that only about 12 percent of the borrowers with outstanding bank loans were regular in their repayments. Of those who borrowed loans for asset purchases, about half no longer had the asset, about 16 percent did not purchase any asset, and 27 percent reported that the asset died or was stolen. The misuse of loans and defaults was more pronounced for IRDP loans than for regular bank loans. Borrowers often presumed that formal sector loans would be waived especially during the times of elections, which have been frequent in the last decade (Mahajan and Ramola, 1996).

The latest detailed study, conducted in 1988, reported that the largest proportion of overdues for loans made in 1986 was for large farmers who borrowed from commercial banks, for small farmers borrowing from RRBs, and for landless laborers borrowing from cooperatives. The highest proportion of delinquencies for both current and past loans were for small farmers in both cooperative and commercial bank portfolios, but delinquent large farmer loans were important for the RRBs; marginal farmers were the least delinquent (AFC, 1988). Large farmers were delinquent on past loans with the RRBs and on current loans made by commercial banks. Small farmers tended to delay payments on past loans obtained from the PACS and on current loans from the RRBs. Lax supervision and weak contract enforcement for loans have contributed to this situation.

Besides the alarming problem of low loan recovery, transaction costs are high for the lenders. Satish and

Swaminathan (1988) sampled some 300 rural financial institutions nationwide in 1984/85 and computed their costs and margins in making agricultural loans. The results are summarized in Table VIII.8. It was concluded that interest rates were inadequate to cover costs. The total lending costs were highest for cooperatives followed by commercial banks. RRBs registered the lowest costs next to the land development banks. Gross margins, calculated as the difference between interest income and cost of funds, were highest for commercial banks and lowest for cooperatives because of the high cost of funds for the latter. Commercial banks can access cheap deposits while cooperatives depend on funds from the apex institution. The transaction and risk costs, however, were lowest for cooperatives. Assuming a default rate of 20 percent on overdues (which may be low), the interest rates charged were inadequate to compensate for costs in all types of institutions.

The break-even nominal interest rates were shown to be around 28, 34, and 27 percent for cooperatives, RRBs and commercial banks, respectively, while these formal lenders were limited to charging only 12 percent nominal rate per annum on rural loans until 1992. Low interest rates, high transaction costs and low loan recovery rates obviously affected bank profits. A follow-up study by NABARD in 1993 confirmed that the break-even interest rates to cover costs were much higher than the interest rates the lenders were permitted to charge (NABARD, 1997).

Transaction costs for borrowers were also very high. Mahajan and Ramola (1996) reported that the transaction costs of borrowing were 17 to 22 percent of the amount borrowed from commercial banks; the effective interest rate, including transaction costs, was 26 to 38 percent per annum. Transaction costs for using savings facilities with banks were also high: 15 percent of the average monthly savings assuming one transaction per savings account per month. A study in Tamil Nadu found that the transaction costs incurred by borrowers on regular bank loans represented 4 to 6 percent of the loan amount, while they were 21 percent of the loan amount for subsidized IRDP loans (Nagarajan et al., 1996).

Table VIII.8: Cost and Margins for Agricultural Lending
by Type of Rural Institution
(All costs and margins expressed in Rs for a loan of Rs 100)

Items	Cooperatives	RRBs	Commercial banks
Estimates of Agricultural Credit Review Committee (1987/88):			
Financial costs[1]	9.43	5.80	7.48
Transaction costs[2]	5.21	5.50	6 to 7.50
Risk costs[3]	1.00	1.25	1.00
Total costs[4]	15.64	12.55	14.48 to 15.98
Interest charged[5]	12.06	9.60	11.62
Gross margin[6]	2.63	3.80	4.14
Break-even interest rate when default is 20%[7]	28.5	34.2	27.5
Estimates of NABARD (1992/93):			
Total costs[4]	21.4	21.0	17.0
Break-even interest rate when default rate is 20%[7]	34.2	36.5	29.1

[1] Financial costs: Costs in raising funds for on-lending.
[2] Transactions costs: Lending and operational costs
[3] Risk costs: Costs due to actual write-offs and/or reserve funds created for that purpose.
[4] Total costs: Sum of financial, transaction, and risk costs.
[5] Interest charges: Average of interest rates typically charged on loans.
[6] Gross margin: Difference between income realizable and financial loans
[7] Break-even rate: Sum of total costs and 20 percent of overdues divided by 1 minus the assumed default rate of 20 percent.

Source: Satish and Swaminathan (1988); NABARD (1997).

DEPOSIT MOBILIZATION

The savings performance of formal financial institutions, based on the average annual savings rate from 1950 to 1996, progressed in six distinct phases: (i) low savings phase, 1950–1968; (ii) increasing savings phase, 1968–1976; (iii) high savings phase, 1976–1979; (iv) stagnation phase, 1979–1985; (v) recovery phase, 1985–1993; and (vi) new high saving phase, 1993–1997 (Reserve Bank of India, 1997). Deposits mobilized by the commercial banks in rural areas increased at an average annual rate of 27 percent in the 1970s, 19 percent in the 1980s, and 24.5 percent during 1993–1997. For the RRBs, the average annual growth was 123 percent in the 1970s, 68 percent in 1981–1983, and 33 percent during 1983–1989. The total deposits collected by cooperatives increased at an annual rate of 18 percent in the 1970s, declined to 15 percent in the 1980s, and picked up to 18 percent in the 1990s (AFC, 1988; Reserve Bank of India, 1997). Rural deposits accounted for only 12.5 percent of total deposits mobilized by commercial banks in 1986, even though about 43 percent of their total branches were located in rural areas.

The RRBs were not innovative in designing deposit instruments, and the public lost confidence in cooperatives as safe institutions for deposits due to several instances of failed primary agricultural cooperatives. Therefore, although cooperatives were permitted by the RBI to pay 0.5 percent nominal interest more than commercial banks on deposits, cooperatives mobilized fewer savings than did commercial banks. However, performance has improved in the 1990s. The annual growth rate of deposits in the formal sector was 20 percent during 1990–1995, and 22.1 percent in 1998. This growth is impressive considering the country's low growth rate in per capita income.

The shares of the major rural financial institutions in total institutional credit disbursed and savings mobilized, and their credit-to-deposit ratios are reported in Table VIII.9. The data show that commercial banks provide more than half of the total credit made by the formal sector in rural and semi-urban areas and mobilize more than 75 percent of total formal sector deposits in those areas. The credit-to-deposit ratios indicate that commercial banks and RRBs mobilize more deposits from rural areas than they lend in those areas, while the cooperatives loan more than the deposits they mobilize. Credit-to-deposit ratios have generally declined for all rural financial institutions, especially commercial banks, over the past decade. There has been a vast potential in rural areas for deposit mobilization and commercial banks have been vigorous in exploiting it.

In addition to the formal sector, several self-help groups, microfinance organizations operated by NGOs, and nonbank financial institutions mobilize deposits in rural areas. A study in 1997 revealed that many deposit mobilizers are unreliable. Over half the sampled households interviewed in both rural

Table VIII.9: Credit-to-Deposit Ratios, Credit, and Deposit Shares of Major Rural Financial Institutions

| Item | Commercial banks | | RRBs | Credit cooperatives | | Total for all rural institutions |
	Rural	Semi-urban		Short term	Long term	
Credit-deposit ratios						
1985/86	0.66	0.52	0.44	1.62	22.8	0.81
1990/91	0.80	0.57	0.15	1.35	14.9	0.80
1991/92	0.58	0.46	0.19	1.31	19.8	0.67
1992/93	0.55	0.44	0.19	1.57	17.9	0.71
1993/94	0.50	0.39	0.16	1.40	14.9	0.64
1994/95	0.49	0.39	0.21	1.59	15.3	0.66
1995/96	0.48	0.37	0.23	1.61	15.8	0.67
1996/97	0.45	0.41	0.27	1.39	16.2	0.64
Share in total credit disbursed by all rural institutions (1990–1997)	24.0	25.7	2.1	46.2	2.1	100
Share in total deposits mobilized by all rural institutions (1990–1997)	31.1	41.3	6.4	21.0	0.1	100

Source: World Bank (1998d).

and urban areas reported losing their investments with nonbank financial institutions (Sa-Dhan, 1998). The lack of regulatory rules for nonbanks and lack of deposit insurance to cover investments with nonbanks mean that investors with nonbanks are unprotected.

MICROFINANCE

Microfinance has been oriented towards "poverty lending" to marginal clientele with little emphasis on the profitability of operations. Microfinance has been provided by governmental programs such as IRDP and the linkage program sponsored by NABARD, by NGOs,. and by a few banks. Anecdotal evidence suggests that there are about 10,000 NGOs in the country currently engaged in providing financial services. There are about 10 replications of the Grameen Bank that have received technical assistance from the Grameen Trust in Bangladesh. The overall outreach of the microfinance programs remains very low. It is estimated that about 2–2.5 million persons are assisted by IRDP every year. The NABARD linkage program has so far reached about 250,000 people. It is unlikely that NGOs reach more than 500,000 borrowers. Few of the programs are sustainable.

Like commercial lending, microfinance is not free from governmental intervention. The NABARD program to link informal self-help groups (SHGs) with banks is an effort to downscale the banking sector to service the rural poor and provide microfinance at the least cost. The program uses three models to link SHGs with banks. In model I, the SHGs are directly linked with the banks. Model II uses NGOs as facilitators/guarantors for this linkage. NGOs are used as financial intermediaries to link SHGs in model III. As of March 1998, over 14,000 SHGs had been linked to the formal sector and NABARD has refinanced Rs214 million of the Rs236 million lent out by banks under the program. Some 265 NGOs have collaborated with 148 formal financial institutions, of which

30 are commercial banks, 101 are RRBs and 17 are cooperatives. The program has covered about 250,000 families in 21 of the 27 states in the country. The majority of the groups are linked using NGOs as guarantors/facilitators, followed by NGOs as intermediaries. Direct lending to the SHGs has been minimal and has been used only for well-established groups with long-standing relationships with banks. The majority of loans have been disbursed to groups linked with NGO facilitators such that loans can be secured by an NGO guarantee (NABARD, 1998).

A study of 300 SHGs linked to banks through two large NGOs, MYRADA and SHARE, in southern India, showed that 45 percent of the borrowers reported starting an income-generating activity with their loan. The repeat borrowers reportedly borrowed less from informal lenders, accumulated assets, and increased their incomes (Quinones, 1997). The average repayment rate has been over 98 percent for all the SHGs linked through the program (NABARD, 1996).

The costs incurred by banks to lend to the rural poor directly and through NGOs and SHGs were examined by Puhazhendi (1995). The study concluded that lending through NGOs and SHGs reduced transaction costs for the banks in screening, client selection, and contract enforcement. The estimated average transaction costs of lending per borrower amounted to 4 percent of the loan amount if the loans were made directly to the poor, but only 2.5 percent when NGOs and SHGs were used as intermediaries. The transaction costs for borrowers accounted for about 40 percent of the loan amount if the loan was obtained directly from the bank but fell to 6 percent if borrowed through a SHG. The default rates were estimated at 22 percent under direct lending, but close to zero when SHGs were used as intermediaries. While the results are encouraging and support the linkage approach used by NABARD, the magnitude of the costs incurred by NGOs and SHGs, and who bears those costs, are unclear.

Quinones (1997) evaluated 10 NGOs operating as microfinance organizations (MFOs); data on their outreach and sustainability are provided in Table VIII.10. These MFO NGOs are amongst the largest MFOs in India, with the maximum outreach and sustainability. Nonetheless, the outreach per field staff of the best MFO in the sample (SEWA) was only 4,712 clients with loans amounting to Rs3.9 million and total deposits mobilized of Rs7.1 million.[8] This means an average loan size of about Rs840 per client and an average deposit of Rs1,520 per client. The smallest outreach per field staff in the sample (Shantidhan) was 73 clients with Rs106,000 in loans and Rs67,530 in deposits mobilized. This represents an average loan per client of Rs1,456 and an average deposit of Rs925 per client. It is interesting to observe that the field staff of only two MFOs mobilized more deposits than the volume of loans made. The loan sizes per client were generally less than Rs5,000 or 38 percent of per capita GDP, indicating the depth of outreach of these MFOs.

Table VIII.10: Outreach and Efficiency of Selected Microfinance Organizations as of 1997

Name of MFO	Outreach per field staff			Sustainability (%)	
	No. clients	Loans in (Rs'000)	Savings in (Rs'000)	Operational[1]	Financial[2]
SHARE	136	209	40	19.6	15.0
Nari Nidhi	124	91	22	23.8	15.0
WWF	391	106	26	49.5	47.9
SEWA Bank	4,712	3,941	7,195	132.1	na
Shantidhan	73	106	67	109.7	89.0
MYRADA	181	251	77	6.8	5.8
SPMS	262	616	403	89.2	73.6
Anarde	364	28	52	10.1	10.1
Lalbhai Group	83	50	48	44.2	44.2
ASAG	1,214	1,072	359	182.0	182.0

[1] Percentage of operational expenses covered out of interest and other earnings without external subsidies.
[2] Percentage of loan loss reserves, inflation risks, and operational costs covered out of interest and other earnings without external subsidies.
na = not available
Source: Quinones, 1997.

---

[8] The exchange rate in 1997 was $1 = Rs38.

Several of these MFOs are not sustainable. Only three (SEWA, Shantidhan, and ASAG) are operationally sustainable in covering operating costs with interest income. Only one (ASAG) is financially sustainable in terms of covering loan losses, inflation risks, and operating costs through interest income. None can also cover the cost of funds and become subsidy free (Quinones, 1997). SEWA has the maximum outreach and is also operationally sustainable, thus refuting the argument of trade-offs between sustainability and outreach. Similarly, ASAG is both operationally and financially sustainable, and ranks second in terms of outreach to clients per field staff. The Grameen replications included in the study (SHARE and Nari Nidhi) are neither achieving good outreach nor are they sustainable. The age of the MFOs may influence their outreach and sustainability: SEWA and ASAG are the oldest, while the Grameen Bank replications have been in operation for less than five years.

The 1997 Microcredit Summit set a target of reaching 100 million families through microcredit by 2005. India's share in the target is estimated to be around 25 million and a sum of about $4.5 billion is required by the year 2005 to reach the objective. Finding the resources may not be a major problem because four apex institutions exist to fund MFOs. They include Friends of Women's World Banking (FWWB), *Rashtriya Mahila Kosh* (RMK), Small Industries Development Bank (SIDBI), and NABARD. All except FWWB are owned by the Government. As of December 1997, RMK and SIDBI had provided loans to SHGs and NGOs reaching a total of about 370,000 households, while FWWB had made loans to 50,550 women through NGOs and SHGs. In addition, there are four large NGOs that function as mini-apex organizations to foster the development of MFOs. Although resources to fund MFOs may not be a problem, the capacity of MFOs to utilize the resources effectively and provide sustainable services is inadequate. The apex operations have not made a significant impact in creating vibrant and sustainable MFOs in the country (Nagarajan and Gonzalez-Vega, 1998a).

The future of microfinance in India hinges upon the creation of a favorable environment for MFOs to grow and innovate. Restrictive policies on deposit mobilization and negative externalities from subsidized programs such as IRDP are an impediment. Also, MFOs need more discipline to become sustainable. It is not clear if they can successfully provide financial services in rural areas. However, microfinance may become more important in the future in the diversification of farm households into small microenterprises due to declining farm sizes and the inability of the traditional bank products to reach such clientele. MFOs may be necessary to serve poorer clients.

The proliferation of MFOs has created a need for formulating regulatory and supervisory guidelines that would set standards but not hamper their creativity. It may become difficult for RBI to supervise the growing number of MFOs. The recently formed association of 20 large community development institutions, Sa-Dhan, could be evaluated as a possible self-regulatory agency of the MFOs.[9]

INFORMAL FINANCE

The importance of informal finance for rural households is subject to debate due to the lack of nationwide time-series data. Some studies suggest that the share of informal finance in total household borrowing declined with the expansion of formal finance. The results of decennial surveys presented in Table VIII.11 show that the share of informal loans declined from 93 percent in 1951/52 to 39 percent by 1980/81, while the share of the formal sector increased from 7 to 61 percent during the same period. However, a recent study by the World Bank, based on surveys of selected villages in five states in 1994 and

---

[9] The association was formed in September 1998 and was recognized by RBI in November 1998. The association intends to lobby for MFO interests, and to set and implement standards for the microfinance industry (Anon., 1998b).

1997, found that the proportion of total informal debt outstanding for rural households was 78 percent and only 22 percent for the formal sector. There was no significant difference in these proportions between the two survey years. In the absence of time series and panel data, it is difficult to conclude that there has been any marked change in the share of informal finance (World Bank, 1995c, 1997c).

Table VIII.11: Share in Rural Household Debt by Various Types of Lenders: Results of Decennial Surveys, 1951–1981

Lenders	1951	1962	1971	1981
I. Institutional lenders	7.1	14.8	29.2	61.2
Cooperatives	2.9	9.1	20.1	28.6
Commercial and regional rural banks	1.1	0.4	2.2	28.0
II. Noninstitutional lenders	92.9	85.1	70.8	38.8
Money lenders	43.8	14.9	13.8	8.3
Farmer lenders	24.8	45.9	23.1	8.6
Trader lenders	6.1	7.7	8.7	3.4
Landlords	2.0	0.9	8.6	4.0
Friends and relatives	14.4	6.8	13.8	9.0
Others	1.8	8.9	2.8	5.5

Source: Reserve Bank of India (1997, p. 543.)

Household surveys confirm that informal finance is clearly important for the poorer population in rural areas. The proportion of informal sources in outstanding household debt of the rural poor in 1980/81 was about 92 percent, formal sources accounting for the remaining 8 percent. World Bank studies conducted in 1994 and 1997 indicated the same pattern for households categorized in the lowest income decile.[10] The

---

[10] For people who owned assets valued at less than Rs20,000 (the poverty line is drawn at a per capita income of Rs11,000 per year), informal sources accounted for 64 percent of total borrowings, while the rest came from formal sources. In contrast, for people who owned assets above Rs0.5 million, the share of informal sources was 16 percent.

studies showed that 93 percent of the total household debt of the rural poor was borrowed from informal sources. Only a quarter of the poor households reported using formal sources, in contrast to over half of the richer households that held more than 35 percent of their debt with formal sources (World Bank, 1995c, 1997c). These results indicate that informal financial sources remain important, at least for the poor rural households.

Informal loans are a major source of consumption loans (Ghate, 1992). A study by Swaminathan (1991), based on panel data, showed that in 1977, loans from informal lenders financed 63 percent of loans for consumption purposes, but the proportion fell to 37 percent by 1985. The World Bank studies (1995c, 1997c) indicated that nearly 17 percent of rural household consumption expenditures were met through external financing, of which 97 percent came from informal sources. Informal lenders were the major source of consumption credit for both poor and rich households in both studies.

The expansion in formal finance has not reduced informal interest rates. On the contrary, a recent study (Dreze, Lanjouw and Sharma, 1997) reported an increase in informal interest rates. The nominal informal interest rates in the 1990s were reported to range from 35 to 60 percent per annum, while they were reported to be around 6 to 20 percent in the 1970s and 1980s. Iqbal (1981) reported a reduction in the 1970s of about 3 percent in informal interest rates in villages with a commercial bank branch.

The commercialization of the rural sector has induced a change in the importance of various types of informal lenders. The shares of traditional moneylender and farmer-lender loans declined from 44 and 25 percent in 1951 to 8 and 9 percent in 1981, respectively (Table VIII.11).[11] Swaminathan (1991) found

---

[11] Commission agents sell inputs to borrowers with the promise that they will exclusively auction or sell their produce to them at harvest time. The lender-commission agent then realizes a commission of 2 percent from the buyer in addition to the interest payments from the borrower (Swaminathan, 1991).

that the share of moneylender loans in total loans of rural households declined from 59 percent in 1977 to 11 percent in 1985, while the share of loans with traders and commission agents increased from 9 to 23 percent. The informal lenders increasingly financed productive activities in addition to making consumption loans. The expansion of the formal sector into pawnbrokering has also reduced the share of informal lenders in this type of financing. The number of informal pawnbrokers in selected villages in the state of Maharashtra, for example. declined from 250 in 1974 to 95 in 1985 (Bouman and Bastiaansen, 1992).[12]

Informal finance has played an important role in mobilizing rural deposits. The rotating savings and credit associations (called chit funds) and nonrotating savings and credit associations (called *bishis*) are a very popular means of savings in rural India (Ghate, 1992). Nayar (1992) reported that the average annual growth rates of deposits mobilized by the informal sector such as in chit funds were 33 and 22 percent in 1980 and 1986, respectively, while formal sources grew at 18 percent in both years.

There has been an important attitudinal change regarding informal finance. The paradigm shift is noticeable in the current enthusiasm of policymakers about the importance of linking SHGs with the formal sector, and in the use of informal lenders such as traders and commission agents as conduits for bank loans. However, care must be taken that this enthusiasm does not lead to regulations that stifle innovations and creativity in informal finance.

---

[12] The trend could also have resulted from the effect of the Debt Relief Act of 1975 that scaled down debts with moneylenders and pawnbrokers, and even made them return pledged assets to the borrowers without any compensation.

IMPLICATIONS OF THE FINANCIAL CRISIS

India has experienced at least four balance-of-payment crises due to insufficient reserves. The crises in 1965–1967, 1973–1975, 1978–1981, and 1990–1991 were induced by exogenous shocks such as adverse weather conditions leading to poor harvests, and by poor inward-looking policies. However, the response to some policy reforms implemented since 1992 has been positive, leading to a growth in GDP, increased reserves and control on inflation. These developments may minimize further balance-of-payment crises (Jayasuriya, 1998). To date, India has not been greatly affected by the current financial and economic crisis in Asia. India's monetary policies have been conservative with regard to opening capital accounts and this has limited the impact of the financial crisis. Ironically, the slow pace of the financial sector reforms and the limited use by Indian banks of foreign resources has served as a blessing in disguise.

The current crisis may affect the country directly and indirectly in the future. Revenues may fall due to a decline in exports to Southeast Asian countries, and to increased competition in world markets due to the devaluation of currencies of other countries. These effects may be attenuated, especially in rural areas, due to the country's large domestic market. But the effect could be significant for India if the global economy is caught in the contagion. The effect could also be dramatic for the rural economy if there is a significant reverse migration from urban to rural areas and a decline in urban consumption of rural produce that may occur with falling urban incomes due to the crisis.

Several lessons have been learned from the financial and economic crisis in Asia with respect to financial reforms: a currency crisis may be induced by rapid liberalization of the financial sector without strengthening regulatory and supervision capacity, a lack of transparency, and a high degree of governmental intervention in the financial sector (Stiglitz, 1998b). Some analysts argue that India's slow pace in financial market liberalization may be a better approach to avoid potential crises.

But with increasing capital inflows, substantial and swift reforms are required to reduce governmental intervention and improve the regulatory environment to make the financial sector crisis-proof. Furthermore, improving access to information is paramount for creating a strong and transparent banking system. If the country continues to lag in improving the environment for the financial sector so that it can function on market principles, a crisis may be unavoidable in the future.

CURRENT POTENTIAL AND CONSTRAINTS FOR RURAL FINANCE

The financial sector has significantly expanded over the past three decades in numbers of banks and bank branches, especially in rural areas. The wide networks of financial institutions in rural areas offer an excellent infrastructure to reach the rural population. The high level of rural bank branch penetration and the increase in absolute volume of credit to the rural sector from the formal institutions are a positive impact of the interventionist policies. Rural deposit mobilization has been vigorous, especially by the commercial banks, and this has placed India first among South Asian countries in growth in deposit mobilization (Khanna, 1995). Increases in deposits may increase the capital base of the banks and reduce their dependency on governmental funds. Eventually, the banks may become more independent and resist governmental pressure to disburse funds imprudently.

There has been a gradual policy shift in the 1990s toward a more market-based financial system. The 1992 financial sector reforms placed greater emphasis on the viability and sustainability of institutions, competition among financial institutions, transparency of operations, quality services, and reduced State control of the financial sector. By redefining priority sectors, financial institutions can more easily meet their mandatory quotas by lending to larger clientele and less risky activities. A debt tribunal has been created to address the problem of debt foreclosures. These measures can improve the potential of the financial sector to offer better services.

Several factors constrain the effective functioning of rural financial markets. The indiscriminate expansion of bank branches in the 1970s and 1980s through mandatory requirements and subsidization led to many nonviable, rural financial institutions. There are far too many bank branches and there is limited institutional capacity to supply services. The financial technology used and the level of employee skills have been inadequate to service the demand for term and consumption loans. Therefore, despite the rapid expansion of rural bank branches, the supply of formal sector loans has been limited. Informal finance continues to be important, particularly for the rural poor for consumption loans, and there is no clear indication of a decline in informal interest rates despite the expansion of the formal sector. The problem of low loan recovery, especially on loans made in rural areas, has persisted over the past two decades. Several RRBs and PACS are reported to be bankrupt.

The Indian approach to cooperatives during the past two decades has neglected deposit mobilization, and the primary agricultural credit societies have been used mainly to channel funds from the apex cooperative organization to the final borrowers. This reduces the incentives for the cooperatives to mobilize deposits.

Directed credit programs and subsidized lending such as in the IRDP have damaged the financial discipline of borrowers. Overdues were as high as 94 percent in 1997 (NABARD, 1997). Furthermore, the easy refinancing of directed credits has destroyed the incentives for banks to engage in prudent lending. Considering the evidence that the program has had little impact on the borrowers, the IRDP appears to be an expensive program for poverty alleviation and a great drain on resources. The NABARD linkage programs have created an awareness of the importance of SHGs, but the sustainability of the program has not been adequately addressed.

The financial sector reforms have limitations: they are not comprehensive and have been half-heartedly implemented.

First, the Government still plays a dominant role in formulating financial sector policies and uses the banking sector to disburse subsidized IRDP loans for poverty alleviation. Fortunately, loan waivers have been resisted since 1991 despite recent natural disasters that led to crop failures and mounting overdues in several parts of the country. However, due to political pressure there were disguises of waivers, such as increased funds for refinance programs to disaster-affected states. But the actual disbursements were low because the majority of farmers reduced their demand for agricultural loans (NABARD, 1998). Their demand for consumption loans and term loans to diversify into disaster-proof enterprises cannot be met through existing financial technologies and funding sources.

Second, although the mounting overdues are a concern, financial institutions have only limited freedom to collect loans. Political groups still lobby for relaxation in recovery procedures, especially during crisis times, thus undermining the collection efforts of institutions. The recent debacle with farmers in southern India who were subjected to several natural disasters since 1996 highlights this situation. The reason quoted for the 150 suicides among cotton and spice farmers during 1997–1998 was their inability to pay back huge overdues because of continuous crop failures (Assadi, 1998; Halarnkar, 1998). The political parties condemned the banks for collecting loans during the crisis and lobbied strongly for loan waivers. It was difficult for the banks to resist the political pressure so they had to settle for loan rescheduling, thus aggravating the overdues problem.

Third, while the RRBs and cooperatives are allowed to charge interest rates to cover costs, the commercial banks still face an interest rate ceiling for small loans. Competition, therefore, has been thwarted. In addition, the RBI guidelines are not mandatory for the cooperatives because they are controlled by state governments through the registrar of cooperatives. Several state governments, for political reasons, are reluctant to deregulate interest rates. Therefore, the flexibility offered by RBI to determine interest rates has not been fully utilized by cooperatives and RRBs. Furthermore, the rates were deregulated before the RRBs and cooperatives could acquire the necessary skills to screen borrowers and charge rates according to risk.

Fourth, mandatory lending for the priority sectors has been reduced, but still exists. Fifth, although the viability of many rural branches is low, due in part to low volume of business, additional institutions such as urban cooperatives are now permitted to operate in rural areas. This may result in more overcrowding and create even more nonviable institutions. However, if the Government avoids bailouts, competition may weed out nonviable branches and institutions, leaving the fittest to survive. A problem is that there are few clear exit options for nonviable institutions. Sixth, the skill level of banking sector employees is generally too low to access and process information efficiently.

A high-level committee was recently commissioned to formulate rural credit policies in line with the financial reforms (RBI, 1998). Although the committee represents yet another Government intervention, it has recommended several useful changes in loan screening and monitoring procedures to improve the quality of loan portfolios, and to increase transparency in reporting requirements. Implementation of these recommendations, however, is highly dependent on politicians who have blocked the autonomy of the RBI to carry out effective reforms. There are several issues that deserve attention: policy environment, financial infrastructure, and institutional development.

Creating the Policy Environment

The financial reform process has been slow due to political instability, but has protected the country from experiencing a financial crisis. The recent crises in Southeast Asian countries that rapidly liberalized their financial sectors have set back the enthusiasm for reforms in India. However, carefully planned and rapidly implemented financial reforms are now crucial to ensure the country's future economic growth. There is a need to create a favorable policy environment and clear-cut guidelines regarding the sequencing of reforms. Lessons need to be learnt from the causes and consequences of the crises elsewhere and applied to the country's current endeavor to reform the financial sector.

The commitment of shifting from the old directed credit policies to a market-based financial sector has not been strong due to political objectives. The practice by the Government of advocating policies from both the old and new paradigms creates a confused environment for private sector initiatives. It will be important to create a policy environment that is freer of short-term political motives.

Interest rate subsidies must be phased out, and ceilings on lending and deposit rates should be completely deregulated for all institutions. This is the only way for true competition to emerge and to give institutions the possibility of covering costs. Targeted lending programs must be narrowly focused and used judiciously to achieve the best results at lowest cost and with the least negative spillovers into nontargeted sectors. Donors need to support a more intensive policy dialogue on interest rates between the Government and financial institutions. Donors can also help disseminate the successes and limitations of targeted programs in other countries.

Clearer policy guidelines are needed so that the RBI has the autonomy to curb political interference. The concept of NABARD as an apex refinancing institution needs to be examined in light of the huge potential to mobilize deposits from the public. As the public becomes more of a stakeholder in financial institutions, there will be pressure to discipline the institutions and encourage them to function more prudently.

Creating and Strengthening the Financial Infrastructure

Financial reforms need to be strictly preceded by efforts to strengthen the financial infrastructure, including the supervisory and regulatory system. Although there are fairly clear guidelines and adequate human resources to regulate and supervise the sector, there has been a reluctance to enforce standards and penalize violators due to political interference. Once again, achieving autonomy is crucial if the infrastructure is to work properly.

Computerization of the banking sector is important in order to process information efficiently and improve the transparency of banking records. Dissemination of information on best practices is required through electronic and print media. The government and donors can also contribute to the creation of credit bureaus and credit-rating agencies that will improve the generation and dissemination of information, leading to better screening of applications.

Institutional Development

The majority of the financial institutions in the country are faced with mounting overdues. Strong institutions cannot be built on weak portfolios. There is an urgent need for rigorous debt collection efforts through debt tribunals backed by enforceable laws. Loss-making bank branches need to be liquidated quickly and nonviable institutions should be closed. Proper exit mechanisms should be devised for closing down nonviable institutions. If clear guidelines are lacking for liquidation procedures, they need to be developed to ensure the smooth exit of nonperforming institutions.

Low loan recovery reflects the cumulative effect of a deteriorating credit culture exacerbated by frequent loan waivers announced by politically motivated governments. The lack of information and skills among bankers to screen applicants effectively and make good loans, as well as the lack of effective enforcement mechanisms, also contributes to recovery problems. The institutions need to become more proactive in order to withstand governmental interference in loan collection efforts. Improvement in the repayment culture can only occur in an environment free of political involvement and by applying tough sanctions against defaulters. Strategies such as penalties for delinquent borrowers, and incentives for early and prompt payers should be introduced; they have been used effectively by the Bank for Agriculture and Agricultural Cooperatives in Thailand and Bank Rakyat Indonesia.

Strong institutions are run by skilled and satisfied employees. The skill levels of the bankers must be improved so they can better screen applicants and make good loans. Training programs need to be strengthened in all the states. Enhancing the skills of bank employees will have limited impact, however, if they are not well rewarded and provided with sufficient resources to perform well. Financial incentives are needed for the best performing bank staff as well as penalties for those whose performance is below standards. Performance-based compensation and incentive packages are required in order to attract and retain quality personnel in rural areas. Loan recovery should be one of the criteria for compensation. Modern equipment is essential to utilize properly the knowledge gained by personnel through skill-enhancement programs. A one-time subsidy from the Government or donors to financial institutions to update the latter with modern banking equipment and software may produce a much higher return than directly subsidizing interest rates.

The feasibility of introducing technological innovations such as automatic teller machines (ATM) and credit cards needs to be carefully examined as a means to reduce transaction costs. The quality of financial services in rural areas must be improved and low-cost and flexible products for loans, deposits, and insurance need to be designed. Some government banks may have to be privatized in order to attract private resources into banking and reduce the drain on public funding.

India is a vast country with wide geographic variations, but research to understand the changes in the demand for and supply of financial services has been traditionally concentrated in only a few locations. More research covering diverse regions is required in order to document the results of various experiments that are underway to help build institutions to address location-specific issues. There may be some advantage in decentralizing the central bank to deal with location-specific variations. It may also be advantageous for donors to identify and work with states with stable governments that are willing to experiment and have a stake in the new initiatives in financial sector development. Donors could also help to improve the research capacity of banks and research institutions and bring them closer to international standards.

India presents a challenge for donors interested in helping it to improve its rural financial markets. On the one hand, a number of recent reforms are moving the system in the right direction such that the current environment is somewhat encouraging for donor involvement. On the other hand, India is not a country that is entirely open for donors to implement a complete overhaul of the system or to introduce new institutions or financial products. Donors must work within the restrictions imposed by the political environment, diversity in financial market philosophies, and institutional capacities. The continued presence of donors who take responsibility for their initiatives and actively work on the financial system may facilitate shifts in the right direction in the long run.

IX RURAL FINANCIAL MARKET DEVELOPMENT IN THE KYRGYZ REPUBLIC: FAST-TRACK TRANSITION

T he Kyrgyz Republic became an independent country in December 1990 along with several other republics in Central Asia. The republics had long been under the central planning system of the USSR. They were dependent on each other for natural, human, and financial resources, and on Russia for governance. The transition from a centrally planned economy to a market economy has been a challenge for all the newly independent republics in Central Asia, including the Kyrgyz Republic. They entered the transition period with a large-scale, low-productivity, highly inefficient, poorly managed, and inflexible enterprise and agriculture sector (Rosegrant and Hazell, 1999). Selected indicators for the newly independent Central Asian republics are presented in Table IX.1. The data indicate that the Kyrgyz Republic is among the poorest of these countries.

The Kyrgyz Republic, nonetheless, was the earliest reformer among the newly independent republics and is now considered to be the most liberal and open of them in terms of political and economic conditions (Table IX.2). A rapid transition path modeled after the central European countries was adopted in 1991 with a strong emphasis on macroeconomic reforms (ADB, 1996). Consequently, while the GDP declined quite sharply for four consecutive years, it became positive in 1995 and has been growing steadily since then. Inflation declined from 225 percent in 1992 to 17 percent in 1997 (IMF, 1998a; Rosegrant and Hazell, 1999).

Furthermore, microeconomic reforms have been implemented. Csaki and Nash (1998) report that substantial

Table IX.1: Comparison of Selected Indicators for Central Asian Republics

Country	GNP per capita ($, 1996)	Average annual growth rate (%, 1990–1996)		Agriculture value added: (% of GDP, 1996)	Population in rural areas (%, 1996)	Rural population living below $1/day (1993)
		GDP	Agriculture			
Azerbaijan	480	-17.7	-6.0	23	44	2.0
Kazakhstan	1,350	-10.5	-15.3	13	40	18.9
Kyrgyz Republic	550	-12.3	-4.6	52	61	
Tajikistan	105	-16.4			68	4.9
Turkmenistan	940	-9.6			55	
Uzbekistan	1,010	-3.5	-1.8	26	59	

Source: World Bank (1998e).

Table IX.2: Resources, Distortions, and Reform in Central Asian Republics (from de Melo et al., 1997)

	Azerbaijan	Kazakhstan	Kyrgyz Republic	Tajikistan	Turkmenistan	Uzbekistan
Natural resources	Rich	Rich	Poor	Poor	Rich	Moderate
Liberalization index[a]	0.38	0.48	0.67	0.31	0.20	0.41
Political freedom[b]	3.2	4.4	6.8	1.8	1.4	1.6
Macroeconomic distortions[c]	1.0	1.07	1.03	1.01	1.27	1.15
Structural distortions[d]	-0.03	-0.62	-0.53	-0.49	-0.87	-1.15
Neighbor with thriving market economy[e]	No	No	No	No	No	No
Liberalization index 5 years after reforms[f]	0.44	0.61	0.82	0.39	0.22	0.58

a   Average of the liberalization index (input, output markets, and privatization); the higher the better.
b   Average of the index of political freedom; the higher the better.
c   Degree of macroeconomic distortions; the lower the better.
d   Degree of structural distortions; the closer to 1 the better.
e   If the country has a thriving market economy as a neighbor? (yes/no).
f   Source: Macours and Swinnen (1998). Liberalization of internal and export markets, enterprise privatization, and banking reforms are included in this index.

changes have occurred in the country, especially in agricultural reforms. The information in Table IX.3 shows that, compared with its neighbors, the country ranks first in terms of implementation of land, rural finance, and input-market reforms. Despite the reforms, the proportion of households considered to be poor steadily increased from 35 percent in 1992 to 40 percent in 1993 to 49 percent in 1996 (World Bank, 1997b). As of January 1997, the shares of poor and very poor in the urban population were 39 and 16 percent, respectively, while they were 58 and 31 percent, respectively, in the rural population (Badu, 1998).

About 3.8 million people, 82 percent of the population, are dependent on agriculture for their livelihood. The agricultural sector accounts for 42 percent of employment and its share in GDP increased from 35 percent in 1991 to 52 percent in 1997 (IMF, 1998a). It is believed that the agricultural sector has growth potential and has a clear advantage, at least in the medium run, over the industrial sector to lead economic growth.

Table IX.3: Status of Agricultural Reforms in
Central Asian Republics

Country	Scores			
	Land reform[a]	Input supply[b]	Rural finance[c]	Total
Azerbaijan	6	5	4	15
Kazakhstan	5	7	5	17
Kyrgyz Republic	6	6	6	18
Tajikistan	2	5	3	10
Turkmenistan	2	1	1	4
Uzbekistan	1	1	1	3

[a]   Land reform. 1-2: large state farms; 3-4: implementation launched recently to privatize farms; 5-6: advanced stage of privatization but not yet complete; 7-8: most land privatized but titling not done; 9-10: private ownership.

[b]   Input supply. 1-4: State controlled; 5-7: privatization in progress; 8-10: privatized markets.

[c]   Rural finance. 1-2: Soviet-type system with specialized agricultural bank to channel loans to agricultural sector; 3-4: new banking regulations introduced but commercial banks yet to emerge; 5-6: restructuring of existing banks and emergence of commercial banks; 7-8: emergence of financial institutions servicing agriculture; 9-10: efficient and competitive financial system that serves agriculture.

Source: Csaki and Nash (1998, p. 12).

Therefore, agricultural development has become a priority for policymakers (Mudahar, 1998). In addition, the Government declared 1998 as the year of renaissance for rural areas and initiated a comprehensive poverty alleviation program called *Araket* (meaning 'initiative'). Development of the small and medium enterprise (SME) sector in rural areas through implementation of microcredit projects has been identified as one of the major strategies to facilitate rural development. It is in this context that the strengthening of rural finance has become an important issue.

OVERVIEW OF THE FINANCIAL SECTOR

The financial sector in the country is still evolving and information about its current status is fragmentary. The information presented in this section is drawn from the existing literature and anecdotal evidence provided by people familiar with the country's financial sector.

The Government and several multilateral donors are simultaneously involved in developing new institutions and restructuring old ones that were in place at the time of Independence. Rapid financial sector reforms have been implemented under the heavy guidance of and with funding from the IMF and the World Bank. The Government has been enthusiastic in implementing the reforms because they are expected to ease financial constraints faced by the newly privatized and private sectors that are perceived to be the engines of economic growth. Furthermore, the extensive financial support previously provided by the former USSR for governmental activities had to be replaced by a reformed banking sector.

The financial sector has transcended from a monobanking system in the early 1990s to a complex system composed of State-owned and private commercial banks, and nonbank financial institutions. Currently, financial services are provided by Savings and Settlement Companies (SSCs), two large system banks primarily owned by the Government, eight commercial banks owned partially by the Government, six private commercial banks with foreign collaboration, several nonbank financial institutions (such as the Kyrgyz Agricultural Finance Company (KAFC), rural credit cooperatives (RCCs), several donor-funded rural and microfinance programs, including credit unions and village banks), and informal finance (ADB, 1997d).

With the transition to a commercial financial system, there has been an impressive expansion in the number of banks and bank branches since 1992. The four State-owned banks expanded rapidly and private commercial banks were allowed to emerge. The share of the State-owned banks in total bank assets declined from 100 percent in 1990 to 80 percent in 1992 and to about 11 percent in 1997 (EBRD, 1998). However, they became accustomed to injections of funds from the State and suffered losses when the State could no longer support them.

The overdues in the banking system at the beginning of 1996 accounted for over 3.6 percent of GDP and the volume of nonperforming loans exceeded 60 percent of the banking sector's lending portfolio. As a result, some banks have declared bankruptcy and several others have lost their licenses to conduct banking operations. Seven banks, including the State-owned Agroprombank that primarily serviced the agricultural sector and the State-owned Elbank that mobilized deposits, were closed. In addition, two State-owned banks, Promstroi Bank and AKB bank, were recapitalized so that they could continue to service the rural sectors (Lailieva, 1998). Furthermore, the Government, with the help of the World Bank, created a nonbank financial entity called KAFC in 1996. The Elbank was replaced in 1996 by SSCs, which are State-owned entities, to mobilize deposits and effect payments. A debt-resolution agency was created to collect and write off nonperforming loans made by Agroprombank and liquidate the assets of Elbank.

A favorable environment now exists for financial sector reforms but several problems remain. Laws on banks and banking have been enacted but the effectiveness of the banking laws has been weak due to enforcement problems (EBRD,

1998).[1] The legal rules are unclear. For example, the new law on pledging was enacted in 1997 and allows for registration of titles and provides clear guidelines for contract rights. However, the delineation of rights between creditors and third parties who purchase the collateral is not clear. Therefore, there are problems in foreclosing the collateral in case of default. In addition, the laws are not clear on the physical possession of the collateral during the contract period and the banks still insist on exclusive physical control over it. For example, pledged apartments are required to remain unoccupied and vehicles and mobile machinery should be left with the bank (Lee and Meagher, 1999).

The legal and regulatory frameworks for nonbanks, such as insurance and leasing companies and pension funds, are being developed but procedures for implementation are unclear. New regulations have been issued for loan provisioning. Competition is encouraged as evidenced by licenses being issued for three new foreign banks in 1997. However, the banking sector is still highly concentrated, as indicated by the share of the five largest banks, which own about two thirds of bank assets (EBRD, 1998).

Private savings and financial intermediation remain low. The banking sector lacks skilled staff who can evaluate risks and borrower business plans. Mechanisms for asset registry and collateral valuation, and the legal framework for foreclosure of collateral are underdeveloped. The regulatory guidelines, although formulated, have been difficult to implement due to the lack of skilled personnel. Very little information exists that is useful for conducting market-based transactions. The old system of concealing information from the public is still evident. It has been difficult to convince the bankers to provide transparency in banking operations. Although data on balance sheets and income statements of

---

[1] The legal rules are unclear and sometimes contradictory, and supervision activity is ad hoc. There are few procedures to enforce the law and there is a lack of trained staff for implementation.

all commercial banks are now being collected and published by the central bank in a monthly bulletin called Banking Herald, the data are not up to international accounting standards (Lee and Meagher, 1999).

At the microlevel, although the population is generally familiar with banks and trusts Government-backed financial systems, it has been difficult to garner trust for new institutions. Indigenous initiatives for creating institutions supported by local resources have been limited. Financial reforms have been largely top-down initiatives and the basic structural transformation of the economy to induce a change in the financial system has been lacking.

The financial sector has evolved rapidly over a short time, but major challenges remain, especially in serving the rural economy. The Government has been reluctant to shift completely to the new paradigm of a market-oriented financial market out of fear of underserving rural areas.

APPROACH TO RURAL AND AGRICULTURAL FINANCE

The country experienced a sharp drop in growth of real GDP from 7.5 percent per year in 1989 to negative 10.9 percent in 1996. Output in 1996 was only 56 percent of the 1991 level. Growth in the agriculture sector declined less than overall GDP but the agricultural value added in 1996 was only 95 percent of the 1991 value (Rosegrant and Hazell, 1999). There was a shift back from commercial to subsistence farming.

The country's fall in agricultural output and the shift backward into subsistence farming have been attributed to credit constraints. Therefore, expanding rural finance is considered important to increase agricultural production, but it is assumed that market-oriented banking will be biased against the agricultural sector. As a result, while banking generally has been liberalized, many restrictions remain regarding rural banking. The old paradigm of directed credit is still prevalent in the form of emergency credits for agriculture, which is considered to be one of the priority sectors.

Rural financial institutions are few, weak, and not yet financially viable. As mentioned, two loss-making banks that serviced rural areas were closed and two new institutions, KAFC and the SSCs, were created with heavy donor involvement, while two other banks were recapitalized so that they can continue to service rural areas. Real interest rates were initially negative for formal financial institutions but became positive in real terms beginning in 1996. However, there is wide variation in nominal interest rates charged by the various credit schemes implemented by the Government and donors in rural areas. They ranged from 12 to 39 percent per annum during the 1995/96 crop season; the inflation rate was 35 percent in 1996.

A huge demand exists for financial services in rural areas. It was estimated that by 1999 small enterprises in rural areas would require about $30 million in short- and long-term credit. The total demand for credit in rural areas, excluding households, may exceed $80 million. The Government budgetary allocations and bank and donor credit to the sector are far below the estimated requirement for external financing (World Bank, 1997b). In addition, there has been an increase in the demand for deposit services. Substantial potential exists in rural areas for deposit mobilization, and it has been suggested that rural households could save up to $84 million and small enterprises up to $8 million annually (ADB, 1997d). Although local deposits could finance the demand by rural enterprises for external finance to a significant extent, less emphasis has been placed by the formal banking sector on deposit mobilization.

An ADB survey observed that less than 10 percent of the demand for savings and credit services for all private enterprises and households in rural areas was met by the banking sector. Commercial bank lending to the agricultural sector in 1995 dropped by 43 percent in real terms compared to 1992; the decline was only one percent for industries and the construction sector, and 16 percent for other sectors. The share of household loans in the loan portfolio of the rural branches of commercial banks was less than 4 percent in 1996 (ADB, 1997d).

Much of the private farming in the country has little access to short- or long-term credit. The use of farm inputs such as fertilizers and chemicals has significantly declined, reportedly due to liquidity constraints. This has resulted in reduced returns to farming (see Box IX.1). In addition, a survey of agribusiness enterprises in rural areas revealed that emerging private firms face considerable constraints in accessing external finance due to lack of collateral (World Bank, 1997b).

Box IX.1. Is Credit a Constraint to Farm Profitability?

A study by the World Bank (1997b) argues that underutilization of land and inputs by private farmers is likely due to credit constraints. It was reported that the consumption of chemicals and fertilizers declined from 210 and 4,530 thousand metric tons (t), respectively, in 1990 to 81 and 2,380 thousand t, respectively, in 1993. A simulation exercise based on data from interviews with private farmers showed that releasing credit constraints would clearly improve the rates of return from farming, especially for small farms. Farms without credit constraints were assumed to have access to loans at 30 percent per annum. Credit programs that provide loans at reasonable cost should be able to improve profitability. The rates of return for private farms with and without credit constraints, derived from simulations, are provided in Table IX.4.

Table IX.4: Returns to Farming With and Without Credit Constraints

Private farm size (ha)	IRR (%) - With credit constraint	IRR (%) – Without credit constraint
Up to 5	5	10
5–10	5	9
10–20	6	9
Above 80	6	11

IRR: Internal rate of return
Source: World Bank (1997b).

THE EVOLUTION AND CURRENT STATUS OF KEY RURAL FINANCIAL INSTITUTIONS

Currently, two banks service rural areas. The Promstroi Bank provides loans to the agriculture sector through 23 of its 26 branches and the AKB-Kyrgyzstan services the rural nonfarm private sector through 20 of its 25 branches. As of 1997, it was reported that 60 percent of loans outstanding at the Promstroi bank and 65 percent at the AKB-Kyrgyzstan were rated as nonperforming. Agricultural loans made by the AKB-Kyrgyzstan in 1996 to collective and state farms accounted for 10 percent of its loan portfolio (ADB, 1997d). All the agricultural loans were considered to be nonperforming and it has stopped lending to the agriculture sector. In addition, nonbank institutions such as KAFC and the SSCs provide loan and deposit services in the place of Agroprombank and Elbank. There are also several donor-initiated microfinance programs that provide small loans primarily to the agriculture sector.

The chronology of major events in the evolution of formal financial institutions relevant to rural finance is provided in Table IX.5. The allocation of credit to the agricultural sector began in 1991 with the conversion of the former branches of Agroprombank-USSR that were located in the Kyrgyz Republic into Agroprombank-Kyrgyzstan. The bank was made responsible for servicing the agricultural sector and was primarily funded through budgetary provisions to direct credit to rural areas. The majority of loans were short term in nature. The market share of Agroprombank in total short-term lending by banks was about 89 percent in 1993. These loans accounted for one third of the total loan portfolio of Agroprombank (Table IX.6). The short-term loans were generally allocated to the rural nonfarm sector; the majority of farm borrowers were state and collective farms (World Bank, 1995b).

Until 1993, credit directed to agriculture through the banks was highly subsidized and provided under special programs. For instance, Agroprombank was directed to provide Som136 million ($22.19 million) in special credit to State and collective

Table IX.5: Chronology of Events Relevant to
Rural Finance in the Kyrgyz Republic

Year	Events
Until December 1990	Part of Soviet Union financial system.
June 1991	National Bank of Kyrgyz Republic (NBKR) established.
December 1991	Kyrgyz branches of three former Soviet Union State banks reconstituted into Promstroi Bank, Agroprombank (agricultural bank), and AKB Kyrgyzstan. Elbank declared as nation's savings bank.
1992	Two-tier banking system introduced with NBKR as central bank.
1993–1996	Subsidized crop loans issued under state budgetary provisions.
1994	Deposit and lending rates liberalized; proposal to discontinue directed credit; reduction of domestic financing of budget deficits.
December 1994	Government initiated a resolution program for nonperforming direct loans and Agroprombank was significantly affected.
1995	Government set up an interministerial working group on rural finance to provide emergency seasonal credit and develop effective rural financial system for medium- and long-term loans.
1995	Nonbank financial institutions encouraged to expand.
November 1995	Rural credit cooperatives (RCCs) established by the Ministry of Agriculture and Food as nonbank financial institutions to channel in-kind loans to farmers.
June 1996	NBKR undertook comprehensive reform of financial sector.
1996	Closure of Elbank (savings bank) and Agroprombank (agricultural bank).
July 1996	Settlement and Savings Companies (SSCs) set up to mobilize savings; use branches of former Agroprombank and Elbank, and post offices.
1996	Kyrgyz Agricultural Finance Corporation (KAFC) established for rural lending as replacement for Agroprombank (supported by funds from the World Bank).
1997	Asian Development Bank supports a project to set up rural credit unions to mobilize deposits and provide production credit.
1997	Tacis-EU initiates regional agricultural credit development project on a pilot basis.

Sources: Compiled from ADB (1997d); Tacis (1997a, 1997b); World Bank (1998e).

Table IX.6: Short-term Credit to Agriculture from All Banks and
Agroprombank, as of September 1993

Percentage of banks' credit for long-term agricultural loans	1.9
Percentage of banks' credit for short-term agricultural loans	17.7
Percentage of Agroprombank credit for short-term agricultural loans	31.8
Market share of Agroprombank in total short-term lending by banks to agriculture	89.4

Source: World Bank (1995b).

farms. The central bank (National Bank of Kyrgyz Republic) provided funds to Agroprombank at a nominal annual interest rate of 190 percent with an agreement that the Government would subsidize the interest rate by 90 percent. This allowed the bank to charge borrowers a nominal rate of 103 percent with 3 percent as its spread. Given the inflation rate at that time, this implied a real interest rate of a negative 74.6 percent (World Bank, 1995b). Indeed, these directed credits were disguises for outright grants to the agricultural sector since the repayment rate was very low.

Producer prices for farmers were very low in 1993–1994. Real interest rates, although negative, were rising and small private farms were unable to service their debts. Many private farms voluntarily stopped borrowing from banks as nominal interest rates exceeded 300 percent by fall 1993. Several illiquid collective farms were unable to privatize because shareholders were reluctant to assume their debts and they were also unable to access new loans. Hence, these farms shifted from the production of commercial crops, such as cotton, to subsistence farming of food crops. The arrears problem, rapid inflation, and rising interest rates led the State and collective farms increasingly to substitute barter exchanges for cash transactions (World Bank, 1995b). The default rates at the Agroprombank increased from zero percent in 1991 to 13.5 percent by the end of 1993, and there was a substantial decline in the bank's profitability. The Government, however, did not bail out the bank but reduced the subsidies and liberalized lending and deposit rates by 1994. As a result, Agroprombank could not service its old loans from the central bank and became ineligible for new loans (World Bank, 1995b). The bank reduced its volume of lending to the agricultural sector and finally suspended all its loan operations in December 1995. It continued to try to collect on old loans but was eventually closed in 1996.

Although closure of Agroprombank left a void in rural financial markets, the general conclusion was that it was a step in the right direction to close the bank rather than bail it out. The costs involved in recapitalizing it would have far exceeded the benefits because the bank was poor in both liquidity and skilled personnel. Moreover, the bank could not shed its image as a public bank that made cheap loans and was lax on loan collection.

Along with financial reforms, the Government has continued to provide subsidized farm credit through local government budgetary provisions. A summary of these budgetary provisions is provided in Table IX.7. The allocations were justified as a stop-gap arrangement until an alternative replaced the Agroprombank. The Government provides these subsidized funds to agriculture under the Emergency Financial Support Program (EFSP) through regional and district authorities. The loans have been made at an explicit nominal interest of zero to 30 percent per annum while inflation in 1996,

Table IX.7: Allocation of Budgetary Resources for Farm Credit, 1992–1996 (million som)

Year	Exchange rate (som per $[1])	Budgetary allocations	Other sources
1992	192.80	21.0	
1993	6.13	40.0	
1994	10.84	140.0	
1995	10.82	258.0	
1996	12.81	278.0	125
1997	17.36	130.0	

[1]   For 1993–1997, the data refer to som per $. For 1992, the data represent Russian rubles per $. Data for exchange rates obtained from ADB Economic and Statistics Website, October 1998. *Available: http://www.asiandevbank.org.*
Data source: Tacis (1997a).

for example, was 35 percent. Up to 1996, the Ministry of Agriculture and Food disbursed farm inputs as in-kind loans to farmer groups that were constituted as credit unions under the EFSP to a value of Som875 million ($63.31 million) as of 1996. These disbursements constituted a major portion of total credit to the agricultural sector during 1994 to 1997. However, the total outreach of these various budgetary allocations is reported to be very small.

The rural credit cooperatives (RCCs) were formed in 1995 as an alternative financial network to replace the ailing Agroprombank. They were established under the direction of the Ministry of Agriculture and Food with 85 percent of the funds provided through budgetary allocations and the rest as grants from Japanese and EU sources. However, they have been a failure in terms of outreach and loan repayment. Most of the funds from these RCCs were channeled to State, collective, and private farms that were rejected from bank finance due to poor performance. Member loyalty, crucial to a cooperative institution, was missing because the RCCs were formed by the local government. Currently, the RCCs play a very minor role in financing the rural sector (ADB, 1997d).

There was a need for an alternate formal financial institution, because the budgetary allocations, the RCCs, and the banks could not effectively service the agricultural sector. Therefore, the KAFC was formed in 1996 as a nonbank financial institution to develop a community-based rural finance system and to fill the perceived void created by the closure of Agroprombank. The KAFC was scheduled to begin its operations by mid-1997 but was delayed due to several logistical problems.[2] It is too early to assess the importance and role of this institution in servicing the rural sector.

The terms and conditions of the KAFC have been designed to provide short-, medium- and long-term finance to private farmers, former collective farms, state farms, and agroprocessing

---

[2] Therefore, the Government had to continue to provide emergency credit for the 1997 crop season through budgetary resources (Tacis, 1997a).

firms. The purposes of loans include working capital, onfarm investments in buildings and irrigation infrastructure, purchase and lease of farm machinery and equipment, and improvement in the quality of livestock. The main activity of the clients should be agriculture and they should not have defaulted on any previous loan; the reputation of the client is important in addition to collateral. Short-term loans are those made for less than a year, medium-term loans are up to three years, and long-term loans are made for three to five years. The Corporation accepts Government securities as the most preferred collateral, followed by real estate. The value of collateral is expected to cover the principal and interest due. Interest rates are determined based on the term of the loans, with lower rates for short-term than for long-term loans (KAFC, 1997). While the criteria for loans from KAFC are strict and market based, they may be difficult for private farmers to meet due to limited collateral. The Government will continue to be the sole shareholder of KAFC in the immediate future but shares will eventually be issued to the private sector. This may reduce governmental intervention in the institution, but care may be required to prohibit monopolistic behavior of few shareholders. The activities of KAFC need to be carefully monitored because the regulatory framework to supervise nonbank financial institutions has yet to be strengthened.

While the KAFC was created to replace the agricultural lending previously done by Agroprombank, there remained a need for an institution to replace the rural deposit mobilization and payment services provided by Elbank. For this purpose, the SSCs were established in July 1996. They were designed solely to mobilize deposits through a network of 49 branches of the former Agroprombank and Elbank. Of these 49 branches, 47 are located in rural areas. Savings and demand deposits, payments and cash transfers, debit card services, safety deposits, and foreign currency and security services are provided by the Companies. The current volume of deposits mobilized in rural and urban areas is unknown.

Tacis-EU (Technical Assistance for Central Asian Independent States by the European Union) proposed a Pilot Agricultural and Food Development Program in Kul *oblast* (district) in 1998 as a regional, agricultural, credit development project to establish a sustainable credit institution. The project is structured as a regional, secondary agricultural bank to service local requirements. The repayment of funds disbursed to farmers by the Ministry of Agriculture and Food since 1995 will be used to form a revolving fund. Private farmers' associations will be formed based on crops cultivated and these associations will be used as a means to provide supervised credit, technical and marketing services, and other facilities required to support agricultural production (Tacis, 1996, 1997a). Although the program was designed as an alternative to the cooperatives and credit unions supported by other international donors, it appears to be a revival of old models for directed credit. It is too early to determine how this program will be implemented and what the results will be.

MICROFINANCE

Donors and the Government are active in providing small loans and microloans to farmers and microentreprenuers. It is reported that most donor programs are not legally authorized to provide financial services, but several function under special arrangements with the central bank under bilateral agreements. These initiatives are directed towards poverty eradication through employment creation. A national microcredit summit was held in the Kyrgyz Republic in July 1998 to focus on issues and lessons learnt by the service providers. This was the first of its kind to be held in Central Asia.

There are currently 19 donor-assisted microfinance schemes that service the rural areas. A profile of these programs is provided in Table IX.8. The programs include schemes sponsored by Tacis-EU, US-Kyrgyz joint Agricultural Commission, CARITAS/HELVETAS, German Agency for

Technical Cooperation/German Development Bank (GTZ/ KfW), European Bank for Reconstruction and Development (EBRD), United Nations Development Programme (UNDP), Mercy Corps, FINCA (Foundation for International Community Assistance), ADB, and an IDA (International Development Association)-World Bank sponsored pilot program called Peoples Development Project. All programs, except for the GTZ/KfW and EBRD-sponsored programs, focus on short-term lending for the purchase of farm inputs. They employ diverse lending methodologies although the majority lend through groups. These are different from the Grameen-type groups that are based on joint liability. Here the members are organized into groups but the loans are provided on an individual basis with individual liability. The groups are used only to apply peer pressure. Most of these programs, except for those of FINCA and ADB, provide credit services only. FINCA and ADB promote voluntary savings through village banks and credit unions, respectively. The donor programs that do not explicitly require collateral use several types of substitutes: FINCA uses a group guarantee and graduated lending while the ADB-assisted credit unions use group pressure as collateral.

These programs generally charge high interest rates that are positive in real terms and most record repayment rates of outstanding loans of between 70 and 100 percent. The higher repayment rates are found in programs that use individual borrowing within voluntarily formed groups, such as farmers' associations or credit groups. Higher repayment rates have also been found in programs that provide technical assistance along with credit. The group members, although not liable for the loan, apply pressure on their peers to repay loans on time so that their group's reputation can be maintained (UNDP, 1998). In-kind loans are generally preferred to cash loans, which is consistent with the observation that credit-constrained private farmers also face difficulties in accessing input markets.

The size range of short-term loans made through these donor programs is usually $100 to $1,000. The Ministry of Labor and Social Protection, Mercy Corps, GTZ/KfW project, credit unions supported by ADB, the United States-Kyrgyz

Table IX.8: Donor Programs for Microfinance and Agricultural Finance

Program	Activity	Average loan size	Nominal annual interest rate (percent)	Length of loan	Comments
Central Asian American Enterprise Funds	Debt and equity investment to private businesses	$300,000 to $5 million			Funded by US Congress
Fund for Enterprise Restructuring and Development	Loans to private businesses	Up to $1 million	12.5 on US Dollar loans	Up to 2 years	
GTZ/KfW (German development bank)	Loans to private businesses		9 on DM loans	5–7 years	Investment loans
European Bank for Reconstruction and Development (EBRD)	Loans to private farms	$50,000 to $500,000	13–15 on Dollar loans	5 years	Business development services provided
US-Kyrgyz Commission on Agriculture and Rural Development	Loans to farmers and agricultural enterprises	Som18,000 to 250,000	80% of inflation		Implemented through Mercy Corps
CARITAS/HELVETAS	Private farmers; women microentrepreneurs	$500–$10,000 for farmers; $500–$5,000 for women	12 for farmers; 15 for women	6 months to 3 years for farmers and women	Established in 1997
Asian Development Bank-Credit Unions	Loans and deposit services	Som25,000	36		Scheduled to expand to 260 branches
Mercy Corps	Production loans to farmers	Som10,000 for farmers with 5–50 ha.	2 for first 6 months; 5 for 7th and 8th months, 10 thereafter	6–12 months	Established in 1995

(Continued next page)

Table IX.8 (cont.)

Program	Activity	Average loan size	Nominal Annual interest rate (percent)	Length of loan	Comments
Mercy corps	Microenterprise loans	Som2,000	4.5 per month	6–12 months	Only for women; pilot project
United Nations Development Programme	Loans for poverty alleviation	$250 per person in a group of 3 to15 persons for productive purposes	40–42	8–12 months	Funded through NGOs that organize credit groups; also provide training to NGOs and borrowers
FINCA	Loans and deposit services to women	$152 per member			Village bank methodology
Agriculture Business and Credit Advisory Service (Tacis), Pilot Agriculture Finance Development Project (Tacis)	Technical assistance to agricultural firms				
Agriculture training and services (Tacis)	Extension services to farmers				
Policy advice and business support (Tacis)	Business services for agricultural enterprises				

Sources: ADB (1997d); Oliver (1997); Tacis (1997b)); FINCA (1998).

Commission on Agriculture and Rural Development, and KAFC provide loans to nonpoor rural clients of up to $2,800. FINCA provides small loans, promotes savings programs, and provides technical support for the self-employed poor through village banks;[3] the average size of the first loan is about $152. While all programs require a business plan, FINCA does not insist on it if the loan is less than $100. Several require participation in training programs. Loans from the Mercy Corps are made only to members of farmers' associations, and ADB-supported credit unions target only their members, but all other programs are open to all rural clients (Martino et al., 1997).

The geographical coverage and outreach of the 19 donor programs have been limited. It is estimated that less than 12 percent of private farmers currently participate in these programs (World Bank, 1997b). The total amount of lending for the agricultural sector under all these schemes is estimated· to be less than $1.5 million per agricultural season, while the estimated demand for loans by the sector is around $80 million. In addition, although 45 percent of the population lives under the poverty line, most of these programs do not support the very poor. The World Bank has proposed to support a Small Farmers Credit Outreach Program that would target households slightly above the poverty line. KAFC and the ADB-supported credit unions also target households above the poverty line. A proposal to target exclusively the very poor households through the Kyrgyz People's Initiative Project is currently being discussed (World Bank, 1997b). FINCA began operations in

---

[3] Savings and credit groups or village banks are the mechanisms used by FINCA to make loans. The village banks are composed of 10–30 members, primarily women, who operate as a mutual support group to facilitate disbursement of credit, recovery of loans, and management of group savings. The groups meet every week over the course of a four-month cycle to repay loans and make deposits. The group members are required to save about 20 percent of the loan amount in the group's internal fund, which is controlled by the group to use as a secondary source of capital to lend for short-term loans to group members. As of July 1998, the clients had saved over $342,250. Banks that have larger savings are able to obtain larger loans from FINCA (FINCA, 1998).

1995 and appears to reach poor women. Up to July 1998, about 90 percent of its 34,946 short-term loans worth $3.6 million were made to poor women with a repayment rate of 98 percent.

In addition to donor programs, the Government in 1997 disbursed microloans to women in the amount of about Som5,000 per borrower in each of six districts (Badu, 1998). However, outreach to poor clients under the Government microcredit programs has been very poor. Less than 20,000 clients have been serviced and the proportion of very poor clients is small.

Few of the above microfinance programs focus on savings mobilization. Institutional and financial viability are not fully understood and there has been a lack of an enabling environment to promote microenterprise activities (UNDP, 1998). Except for FINCA, the financial viability of the microfinance programs is poor (ADB, 1997d).

Generally, the criteria for participation in all the above microfinance programs are based on a minimum land holding and/or membership in a farmers' association (Wadwa, 1998). While the criteria help to screen applicants and monitor them at low cost, they may also exclude landless applicants demanding external financing.

INFORMAL FINANCE

Although informal finance exists, its share in the total financial transactions of households has been very small. A recent ADB survey stated that only 5 percent of rural households and 2 percent of rural nonfarm enterprises reported receiving loans from informal sources such as family and friends. None had loans from moneylenders. Informal loans were small, averaging about $285 for households and about $405 for rural enterprises (ADB, 1997d).

Some private farmers reported using informal finance for buying inputs. The arrangements generally involved in-kind loans for farm inputs made by traders and farmers with a promise to repay a prenegotiated volume of farm product at harvest. The inputs lent out by farmers were surplus items from subsidized in-kind loans made by the Government. This indicates that governmental programs suffer from targeting leakage because loans are being provided to those who may not require them. Several of these informal contracts were based on barter such that interest rates were not transparent (World Bank, 1997b).

CURRENT POTENTIAL AND CONSTRAINTS FOR RURAL FINANCE

Within only eight years since independence, the country has moved from a monobanking system to a financial system composed of several financial institutions. However, it has been difficult to develop a comprehensive rural finance strategy due in part to diverse opinions regarding the estimates of the demand for finance in rural areas. While the World Bank estimates farm credit demand at $82 million in 1999, the Kyrgyz agricultural department estimates it at $55 million (UNDP, 1998). The difference in the estimates is due in part to diverse methodologies and a lack of detailed information.

The demand for financial services in the future will be determined by the evolving structure of the rural economy (see Box IX.2). By 1996, more than half of the former collectives were dismantled and land was distributed to private farmers. In addition, land rights have become tradable since 1995 (Bloch et al., 1996). It has now become important for small peasant and private farms to form cooperatives voluntarily to purchase inputs and sell products in order to achieve economies of scale, and obtain loans from the banks (Kawai, 1996). With economies of scale and tradable land rights there may be more consolidation of farmland through purchases; voluntary associations and cooperatives may emerge to buy inputs and market production collectively.

Box IX.2. Evolving Structure in Rural Kyrgyz Republic

Land reforms were launched in 1991 and vigorously pursued until mid-1994, and again since 1996. Several farm types, such as peasant farms, private farms, cooperatives, associations of peasant farms, joint-stock companies, and small enterprises, were formed out of the former collectives and State farms. Former members of collectives were allowed to lease land for 99 years from the collectives and State farms, and farm them as private and peasant farmers (Bloch et al., 1997; Rosegrant and Hazell, 1999). The peasant associations and cooperatives were formed by the voluntary consolidation of peasant and private farms. The collectives were also allowed to reorganize themselves as joint-stock companies or to declare bankruptcy, with property divided among the former members.

The information in Table IX.9 shows that since 1991–1993, the proportion of farmland of private and peasant farms, and associations of peasant farms has increased, while that of collectives and State farms has decreased. However, from 1993 to 1995, the average farm size of peasant farmers declined from 18 to 12 ha, and the average size of cooperatives fell from 13,000 to 699 ha. Some peasant farms were smaller than 0.25 ha. (Bloch et al., 1996). Contrary to the expectation of the Government, about 45 percent of the farmland still remained as collectives and State farms as of 1996 (World Bank, April, 1998). It was estimated that at the end of 1997 there were 23,000 private farms, 1,500 family farming associations, 860 voluntary collectives, and 15 joint-stock farm enterprises (Martino et al., 1997).

It is reported that lack of access to external capital restricts the members of the collectives from claiming private plots for farming. Furthermore, while the limits on maximum farm sizes were eliminated in 1994, the limits on minimum farm sizes were fixed at 1 ha for individual farmers and 5 ha for associations of peasant farmers. This has led to the consolidation of peasant and private farms (World Bank, 1998e).

Table IX.9: Percentage Share of Various Farm Types in
Total Area of Agricultural Land

Type of farm	1991–1993	1994	1995
Peasant and private farms	8	13	12
Associations of peasant farms			12
Cooperatives	13	9	11
Collective farms	32	35	25
State farms	37	31	23
Others (joint-stock companies, etc.)	9	12	17

Source: Bloch et al. (1996).

The consolidation of farmland may require long-term mortgage loans for purchases and long-term loans to buy machinery and equipment. In addition, loans to individual farmers within a voluntary association may be required. However, the collateral laws are inadequate to deal with voluntary collective farms where titles are individually owned but decisions are jointly made. Little information is collected to use in creating a credit history for these farms. In addition, leasing may emerge as an option to purchasing farm equipment and machinery for voluntary associations. But the leasing laws are poorly developed. Furthermore, information is scanty on the governance structure of these new types of voluntary collectives.

Providing financial services to the evolving rural economy will require flexibility by the financial institutions. The current status of the banks is inadequate to deal with the changing rural sector. Even though the donor-initiated cooperatives and credit unions may be useful, they face constraints, including a weak legal and regulatory framework. In addition, there is no national cooperative administration and it will take a long time to institute one. Also, the ability of the credit unions to provide agricultural production credit is unknown.

There is a need to provide deposit services in rural areas but a paradox exists wherein donors initiate projects based on donor capital even though there is a vast potential to mobilize local deposits. Few donor programs have incorporated savings components into their programs. Although the Government created the SSCs to mobilize deposits and they have a wide network, there may be problems if they cannot profitably make the loans necessary in order to pay attractive interest rates to their depositors.

There has been a gradual liberalization of interest rates and a decline in the disbursement of subsidized loans through budgetary allocations. As a result, the country has been acclaimed as the leader among its neighbors in the effective implementation of financial sector reforms. Political intrusions, however, remain in the form of emergency loans to agriculture. Furthermore, reforms have yet to be initiated in the areas of prudential regulation and supervision, especially measures for the mushrooming nonbank financial institutions. The skill levels of bank employees remain low and access to information in remote rural areas has been difficult. All these constrain the provision of rural financial services.

It has been very expensive to litigate and courts are often corrupt because judges and prosecutors are paid very low salaries. A survey in 1996 of business persons in urban areas found that the justice system is rated as unfair. It is estimated that court fees account for 10 percent of the amount in controversy. It was reported that weak legal institutions constrain the financial health and growth of private firms (Lee and Meagher, 1999). These types of problems may be even more severe in rural areas. It is important to improve the court systems to enable creditors to be confident that financial contracts can be effectively enforced. In the absence of an effective legal system, the banks tend to be very conservative and insist on a high level of safe collateral that few borrowers can afford to offer.

FUTURE DIRECTIONS

Much has been achieved within a short period in transforming the financial sector, but a careful assessment of performance is now necessary in order to identify remaining bottlenecks and gaps. Several isolated and small projects are in place but information on their achievements and problems encountered is very limited. As a result, it is difficult to identify specific policies, projects, or interventions that are needed now for development of a strong financial sector. In the absence of reliable specific information, the priorities identified for financial sector development in other transition economies are used as a guide here.

In other transition countries, it has been found that the process of building a strong financial sector has encountered problems because of the lack of an appropriate policy environment and financial infrastructure needed to facilitate a market-based economy (World Bank, 1996b). There is a serious lack of information about these basic problems of policies and infrastructure in the Kyrgyz Republic. Although well intentioned, the donors' approach so far has focused more on building institutions to channel funds than on strengthening the policy environment and infrastructure. Initially there was logical concern about a collapse in production that might be caused by liquidity constraints. In the rush to keep funds moving and to build new financial institutions, some of the fundamentals were ignored. There is a need to re-order priorities with greater attention to creating an appropriate policy environment and institutional infrastructure. Moreover, donor efforts to create institutions seem to be uncoordinated and it is not clear how these efforts will lead to an integrated financial market. Correcting fundamental problems may be the highest priority in the Kyrgyz Republic and resolving them may produce higher returns in financial sector development at this stage than investing in small and isolated projects to create and build financial institutions.

Creating the Policy Environment

The current policy environment in Kyrgyz Republic is generally favorable for implementing policies that will strengthen the financial sector and help it meet the growing demand for financial services. However, efforts are still required to convince policymakers to shift to the new paradigm in providing financial services in rural areas. It may be time for donors to stop supporting directed credit programs and instead take the lead in disseminating the largely negative results of directed credit in this country and elsewhere.

In the short run, there is an urgent need for the Government to create a comprehensive rural financial policy in consultation with the donors who may fund some of the activities to implement it. It is crucial that the fragmented and isolated donor initiatives should be legally recognized and be folded into a more integrated approach to developing the financial markets. If left uncoordinated and disconnected, these well-intentioned individual efforts to increase liquidity in rural areas may actually raise total costs of providing services and undermine the creation of a true financial market. Donors intending to work in the financial sector should make a long-term commitment to the task as an incentive for the country to stay on course with its financial reforms.

The current endeavor to stabilize inflation and increase competition among the financial institutions is a step in the right direction and should be continued along with efforts to liberalize interest rates. The rural financial policy needs to consider trends in inflation when determining the price for financial services, especially interest rates for loans and deposits. However, determination of inflation rates has been difficult in transition countries due to rapid changes in the economy and lack of appropriate methodologies to measure inflation accurately, especially in rural areas (World Bank, 1996b). It is important to continue the currently successful efforts to stabilize exchange rates and inflation, and to develop robust methodologies to collect information required for calculating inflation.

The Kyrgyz banking legislation enacted in mid-1997 authorized the central bank to regulate and supervise the banking sector. However, the law still allows the central bank to function as a fiscal agent for the Government by establishing a link between the banking and tax systems that is prone to abuse (Lee and Meagher, 1999). Reforms are required to separate the banking and fiscal systems.

Creating and Strengthening the Financial Infrastructure

While some of the legal and communication infrastructure inherited from the former USSR has become obsolete for a market-based financial sector, new infrastructure has been created since Independence. However, immediate attention is required to explore ways to both create and strengthen the financial infrastructure, which involves information, legal and regulatory systems, transportation, and communication systems. Experiences in Russia and Romania have shown that poor infrastructure, especially in regulatory and information systems, may constrain the growth of the financial sector.[4]

In the short run, governmental intervention is essential to create a strong bank regulatory and supervisory capacity. As the central bank assumes the responsibility of regulator, it will be important to assess its capacity to handle challenging tasks in two areas. First, a system is needed for the supervision of nonbank financial institutions and NGOs without stifling their innovative methodologies to provide services at low cost. This is an immediate priority since the KAFC is a nonbank institution and several donor-initiated rural and microfinance projects operate as NGOs. Second, the country so far has been immune to the financial and economic crisis in Asia because the capital account has been controlled and foreign direct investments have been limited.[5]   However, the situation may

---

[4] Analysis underway in Romania is documenting how an inadequate legal framework for creating, perfecting, and enforcing security interests constrains and drives up the costs of lending (Fleisig and Pina, 1998).

[5] Also, trade has been limited with Russia, a country that has been severely affected by the financial crisis. Less than 20 percent of total exports go to Russia and the GDP exposure due to the trade is less than 9 percent. Most of the exported goods are nonagricultural in nature (EBRD, 1998).

change if trade becomes liberalized and more important in the country. If this occurs, it may induce a higher level of hard-currency borrowing by domestic banks and firms. The recent experiences in Southeast Asia show that such a trend must be supported by a proper regulatory capacity.

It is also essential to develop information collection and dissemination systems about borrowers. There has been little information flow among financial intermediaries to facilitate the learning process and to conduct assessments needed for corrective measures. Donors can play an active role in this area. First, an assessment should be made of the current information systems and bottlenecks for operation of independent credit bureaus. Second, there is a need to create an information-sharing culture among the financial intermediaries. Third, the intermediaries need to be trained to collect information, such as their client's financial liabilities and repayment performance, which can be used to assess the creditworthiness of applicants. In all these efforts, it is important for donors to build up local human resources to become independent in information management by the time the donors leave the scene.

Experience to date has shown that there is a need to strengthen asset registry and valuation systems for both movable and immovable properties because collateral is important to consummate transactions in the early stages of banking sector development. Observers have also noted that leasing laws need to be perfected for them to become an alternative way to acquire fixed inputs. The donors can help by funding exploratory travel for Kyrgyz nationals to learn about successful asset registry and leasing systems in other countries.

Institutional Development

The current donor approach to institutional development in the country is questionable for several reasons. It involves many uncoordinated efforts and heavy subsidization leading to unsustainable operations. Client targeting has resulted in leakages and limited outreach. Furthermore, the development of separate institutions to provide loans and mobilize deposits in rural areas may be unwise and hamper the financial viability of institutions because of the foregone economies of scope and scale. An immediate priority is to assess the implications of this approach for the entire financial sector and the rural economy before attempts are made to build more institutions.

The microfinance initiatives of the donors and Government are in their early experimental stages. These initiatives should be carefully monitored and information should be exchanged among the programs. The legal status of microfinance needs to be resolved to enable the new programs to evolve into a more permanent status. Given the limitations of microfinance in serving the agriculture sector, it may be better suited to serve rural nonfarm than farm enterprises. The microfinance organizations need to be sensitive to local conditions and avoid the blind replication of models proven successful elsewhere. A few programs have modified the Grameen group-lending approach to suit the Kyrgyz culture, which has an aversion to group liability. However, collateral substitutes have yet to be developed to replace adequately collateral and group liability. Donors may usefully support skill development of personnel and provide start-up capital. However, there is a clear need for performance-based projects with clear exit strategies. The donors should exit once the capacity has been built to mobilize local resources through local deposits or through linkages with local banks.

Strong institutions are run by skilled employees. After evaluating the skill levels of the employees, opportunities for continuous skill enhancement should be provided to them as part of institutional development. The donors should assess the local capacity for training bank employees and initiate projects to create bank training institutes if none exists. There may be opportunities to achieve economies of scale in training by developing a regional-level training institute for banking employees in the Central Asian region.

It will be important to monitor the AKB-Kyrgyzstan and Promstroi banks to evaluate how they are performing after recapitalization. Information is sparse regarding the structural reforms that may have accompanied the injection of new funds. Key issues will be the status of loan recoveries and whether or not revenues are covering costs. If problems persist, it may become necessary to close down these operations or consider privatizing them.

X RURAL FINANCIAL MARKET DEVELOPMENT IN THE PEOPLE'S REPUBLIC OF CHINA: A PROCESS OF PLANNED TRANSITION

I n 1979, the PRC embarked simultaneously on two transitions: (i) from a centrally planned economy to a market-based economy, and (ii) a structural transformation from an agricultural-based to a nonagricultural-based economy. The transitions have not been smooth, but much has been achieved in a short time in the PRC compared with other transition countries. Real GDP per capita grew at an annual rate of almost 9 percent during 1980–1995 compared with 6.5 percent for Thailand and 3.5 percent for India.

The rural real GNP per capita in 1995 was 3.75 times that in 1978 when the transition began (Morduch, Park, and Wang, 1998). Although 70 percent of the population still live in rural areas, rural poverty is reported to have declined from 250 million people in 1978 to 58 million in 1996. The gross value of rural social output, an indicator of overall growth of the rural areas including agriculture, industries, commerce, and construction, grew by 9.3 percent annually in real terms between 1978 and 1991. The gross value of agricultural output increased at a real rate of 5.6 percent per year during the same period.

The structural transformation was accompanied by an increase in demand for a variety of financial services. The increase in incomes raised economic surpluses and the demand for deposit services. The household savings rate during the transition was significant, averaging about 33 to 37 percent of GDP between 1978 and 1995, the highest in the world (World Bank, 1997d). The level of financial deepening indicated by the ratio of money circulated through banks to GDP (M_2/GDP) grew from 79 in 1990 to 106 in 1996 (ADB, 1997e). It became a challenge to channel the impressive levels of domestic savings into productive investments. The financial systems in centrally planned economies were inadequate to allocate resources efficiently between surplus and deficit units. As a result of the economic changes, the stage was set for moving towards a market-based financial system.

OVERVIEW OF THE FINANCIAL SYSTEM

Beginning in 1979, financial sector reforms were implemented along with land and input- and output-market reforms. However, financial sector reforms have progressed slowly compared with reforms in other sectors, and a market-based financial system has yet to fully evolve (Tuan, 1993). Significant changes occurred in the financial sector as it was transformed from a simple monobank-based system in 1979 to one with multiple financial institutions in the 1990s. Four State-owned specialized banks, three policy banks, 14 small commercial banks, and a huge network of urban and rural credit cooperatives characterize the current financial system. Recently, the nonbank financial institutions, consisting of trust and investment companies (TICs) and insurance companies, have been growing at a significant pace.[1] In addition, there are now quasi-State-owned financial institutions called rural credit foundations (RCFs), and microfinance programs initiated by the Government and donors. Capital markets are also rapidly emerging, but strict controls remain regarding participation. A new securities law is expected to be implemented in 1999.

---

[1] For more information on nonbank financial institutions, see Kumar et al. (1997).

The financial sector transformation in the PRC can be better understood by examining the changes that occurred during four distinct phases: (i) pre-reform phase: before 1979; (ii) reform phase I: 1979–1984; (iii) reform phase II: 1984–1993; and (iv) current reform phase: after 1993. A brief chronology of events under the four phases is provided in Table X.1. The pre-reform period was characterized by a monobank, called the People's Bank of China (PBC), and Rural Credit Cooperatives (RCCs). The PBC was primarily used as a mechanism to mobilize deposits from the public to fund State-owned enterprises. The RCCs were controlled by the PBC and were responsible for deposit mobilization and the provision of loans to rural households and collectives.

The phase I reforms between 1979 and 1983 marked the introduction of a two-tier banking system. The financial system in the PRC was expanded to include four State-owned specialized banks (the Agricultural Bank of China (ABC), the Bank of Industry and Commerce (BOIC), the People's Construction Bank of China (CBOC), the Bank of China (BOC)), and a central bank– the previous People's Bank of China (PBC). These State-owned specialized banks operated within their designated lending areas. During phase II, several nonbank financial institutions, such as trust and investment companies, were allowed to emerge and compete with the State-owned banks. Competition began to emerge among the financial intermediaries.

The phase III reforms commenced in 1994 with the creation of three policy banks to disburse government-directed loans so that the State-owned specialized banks could be converted to commercial banks. The other State-owned commercial banks that existed since 1979 were provided with greater autonomy in lending decisions; the creation of new privately-owned commercial banks was encouraged. A unified interbank market, auctions for treasury bills, and strict asset-liability ratios were established for commercial banks. The reforms also severed the links between banks and nonbank financial institutions, and tightened regulations on stock exchanges; a modern payment system was initiated (World Bank, 1997d).

Table X.1: Chronology of Major Financial Sector Reforms in the PRC

Years	Financial sector	Rural financial sector
Phase I: Pre-reform period, prior to 1979		
Until 1979	Monobank system.	The PBC functioned as central bank and commercial bank. Provided agricultural loans to communes through its branches. RCCs were responsible for loans to households.
Phase II: 1979–1983		
1979	Established four State-owned specialized banks including the ABC.	The ABC finances agricultural sector (but not farm households). RCCs finance rural households and TVEs.
1983	Two-tier banking system created; central bank created out of the PBC; competition allowed among the State-owned specialized banks.	
Phase III: 1984–1993		
1984		Control of RCCS shifted from PBC to ABC. RCCs begin servicing TVEs and households independently.
1985	Financing responsibilities shifted from Government to banks.	Supply of funds to State farms transferred from Ministry of Finance to ABC. TVEs and households in rural areas financed by ABC and RCCs
1987	Competition among all banks and nonbank financial institutions.	Several small commercial banks allowed to lend to all sectors. Nonbank financial institutions allowed to operate.
Phase IV: 1993 to date		
1993	Refinance facilities from PBC restricted.	PBC no longer required to finance budget deficits and to provide loans or refinance the State-owned banks for policy purposes in rural areas. State-owned specialized banks
1993	Comprehensive reforms introduced.	converted into real commercial banks. Diversified financial market established that is regulated and supervised by PBC, and PBC made into a real central bank.

(continued next page)

(Table X.1 Cont.)

Years	Financial sector	Rural financial sector
1994	Establishment of three policy banks.	ADBC established to provide policy loans to priority sectors such as agriculture.
August 1996		Established an interministerial coordination group for rural financial system reform, led by the PBC.
September 1996		Contract responsibility system for ABC. Taxes and targets agreed upon with finance bureau and residual profits retained by ABC.
1998	Competition among specialized banks	All specialized banks allowed to finance all sectors in rural areas. Interbank borrowing and lending allowed.
1998 (proposed)		Merger of RCFs with RCCs or disband RCFs. Increased regulation of RCFs.

Sources: Compilation based on Ruogu (1996); Cheng and Watson (1997); Park, Brandt, and Giles (1997); World Bank (1997d); Morduch, Park, and Wang (1998).

Beginning in 1998, lending quotas for State-owned commercial banks were lifted and banks were authorized to adjust interest rates within a 20-percent band depending on the borrower's creditworthiness. There are plans to consolidate bank branches, including those of the central bank, to maximize staff productivity and to reduce costs of operations and political influence of local governments.

The decision in August 1998 to close the biggest nonbank investment company, Guangdong International Trust and Investment Corporation, and the refusal of the Government to assume its debts sent strong signals to foreign investors that the Government may not bail out State-owned companies that borrow more than they can repay. The Government has also indicated that there will be a reduction in the number of trust and investment companies from 240 to about 20. While the refusal of the Government to bail out a prominent company reduced the confidence of foreign investors, it also indicated the commitment of the Government to reform the financial system (Anon., 1998e, 1998f).[2] This could lead to some reduction in foreign capital inflows and create a credit crunch if the Government does not boost investor confidence.

The implementation of financial reforms has been cautious, but it has contributed to the creation of many types of financial institutions. Several issues remain unresolved. It is not clear if the regulatory system has been adequately strengthened and staffed with skilled personnel to supervise the diverse institutions effectively. There has been a huge problem with nonperforming loans leading to insolvency of the majority of State-owned banks (Ling, Zhongyi, and von Braun, 1998). Official estimates in 1997 show that 20 percent of their loans were nonperforming, and about 5 to 6 percent were unrecoverable, amounting to about yuan (Y) 1,000 billion ($120.5 billion). The loan loss reserves represented less than one percent of the loans (Song, 1998).[3] Most of the nonperforming loans were policy loans made to State-owned enterprises at subsidized rates. The Government is considering a write-off of over Y180 billion ($21.7 billion) during 1998 to 2000 (Oxford Analytica, 1998). This may create some moral hazard problems in that an expectation may develop that future nonperforming loans will also be forgiven.

APPROACH TO RURAL AND AGRICULTURAL FINANCE

In the 1990s, a slowdown occurred in the income growth of farm households. Regional and rural-urban income disparities

---

[2] The closure of the Guangdong corporation also revealed the bad-loan problems faced by nonbank financial institutions and the weak regulatory guidelines for them.

[3] A recent World Bank report suggested that a systemic crisis will occur if nonperforming loans exceed 15 percent of total loans (Caprio et al., 1998).

became more pronounced. Farm household incomes per capita grew by only 1.4 percent during 1991 compared to 5.8 percent in urban areas. Income per capita grew more rapidly in rural areas located in the coastal regions compared to rural areas in the interior. Of the total income inequality, rural-urban disparities explained about 60 percent, while regional disparities contributed less than 20 percent (Tuan, 1993). This has caused concern because the majority of the population lives in rural areas and generates surpluses through savings. Rural finance is considered to be an important tool to improve rural incomes, especially agricultural incomes, and to generate surpluses that can be used to finance rural nonfarm enterprises.

Rural financial reforms were a significant part of overall financial sector reforms. The phase I reforms between 1979 and 1983 marked the initiation of the household responsibility system, leading to emergence of about 230 million peasant farms and an enormous demand for financial services (Ling, Zhongyi, and von Braun, 1998; see Box X.1). The ABC was created as a State-owned specialized bank to finance agricultural purchases by the marketing boards. The RCCs, under the direction of the PBC, were made responsible for servicing the rural households. With the phase II reforms, the control of the RCCs shifted from the PBC to the ABC. The ABC and the RCCs, due in part to political reasons, began financing the township and village enterprises (TVEs) that emerged in the 1980s.[4] Cheng and Malcolm (1995) claimed that the phase I reforms facilitated the dismantling of the collectives and increased farm production and incomes, and that phase II reforms coincided with the transition from subsistence farming to commercialized

---

[4] TVEs are industrial enterprises owned by local governments and citizens and generally produce consumer goods for domestic and foreign markets. The TVEs have so far created about 95 million jobs and their share in GDP rose from 13 percent in 1985 to 31 percent in 1994. Because the local governments can retain the revenues from TVEs, they have been efficiently managed and often the loss makers are closed down. They are usually financed by local financial institutions and some foreign investors (World Bank, 1996b).

production in rural areas. Phase II was characterized by slower growth in agricultural production and incomes, a rapid growth of TVEs engaged in nonfarm production activities, and a shift in labor from agriculture to the nonfarm sector.[5]

The phase III reforms included two major components relevant for the rural PRC: (i) the separation of the Agricultural Development Bank of China (ADBC) from the ABC in 1994 with the ADBC responsible for providing policy loans including loans for the purchase of farm goods, poverty alleviation, and

---

Box X.1. Household Responsibility System

The household responsibility system, ratified by the Government in early 1981, assigned collectively owned lands to households under a 15-year lease. The profits and production decisions were transferred from the communes to the households. It was estimated that the proportion of households participating in the household responsibility system increased from less than one percent in 1979 to 99 percent in 1984. It is also reported that the system alone contributed to nearly half of the growth in agricultural output between 1978 and 1984. Grain yields increased rapidly in the 1960s with the advent of the green revolution but declined after that until 1979. The average growth of grain yields during 1960–1970 was 5.3 percent, but only 2.9 percent during 1970–1978. However, with the introduction of the household responsibility system, the average growth of grain yields increased to 5.7 percent during 1978-1984 (World Bank, 1997d).

---

[5] The share of the labor force in agriculture dropped from 76 percent in 1975 to 69 percent by 1995. The annual growth rates in the agricultural labor force declined from 0.77 percent in 1970–1979 to negative 0.08 percent in 1990–1993. The decline in agricultural labor resulted in a shift of the labor force, not from rural to urban areas, but to the rural nonagricultural sector. This shift is estimated to have contributed to about one percent per year to real GDP growth.

agricultural development; and (ii) the separation of the RCCs from the ABC in 1996 with the RCCs mandated to service rural households and small rural enterprises independently. With the separation of the development portfolio in 1996, the ABC was left to operate as a State-owned commercial bank (Cheng, Findley, and Watson, 1997). The central bank required that the ABC and the RCCs become responsible for their losses without help from the State. Thus, they became cautious in rural lending, and as a result access to loans for rural households and TVEs has declined. Furthermore, low and regulated deposit rates created poor incentives for rural households to save with the RCCs and ABC. This facilitated the emergence in 1988 and 1991 of nonbank institutions such as the rural credit foundations (RCFs).

The rural financial sector is currently composed of formal financial institutions, donor- and government-sponsored microfinance programs, and informal finance. The formal financial institutions include the State-owned specialized bank, the ABC; the policy bank, the ADBC; and the nonbank financial institutions, the RCCs, RCFs, and mutual associations and credit groups (MACGs).

The reforms that have occurred in the financial and other sectors since 1979 have shaped the present rural PRC. The growth rate of value added in agriculture per annum was significantly higher during the reform phases than during the pre-reform phase: it was about 8 percent during 1979–1994 compared to 2.8 percent prior to 1979 (Rana and Hamid, 1995). In addition, the rural industries were dominated by TVEs in the 1980s due to restrictions on operation of private industries. Private and individually-owned rural enterprises emerged only in the 1990s. The emergence of private rural enterprises can be attributed to the rise in agricultural prices that increased rural incomes and savings, thus generating capital for nonfarm activities. Also, the availability of labor freed from the communes coupled with the demand for nonagricultural commodities due to increased incomes, created opportunities for starting rural nonfarm enterprises. The Government also encouraged urban industries to subcontract work to rural enterprises. As a result, the share of rural enterprises in industrial output, which accounted for only 22 percent in 1978, increased to 30 percent in 1984 and to 36 percent by 1990 (World Bank, 1997d).

Access to financial services in rural areas, however, has been limited in spite of innovative new rural financial institutions such as the RCFs (Park, Brandt, and Giles, 1997). The ABC and the RCCs that service the rural areas have consistently earned negative profits in the last few years. Rural deposits from farmers and households have been increasingly channeled to finance TVEs and urban enterprises rather than to farmers and nonfarm households in the rural areas (Huang et al., 1998).

THE EVOLUTION AND CURRENT STATUS OF KEY RURAL FINANCIAL INSTITUTIONS

Participants

The ABC, created in 1979, is the oldest and largest of all rural financial institutions in terms of assets, followed by the RCCs (Table X.2). The ABC is now primarily responsible for financing farming activities of State farms and for mobilizing deposits from individuals, collectives, and RCCs. There are currently 20,000 branches of the ABC to mobilize deposits at the township level. In 1994, policy loans were divested from the ABC and moved to the newly created policy bank, the

Table X.2: Gross Assets of Rural Financial Institutions

Institution	1996 ($ Billion)
ABC	180
ADBC	70
RCCs	160

Source: Park, Brandt, and Giles (1998).

ADBC. Since then, the ADBC has been responsible for financing grain purchases by grain cooperatives, and for policy loans directed towards poverty alleviation, agricultural development, and infrastructure development in rural areas.[6] The ADBC utilizes the ABC branches in addition to its own branches that were carved out of ABC for its operations. Most of the loans from the ADBC are financed by the PBC, under its allocation for policy loans.

In addition, there is a wide network of RCCs responsible for servicing rural households and collectives with loans and savings services. These nonbank financial institutions are strictly regulated by the PBC. Currently, there are about 2,400 at the county level, 49,500 at the township levels, and 58,000 branches and 260,000 agents at the village level with an average of 4,000 members per RCC (ADB, 1997e). Although the RCCs are legally owned by their members, the influence of local governments has been significant. Until August 1996, the RCCs were managed by the ABC and functioned almost as resource providers to the ABC, but have since become autonomous.

The MACGs were established by the Ministry of Civil Affairs in about 173,000 villages to provide relief and emergency loans in poor and disaster-prone areas. Several groups also provide consumption loans and a limited volume of production loans up to Y500 for one year to poor households (Ling, Zhongyi, and von Braun, 1998). As of 1993, it was estimated that the MACGs had about Y1.2 billion in outstanding loans in rural areas. However, the MACGs are reported to suffer losses due to negative real interest rates and poor repayment rates (Park, 1998).[7]

---

[6] Recently, huge losses due to corruption have been detected in the grain purchase bureaus financed by ADBC. The losses are estimated at 3 percent of the total economic output of the country. The head of the ADBC was removed from office for making loans to the grain stations that were involved in the scandal (Anon., 1999a).

[7] Most loans were perceived as gifts from the Government and were not repaid. These are called *huzu* or *chujihui* in Chinese.

The RCFs expanded in the 1990s to cater to the increased demand for loans and deposit services.[8] They developed voluntarily to manage the collective assets and funds that remained after the disbanding of communes. They are quasi-State-owned financial institutions at the township level under the Ministry of Agriculture and are owned by the collectives and households. The most important source of initial capitalization has been deposits and capital from the collectives. Currently, most RCFs are capitalized by household shares and deposits. The stated goals of the RCFs are to meet the demand for funds by agricultural households and to support the agriculture sector and rural households.

The volumes of loans made by the RCCs, ABC, and ADBC to households, TVEs, and agricultural collectives are reported in Table X.3. Aggregate data for the RFCs were not obtained. The data show that the volume of loans to all sectors has generally increased, especially after 1984. The ABC made more loans than did the RCCs in the early 1980s. Since then, the RCCs have become more important in providing rural loans. The RCCs made an almost equal volume of loans to households and TVEs until the 1990s, when loans to TVEs surpassed those to households, and currently represent twice the volume of loans made to households. In practice, the ABC does not make any household loans in the majority of industrial areas. It has generally serviced agricultural collectives more than the TVEs, except during 1986-1989. In general, the TVEs have obtained more loans from all three institutions than have households and collectives, indicating a bias of the major rural institutions towards TVEs. This bias may be influenced by favorable governmental policies for light industries and linkages with local governments. A case study of investments made in poor

---

[8] Although the RCFs were allowed to operate as unregulated rural institutions in 1986, their initial growth was slow. They expanded rapidly in the 1990s due in part to the tightening of funds for rural households from RCCs and the ABC. The first RCF was established in 1988 in the province of Sichuan.

counties in Shaanxi Province revealed how loans made during 1984 to 1991 increasingly shifted in favor of TVEs and county enterprises as part of the poverty reduction effort. However, loans made to households seemed to make a larger impact on growth (Rozelle et al., 1998).

Performance of Major Rural Financial Institutions

There are no studies at the national level on the performance of rural financial institutions. Here, we rely on a few cross-section studies conducted in selected provinces in recent years. Park, Brandt, and Giles (1997) studied the RCCs, RCFs, and the ABC in six provinces in 1996 and compared their outreach and performance. The results are summarized in

Table X.3: Loans from RCCs, ABC, and ADBC to Rural PRC in Billion Yuan (1985 prices), 1978–1996

Year	Loans from RCCs to			Loans from ABC to		ADBC loans to agriculture
	Households	Collectives	TVEs	Collectives	TVEs	
1978	1.4	2.8	1.6	10.7	2.5	
1979	1.4	2.8	1.8	12.0	3.8	
1980	1.9	4.1	3.7	12.7	6.3	
1981	2.9	4.1	4.1	13.3	7.2	
1982	5.0	3.9	4.8	14.3	8.3	
1983	8.4	3.2	6.7	15.5	9.0	
1984	19.7	4.2	14.7	19.4	17.2	
1985	19.4	4.1	16.4	19.7	18.8	
1986	24.3	4.2	25.1	23.4	27.2	
1987	30.6	5.7	31.6	26.4	30.8	
1988	27.6	5.9	33.8	25.8	30.3	
1989	26.2	8.5	34.0	25.4	26.5	
1990	32.0	12.0	43.2	36.2	26.7	
1991	37.9	16.0	54.6	43.3	29.9	
1992	43.2	22.8	73.6	50.2	33.1	
1993	44.2	30.1	89.6	45.1	38.9	
1994	44.6	33.1	94.0	38.4	38.8	9.4
1995	48.9	37.3	100.0	42.6	39.8	11.9
1996	52.9	58.6	104.4	49.6	43.8	17.1

Source: Huang, Rozelle, and Nyberg (1998).

Table X.4. The study found a greater bias towards TVEs and collectives in the loan portfolios of the ABC than in the portfolios of RCCs and RCFs. Indeed, the RCF loans were more strongly oriented towards rural households than were those by RCCs and the ABC. Due to their low level of capitalization, most RCFs were not allowed to make fixed capital loans to TVEs until 1997. It is unclear whether the focus on households will change as a result of their current eligibility to make fixed capital loans to TVEs.

Table X.4: Performance of the ABC, RCCs, and RCFs as of 1995
(Based on a survey of six provinces, mean values reported)

Items	ABC	RCCs	RCFs
Share of households in total loan portfolio	10	43	45
Share of TVEs and collectives in total loan portfolio	30	35	24
Value of outstanding loans per borrower (yuan)	243	189	67
Overall loan-to-deposit ratio	0.15	0.18	0.20
Interest rate spreads (%)	na	7	7
Repayment rate from TVEs and collectives (%)	81	67	76
Repayment rate from households (%)	82	80	82
Share of interest costs in total costs	80	75	65
Share of office expenses in total costs	11	10	14
Loans to gross value of output of industries and agriculture	18	12	1
Profitability (ratio of profits before taxes to total funds)	0.4	1.2	4.7

Source: Park, Brandt, and Giles (1997).

In general, the loan-to-deposit ratio was the highest in RCFs followed by RCCs and the ABC. RCF loans were small, averaging about Y67, compared to Y243 and Y189 from the ABC and RCCs, respectively. This may be because of the smaller proportion of loans to TVEs and collectives from RCFs than from the ABC and RCCs. Another study by Cheng, Findley, and Watson (1997) also reported that the RCF loans were small, usually less than Y50,000, were lent for short terms, usually 3 to 6 months, and were only to meet agricultural working capital requirements. Given the annual GDP per capita of Y5,568 in

1996, the RCFs appear to reach the poor with small loans.[9] However, anecdotal evidence suggests that RCFs tend to be located in industrial towns rather than in poor rural areas.

The study by Park, Brandt, and Giles (1997) also showed that the RCFs charged the highest nominal annual interest rates, about 20 percent, followed by the RCCs at 18 percent and the ABC at 15 percent. The interest rate spread was about 7 percent for both the RCFs and the RCCs. The nominal interest rates for RCFs varied by location, indicating flexibility in adjusting interest rates according to local market conditions, in contrast to the RCCs and the ABC, which are regulated by the PBC.

The repayment rates for TVE loans, calculated as a percentage of loans paid on time to loans outstanding, were 81 percent for the ABC, 67 percent for RCCs, and 76 percent for RCFs, while for households they were 82, 80, and 82 percent, respectively. However, there was a large regional variation in the repayment performance for RCFs compared to that for RCCs and the ABC. The spreads reported above obviously cannot compensate for these low recovery rates. Therefore, interest rate controls and low recovery rates affect the viability of the institutions.

RCFs were observed to be more profitable than the ABC and RCCs. The average profitability, measured as a share of before-tax profits to total funds, was 4.7 percent in 1995 compared with 0.4 percent reported by the ABC and 1.2 percent by RCCs. However, given the low recovery rates compared with the spreads reported above, the profits reported by RCFs appear to be inflated. Differences in accounting procedures might explain some differences. It is important to follow common accounting procedures such that data provided by these institutions are comparable and accurately reflect their health.

Fifteen of the 54 RCCs reported negative before-tax profits in 1995 compared to three out of 37 in 1988. The profitability of the ABC has also declined significantly since 1988, falling from 6 percent in 1988 to 0.4 percent in 1995. Indeed, the competition

---

[9] $1 = Y8.26 in 1997.

from RCFs has reduced the profitability of RCCs due to falling volumes. In townships with RCFs, the rate of growth of funds in RCCs was only 2.1 percent compared with 17.9 percent in those townships without an RCF. As a result, the profitability of RCCs in the absence of nearby RCFs was estimated at about 1.8 percent while it was almost zero when RCFs were present. It was found that RCCs lack client orientation and uniform policies and procedures for loan screening, and there has been a high volume of nonperforming loans, as well as inadequate management information systems and risk management. The Asian Development Bank is currently providing technical assistance to selected RCCs on a pilot basis to restructure them and help them become financially viable client-oriented institutions (ADB, 1997e).

The research by Park, Brandt, and Giles (1997) also showed that the majority of RCF loans required more collateral from both households and TVEs than did the ABC and RCCs. Generally, more prosperous households used third-party guarantors while poorer households were required to offer a combination of collateral and third-party guarantors for RCF loans. Some RCFs that experimented with making loans without collateral or guarantors registered the lowest repayment rates. Within the RCF loan portfolio, contracts were more strictly enforced for households than for collectives and TVEs. Overall, the average frequency of enforcement actions through law suits and collateral foreclosure was lower for RCFs than for RCCs, indicating the importance of collateral in recovering loans.

RCFs were observed to be the most innovative among the formal, rural financial institutions (Cheng, Findley, and Watson, 1997). For example, they used village agents at the beginning of their operations and paid commissions according to the amount of deposits mobilized and loans collected. Later, agents were not used for households that had established a credit record. RCFs consider the size of operation, reputation of the managers of TVEs/collectives, and asset quality in determining loan size. For loans above a certain limit, the managers of the TVEs need to use their enterprise's assets and their personal assets as collateral, such that they have a stake in the loan. In some areas, RCFs also insist that all members of the household sign loan contracts in which family assets are pledged as collateral.

Although the RCFs have been efficient, the ratio of volume of loans to gross value of output of agriculture and industries in the region was the highest for the ABC (18 percent) followed by RCCs (12 percent), and the lowest for RCFs (1 percent). This indicates the relatively small volume of loans made by the RCFs compared with the ABC and RCCs.

Ling, Zhongyi, and von Braun (1998), based on a survey in 1993 of 1,920 rural households from 12 provinces, found that despite the presence of banks, loans from informal lenders were the major source of funds for over half the borrowers. Bank loans were also smaller than the loans from informal lenders, especially for poor households. Asset-poor households were invariably excluded from formal markets.

As shown above, the increase in rural financial institutions has not generally improved access to loans by rural households. The bulk of institutional loans are made to TVEs, and the next largest share goes to agricultural collectives. Where farm households can access loans for agricultural production purposes, they are unable to obtain loans for nonagricultural purposes even though nonfarm activities are more productive than agriculture.[10] Neither can households access loans for nonfarm activities from informal lenders (Cheng and Malcolm, 1995).

This lack of access to loans for household activities may reduce the productivity of farm credit. For example, Feder et al. (1990a, 1990b) showed that supplying additional formal agricultural credit would increase agricultural output of credit-constrained households only if access to agricultural inputs and loans for nonfarm activities were not constrained. The supply

---

[10] A recent study pointed out that the wages in nonagricultural activities in rural areas are seven times higher than in agricultural activities; the marginal returns from farming were found to be three times lower than from rural offfarm enterprises (World Bank, 1997d, p. 45).

of formal production credit to credit-constrained farm households did not significantly affect farm output, but was associated with increased overall output from both farm and nonfarm activities. This result confirms that formal loans targeted towards production activities are fungible because production credit has apparently been diverted to consumption and nonfarm investment. As a result, expanding the supply of formal credit has had less of an output effect on the agriculture sector per se.

DEPOSIT MOBILIZATION

It was reported that personal savings in banks amounted to Y5.43 trillion ($ 655.8 billion) in January 1999, a 16 percent increase from January 1998. These deposits accounted for 68 percent of GDP, the highest in the world. The savings rate has been increasing despite the cuts in deposit rates from 9 to 4 percent per annum due to lack of alternative investments and less optimism in the economy. It was observed that people now spend less but save more (Anon., 1999c).

Data on deposits mobilized by RCCs and the ABC are provided in Table X.5. No comparable data are available for RCFs. Since the mid-1980s, deposits have generally been increasing at a significant pace in both institutions. The RCCs have been more successful in mobilizing deposits than has the ABC. Household deposits account for a substantial portion of the deposits collected by both institutions. The increased incomes that have accrued to households since the 1980s due to favorable prices and the household responsibility system contributed to the increased surpluses available for savings. In 1996, individual farm household deposits accounted for over 85 percent of total savings mobilized by the ABC and RCCs.

Information in Tables X.3 and X.5 shows that total deposits mobilized by both RCCs and the ABC generally outpaced the total volume of loans made by them in rural areas. However, sectoral differences were noted. The loans from the ABC to

Table X.5: Deposits Mobilized by RCCs and the ABC from Rural PRC
(Y Billion, 1985 prices)

Year	Savings in RCCs from			Savings in ABC from		
	Households	Collectives	TVEs	Households	Collectives	TVEs
1978	7.1	12.0	2.6	1.0	4.1	0.6
1979	9.9	12.4	2.8	1.8	4.8	1.0
1980	13.9	12.5	3.5	2.6	7.3	1.3
1981	19.6	13.1	3.4	3.4	6.4	1.6
1982	25.9	13.7	3.8	4.1	6.9	1.8
1983	35.8	10.3	7.0	4.9	6.8	1.9
1984	47.7	9.8	8.8	7.1	7.8	3.9
1985	56.5	7.2	7.2	9.9	7.0	3.1
1986	72.3	7.9	8.7	15.3	8.8	4.3
1987	88.4	7.9	9.2	23.2	9.4	4.8
1988	84.8	7.3	9.5	26.9	8.0	4.6
1989	88.9	5.8	7.9	32.1	7.0	3.5
1990	113.6	6.6	9.2	44.9	8.3	4.1
1991	138.9	8.1	11.5	54.9	9.7	5.2
1992	163.1	12.2	17.2	64.5	10.8	7.5
1993	179.5	12.4	18.2	71.0	8.8	13.7
1994	198.6	11.6	17.8	78.5	8.0	13.0
1995	222.9	11.4	17.4	88.1	7.8	11.9
1996	260.1	12.7	19.2	102.9	7.7	12.7

Source: Huang, Rozelle, and Nyberg (1998).

TVEs and collectives were four and seven times larger, respectively, than the deposits collected from them. Similarly, loans from RCCs to TVEs and collectives were more than four and five times, respectively, the amount of deposits mobilized from them. In contrast, loans to farm households from RCCs represented only one fifth of the savings they mobilized. These results indicate that deposits by the rural household sector invariably finance rural nonfarm activities and collectives.

About three quarters of the total savings mobilized in rural areas are lent out in rural areas, indicating no major siphoning of resources from rural to urban areas. Indeed, it appears that the ABC has transferred resources from urban to rural areas in recent years (Huang, Rozelle, and Nyberg, 1998).

RCFs are now emerging as competitors to RCCs and the ABC, especially in deposit mobilization. Cheng, Findley, and Watson (1997) estimate that the total deposits in RCFs were around Y100 billion by 1996 compared to Y880 billion in RCCs. The RCFs have been innovative in using local connections to mobilize deposits and introduce new financial products.

MICROFINANCE

The PRC's microfinance movement started in 1994 as a mechanism to alleviate poverty, with the establishment of several Grameen-type institutions. There are currently several types of microfinance institutions operated by international donors and, since 1997, by the Government.

Morduch et al. (1997) reported the presence of at least 15 international donors providing microfinancial services in the 1990s. Five of the programs are variations of the Grameen model and provide group loans, three provide individual loans, four provide revolving funds for groups and individuals, and one provides a loan guarantee for bank loans. Anecdotal evidence suggests that the total outreach of all these programs is only 10,000 clients.

The Government microfinance programs are essentially subsidized loan programs intended for poverty alleviation. These programs cover about 87 counties in eight provinces. Thus far, about 80,000 households formed into about 14,300 small and 2,400 large groups are covered. Most of these Government initiatives are variants of the Grameen model (Morduch, Park, and Wang, 1997).

Park, Ren, and Wu (1998) compared three microfinance programs: (i) initiated and implemented by the Government, (ii) initiated by both donors and the Government, and (iii) initiated and implemented by donors. They also randomly sampled 449 households in 18 villages serviced by the three programs. By sampling design, 305 of the 449 households surveyed were microfinance program members and 144 were nonmembers. The results showed that the government-implemented microfinance programs are fairly young and perform poorly compared to donor-initiated microfinance organizations (MFOs). The results also revealed diversity in program design and attitudes of microfinance clients towards their programs. Client willingness to pay ranged from 2 to 3 percent per month, and the average interest charged by MFOs was around 2.3 percent per month. The interest rates on government programs averaged about 0.24 percent per month or 2.9 percent per annum (about 4 percent less than the regulated PBC rates for such loans). However, it is estimated to cost about 4 percent per month to provide microfinance services for agricultural purposes in the poor areas. Therefore, none of the three programs is currently sustainable.

A profile of the sampled programs is provided in Table X.6. In contrast to microfinance programs in other Asian countries, these programs have provided more loans to agriculture-related activities than to small businesses. Although all programs use the group lending methodology, group cohesion varies across the programs. In governmental programs, group leaders are often appointed and there is less participation of center members in loan processing and at the center meetings. Members have a poorer understanding of the responsibilities of the group members, such as joint liability and attendance at the center meetings. The self-reported repayment rates for the nongovernmental organization (NGO) programs range from 71 to 100 percent, while it is less than 60 percent for the governmental programs. More clients in the governmental programs experience difficulty in paying loans on time than in the NGO programs, implying their inability to generate sufficient income. Nonetheless, part of the reason for the lower repayment rate experienced by the governmental programs may have resulted from a lower expectation amongst their clients of continued access to loans, an incentive for prompt repayment, than from NGO programs.

Many programs had a compulsory savings component. NGOs are currently prevented by the central bank from mobilization of voluntary savings. While some programs return the savings to the members after all group members repaid their loans, some do not return savings until the member leaves the program. Several programs provide complementary services

Table X.6: Profile of Microfinance Programs : Results of a Survey

	Program sponsor		
	NGO	NGO and Government	Government
I. Purpose of loans (percentage of female members reporting)			
1. Agriculture and livestock related activities	89.0	97.0	86.0
2. Small business	2.0	2.20	2.0
3. Other purposes	9.0	0.80	12.0
II. Group cohesion			
Percentage of members who know all other members	98	92	85
Formed group with members since village leader arranged it (percentage of members reporting)	3	24	78
Regular meetings held by the center (percentage reporting)	89	67	42
In the past 10 meetings, how many times were you absent? (average of all responses)	1.6	1.7	2.6
III. Repayment status			
Are you responsible for repaying loans of other members who do not repay on time? (percentage of members reporting yes)	94	77	44
Percentage of members who had at least one late repayment	4.7	32.5	75.8
Percentage of members who did not repay their weekly dues on time	2	5.3	36
If you pay all installments on time, will you get another loan? (percentage reporting yes)	95	47	23
In fact you paid loans. Did you get another loan? (percentage reporting yes)	61	28	

Sources: Morduch et al. (1997); Park, Ren, and Wu (1998).

such as linkages with the input and output markets in addition to credit (Morduch et al., 1997).

The microfinance programs are still in their infancy. They are limited in the following ways: (i) a lack of long involvement of NGOs in developmental activities; (ii) firm government involvement through subsidized microfinance lending; (iii) a large proportion of the population that may demand microfinance in sparsely populated mountainous areas where microfinance best practices, such as group lending technologies, may be costly to implement; and (iv) a large demand for crop-based activities that may not permit frequent loan repayments as recommended by the best practices. Therefore, microfinance programs that are successful in countries such as Bangladesh and Indonesia may not be as appropriate for the PRC, and the Government's use of subsidized lending rates does not conform with microfinance best practices. In addition, unlike Bangladesh, these programs tend to provide agricultural loans. It is a puzzle why programs in the PRC prefer agriculture to nonfarm activities when nonfarm activities, for which microfinance is well suited, are largely unserved by the formal financial system.

INFORMAL FINANCE

No longitudinal data exist to examine changes in the share of informal finance in total household borrowings and in interest rates due to the expansion of the formal financial systems. Anecdotal evidence suggests that informal finance has functioned for the past two decades parallel to the formal financial institutions in rural PRC and meets the demand for consumption loans. Informal finance appears to flourish in places where the concentration of formal finance is high (Ling, Zhongyi, and von Braun, 1998).

Fragmentary information based on cross-section studies conducted since the 1980s provides insights regarding changes in the composition of informal lenders. Feder et al. (1989) noted that informal finance had transcended from rudimentary transactions to commercialized ones during the 1970s and 1980s. Although the most common sources of informal credit were friends and relatives, there had been an emergence of commercial informal lenders such as middlemen who link traders and farmers. These middlemen were found to be socially unrelated to the borrowers and nonresidents of the borrowers' village. They appear to link the credit to farm output. In addition, informal rotating savings and credit associations (called *hui* in Chinese) were also popular.

A 1992 national survey reported that two thirds of farm loans in poor areas are obtained from informal lenders (Ling, Zhongyi, and von Braun, 1996). A survey by West (1990) showed that in 1987 about 62 percent of the poor borrower households reported borrowing exclusively from informal sources. Another study indicated that the share of informal loans in total household borrowing increased slightly with the poverty status of the households. Households in the lowest income quartile reported borrowing more than 53 percent of their loans from informal sources compared to 46 percent by households in the highest income quartile (Park and Wang, 1998).[11] It has also been observed that while nonpoor households borrow more from moneylenders than from friends and relatives, the opposite is the case for poor households (IFPRI, 1998).

The importance of informal finance has remained the same in wealthy areas over the past two decades. The ratio of informal to total debt outstanding ranged from 95 to 50 percent in two of the wealthy, major grain-producing counties. About 20 to 45 percent of the households reported loans from informal lenders in the two counties (Feder et al., 1990a, 1990b). The results were confirmed by the latest study conducted in 1997 by Park, Brandt, and Giles (1997). However, Park and Wang (1998), in a survey of six provinces, found that while informal

---

[11] These are preliminary results based on a survey of 500 households in counties defined as poor according to national poverty statistics.

loans were larger in number, they accounted for only half the value of formal loans, indicating the small size of informal loans.

A larger proportion of informal loans has an explicit nominal interest rate now than a decade ago. For instance, based on a survey in 1996 of 184 villages in six provinces, Park, Brandt, and Giles (1997) found that the number of villages reporting explicit nominal interest rates from informal lenders increased from 42 in 1988 to 82 in 1995 (almost a 70 percent increase). The informal annual nominal interest rates were much higher than the 15 to 20 percent rate charged by the formal institutions. Feder et al. (1989) cited studies that reported loans from friends and relatives with rates up to 3 percent per month; lenders who were not friends and relatives charged about 5 percent per month; loans arranged by middlemen cost between 10 and 30 percent per month. High interest rates were related to low levels of technological development and access to markets, and the lack of collateral assets.

Feder et al. (1989) reported that the majority of informal loans were short term, although several could be for an indefinite maturity through rollovers, depending upon the borrower's ability to pay. Nonetheless, these loans were of longer duration than formal loans. The informal loans were primarily provided by friends and relatives who were more willing to provide loans for a one-time activity that can be reciprocated, rather than finance an on-going activity that may require continuous support. There were several instances in their sample that reported informal loans with medium-term maturity, and they outnumbered the medium-term loans from the formal lenders. Several informal loans from commercial lenders were secured by collateral although some households reported using third-party guarantors. Most loans from friends and relatives were based on reciprocity.

In general, formal and informal credit markets were observed to be highly segmented and did not substitute for one another. West (1990) reported that loans used for weddings, housing construction, and other consumption activities were financed by informal sources, while loans used for working capital in farming, fixed investments in farming, animal husbandry, and fisheries were financed by formal sources. The farmers faced difficulty in diverting loans obtained for construction and social activities to production activities because they could be easily detected. However, formal loans could still be diverted for day-to-day consumption activities and therefore were fungible while the informal credits were not. This indicated that households constrained in their access to formal sources may have been limited in their ability to finance production activities. Anecdotal evidence suggests that informal sources are still not yet fully commercialized to finance farm and nonfarm production activities as occurs in other Asian countries such as India and the Philippines.

CURRENT POTENTIAL AND CONSTRAINTS FOR RURAL FINANCE

The landscape of the financial sector has changed in the PRC since 1979 with the introduction of different types of institutions. There is a strong deposit base due to a well-established savings discipline, and continuous reforms that increase incomes. The huge volumes of deposits have been a significant source of funds for rural financial institutions, leading to some degree of financial independence from the Government. Overall, the presence of several formal institutions has increased competition in rural areas, at least for deposits. But ceilings on deposit rates impede a strong drive by the institutions to mobilize public deposits, to become subsidy free, and to innovate with flexible savings instruments. It is now important to assess whether the current increasing trend in deposits will continue, decline, or stabilize at the current rate, and whether the financial institutions will develop mechanisms to cater effectively to the demand for deposit services in the future. Few studies focus on the demand for deposit instruments in rural areas.

Although competition is encouraged, political intervention continues to influence the portfolio mix of the banks, and interest rate controls still exist. As a result, access to loans for rural households, although they contribute significantly to the capital of the financial institutions through deposits, is very low. The financial institutions are also biased against financing nonfarm enterprises of rural households. With meager informal lending for nonfarm enterprises, many rural households may be unable to access external finance for nonfarm activities. The ongoing structural transformation will alter the rural sector. Small farm households may predominate in the future and will need to diversify into nonfarm activities to augment incomes (Box X.2). But a liquidity-constrained nonfarm sector may not grow as required to contribute to economic growth.

Other issues remain to be addressed regarding the future structure of rural areas. For instance, there may be an increase in the intensification of farming and a greater demand for long-term loans. It will be important to understand the future demand for various types of financial services by small diversified farms so that appropriate institutions and instruments can be developed. The sparse information available constrains our ability to speculate about the future demand for and the supply of services. There is a clear need to assess the future demand for various services and the capacity of institutions to meet that demand.

With limited information about the negative profits recorded by ABC and the RCCs in recent years, there is uncertainty about their viability and their ability to provide more services in the future. It is not clear whether competition from RCFs and their prudent practices, and focused lending for farms and rural households will initiate changes within the ABC and RCCs that will modify their portfolio mix and make them profitable. Political interventions may hamper the efficient allocation of resources within the ABC and RCCs. The recent political effort to lobby for limits on the expansion of RCFs and the suggestion to merge them with RCCs create great uncertainty regarding the commitment of the Government to encourage competition in rural banking.

Although RCFs are innovative and have contributed to a diversified financial sector in rural areas, several concerns remain. Being unregulated may lead them to imprudent

Box X.2 Evolution of Farming Structure in the PRC

The current farming structure in the PRC evolved from small individual farms that existed prior to 1949 to cooperatives and collectives that existed until 1979. The evolution of the farming structure is provided in Table X.7.

The agrarian reforms during 1919 to 1949 resulted in abolition of the feudal system and distribution of land to actual tillers, creating small private farms. The average farm size was about 0.85 ha. Beginning in the 1950s, there were shifts from individual farm households to mutual aid groups and elementary agricultural producers' associations where about 20 to 30 farm households pooled their land and resources. The average farm size of such associations was about 20 ha. The individual farm households became semi-independent owners in such associations.

However, beginning in 1953 with the socialist regime, the associations were converted into cooperatives and collective ownership of land was introduced. The average number of farm households that formed a cooperative was about 150 to 200 with an average farm size of 160 ha. These advanced cooperatives were then converted to people's communes in 1958 with an average of 4,600 farm households and 3,800 ha of arable land per commune. The commune owned the land and the livestock that belonged to the farm households and made the production decisions. However, input purchase and output sales were arranged by the local and provincial governments.

The scenario changed with the introduction of reforms in 1979. The communes were replaced by the household responsibility system wherein farm households were assigned limited ownership of land previously owned by communes. The average farm size per farm household in 1986 was estimated to be around 0.6 ha, smaller than it was in 1950. Beginning in the late 1980s there were frequent appeals for enlargement of the farms since the small farm structure was shown to suffer from diseconomies for scale and fragmentation due to inheritances. Therefore, some tenurial arrangements such

(continued next page)

Box X.2 (continued)

as renting, formation of voluntary collectives, and cooperatives were allowed. As a result, the farm size in the early 1990s ranged between 0.85 ha per household and 20 ha per voluntary collective. However, fewer than 10 percent of farmers who obtained land under the household responsibility system preferred to sell it so that enlargement could occur. Based on the trend, it was expected that the predominance of small farms will continue for a long time even if not profitable, but there will be a coexistence of various types of tenurial arrangements and diversification of small farm households into nonfarm activities (Ruofeng and Jiyuan, 1992).

Table IX.7: Evolution of Farming in the PRC, 1914–1988

Years	Type of farming	Average number of households per farm	Average farm size (ha)
1914–1949	Individual small farms	1	0.85
1950–1953	Elementary cooperatives	20–30	20
1953–1958	Advanced cooperatives	150–200	160
1958–1979	Communes	4,600	3,800
1979–1985	Individual farms under household responsibility system		
1986 and onwards	Single family farms; cooperative farms; collective farms; specialized farms	1; 10	0.8 to 20

Source: Compiled from Ruofeng and Jiang (1991).

behavior. For instance, Cheng, Findley, and Watson (1997) reported that the capital adequacy ratio in several RCFs is less than 12 percent and the loan-to-deposit ratio is over 90 percent, although PBC regulations require the latter to be less than 70 percent. While banks are required to maintain a reserve of up to 13 percent of deposits, the RCFs maintain no reserves. The provisions for loan losses are only about 0.8 percent of total loans made even though delinquency rates are high. In addition, the Government does not insure deposits mobilized by RCFs, and they tend to operate in fairly small areas with limited scope for risk diversification. The RCFs may have a significant positive impact on the rural sector, but without some regulation they may engage in unhealthy competition that could weaken the entire rural financial system.

Although the financial and economic crisis in Asia has not affected the country directly, there are indirect effects through declining exports that have caused a huge build up of inventory, which cannot be absorbed by the domestic markets. There is a serious challenge to increase domestic demand to keep the economy growing and generate surpluses for investments. There has also been a decline in the inflow of foreign capital due to uncertainties in the region (Song, 1998), and the banking system is not strong enough to support investment. Therefore, it is important now to exploit the vast potential for deposit mobilization in rural areas to finance investments. The challenge lies in effectively transferring domestic resources into productive investments. The weaknesses of the banking system will impede this process.

FUTURE DIRECTIONS

The Government has been strongly committed to phased financial sector reforms and has not reversed its policies. The phased reforms effectively created a diverse set of institutions, primarily government-owned, to serve the rural sector. However, these institutions are not viable and access to their services appears limited. There is a need for many reforms, but there is little information for use in examining the full implications of past reforms and the current status of rural financial institutions in order to identify specific problems and offer solutions. An important priority for the Government, therefore, should be to open a dialogue with the financial intermediaries to assess the effects of rural financial sector policies implemented thus far. Donors may contribute to the process by helping with independent audits of the ABC, the ADBC, RCCs and RCFs, to examine their constraints and performance, and to evaluate their potential to service the changing rural sector. This information would help identify which institutions need to be restructured, strengthened, or closed. There is also need to conduct surveys to collect microlevel information from rural households and enterprises to assess the current sources of finance in rural areas, the unmet demand for financial services, and the willingness to pay for these services. The survey results would help pinpoint where new instruments are needed to meet demand.

The country has been able to avoid the financial and economic crisis that has affected other East and Southeast Asian countries because (i) the inflow of foreign capital has been used predominantly to finance long-term direct investments rather than short-term loans, (ii) the currency is nonconvertible for capital account transactions, and (iii) the country has a huge current account surplus and foreign exchange reserves. But the PRC is not completely immune to a financial crisis because it has problems similar to the affected economies. There are instances of insider trading within the banking sector, huge volumes of nonperforming loans, a large proportion of bank portfolios composed of loans to inefficient State firms, and indications of overinvestment in real estate (Oxford Analytica, 1998).[12] These problems imply fundamental weaknesses in the financial system that could lead to a systemic crisis if not addressed through fundamental financial reforms to deal with foreign capital inflows, reduce arrears, and prevent insider trading. Reforms to increase the transparency of operations would also need to address the above problems.

----

[12] It has been reported that Chinese banks have heavily invested in real estate, although market values have declined since 1995. There are millions of square feet of luxury villas, town houses, and office spaces financed by banks in Beijing, Shanghai, and Shenzhen that were found to be unoccupied in 1998 (Oxford Analytica, 1998).

Creating the Policy Environment

Reforms are required to allow the State banks to lend and mobilize deposits largely based on commercial criteria. The interest rates for loans and deposits need to reflect the cost of funds adjusted for inflation and the opportunity costs of capital. State policies artificially control interest rates and hence affect demand such that it is difficult to evaluate the opportunity cost of bank funds used for lending. There is no rationale explaining why State banks have been allowed to deviate up to a maximum of only 20 percent from the fixed lending rates. Donors should promote and contribute to a policy dialogue on interest rates between financial intermediaries and the Government. Experience in other transition countries has shown that rapid increases in interest rates create distress borrowing and financial crises, since it is difficult to raise interest rates on loss-making State firms. A gradual approach to interest rate liberalization combined with reforms to increase competition, and policies that exclude insolvent banks and enterprises from borrowing may help move the system towards market-based interest rates (World Bank, 1996b). Policies should encourage competition and avoid subsidies that undermine it. Moreover, the enterprise reforms need to be expanded and accelerated, with a complete evaluation of State-owned enterprises to identify which ones should be closed or privatized.

The future impact on the PRC of the current financial and economic crisis in Asia is unclear. The weak currencies of other countries in the region put pressure on the PRC to devalue its currency to compete for export markets. This creates a situation of great uncertainty regarding future exchange and inflation rates, which will influence future interest rates. It will be important to stabilize the exchange and inflation rates if devaluation occurs. The current policy to regulate capital inflows and limit currency convertibility may be appropriate given the limitations of the financial sector. The correct sequencing may be first to reform the enterprise sector to complete financial reforms, then open the capital account.

The current governmental approach to alleviate poverty through highly subsidized microfinance lending is counterproductive to the objective of creating efficient competitive financial markets. In other developing countries, this approach has created a dependency syndrome and impeded other market-based initiatives. The Government should focus its scarce resources on improving the environment such that market-based initiatives can successfully introduce new financial products and innovative financial technologies. If the Government must be involved in direct services, it should follow the best practices developed elsewhere. The policy bias towards light industries should be reduced to give nonfarm enterprises better opportunities to emerge.

Creating and Strengthening the Financial Infrastructure

There is evidence of decline in investor confidence due to the recent failure and closure of the Guangdong International Trust and Investment Corporation. It is important for the Government to restore confidence by issuing transparent investment guidelines and regulations for investment companies to discourage investments in risky activities. The entire system of prudential regulation and supervision needs to be evaluated. For example, do good guidelines exist for loan loss provisioning by rural financial institutions, and are they respecting the guidelines? A system of appropriate guidelines and methods to insure compliance is part of the necessary infrastructure for financial institutions. However, the most well designed system cannot be successful if the supervisory personnel are not capable of and efficient in monitoring the financial institutions. Training programs for skill development may be as necessary as the regulatory system itself. There may be a role for donor projects in both developing the systems and training the staff.

Access to good and timely information is the lifeblood of financial institutions. There is no information on the internal

methods used by rural financial institutions to collect and
analyze information as part of their technology to screen and
select clients, and determine loan sizes and terms. These
methods need reviewing to evaluate the extent to which they
may be responsible for the low loan recovery rates.
Alternatively, this analysis might reveal that problems of
property rights and the legal system are the chief causes. The
second potential problem concerns access to external
information. A financial institution must efficiently access
information about a potential client's past credit history and
the nature of any claims outstanding against property offered
as collateral. No information is available on how such
information is currently collected, stored, and exchanged in the
PRC, or the potential need to create public institutions such as
real estate registries or credit bureaus. Third, the regulatory
authorities, donors, and investors must be assured that
established accounting procedures are followed by financial
institutions such that their accounts reflect the true situation.
The information available does not inspire confidence that this
area of information generation is accurate or efficient.

Institutional Development

Experience to date in transition economies indicates that
institution building is a difficult process that requires a long-
term commitment from donors and government (World Bank,
1996b). It is not clear that the PRC has yet developed the
institutions needed for the future. The decision to create policy
banks may allow the State banks to function more like
commercial banks. But specialized policy banks may meet the
same fate as agricultural development banks in other countries.
They suffer from limited portfolio diversification due to
restrictions on their portfolio mix, inflexibility in interest rates
due to political interventions, and disincentives to mobilize
deposits due to access to cheap funds from the government.
In the PRC, the transfer of bad loans from the ABC to the ADBC
may simply erode the latter's profits and require it to be

recapitalized in the future. This bad debt problem needs to be resolved, and the ADBC needs to be allowed to compete for household deposits with RCFs and RCCs by offering market rates and flexible products.

A cost-benefit assessment should be conducted regarding the potential prudential regulation and supervision of nonbank institutions such as RCFs. This assessment should determine whether RCFs should be left unregulated, merged with RCCs, or closed. They meet a demand and have been innovative, but there are possible losses to depositors to be considered in whatever course of action is taken.

XI RURAL FINANCIAL MARKET DEVELOPMENT IN INDONESIA: MIXING MARKETS AND MANDATES

OVERVIEW OF THE FINANCIAL SYSTEM

Indonesia has a long history of deregulation of its economy and the financial sector, mixed with a high degree of State intervention designed to allocate credit on the basis of preferential programs. This mixed policy environment is attributed to more than 30 years of authoritarian rule in which policy decisions have been shaped by bureaucrats operating largely unconstrained by organized political action from societal groups. The State's domination of political life has been matched by its large presence in the marketplace. For example, the public sector was reported to account for 30 percent of GNP in 1988. The State banks have been shaped with little concern for the preferences of bankers, and they have accounted for 80 to 90 percent of all loans extended since the late 1960s. Credit subsidies have been allocated on the basis of economic priority. Agriculture, and particularly rice farmers, have been systematically favored as political leaders attempted to win friends and preserve mass support in the countryside (MacIntyre, 1993). This explains the persistence of State intervention as part of the movement towards market-oriented policies in the 1980s. The major exception to these generalizations is the freedom granted to rural financial institutions in recent years to set interest rates and design products that meet their requirements for sustainability.

The country has gone through several episodes of regulation followed by deregulation and re-regulation. Heavy State involvement in the economy began in the late 1950s with the nationalization of Netherlands-owned firms, the nationalization of banks, and the disappearance of foreign banks. After Suharto assumed power in 1966, some nationalized businesses were eventually returned to their former owners, efforts were made to attract foreign capital, and Bank Indonesia (BI) was returned to a more traditional central bank role, but closely tied to the Government. The five State commercial banks were assigned to serve particular sectors of the economy. Bank Rakyat Indonesia (BRI) was assigned rural development and smallholder agriculture, while Bank Bumi Daya was to serve estate agriculture and forestry. A major growth spurt occurred in the deposit base of the State banks beginning in 1968 when they were ordered to increase dramatically the interest rates on term deposits (MacIntyre, 1993).

Following the 1967–1968 banking reforms, State intervention in credit markets via BI influenced credit distribution in three ways. One was the direct provision of preferential loans to priority borrowers. The second was central bank control of the deposit and loan rates offered by the State banks, in which differing rates were set for borrowers according to economic priority. The third mechanism was through central bank preferential refinancing known as liquidity credits. The higher the priority of the economic sector, the higher the proportion of the loans eligible for rediscounting, and the lower the rate of interest charged by BI. The Bimas rice intensification program, for example, was eligible for 100 percent refinancing.

The first major financial deregulation occurred in 1970 with the adoption of a unified exchange rate and the opening of the capital account to the free inflow and outflow of funds (McLeod, 1999). To strengthen indigenous Indonesians, new programs for short-term (*Kredit Modal Kerja Permanen*, KMKP) and long-term (*Kredit Investasi Kecil*, KIK) loans were created, and the medium-term investment program KI (*Kredit Investasi*) was reserved for firms with indigenous majority ownership.

The inflationary pressure created by the inflow of funds, however, led to the introduction of credit ceilings for each bank on the assumption that tight restrictions on nonpriority sectors would encourage lending to priority groups. This added a fourth mechanism to the State's credit allocation arsenal. By 1982, it was estimated that the State banks were responsible for 83 percent of all outstanding loans, and central bank credit subsidies amounted to 50 percent of outstanding credit (MacIntyre, 1993).

The collapse in petroleum prices prompted the 1983 reforms that were introduced to mobilize private savings, replacing the oil-funded subsidized credit system. All four measures of credit allocation were altered: 1) credit ceilings were abolished, 2) State bank deposit and loan rates were deregulated, 3) central bank preferential refinancing was curtailed, and 4) the central bank's subsidized direct lending was also curtailed. An additional deregulatory package (PAKTO 88) was introduced in 1988. It eased the licensing of new private domestic and foreign banks, relaxed regulations on bank branching, and permitted banks to design their own saving deposits (McLeod, 1999). A new type of People's Credit Bank (*Bank Perkreditan Rakyat*, PBR) was created with special incentives granted to indigenous entrepreneurs to enter banking. In 1989, controls were removed on offshore borrowing by banks.

One of the last deregulatory reforms was the further reduction in subsidized loan programs in 1990, and an upward adjustment in refinance rates. However, banks were required to extend at least 20 percent of their total loans to small and medium enterprises. A new banking law in 1992 removed the distinction between development and savings banks. New private and foreign banks mushroomed in urban areas with the lowering of entry barriers, and a major expansion in small PBRs occurred in rural areas. By the end of the 1980s, private banks accounted for a third of all outstanding credit. Financial deepening began to grow at a rapid rate. The M_2/GDP ratio (the ratio of money in circulation to GDP) ranged between 10 and 20 percent from 1970 to 1984, then climbed to almost 40 percent by 1990. The financial system had evolved so there was greater competition between private and State banks and flows of credit and interest rates depended mainly on market forces (Chant and Pangestu, 1996).

Deregulation effectively ended in 1991, when liquidity loans to financial institutions began to expand and controls were reimposed on overseas borrowing by banks. The near collapse of some private banks and the 1994 scandal with *Bapindo*, the Indonesian Development Bank, prompted a wave of new prudential regulations, supposedly to prevent banking abuses. Credit controls were reimposed in an attempt to control inflation and, in December 1995, the central bank moved to exercise control over nonbank financial institutions. In 1996, the Government adopted the policy of being more selective in the licensing of new bank branches out of fear that excessive competition would emerge between banks.

Following devaluation of the Thai baht in July 1997, the rupiah came under speculative pressure and by April 1998 its value had fallen by 70 percent. The Government closed 16 private banks that failed to abide by prudential regulations. Inadequate capital and highly concentrated lending to companies with close ownership links with the banks were reported to be the principal concerns (McLeod, 1999). The political and economic crisis that followed continues to this day and has inspired several subsidized credit programs as part of the Government and donor response to the economic and social problems.

APPROACH TO RURAL AND AGRICULTURAL FINANCE

Indonesia has employed a variety of agricultural and rural development strategies that have influenced the evolution of rural financial markets. Rice self-sufficiency was the priority in the 1960s and early 1970s. The Fourth Five-Year Development Plan (1983–1989) aimed to make the villages self-supporting, while the Fifth Plan (1989–1994) emphasized rural poverty and the poorest of the poor. Infrastructure investments were made and direct cash grants were given by the central Government to individual villages. Self-help groups and cooperatives were given special roles to support food self-sufficiency and small-scale rural enterprises. Programs were implemented to intensify agriculture, to stimulate rural nonfarm enterprises, and to increase rural employment (Teuku, 1994). Transmigration projects were implemented to create employment and reduce population density.

The country has developed an unusually rich and complex set of formal and informal financial organizations. Some have been explicitly linked to agricultural and rural development strategies, while others aimed to extend financial services into rural areas. The widespread network of government programs means there has been less scope for NGOs than in other Asian countries. Therefore, microfinance by NGOs is much less significant than elsewhere (McGuire, Conroy, and Thapa, 1998).

The Indonesian approach to the development of rural finance has evolved over time. First, in the 1970s and 1980s, the Government actively intervened in financial markets by creating a special program with regulated terms and conditions for every purpose that seemed important. In 1982, 19 categories of short-term credit were specified with seven different lending rates, three discount rates, and eight rediscount percentages (Gonzalez-Vega, 1982). This approach may have made a contribution to economic growth, but the price was high transaction costs. For example, one branch of BRI was found to manage 126 separate credit programs, each with its weekly, monthly, and quarterly reporting requirements, its terms and interest rates, and its procedures and criteria for borrower selection (Gonzalez-Vega, 1982). In recent years, the provision of financial services to the poor has become more important. But it has occurred more as the result of competition among financial institutions striving to provide market-oriented services than to an NGO-dominated attempt to reach the poor.

Second, both the national and provincial governments have employed a variety of grants, capital transfers, and subsidies to start and strengthen financial institutions. Usually the goal was to avoid creating subsidy dependence and encourage sustainable financial intermediaries. The Government departed from this approach in recent years, however, and reverted to creating subsidized poverty-oriented projects. New government and donor programs created in the wake of the 1997 and 1998 crisis also employ subsidized credit.

There are some good descriptions of the major rural finance programs, but little formal analysis of the evolution of rural finance markets in the country (Gonzalez-Vega and Chaves, 1993). The *Badan Kredit Kecamatan* (BKK) system in Central Java and the nationwide BRI unit desa system are well documented, but many provincial and rural banks provide rural services along with government and donor programs. Although priority was given to State banks, 27 regional development banks were created in the Sukarno era, one for each province, and by 1970 there were nearly 300 People's Credit Banks at the district level (Lapenu, 1998). By 1981, Gonzalez-Vega (1982) estimated that almost 6,000 secondary banks and over 1,000 nonbank financial institutions, in addition to over 3,500 BRI unit desas, were operating in the country. Government-sponsored cooperative credit programs have also been important in some areas.

Two nationwide programs were specifically created to benefit the rural economy: the Bimas (*Bimbingan Massal*) rice intensification scheme, and the small investment (KIK) and permanent working capital (KMKP) schemes. Indonesia faced a growing rice deficit in the 1960s, and achieving rice self-sufficiency became a top priority. The green revolution offered new production opportunities but required huge investments in irrigation, and it was assumed that farmers had to be enticed with cheap credit to use purchased inputs for the new high-yielding varieties. To accelerate the green revolution, the Bimas rice intensification program was established in 1969. The BRI unit desas were selected to channel subsidized credit to rice farmers. Units were established on the basis of how many rice fields could be covered from a given location, and this area ranged from 600 to 2,000 ha (Patten and Rosengard, 1991). Each unit operated as a window of a district office rather than as a separate financial entity, and the units had little authority to choose their clients.

The extension staff of the Ministry of Agriculture chose the borrowers by certifying those farmers who agreed to participate in all aspects of the Bimas program. BI supplied BRI with funds at 3 percent per year, while the farmers paid 12 percent, a rate below the annual inflation rate and the interest rate paid on small savings. The program covered 75 percent of loan losses, and provided an administrative subsidy for some of the unit desa costs. In 1974, a loan window was created primarily for nonfarm activities (*Kredit Mini*); in 1976 the unit desas were authorized to mobilize rural savings through the national saving program (TABANAS or *Tabungun Nasional*); and *Kredit Midi* was introduced in 1980 for making larger nonagricultural loans. All these loan programs carried a nominal annual interest rate of 12 percent.

The number of unit desas expanded quickly until a peak of 3,626 was reached in 1984 with a staff of over 14,000 (Patten and Rosengard, 1991). Total Bimas lending peaked at rupiah (Rp) 55 billion in the 1975-1976 planting season, fluctuated in the Rp35–50 billion range for several years, then fell to Rp14 billion by 1983-1984. The default rate rose steadily to reach almost 55 percent (Table XI.1). A factor that contributed to the high default rate was the periodic debt forgiveness programs, which created the expectation among borrowers that sooner or later unpaid loans would be pardoned (Gonzalez-Vega, 1982). Annual operating losses exceeded Rp20 billion in 1983 and 1984. The Bimas program ended in 1983. The country achieved rice self-sufficiency in 1984, but at a considerable cost by essentially bankrupting BRI (Martokoesoemo, 1994).

The second nationwide credit program, KIK/KMKP, was introduced in 1974 to improve credit access for small businesses, especially for indigenous Indonesians. The banks lent at a 12 percent nominal annual rate and the loans were refinanced by BI at 3 percent. In addition, 75 percent of the loan losses were insured by the State-owned loan insurance company

Table XI.1: Bimas Credit Statistics by Planting Season for Rice,
1970/71–1983/84

Planting season	Number of borrowers	Amount lent (Rp'000)	Amount overdue (Rp'000)	Default rate (%)
1970/71	1,326,714	8,454,655	283,918	3.36
1971	356,607	2,508,981	140,936	5.62
1971/72	1,181,770	7,306,117	215,123	2.94
1972	356,654	2,558,494	148,866	5.82
1972/73	1,714,733	12,772,340	624,828	4.89
1973	540,684	4,942,043	319,512	6.47
1973/74	2,550,242	31,550,210	2,586,425	8.20
1974	987,704	12,537,608	1,311,011	10.46
1974/75	2,615,451	40,558,848	3,483,830	8.59
1975	1,104,904	17,214,042	2,472,542	14.36
1975/76	2,476,963	55,074,430	5,242,564	9.52
1976	914,105	22,442,485	3,605,253	16.06
1976/77	2,089,933	48,871,790	7,026,623	14.38
1977	635,349	17,534,636	5,028,980	28.68
1977/78	1,799,120	44,550,076	6,176,217	13.86
1978	643,299	17,744,210	3,876,982	21.85
1978/78	1,403,017	42,235,323	6,740,321	15.96
1979	412,837	12,983,968	2,178,760	16.78
1979/80	1,161,317	36,313,088	5,389,251	14.84
1980	432,512	14,221,010	2,605,034	18.32
1980/81	1,087,330	35,094,157	7,876,394	22.44
1981	555,893	18,892,722	4,393,003	23.25
1981/82	1,104,280	43,609,046	15,314,124	35.12
1982	303,306	13,755,901	7,714,392	56.08
1982/83	900,600	45,597,802	22,285,583	48.87
1983	199,468	9,411,605	4,801,750	51.02
1983/84	363,555	14,081,566	7,679,457	54.54

Source: Reproduced from Patten and Rosengard (1991, p. 63).

(PT Askrinde)[1] with much of the insurance premium also paid by BI. Like Bimas, these programs encountered heavy losses, widespread fraud, and high default rates. Banks were under heavy pressure to disburse, often lending to new customers with no previous bank or business experience. These programs were terminated in 1990 as part of the Government's effort to cut subsidies (Martokoesoemo, 1994).

---

[1] No information was obtained about this company.

With the termination of Bimas, a modest small-farmer lending scheme (*Kredit Usaha Tani*, KUT) was introduced, to be handled by officially backed village cooperative units (*Koperasi Unit Desa*, KUD). It was one of the few programs to continue receiving 100 percent refinancing at 3 percent per annum from the central bank. It provided credit to farmers' groups at a subsidized 12 percent nominal rate per annum. By the end of 1993, KUT arrears had risen to some 17 percent of total loans disbursed since 1985 (Martokoesoemo, 1994). There is suspicion that this program tended to reach wealthier villages with better political connections.

Several other national and provincial efforts have expanded financial services into rural areas during the past two decades. Development banks have been set up in all provinces. In East Java, 220 KURKS (*Kredit Usaha Rakyat Kecil*, credit for activities of the poor) were organized as regional enterprises rather than banks. They were capitalized largely by the provincial governments (Lapenu, 1998). The PAKTO 88 reforms created the People's Credit Banks (*Bank Perkreditan Rakyat*, BPR), which required a minimum capital of only Rp50 million compared with Rp10 billion required for a primary bank at the time. These small partial service banks were intended to serve only rural areas, and by June 1998 a total of 2,227 existed, mainly in Java and Bali (Reille and Gallman, 1998). Other provinces developed other types of institutions known as LDKP (*Lembaga Dana dan Kredit Pedesaan*) or rural funds and credit institutions. The 1992 banking law required that they be closed if they did not obtain a BPR license within five years.

The major remaining directed credit program is *Kredit Usaha Kecil* (Credit for Small Activities, KUK) that was started in 1990 to support the development of indigenous small Indonesian businesses in the face of ethnic Chinese dominance of larger enterprises (McGuire, Conroy, and Thapa, 1998). All banks are required to lend at least 20 percent of their total loans to small and medium enterprises originally defined as firms with assets less than Rp600 million. Since 1997, the maximum loan allowable is Rp350 million (approximately $145,000). Private commercial banks, especially those involved in corporate lending and without extensive branch networks, have had difficulty in meeting this requirement, and one response has been to channel funds through the rural banks (BPRs). This led to the creation of the DABANAS Foundation as a joint enterprise of the Association of Indonesian Private Banks and the Association of Indonesian Rural Banks. It mobilizes funds from the commercial banks at the nominal annual rate of 16.5 percent, adds a one-percent fee, and lends the funds to the rural banks. It also provides banks with technical assistance and may eventually provide some regulatory and supervisory functions for the rural banks.

Two major rural poverty programs were created with little concern for their future sustainability (McGuire, Conroy, and Thapa, 1998). The first program is *Impres Desa Tertinggal* (IDT), an interministerial effort that commenced in 1993 with the goal of assisting backward villages. Initially 28,000 villages were identified to receive the following: 1) a capital injection of Rp20 million per year for up to 3 years for income-generating activities, 2) facilitators to help self-help groups become economically active, and 3) physical infrastructure up to the value of Rp100–130 million. The capital is essentially a revolving fund with local groups free to decide the terms of lending to members. By March 1997, over 120,000 self-help groups had been created with some 3.3 million members. After about three years of funding, about one third of the groups were judged ready to enter the PHBK project described below.

The second poverty initiative, the Prosperous Family Program created in 1996, is funded by a levy of 2 percent on the income earned by persons and corporations in excess of Rp100 million per year. It is implemented by BKKBN (the National Planning Coordination Board) which has an infrastructure in practically every village. Women's groups are set up and the poorest are enrolled initially in the TAKESRA savings scheme in which each woman receives a tiny initial grant of Rp2,000 (less than $1.00), and a bonus of Rp2,000 if she saves Rp100 each month for six months. When they accumulate Rp25,000, the women become eligible for loans of Rp20,000 under the KUKESRA credit program at the subsidized nominal rate of 6 percent per annum. Up to April 1997, some 9.8 million Indonesian families had received funding through this scheme. This number swamps the large BRI unit desa clientele of 2.3 million borrowers.

These two poverty programs represent a break from the pattern of establishing sustainable finance in rural areas. Neither program must set rates to cover costs and they depend on intensive support from government field staff. They sometimes overlap in areas in which other types of sustainable finance are being developed. The groups that participate are supposed to graduate to commercial funding sources, but that seems unrealistic given the expectations created among borrowers about access to subsidized funds.

Several other government and donor programs were initiated in recent years to expand banking services to the poor. For example, the Ministry of Agriculture encouraged the development of Grameen-type joint liability lending programs, and donor-funded projects have linked local self-help groups and village associations with financial institutions.

THE EVOLUTION AND CURRENT STATUS OF KEY RURAL FINANCIAL INSTITUTIONS AND PROGRAMS

Participants

There are no comprehensive data available on which to assess the overall performance of the rural financial system in Indonesia. Data are insufficient at the macro level to evaluate aggregate trends in the amount of agricultural or rural loans disbursed or outstanding, and to calculate the ratio of credit to agricultural GDP. Comprehensive micro studies have not been done to analyze which firms and households have access to formal and informal finance, and which do not. Therefore, this section is limited to discussing selected institutions and programs. Two key institutions have been analyzed in detail by researchers. The first is BRI, which transformed itself after the collapse of Bimas, and the second is *Badan Kredit Kecamatan* (BKK) created in Central Java in 1972.[2] Both have undergone fundamental reforms with differing degrees of success. Information is also provided on the South Kalimantan BKK-type provincial bank and the PHBK credit project.

Discontinuation of Bimas meant that BRI faced the problem of what to do with the significant financial infrastructure of 3,600 unit desas and 14,000 employees. Closing the units would have wasted an important resource and destroyed the goodwill built up with their clientele. An important problem was the low interest rates charged on loans relative to the cost of funds in the Kredit Mini and Kredit Midi programs. The financial reforms of 1983, which liberalized interest rates, provided the opportunity to design new products and establish an appropriate pricing structure.

Following the collapse of Bimas, three key policy changes were introduced in 1983/84 to reform the unit desa system: 1) the units were transformed into full-service rural banks, 2) each unit would be treated as a discrete profit or loss center within BRI, and 3) they would be evaluated on profitability rather than on hectares covered or money lent. A new credit program, KUPEDES (*Kredit Umum Pedesaan* or General Rural Credit), was created to provide loans for a wide range of purposes. Nominal interest rates were set at a flat 1.5 percent per month on the original loan balance for working capital, and a flat 1 percent per month for investment loans. These terms worked out to effective rates of 2.6 and 1.7 percent per month, respectively. A portion of total interest payments would be rebated to borrowers who paid on time. Few restrictions would be placed on the use of borrowed funds but, unlike many of today's microfinance programs, collateral would be required to cover the value of the loan.

---

[2] Unless specific references are noted, the information presented about these two institutions is drawn from Patten and Rosengard (1991).

Changes were introduced in which each unit desa was treated as a separate accounting entity such that the staff could be held accountable for its performance. Demand for credit for other types of activities surpassed demand for agricultural production credit; some unit desas were converted into village service posts, and they released staff for reassignment to those unit desas that experienced a rapid growth in loan demand.

The SIMPEDES (*Simpanan Pedesaan*) savings instrument was introduced in the unit desa system in mid-1986 as an alternative to the national voluntary savings program (TAMADES). The design of SIMPEDES was based on market research with rural clients. It offered low interest rates on small savings, but higher rates for larger savings accounts. Unlimited withdrawals were permitted, savers were given coupons for participation in a semi-annual lottery, and the BRI guaranteed deposit safety. The first two features were attractive for rural savers and the savings volume subsequently grew relative to other higher-interest-rate products with withdrawal restrictions. Time deposit and giro (demand deposit) accounts were also created.

One of the unique features of the unit desas compared with other important microfinance organizations, such as the Grameen Bank and most NGOs in Bangladesh, is that they make individual loans based on collateral, often in the form of land, and loans are made for one to three years. Local village officials are involved in loan screening by acting as character references for the borrowers. Agricultural loans including livestock and fisheries are estimated to represent 18 percent of the total portfolio; 25 percent of the borrowers are women, and the units serve a large number of local savers and borrowers. All borrowers are charged an up-front penalty fee of 0.5 percent per month that is refunded if all payments are made on time. The proportion of loans in arrears in 1996 was only 3.64 percent. As such, the unit desa system ranks as one of the most effective rural financial institutions in a developing country.

The second, major well-studied financial institution, the provincial BKK system, was created in Central Java in 1972 to provide small, short-term loans to rural families primarily for nonfarm productive purposes. The creation of this system was part of a set of activities sponsored by the provincial government to reduce dependence on agriculture, shift resources to targeted ethnic groups, and promote economic activities of the poor. The provincial government provided start-up capital through the Central Java Regional Development Bank (BPD), which also supervises BKK operations. Two hundred BKKs (units) were initially formed and the number eventually grew to almost 500. These units created over 3,000 (*pos desas*) village posts (out of a total of about 8,500 villages in the province) that are staffed once a week, usually on local market days. Unlike the original BRI design, the BKKs are locally administered and are financially autonomous. The system has political accountability because it is incorporated into the local government structure.

Six BKK loan products were created, ranging in maturity from 22 days with nominal monthly interest rate of 4.8 percent, to six months with monthly interest rate of 2.0 percent, the interest rate decreasing with length of loan period. As in BRI, loans are made to individuals. Savings are mandatory to provide capital for loans and instill the savings habit. In theory, access to savings is possible after full loan repayment but, due to fund shortages, many BKKs did not allow or encourage such withdrawals. An unfortunate concept was the creation in 1974 of a *khusus* (special) window for the credit programs of the province's *dinases* (technical service agencies), which included a wide range of agricultural and rural development activities. The clients were selected by the *dinases*, so the BKKs were in the position of being only a collection agency rather than screening their clients and building a long-term banking relationship. Furthermore, the BKKs were allowed to charge only a one-percent-per-month nominal interest rate.

The performance of the BKKs was not good in their early years. By 1979, many were nonviable and about a third had closed or were operating at low levels. A Provincial Area Development Project financed by the United States Agency for International Development, injected fresh capital and provided technical assistance, and the central Government provided a Rp3 billion loan to assist with rehabilitation and expansion.

Between 1981 and 1989, the number of weak BKKs (Class V) fell from 1,984 to 6. Beginning in 1986, several reforms were introduced, in part due to competition from other lenders. The maximum loan-size ceiling was raised, an interest rebate for loans paid on time was introduced, and the national voluntary savings program (TAMADES) was introduced on an experimental basis. To improve services, the system of village posts was expanded and by 1991 there were posts in roughly half the province's villages.

The South Kalimantan provincial government started a BKK-type program in 1985 (Ravicz, 1998). The province first created BKK units to accept deposits and they now number 34. After the 1992 banking law, the province began creating *Lembaga Pembiayaan Usaha Kecil* (LPUK) units that do not accept deposits. They now number 76, such that one or other of the two types is found in all the province's 109 subdistricts. The units rarely pay taxes and are not subject to the reserve requirements that apply to commercial banks. The provincial development bank (BPD) essentially makes all policy decisions, determines the products offered, selects the staff to be hired, and supervises them. Prospective borrowers must have a business or employment to obtain a loan. Loan terms vary between 10 weeks and 18 months. Nominal interest rates range from a low of 3.5 percent per month on a declining-balance basis to a high of one percent per week on the initial loan balance with a 10-percent savings requirement. Minimum loan sizes are about Rp50,000 (about $20) with a maximum of Rp1 million (about $440).

A major distinction compared with BRI and the Central Java BKK system is that in 1985 the South Kalimantan BKK system began experimenting with group lending in which "channeling groups" pass loan funds down to their members and forward repayments to the BKK unit. Each member is responsible for paying his/her share but, in the event of default, the remaining group members are liable for any unpaid amounts. Penalties are not charged for late payments nor are interest rebates given for on-time payment. Only the original 34 BKK units accept voluntary savings or require forced savings. Savings earn a nominal annual interest rate of 9 percent.

The *Program Hubungan Bank dan KSM* (PHBK) is an example of a donor program designed to increase access by the poor to financial services through group lending (Ravicz, 1998).[3] It is sponsored by BI and the German Agency for Technical Cooperation (GTZ), and in 1989 it began to provide technical assistance to borrower groups, and to banks and NGOs that lend to the groups. Since 1992, no liquidity support has been provided for the loans. The program operates in several provinces and three lending models are used. In the first, borrower groups act as financial intermediaries (KSP) because they on-lend to members the funds provided to them by banks. NGOs identify and train groups but the banks retain the credit risk. The program pays the costs of the NGOs that provide training in bookkeeping and financial skills. Model two is similar except that the banks lend to the NGOs that on-lend to the groups and retain the credit risk. This model is now discouraged because few NGOs had the capacity to function as viable financial intermediaries. In model three, the banks lend to a channeling group (KPM), and the loans are usually divided equally among the members who are responsible for each other's loan repayments. The program trains the banks that are expected to organize and train the groups. Each group has a well-respected leader known to the bank prior to issuing the loan.

---

[3] The Asian Development Bank has two projects underway that have financial components. The first is a $25 million microcredit project, in which BI lends to rural banks (BPRs) and to regional development banks (BPDs) that on-lend to nonbank financial institutions and to NGOs. Each participating institution is free to on-lend to individuals and borrowing groups on the basis of commercial viability with terms and conditions set by market forces. The project aims to expand microenterprises for poverty alleviation. The second is a $78 million project designed for rural income generation (cofinanced by the International Fund for Agricultural Development). It includes a savings and credit component operated by BRI. The project supports the creation of self-help groups composed of persons living below the poverty line. BRI provides a savings channel for the groups and group loans for productive activities.

Outreach

The transformation of the BRI unit desa system in 1983-1984 produced spectacular results in outreach and financial performance. The number of outstanding KUPEDES loans rose steadily from 360,000 in 1984 to over 1.6 million in 1989 (Table XI.2). SIMPEDES savings reached almost 70 percent of total savings by the end of 1989, while total unit desa savings exceeded the volume of total KUPEDES loans outstanding by 13 percent. The total number of savers roughly equaled the number of loans outstanding. Whereas the unit desas had produced substantial losses up to 1986, by 1991 they contributed about two thirds of total BRI profits (Robinson, 1992). Because of this positive experience, unit desas were opened in selected urban neighborhoods and achieved similar positive results.

Recently published data for the unit desas for 1996 show continuous growth (Charitoneko, Patten, and Yaron, 1998). The number of loans outstanding was 2.5 million with a total volume of $1.7 billion. Average loan size was $1,007 and the average outstanding loan balance was $685. Minimum loan size was Rp25,000 (about $11) and maximum was Rp25 million ($11,000). Savings were even more impressive: 16.2 million savers (over 6 savers for each loan), Rp7.1 trillion in total savings ($3.0 billion), and an average savings account balance of approximately $184. A flat nominal interest rate of 1.5 percent per month was still charged on loans, and the average annual effective yield for prompt payers was 32 percent.

The performance of the Central Java BKK system has been less impressive as reported in Table XI.3. The system reached about 500,000 loans outstanding by 1987, then growth tapered off. The total loan portfolio was almost Rp50 billion at the end of 1992 (roughly $23 million) with an average loan size of about $47. The number of savers also leveled off at just over 500,000 but voluntary savings grew substantially, representing half of the total 1992 savings of some Rp12 billion ($6 million) with the average account equivalent to $12. Cumulative delinquencies fell steadily from 1972 and the system was becoming profitable.

Table XI.2: Growth of BRI Unit Desa Operations, 1984–1989

Date	Total KUPEDES lending during semester		Total KUPEDES outstanding at end of semester		Cumulative KUPEDES lending		Total savings at end of semester (Rp billion)				Total		Ratio of total savings to KUPEDES loans outstanding (%)
	Rp billion	Thousands of loans	Rp billion	Thousands of loans	Rp billion	Thousands of loans	TABANAS	SIM-PEDES	Giro	Deposito berjangka	Rp billion	Thousands of savers	
June 1984	81.1	302	71.6	360	81.1	302	26.9	0.0	2.6	0.0	29.5		41.2
Dec. 1984	90.2	337	111.1	641	171.3	639	39.1	0.3	2.0	0.8	42.2		38.0
June 1985	156.1	474	180.1	854	327.4	1,114	39.5	0.5	1.9	1.1	43.0		23.9
Dec. 1985	182.7	518	229.0	1,035	510.1	1,631	63.8	5.1	13.8	2.2	84.9		37.1
June 1986	225.7	572	284.9	1,164	735.8	2,203	66.5	15.5	11.8	3.0	96.8		34.0
Dec. 1986	256.3	578	334.4	1,232	992.1	2,782	78.4	82.6	10.9	3.9	175.8	3,544	52.6
June 1987	299.1	599	403.2	1,301	1,291.2	3,381	66.7	121.8	16.6	5.3	210.4	3,854	52.2
Dec. 1987	298.7	538	429.2	1,315	1,589.9	3,918	79.5	182.6	12.5	12.7	287.3	4,184	66.9
June 1988	348.1	568	492.6	1,379	1,938.0	4,486	70.3	214.7	9.8	21.8	316.6	4,251	64.3
Dec. 1988	359.6	546	538.7	1,386	2,297.6	5,033	89.5	342.0	16.6	44.4	492.5	4,998	91.4
June 1989	483.0	658	690.6	1,490	2,780.6	5,690	86.4	454.9	8.4	71.6	621.3	5,365	90.0
Dec. 1989	589.7	722	845.6	1,644	3,370.3	6,412	113.6	699.8	26.3	117.3	957.0	6,262	113.2

Source: Reproduced from Patten and Rosengard (1991, p. 77).

Table XI.3: Expansion and Portfolio Quality of the BKK Program

Year	Loans outstanding Number	Amount (Rp'000)	Cumulative delinquencies (% of cumulative loans) Number	Amount	Savers (number)	Savings (Rp'000)
1972		213,429	16.03	7.11	73.456	38,389
1977	260,253	1,400,382	7.03	3.15	244,469,	356,273
1982	310,167	4,817,823	4.36	1.92	283,841	1,002,394
1987	516,065	18,223,750	3.26	1.98	415,842[a]	2,865,724[a]
					3,339[b]	29,550[b]
1992[c]	498,591	48,946,000			414,797[a]	6,268,000[a]
					91,461[b]	6,193,000[b]

[a]   Mandatory savings
[b]   Voluntary savings (*TAMADES*)
[c]   Data for loans outstanding and savings for 1990–1992 available only rounded to millions
      and thousands of rupiah, respectively.

Source: Riedinger (1994).

A 1989 survey of over 600 clients in 20 BKKs revealed that petty trading was the primary activity for more than half of the respondents and farming was a secondary activity for about half of them (Patten and Rosengard, 1991). Sixty percent of the borrowers were women, half the borrowers owned land, and most lived in the village where the loan transaction took place. More than a third had received credit from other sources and more than 40 percent had savings accounts outside the BKK. Average borrowers quadrupled their loan size within four years and received a total of more than 13 loans.

Analysis of the South Kalimantan BKK system for 1995 revealed 34,518 loans outstanding for the 110 units for a total Rp7.8 billion ($3.4 million) or about $100 per loan (Ravicz, 1998). The growth between 1993 and 1995 was due almost entirely to increased average loan size rather than to a larger number of loans. Most of the borrowers were petty traders and approximately 40 percent were women. Loans were not written off such that, after adjustments were made for old loans, the arrears rate in 1995 for loans more than 90 days overdue was 6 percent. Return on equity was estimated to be –29.7, 7.5, and

12.0 percent for 1993, 1994, and 1995, respectively. All BKKs needed additional liquidity. For those units that mobilize savings, voluntary savings were equal to only 31 percent of outstanding loans in 1995. The fact that the new units do not accept savings will retard their growth, deny an important service to clients, and deprive loan officers of an important gauge of client creditworthiness. These units may be especially vulnerable to competition from BRI and other banks in the region.

An evaluation of the PHBK project was conducted in 1997–1998 (Steinwand, 1998). It included interviews with 23 rural credit banks (BPR), approximately 10 KPM (financial intermediaries) per bank for a total of 200, and two members from each KPM for a total of 400 members. Most of the BPR were newly created with 10 years or less of experience. The PHBK project is oriented toward sound banks, but seven sampled banks had serious problems due to high arrears or internal problems such as misuse of funds.

The banks tend to be small and chose to participate in the program to lend to small entrepreneurs and microentrepreneurs because they cannot compete with commercial banks for larger clients. Nearly a third made loans as small as Rp50,000 ($10) and the median minimum loan size was Rp100,000. The median minimum requirement to open a savings account was only Rp2,500 ($0.50). The banks provide door-to-door service in collecting savings and loan installments at their client's homes. Productivity per staff member varied considerably from 26 to 119 credit accounts per staff member and 80 to 318 savings and time-deposit accounts. Margins varied from 20 to 43 percent but, because of high costs, profits were either negative or reached a maximum of 3 percent of average productive assets. Future profits will depend heavily on the disposition of classified loans, which varied from 6 to 30 percent of productive assets.

The banks are vulnerable to losing deposits because only a few people hold most of the time deposits in a bank. There was no clear evidence that group lending reduced the costs and risks of lending compared to individual loans, but it may have assisted the banks to reach a poorer clientele. Group lending seemed to perform better in Central Java than in the other provinces and staff productivity was higher.

Analysis of the PHBK borrowing groups (KPM) revealed an average of 11 members. The overall membership was 56 percent men with 26 percent of the groups being men-only, 21 percent women-only, and the remainder mixed gender. Only 26 percent of the groups met regularly, and nearly half were new and had only received one loan. Most groups divided the total loan among the members according to an estimate of need. With the exception of Central Java, about three quarters of the groups restricted loans to productive purposes. Even though most groups employed joint liability, most banks required collateral, frequently in the form of blocked savings accounts. About half of the groups had no arrears. The better paying groups were formed at their own initiative, were smaller in number of members, kept total group size unchanged over time, selected their own managers, and met more regularly. Surprisingly, loan collateralization made little difference in repayment. The best repayment rate was observed when the group managers collected from members and delivered the funds to the bank rather than when the bank staff picked up payments from the group.

Analysis of the member interviews revealed that about half reported trade as their primary business with agriculture being second most important. Most members reported using the loan for expanding a current business rather than starting a new one. Nearly half had never visited their lending BPR because the services were received at their homes. The median distance from the BPR to the member's home was eight kilometers. Surprisingly, their closest bank was only three kilometers away on average, and it was often a BRI unit desa. This result reflects a possible segmentation in the clientele. Clients able to borrow somewhat larger loans on an individual basis may choose BRI, while clients who enjoy the greater level of service provided or who cannot or choose not to provide as much loan collateral, select the BPR.

Access to formal loans appears to be widespread in rural Indonesia. Borrowers without sufficient loan collateral face problems in getting loans from BRI and the other lenders that require physical collateral. Seeking loans from joint liability group lenders is one way for rationed borrowers to solve this problem. However, Indonesia represents an especially interesting case because several organizations successfully provide individual loans without requiring collateral. Instead, they employ local authorities such as village leaders to screen clients. This experience is in sharp contrast to organizations in other parts of rural Asia that conclude that group lending is the only way to improve access by the poor to formal finance.

Sustainability

The sustainability of Indonesian rural financial institutions is quite varied. The BRI unit desas represent one extreme. The gross financial spread for the unit desas in 1996 was reported to be 18 percent and the adjusted return on equity was an extremely large 134 percent. The unit desas were financially self-reliant and subsidy independent. In effect, they were subsidizing the rest of BRI, such that rural borrowers were subsidizing the more affluent urban clientele. It was estimated that in 1995, the unit desas could have reduced the yield on their loan portfolios from 31.6 to 16.3 percent and still remained subsidy independent (Charitoneko, Patten, and Yaron, 1998).

Several weaknesses have been identified in the Central Java BKKs, especially when compared to the BRI unit desas, and they raise questions about BKK sustainability (Riedinger, 1994). First, the low-interest-rate experience with the *khusus* loans revealed the importance of correct pricing to cover lending costs and risks. Second, many of the BKK failures in the early 1980s were in urban areas where corruption may more easily occur. Third, total outreach is limited because of an incomplete network of village posts. Fourth, the trend towards larger loan sizes may reduce female participation. A study of BRI and other BKK-like financial institutions found a negative relationship between increasing loan size and the share of female borrowers (Holt, 1991). Fifth, savings mobilization lags behind BRI and other BKK-like institutions. One reason is that poorer customers seem to prefer passbook savings rather than the certificates of deposit of the TAMADES program operated by the BKKs. The proximity of the BKK units to their clients offers an advantage relative to competitors, but it may not be sufficient to retain their savings as interest rates rise elsewhere.

No definitive judgement can be made about the lasting impact and sustainability of the PHBK. Since the participating banks are small, they may choose to continue serving this clientele after the project subsidy ends. No clear evidence exists on whether or not group lending reduces lending costs or risks, but groups may help somewhat poorer clients gain access to financial services. The regional differences in the results imply that Central Java is a more favorable area for group lending than the other less densely populated provinces.

A major conclusion is that there is a considerable range in the sustainability of the rural financial organizations. On the top of the list are the unit desas that could substantially reduce their interest rates and still be subsidy independent. This is due to their high interest rate policy and level of efficiency. BRI also has attractive savings products even though very small deposits earn no interest. Many of the other financial organizations, however, rely on subsidies. They do not price their loans high enough to cover costs and have not developed attractive saving products to mobilize savings. Rather than compete with BRI on interest rates for savings, some institutions emphasize the service of door-to-door savings collection. The special poverty-oriented programs funded by the Government and donors tend to be highly subsidized, represent a departure from the Government's drive to create sustainable finance, and run the risk of collapsing if the flow of subsidies is discontinued. Any success they achieve in furnishing financial services to the poor, therefore, would only be transitory. Their loan recovery rates are also inferior to the BRI unit desas and this saps their viability.

The relative success of BRI and some other rural financial institutions is due in part to Indonesia's dynamic economy and comparatively stable macroeconomic and political environment until mid-1997. This contributed to a strong demand for credit and savings services. This demand and the generally good repayment performance of borrowers stimulated the emergence of rural financial institutions.

Several key features of institutional design also explain the successful performance of many of the important financial intermediaries (Chaves and Gonzalez-Vega, 1996). First, important information problems in lending have been resolved by establishing a network of semi-independent, locally operated financial institutions with a comparative advantage in gathering information about clients, monitoring loans, and enforcing loan contracts. Loans, therefore, are often based more on character than collateral. Second, to resolve the agency problem, incentives in the form of performance-based remuneration and efficiency wages[4] have induced financial managers to behave in ways consistent with the financial health of the institutions. Third, managers of the financial institutions have been given considerable autonomy over interest rates and other key performance variables. Fourth, one-time subsidies in the form of start-up loans and grants nurtured the organizations without creating a dependency for continuous subsidies. The modest levels of this support prevented the development of expensive fixed-cost structures. Fifth, clients value their banking relationship due to rapid loan disbursement, low transaction costs, and the possibility of pledging nontraditional forms of collateral such as character references. Loan recovery is high because borrowers want to protect their reputations and their access to future loans.

---

[4] Efficiency wages refer to wages paid above employee opportunity costs. This increases the cost of job loss and encourages workers to put forth adequate effort.

DEPOSIT MOBILIZATION

Indonesia has explicitly included savings mobilization in its policies to expand financial services. As noted above, the number of savers in the BRI unit desas far exceeds the number of borrowers. This experience reveals the importance of designing financial instruments desired by customers. TABANAS (national savings program) and TASKA (insurance savings scheme) were introduced in 1971. Various financial institutions were authorized to accept deposits. Interest income was tax exempt, BI guaranteed the deposits, depositors received special incentives through lotteries, and the deposits could be used as loan collateral. The banking reforms, which reduced reserve requirements, removed easy access to refinance funds and permitted banks to develop their own financial products, thereby unleashing a scramble for savings and deposits. Interest rates have often been negative in real terms but, rather than raise rates, some banks have attempted to attract funds through reducing transaction costs to savers by offering door-to-door savings services. The banking law of 1992, however, limited deposit taking to those banks defined as commercial banks and rural credit banks.

The most well-analyzed rural savings experience is that of BRI and the introduction of SIMPEDES. The reforms of BRI were based on the idea that there was an unmet rural demand for savings that could be effectively mobilized for lending. BRI participated in the national TABANAS program beginning in 1976 and offered other savings instruments but only in its branch offices. TABANAS was found to have limitations for rural people because it permitted only two withdrawals per month so SIMPEDES was designed to permit unlimited withdrawals. It also provided savings opportunities for the previously untapped market of formal and informal rural organizations such as village treasuries, schools, development programs, sports associations, and informal savings and loan associations. The SIMPEDES design was first tested in 1984 with a 12 percent nominal annual interest, but with the added labor costs it proved to be too expensive. It was redesigned such that no interest was paid on small accounts of Rp25,000 or less, and 12 percent on accounts above Rp200,000. Over time, the interest rates were raised on the larger accounts, but generally not as high as the TABANAS rates (Robinson, 1992). The features of unlimited withdrawals, BRI guarantees of safety, and participation in savings lotteries proved to be the attractive features of SIMPEDES in rural areas. This stimulated its rapid growth as noted in Table XI.2.

The cost of mobilizing savings in the BRI unit desa system was recently estimated at about 15 percent (Maurer, 1997). This high cost has been balanced by a funds transfer price within BRI of about 15.5 percent. Therefore, besides providing a valuable service to savers, units can make profits by channeling excess funds to branches. Some 95 percent of the units are net fund providers to branches. More than a third of interest income in 1996 came from branch interest, and two thirds came from KUPEDES loans. The transaction costs to savers have been kept low through the customers' physical proximity to the BRI units. Units or village service posts, however, do not cover many remote areas; thus, opportunities still exist to tap savings by expanding the BRI network or by more aggressive savings mobilization by competing financial institutions.

MICROFINANCE

Microfinance does not play as visible a role in Indonesia as in some other Asian countries. Seibel and Parhusip (1998) prepared a summary of the loans and deposits reported for the BRI unit desas and the major categories of microfinance organizations as of December 1995 (Table XI.4). These data give a partial picture of access by the poor to financial services. Some 12,000 total rural banking outlets were reported with 4.7 million outstanding loans. BRI had about a quarter of the outlets and reported almost half the total loans with over 60 percent of the total volume. The Rp5 billion in total loans, however,

Table XI.4: Number and Market Share of Major Rural Financial Organizations, December 1995

Type of financial institution	Number	Outstanding Loans				Funds Mobilized			
		Accounts ('000)	Percent of total	Amount (Rp billion)	Percent of total	Accounts ('000)	Percent of total	Amount (Rp billion)	Percent of total
1. BRI – unit desa	3,482	2,264	48	3,194	63	14,483	76	6,016	81
Major microfinance organizations:									
2. BPR (Rural Credit Bank) and Secondary Banks	1,948	1,232	26	1,566	31	2,969	16	1,226	17
3. LKPDs (Small Financial Institutions)	1,978	261	6	224	4	456	2	118	2
4. BKDs (Village Credit Body, include BPR)	5,435	955	20	93	2	1,176	6	63	<1
Total rural	12,843	4,712	100	5,077	100	19,084	100	7,423	100
5. Commercial Banks	240	91,168		234,611		49,904		214,764	

Source: Adapted from Seibel and Parhusip (1998).

represented less than 2.2 percent of the total loans reported by commercial banks.

The remarkable feature of Indonesian microfinance is the 19 million saving and deposit accounts that represent 38 percent of the total number of accounts reported by the commercial banks. The unit desas were responsible for three quarters of these accounts, with over 80 percent of the total value. The other three categories of rural microfinance organizations perform less well in mobilizing savings. Their savings-to-loan ratio is less than one, indicating that they obtain resources from other sources to finance their loan portfolios. Considering that the commercial banks have rural operations and assuming that most rural households have only one account, it can be concluded that in 1995 some 20 million rural households had formal savings accounts and some 5 million had loans. Many clients would be defined as poor so this represents significant outreach.

As noted above, the geographic distribution of financial outlets appears to be most heavily concentrated in Central Java and other regions with high population densities. Some villages are served by competing banks, while more remote areas are likely to be underbanked.

The depth of outreach also seems substantial. The country's per capita GDP was reported to be just over $1,000 in 1995. The unit desas in 1996 reported average loan size roughly equal to that amount, but make loans as small as $11. The average loan size of the Central Java BKK was $47 in 1992. It is often thought that joint liability group lending is capable of reaching poorer clients than is individual lending, but the South Kalimantan BKK, which makes some group loans, reported an average of $100 per loan in 1995. The 1997–1998 evaluation of the PHBK project, however, reported that nearly a third of the small banks made loans as small as $10. Although BRI can make loans as small as the other banks, on average its loans are somewhat larger. Therefore, the poor may find it easier to get smaller loans to meet their demands in regions and villages where the other microfinance organizations are located. However, on the savings side, the unit desas do a much better job than other organizations in attracting small savings. The government guarantee of BRI deposits helps explain why savers moved their funds into BRI during the financial crisis as discussed further below.

INFORMAL FINANCE

In his comprehensive study of informal finance, Ghate (1992) noted there are fewer studies on informal finance in Indonesia than in many other Asian countries. There is little information on which to evaluate the types and total volume of informal finance, who uses it, and the terms and conditions. The following types of informal finance mentioned in the literature are presumably still common.

An ancient and widespread form of rotating savings and credit associations (RoSCAs) called *arisans* is found in both rural and urban areas. Membership tends to be small and contributions in the form of rice often substitute for money. Hospes (1992) discussed the important role of RoSCAs in a study of the coastal town of Tulehu in the Moluccan province. He noted ways in which formal and informal finance are linked, such as a local cooperative (KUD) opening interest-free deposit accounts for daily savings and depositing the funds in an interest-bearing account in the local BRI unit desa. Loans from itinerant traders, professional moneylenders, and *arisans*, in addition to friends and relatives, are most frequent in both Central and Eastern Java. Moneylenders appear to be prevalent in urban areas; the profession is associated with the ethnic minorities of the Chinese and the Batak tribe.

Informal finance is frequently found in trading. Bouman and Moll (1992) cite a case study of vegetable farmers in West Java in which most of the farmers obtain rice and production inputs from shopkeepers and traders. These loans are interest free, usually without collateral, but inputs bought on credit are priced higher than cash purchases. Loans are also obtained from traders against standing crops. In the *tebasan* system, the crop is purchased only 3 to 10 days before harvest. The *ijon* system involves the sale of the crop long before harvest and is frequently done for rice farming in Central Java, and for tree crops in East Java and other islands. The borrowers shift much of the price and marketing risk to the lender who assumes responsibility for harvesting and selling the crop. Suppliers' credits are used by the manufacturers and retail dealers of hand tractors and powered threshers. Land pawning through usufructuary mortgages also exists through *sewa*, in which land is leased by large landowners from small landowners for a fixed number of crop seasons. The net proceeds of cultivation repay both principal and interest. There is another form called *gadai*, in which the earnings constitute interest only and no fixed maturity is established.

IMPLICATIONS OF THE FINANCIAL CRISIS

The financial and economic crisis in Asia hit Indonesia particularly hard because it occurred when it was experiencing its worst drought in 50 years and international oil prices were in sharp decline. In the space of a year, the currency fell in value by 70 percent, inflation soared to over 50 percent, the economy rapidly contracted, unemployment soared, and the stock market lost much of its value (McGuire and Conroy, 1998). The central bank sharply increased interest rates, which raised the costs of production for borrowing firms. At the same time, the Government tried to preserve a social safety net for the poor by subsidizing food, fuel, electricity, medicine, and other essential items. The political clashes and eventual change of Government contributed to a climate of political and economic uncertainty.

Some fragmentary evidence exists about the impact of the crisis. The primary concern here is to understand how it affected the rural economy and rural financial institutions. At the aggregate level, there was little evidence of a credit crunch for firms up to early 1998, but strong sectoral shifts in funds may have contributed to localized credit problems (Ding, Domac, and Ferri, 1998). First, real deposit growth declined while funds denominated in foreign currency rose, indicating a reluctance to hold rupiah. Second, the market shares of State and foreign bank deposits rose while those of private national banks fell, indicating a flight to safety by depositors. This shift probably implied that borrowers from small private banks faced greater credit constraints than those of State banks. They would probably be small and medium-sized enterprises generally perceived to be risky. Third, the decrease in spreads between lending and deposit rates contributed to bank fragility. Several banks were closed and others were taken over by the Indonesia Bank Restructuring Agency (IBRA).

In January 1998, the Government declared a guarantee on all bank deposits to stem the outflow of deposits from private commercial banks. In mid-March 1999, the country announced the closure of an additional 38 banks, and the nationalization of seven others. A plan was approved by the Government to recapitalize seven State banks, 14 regional banks and 11 nationalized banks (Anon., 1999b). The total stock of bonds to be issued in 1998–1999 to finance the operations of IBRA was estimated to be Rp235 billion (25 percent of GDP). The annual budgetary costs of servicing the bonds and the operational costs of IBRA were estimated to be about 2 percent of GDP (Lane et al., 1999).

The experience of BRI varied depending on the economic sector served. The Strategic Business Unit that deals with corporate finance was hit particularly hard because its clients are large corporate units, many of which borrowed abroad and were seriously affected by the fall in the exchange rate. Most of these loans were nonperforming in August 1998 (Patten, 1998). In the Micro Unit, which includes the unit desas with the KUPEDES borrowers, these borrowers continued to pay back more than 97 percent of their loan amounts falling due. A nominal decline occurred in KUPEDES loans outstanding, but this was attributed more to weak demand than to supply constraints or rising interest rates. Nominal interest rates were raised from 1.5 to 2.2 percent per month flat only in September

1998. Borrowers reportedly feared taking on new debt because of a weakening in demand for their products due to the drought, stagnant incomes, layoffs, and inflation. This seems to imply that loans did not play an important role in consumption smoothing. BRI experienced a rapid increase in savings in both the branches and unit desas. This was explained by the perception of security in State-owned banks as well as an increase in the interest rates paid on savings.

The situation may be less favorable for small banks and special programs serving poorer clients. A survey of selected rural banks (BPRs) suggested that they were exercising caution in extending loans to new clients, were making fewer loans, and were increasing average loan sizes to cope with inflation. Some rural banks reported a rise in arrears, and were providing loans only to established customers and tightening collateral requirements. Some depositors were reported to be withdrawing their funds from BPRs and depositing them in BRI due to the perception of greater security (McGuire and Conroy, 1998). A case study of three BPRs revealed the wide variation that exists among local economies, the circumstances of different financial institutions, and the different management strategies employed to deal with the crisis. While one bank managed to adjust its lending and pricing policies to the changing circumstances, another had more difficulty and may fail (Reille and Gallman, 1998).

In response to the problems faced by rural banks, the central bank announced in June 1998 that working capital credits would be available to rural banks for expanding their financial resources for small enterprises and employment creation. These credits were to be made available at 15 percent per annum and could be relent at a maximum of 30 percent. This rate is below current market rates so there is a concern about sustainability.

There is evidence that NGOs and specialized projects were also experiencing a decline in loan recovery rates. The organizations associated with Catholic Relief Services face the common dilemma of rising operating costs and falling revenues. They have slowed disbursements and permitted selective loan rescheduling. They face the dilemma of focusing on either the

sustainability of the financial institution by raising interest rates or on the welfare of the borrowers who may be in a precarious situation (McGuire and Conroy, 1998).

It appears that State banks have fared better than private banks, and rural financial institutions have been much less affected than their urban counterparts. BRI unit desas have been relatively unaffected. The smaller rural banks and specialized programs face the greatest challenges. If, because of financial stress, the lenders cannot make new loans, they will break the financial relationships built up with borrowers. Borrowers may hesitate to repay if they believe that the lenders lack liquidity to make new loans. But the lenders may become illiquid precisely because of low recovery rates. Furthermore, the group-lending technology may be severely tested. Peer pressure to repay may give way to collective default if group members perceive that another member may not be able to repay. The lack of collateral may make the group lenders more vulnerable in this crisis than the individual lenders who have the ability to threaten to seize mortgaged property in the event of nonpayment. Another threat to the small banks is the recent flood of subsidized credit projects implemented to ease the economic problems created by the crisis. These programs represent threats to institutions trying to become independent of subsidies.

CURRENT POTENTIAL AND CONSTRAINTS FOR RURAL FINANCE

The Indonesian experience provides important lessons for rural Asia about what to do and what not to do in developing a sound and efficient rural financial system. Four lessons stand out. First, the important role played by technocrats, supported by foreign technical assistance, was obvious in effectively redesigning the BRI unit desa system, developing and pricing new loan and savings products, decentralizing responsibility and providing personnel incentive systems, and creating an image of a stable, long-term institution. Second, resources spent on institutional development may have little impact if the policy environment is unfavorable. The huge volume of resources that historically had been invested in BRI and its predecessors made little impact when the institution was saddled with the ill-conceived Bimas program, but contributed to a large payoff when policies and the institutional mission were changed. In fact, the most important contribution of the relatively small amount of donor support that went into the system in recent years may have been political support for technocrats facing pressure to undertake unhealthy practices and policies. Third, the massive amount of rural savings mobilized by the unit desas provides ample proof of the demand for attractive savings products and the capacity of rural people to save. Even within Indonesia this lesson does not seem to have been fully learned by financial institutions that are slow in designing products demanded by a rural clientele. Fourth, policies and institutions can be designed to achieve high levels of outreach, serve the very poor, and attain financial and institutional sustainability using an individual lending technology. The unit desas reach poor clients by using an individual loan technology requiring collateral, but group loans may be useful for reaching even poorer clients.

Although much has been written about rural financial institutions in Indonesia, there are uncertainties about several key questions, such as:

- How far have the formal financial institutions penetrated into rural areas, especially the more isolated regions of the country? What types of households and rural enterprises have and do not have access to formal loans and savings services? Are there specific regions in which the lack of access to formal financial services is a serious constraint for firms and households? How unique is the Central Java economy and culture relative to the rest of the country, and what are the limits to the transferability of lessons learned in that region?
- What financial institutions serve large farms and agribusinesses? How dynamic are they in meeting

evolving demands? How were these financial institutions and firms affected by the financial crisis?

- How well do rural cooperatives and special credit programs and projects perform? Whom do they serve with what products, and what is their potential for sustainability?

- How many formal financial services are provided to farmers largely engaged in seasonal crop production, compared with those to rural entrepreneurs with nonfarm enterprises? What types of financial services are provided to the very poor? Are there limitations in the BRI or other institutional models that affect how well they can be applied to typical farming situations or to very poor clients?

- How important is informal finance either as the sole or complementary source to formal finance? Whom does it serve at what terms and conditions? What lessons can be learned from informal finance to improve formal finance?

- How many subsidized lines of credit exist in rural areas today? How many have been implemented since the crisis, and what are the implications for financial institutions striving to achieve self-sufficiency? How fragmented have the rural financial markets become because of government and donor programs?

- What type of information is collected about clients of formal financial institutions, and how is it processed, analyzed, and shared among financial institutions?

These uncertainties need to be resolved before clear recommendations can be made about the priority needs of the rural financial system at this time. However, a number of issues identified in the literature require attention.

Creating the Policy Environment

The major short-term problem in Indonesia is how to manage the negative effects of the financial crisis, and restore the health of the financial system. The longer-term policy issues concern what needs to be done to prevent a repetition of the financial crisis. The crisis exposed the inherent weaknesses of the entire financial system, and especially the lack of transparency in financial operations. It is commonly known that political considerations distorted decisions about which projects to fund, and at what terms and conditions. The unnoticed "contagion" effect may be the greater acceptance of corruption in small financial transactions because of the corruption observed in large ones. The corrupting influences of family and political connections must be minimized at all levels of the financial system. This requires the creation and effective enforcement of rules about insider transactions and portfolio concentration. Implementing these changes requires strong support from the Government, but that may be difficult to obtain at this time of political uncertainty. Donors also need to insist on these changes.

The costs of restructuring the financial system are projected to be large; perhaps the annual costs will amount to 2 percent of GDP. Financing these costs will crowd out other demands for resources. The question of who will bear these costs may be an important factor influencing the country's future political stability. This experience demonstrates the extreme costs that a country may bear when bad financial and macroeconomic policies are implemented.

The desire to ease the social costs of the crisis is understandable. But the policy of creating unsustainable financial projects cannot be rationalized, given the country's negative experience with directed and subsidized programs. Although the intent may be laudable, these projects create several problems. First, unsubsidized organizations cannot compete by offering market-based products. Second, the lucky beneficiaries may come to expect subsidies and never graduate to become clients of market-based institutions. Third, resources for subsidies will always be limited, especially so in this crisis situation, so the few who get the subsidies gain at the expense of the many who do not. Fourth, weak enforcement procedures may undermine the repayment culture.

Creating and Strengthening the Financial Infrastructure

The major infrastructure challenge is to create an appropriate regulatory and supervisory framework for the financial system. The most prominent banking failures in the early 1990s were caused more by a lack of enforcement than by a lack of regulation (McLeod, 1999). Presumably that problem also contributed to the current crisis. The highly decentralized nature of the rural financial system, with thousands of independent banking units, complicates monitoring the health of the system and performing essential regulatory and supervisory functions. Therefore, the challenge for the lower end of the market is the difficulty of regulating and supervising the thousands of small financial institutions scattered in rural areas. They represent strength in the sense of extending the financial frontier outside the large cities and beyond the reach of BRI, but they pose a problem for effective regulation and supervision. On the one hand, their flexibility in serving local clients with market-determined financial products needs to be preserved while, on the other hand, they need to become more professional in their operations with appropriate safeguards for depositors and owners.

BI may not have the capacity to undertake this vast regulatory task, and it may have compromised its traditional regulatory role by managing donor and government projects designed to channel loans to targeted clients. The same problem exists for BRI because it must ensure the viability of the unit desas at the same time as it channels subsidized funds through its branches. A firewall needs to be built between these two sets of activities such that the problems caused by subsidized funds do not contaminate nonsubsidized operations.

The current patchwork arrangement is insufficient to deal with the regulatory complexities of the rural financial system. The danger, however, is that a heavy-handed regulatory framework will be applied to small institutions, which will raise costs, damage innovation, and strangle the system when the risks and costs to society are fairly small, even if a few small units collapse due to poor management or fraud. Alternative methods of regulation and supervision need to be explored. For example, the rural banks are eligible to join *Perbarindo*, the Association of Indonesian Rural Banks, which might evolve into a method of self-regulation. Likewise, the NGOs have discussed forming an association, but so far this has not occurred (McGuire, Conroy, and Thapa, 1998).

Little information was found in the Indonesian literature about the collection of information and its availability to financial institutions. Information about credit histories is necessary to permit lenders to screen possible clients and to determine the terms and conditions of loans made. It is unclear if there is any type of credit reporting system and who has access to it. If none exists, then consideration should be given to creating one.

Institutional Development

The immediate problems of the financial system imply that some rural financial institutions may require a government bailout to avoid collapse. This is a delicate problem because, on the one hand, the Government has to evaluate the social losses if they are permitted to fail. On the other hand, there is the problem of precedence and the moral hazard problem in that financial institutions in the future may undertake risky behavior if they believe they will also be bailed out if they fail. For the long term, lender-of-last-resort arrangements need to be worked out for rural lenders that face the systemic agricultural risks of droughts, floods, and other natural disasters.

There are several puzzles about the uneven pattern of development of Indonesian rural financial institutions. With the success of the BRI unit desas, it is puzzling why other institutions fail to adopt similar methods of management, and design and pricing of products. It is even more puzzling why donors support subsidized projects. If a dynamic organization such as BRI fails to serve a particular class of customers, such as the very poor, the question should first be asked why this is so. Perhaps there are good reasons to support competing institutions and to provide temporary subsidies to cover the cost of serving particular classes of clients. Unfortunately, the rationale for many institutional strengthening projects does not appear to be based on a good analysis of the underlying problems, and there is little explanation of how a particular project will provide anything more than a temporary respite from the problems.

Since there are many small and weak institutions, an obvious question is how to strengthen them. Consideration might be given to establishing an apex or second-tier institution. Experience has revealed several weaknesses in this approach, however, that have to be evaluated before assessing if this is a good recommendation for Indonesia. Apex organizations work better if there is a willingness by the participating institutions to adopt fundamental changes and a clear understanding of the nature of the improvements required. Apex organizations may also assume a regulatory role, but their promotional role may complicate their effectiveness as impartial agents for regulation and supervision (Gonzalez-Vega, 1998). The same problem may exist for the newly created DABANAS Foundation.

Many projects and programs funded by the national and provincial governments and donors with heavy subsidy elements have emerged in recent years. They focus mainly on loans in spite of the huge demand for rural savings services. These initiatives unfairly compete with nonsubsidized financial institutions and create expectations about entitlements for future subsidized loans. The subsidized pricing of financial services needs to be avoided. If subsidies are justified for nonfinancial services, they should be provided by institutions other than banks. The rationale for creating new rural programs and institutions is unclear in the face of the widespread network of unit desas, the BPRs, and the millions of clients served.

The pricing policy of BRI should be revised. No rationale can be found to justify why the unit desas should tax rural borrowers through excessively high lending rates, and generate huge profits that subsidize the rest of BRI operations, including large loans to richer clients. Unit desa lending rates should be set to cover the cost of funds, operating costs, losses, and costs of new product development, plus building prudent reserves. If any cross-subsidization is desired, it should be to tax the current rural borrowers to allow the unit desas to expand into more distant rural areas and to compensate them for making smaller loans to poorer clients. The unit desas might be given the freedom to lend to other banks and earn an interbank rate rather than be limited to BRI. This would improve resource allocation and expose the implicit subsidy now going to BRI. Alternatively, the rural units might be spun off as a separate institution such that the surpluses generated could be used to lower interest rates, expand the network, serve more clients, and create new products.[5]

---

[5] Apparently consideration was being given to various alternatives in 1998, including creating a separate bank to take over the corporate unit of BRI with its large portfolio of nonperforming loans.

XII RURAL FINANCIAL MARKET DEVELOPMENT IN THAILAND: MAXIMIZING OUTREACH, MINIMIZING SUBSIDIES

OVERVIEW OF THE FINANCIAL SYSTEM

State officials in Thailand have intervened in the economy and the financial sector to a lesser degree than in most other Southeast Asian countries. The monetary authorities have generally maintained positive interest rates, mandated few credit allocation requirements, and imposed only loose controls on international capital movements. State-owned financial institutions have played only a modest role in the banking system (Doner and Unger, 1993). The banking sector, however, has been given considerable protection from competition, and the agricultural sector has benefited from a long history of special credit policies and subsidies. The crisis beginning in 1997 revealed considerable financial sector weaknesses that are being addressed through policy and institutional reforms.

Until the late 1980s, the central bank's (Bank of Thailand, BOT) banking policy focused largely on the stability and solvency of financial institutions and the use of credit instruments to promote agriculture and exports. Occasionally, the BOT promoted competition and reduced concentration among the commercial banks, but simultaneously maintained policies that reduced competition as a way to support the solvency of weaker banks. Commercial banks were encouraged to cooperate on interest rates by creating in effect a cartel because of the fear that price competition for deposits would drive up interest rates and threaten the solvency of smaller banks. Existing banks were protected from competition by the refusal of the authorities to issue new licenses for additional domestic or foreign banks (Muscat, 1995).

Historically, financial operations in Thailand were subject to interest rate ceilings on both deposits and loans, to regulations on portfolio and branching, and to various types of compulsory credits. Deregulation was first undertaken in a gradual way, beginning with interest rate reform after the second oil shock (1979–1980). The ceiling on lending rates was raised from 15 percent to a level deemed appropriate by the Ministry of Finance. The ceiling rate on term deposits with maturity greater than one year was lifted in 1989 followed by the abolition of ceilings on all time deposits in 1990. The cap on savings deposits was removed in 1992 and all interest rates were liberalized except for agriculture (Vichyanond, 1995). These and other major policy changes are listed in Table XII.1.

The BOT implemented a reform plan in the 1990–1992 period that further deregulated interest rates, relaxed portfolio requirements and foreign exchange controls, improved the supervision and examination system, adjusted capital requirements, promoted financial innovations, and improved the payments system. The second three-year BOT plan beginning in 1993 focused on savings mobilization, development of the country into a regional financial center, and improvement of the central bank's operations (Vichyanond, 1995). Liberalization of the financial system without appropriate regulatory safeguards, however, contributed to the country's currency and financial crisis in 1997.

Growth of the total financial system has been impressive as measured by the broad money supply (M_2) and total assets of financial institutions (TAFI) shown in Table XII.2. The banking sector grew steadily from 1977 to 1986 as M_2/GDP rose from 37 to 59 percent while TAFI/GDP grew from 64 to 99 percent. Growth accelerated thereafter and by 1992 the two ratios reached 79 and 139 percent, respectively. The rapid

Table XII.1: Selected Financial Policy Changes in Thailand

Year	Policy
1966	Creation of BAAC
1967	BOT is authorized to rediscount promissory notes arising from agricultural transactions
1971	BOT begins to discount notes for agricultural marketing loans
1975	BOT adopts a quota system in which 5 percent of commercial banks' loans should go to agriculture. Rural branches of commercial banks directed to provide credit equivalent to at least 60 percent of deposits in the local area with one third mandated for agriculture
1976	Commercial bank lending to agriculture set at 7 percent of 1975 deposits
1977	Agricultural quota set at 9 percent of 1976 year-end deposits
1977	Bank branches are required to lend at least 60 percent of their local deposits in the local market area and at least one third must be lent to farmers
1978	Quota set at 11 percent of 1977 year-end deposits
1979-1980	Ceiling on lending rates raised
1987	Broadening of definition of agricultural activities to include small-scale rural industries
June 1989	Lifting of interest rate ceilings on term deposits with maturity greater than one year
March 1990	Removal of interest rate ceilings on time deposits
May 1990	Lifting of foreign exchange controls on current account transactions
January 1991	Broadening rural credit to include wholesale trading and regional industrial estates
January 1992	Removal of interest rate ceilings on savings deposits
June 1992	Removal of interest rate ceilings except on mortgage lending to low-income households
1992	Broadening of rural credits to include credit for farmers' secondary occupations and farm exports
March 1993	Establishment of Bangkok International Banking Facilities

Sources: Meyer, Baker, and Onchan (1979); Vichyanond (1995); Sacay, Randhawa, and Agabin (1996); Vajragupta and Vichyanond (1998).

growth of the economy as well as financial liberalization contributed to these trends (Vichyanond, 1995).

Commercial banks, the majority of which are privately owned, dominate the financial sector. Historically, they accounted for some 70 percent of the total assets of the financial system. Bank concentration is quite high and major banking families control the dominant banks (Donor and Unger, 1993). The five largest commercial banks owned 55 to 70 percent of

Table XII.2: Financial Deepening: M_2, TAFI, and GDP
(B Billion)

	1977	1980	1983	1986	1989	1992
M_2	151.1	251.8	450.5	672.8	1,207.1	2,123.0
TAFI[a]	257.6	449.6	758.5	1,123.2	2,022.3	3,716.7
GDP	403.5	662.5	921.0	1,133.4	1,856.5	2,671.4
M_2/GDP (percent)	37.4	38.0	48.9	59.4	65.0	79.5
TAFI/GDP (percent)	63.8	67.9	82.4	99.1	108.9	139.1

[a] TAFI: total assets of financial institutions.

Source: Vichyanond (1995, p. 310).

total commercial bank assets from 1962 to 1990. In 1990, they had 64 percent of the branches and mobilized almost 73 percent of total deposits.

An important feature of Thailand's financial history has been the relative autonomy of the BOT and its ability to restrain the growth of preferential or directed credit, with agriculture being the primary exception. In spite of the import substitution strategy in the 1960s, the manufacturing sector relied on foreign and domestic financial resources without receiving directed credit. Commercial banks functioned largely as merchant banks financing trade and domestic distribution of imported manufacturing goods. The share of manufacturing in total commercial bank credit rose slowly from 10 to 25 percent during 1958–1990, while the foreign trade share declined from 37 to 11 percent (Table XII.3).

Table XII.3: Allocation of Commercial Bank Credit by Selected Sectors, 1958–1990 (percent)

Sector	1958	1966	1974	1979	1983	1988	1990
Foreign trade	37.0	30.4	29.5	26.2	16.2	13.6	10.7
Domestic trade	16.8	15.5	21.1	22.4	24.6	18.9	17.6
Manufacturing	10.1	16.3	18.5	17.3	21.5	25.8	25.1
Construction and real estate	7.3	13.8	9.3	8.1	8.3	10.6	15.9
Agriculture	3.4	3.8	1.9	5.4	7.4	6.6	6.7

Source: Doner and Unger (1993, p. 105).

Government regulators in Southeast Asia have generally not regulated nonbank financial institutions as closely as commercial banks. Thailand faced major insolvencies in the 1980s and, at a cost of $190 million (about 0.48 percent of GNP), bailed out 50 finance companies that collapsed because of fraud and speculation on real estate and exchange rate transactions. The Government liquidated some finance companies, merged others, and sold some to new investors (Stiglitz and Uy, 1996). In another financial crisis, five commercial banks experienced financial difficulties in 1986–1987 due to a high concentration of unsecured insider loans and high international interest rates. The BOT established a pattern of supporting commercial banks in times of trouble by providing them with soft loans (Christensen et al., 1993). There was no explicit deposit insurance, nor any formal mechanism to take over insolvent institutions. Legal restrictions made it difficult to foreclose on debtors or to collect overdue debts once a commercial bank commenced legal action. The realistic option, therefore, was to provide low-interest loans to failing banks to prevent their failure. Many such loans are still on BOT's books. By bailing out troubled banks, the BOT limited the risks for depositors and shareholders but may have created moral hazard problems that contributed to the 1997 crisis.

APPROACH TO RURAL AND AGRICULTURAL FINANCE

Thailand has traditionally been a food-surplus country and has never implemented major, highly subsidized agricultural credit programs such as the Bimas program in Indonesia or the Masagana 99 program in the Philippines. However, financial support for agriculture has a long history. Since 1916, the Government has experimented with different institutional frameworks to provide cheap credit to the rural sector. The usual method was to encourage farmers to set up credit cooperatives and provide them with funding. The default rate was high and eventually the finance would dry up (Ammar et al., 1993).

Targeted financial support through the banking sector began with the rediscount facility, first introduced in 1958 to support exports, which were essentially agricultural. Initially it financed only rice exports, but was later broadened to include agricultural export products. In 1967 and 1971, the BOT was authorized to rediscount various types of promissory notes involving agricultural operations.

The creation in 1966 of the Bank for Agriculture and Agricultural Cooperatives (BAAC) as a specialized institution under the Ministry of Finance to provide loans to farm households, and its subsequent funding and regulation, represent the country's most important effort to support small and medium-sized farmers. An interesting aspect of financial development in Thailand is how the country has managed to avoid the errors of other countries that also created specialized agricultural finance institutions. The rapid growth of agriculture and the rural economy provided a strong demand for rural financial services, but several problems, including the land tenure system, have constrained the development of competitive financial institutions.

Political pressures in the 1970s pushed the BOT towards a more expansionary and developmental set of economic strategies. This resulted in the first large-scale sectoral credit allocation policy for agriculture, based on the widespread perception that the rural population was not benefiting equitably from the development process. Beginning in 1975, commercial banks were required to lend to agriculture an amount equal to 5 percent of their previous year's total lending. This allocation was gradually increased to its current level of 20 percent of total deposit liabilities outstanding at the end of the previous year. Shortfalls have to be deposited with BAAC where they earn a lower return than is available from alternative uses. Also in 1975, a condition for branch opening was imposed, in which the equivalent of at least 60 percent of deposits must be lent in the local area with one third allocated to agriculture. In 1978, the quota was divided into two categories: the larger one as "agriculture" with individual farmers as the target, and the smaller one being a new category of agribusiness and agro-industries. In 1987, the definition of agriculture was broadened to include small-scale rural industries. The commercial banks have not met their agricultural quotas in several years, but the BOT has chosen to ignore the problem. It is also believed that banks have submitted inflated reports on their quota adherence (Muscat, 1995). As noted in Table XII.4, the reported share of commercial bank credits to agriculture rose after the allocation policy was put into effect in the late 1970s; thus, the quota may have made some impact.

Table XII.4: Bills, Loans, and Overdrafts Outstanding to the Agricultural Sector and to Farm Households[a], 1970–1998
(B Million)

Year	Commercial banks (1)	BAAC (2)	Agricultural coops (3)	Total 1+2+3 (4)	Agricultural GDP (at current prices) (5)	Ratio agricultural credit/ GDP (6)
1970	637	1,209	456	2,302	38,786	0.059
1975	2,824	4,715	1,898	9,437	92,842	0.102
1980	12,588	12,464	3,877	28,929	173,806	0.166
1985	39,355	21,632	5,246	66,233	169,895	0.390
1990	99,354	38,821	7,739	145,914	279,268	0.522
1995	158,940	129,686	18,124	306,749	454,700	0.675
1996	164,019	169,767	20,770	354,556	502,600	0.705
1997	161,695	197,372				
Feb. 1998		195,465				

[a] Some double counting may exist in these data. Some commercial bank loans are extended to BAAC and agricultural coops. Similarly, some BAAC loans are extended to agricultural cooperatives.

Sources: Bank of Thailand, Department of Cooperatives Promotion, and Ministry of Agriculture and Cooperatives.

Several schemes have been established to channel funds to small and medium-sized enterprises (SMEs) that employ less than 200 workers. Rural areas benefit from SME incentives to the extent that they are located outside Bangkok. A Small

Industries Finance Office was created in the 1970s, but it extended very small volumes of credit and fell into serious arrears. Special SME credit windows and guarantees were set up in the 1980s and the funds and guarantees extended grew rapidly, but represented only a small fraction of the total financial system credit for industry (Muscat, 1995). A strong locational bias in favor of Bangkok and the lack of an effective promotional program made it difficult to develop strong support for rural industries. Credit policies were strongly oriented towards agriculture at the time (Akrasanee et al., 1983).

A study of provincial industries in the late 1980s found that interest rate ceilings encouraged financial institutions to concentrate their lending on larger firms with lower unit lending costs and lower perceived risks. Moreover, collateral was usually required in the form of land, plant, machinery, or equipment. It was also found that many firms needed to improve their bookkeeping in order to provide better financial information to financial institutions (Aungsumalin, 1990). Several programs have emerged in recent years to encourage industrial decentralization and rural enterprises. The Ministry of Industry provides workshops and training for small business operators, promotes specific occupational groups, strengthens small enterprises such as rice mills and handicrafts, and arranges contracting between private sector companies and village groups. The Ministry of Agriculture and Agricultural Cooperatives supports farmers in enterprises that add value to rural products (ADB, 1997b).

The broadening of the definition of rural credit in the early 1990s increased the scope for commercial banks and BAAC to lend for nonfarm activities. The BAAC charter was amended in 1992 to allow a fixed percentage of lending for agricultural-related activities operated by farmers. It began such lending in 1994 and in 1997 quickly disbursed an Asian Development Bank loan of $50 million to make medium- and long-term investment loans for activities to increase value-added production. The project also supported BAAC through training and operational reforms. At least one third of the beneficiaries were to be women. More than 7,000 subloans were made with a total value of

$46 million (average of approximately $6,500). A follow-on $200 million project was proposed in 1997 to be disbursed in the poorest 44 provinces (ADB, 1997b).

The country's land tenure system has been a constraint for commercial banks and other financial institutions that use traditional collateral-based lending to screen borrowers and enforce loan contracts. Many farmers on private lands and squatters on public lands do not have legal documents that lenders will accept as collateral. Security of tenure has a substantial effect on the agricultural performance of farmers, since an important determinant of greater productivity on legally owned land is better access to cheaper and longer-term institutional credit enjoyed by titled owners (Feder et al., 1988). Collateral substitutes are needed in this situation. BAAC lends to informal borrowing groups as a way to help resolve the loan collateral problem. Lending to cooperatives and farmers' associations is another way, provided that the members exert peer pressure on borrowers to repay.

THE EVOLUTION AND CURRENT STATUS OF KEY RURAL FINANCIAL INSTITUTIONS AND PROGRAMS

Information is presented here on rural finance in aggregate and on BAAC because of its exceptionally important role in rural areas. There have been no nationwide rural surveys to determine who has and who does not have access to financial services. It is generally believed that market segmentation occurs, in which commercial banks serve large farms and agroindustries; BAAC largely serves small and medium farms, cooperatives, and associations; the poor and landless are served mainly by informal finance and a few government programs and NGOs. Agricultural cooperatives and village-level credit unions may also reach poorer segments of the rural population.

Unfortunately, little can be said about either the top or bottom end of the rural financial market because there is a dearth of information about financial services provided by commercial banks, agricultural cooperatives, and rural credit unions. The limited information available about informal finance is presented below.

Thailand is one of the few Asian countries for which it is possible to track total agricultural lending over time. The total value of loans outstanding to agriculture at the end of 1996 was about baht (B) 355 billion (approximately $14 billion) relative to an agricultural GDP of B503 billion (about $20 billion) (Table XII.4). Since 1970, the volume of agricultural lending has grown faster than agricultural GDP. The ratio of agricultural credit outstanding to agricultural GDP steadily increased from 0.06 to over 0.70 by 1996. The most rapid increase occurred from 1989 to 1993 when the ratio doubled from 0.36 to 0.73. Even discounting some double counting in the data, the increase in total agricultural lending has been large. This finding is consistent with the technological change that has occurred in Thai agriculture, increased mechanization and onfarm capital formation, the emergence of medium- and long-term loans, and the expansion of large agribusinesses that have successfully penetrated export markets.[1]

Participants

Commercial banks, BAAC, and cooperatives are the most important rural financial institutions. The data on commercial bank lending to farmers may be inflated because of a bias in

---

[1] The rapid expansion in lending in recent years may have also contributed to the diversion of fungible funds into nonagricultural activities. This occurred in Brazil in the 1980s under a heavily subsidized credit regime when the agricultural credit/GDP ratio approached 0.80. Therefore, perhaps the expansion in agricultural lending contributed to Thailand's urban real estate bubble of the 1990s.

reports provided to BOT to show compliance with the agricultural lending quota. The commercial banks' total rural lending shows consistent growth in lending to farmers, as well as a rapid expansion in lending to agribusinesses, rural small-scale industries, and other purposes included in the changing definition of rural credit (Table XII.5). By 1996, the reported loans to farmers represented less than 20 percent of the total, while 20 percent went to agribusinesses, and almost half represented loans to unspecified other target groups. The share of bank lending in total agricultural lending rose from 27 percent in 1970 to 68 percent in 1990. Thereafter, the share of BAAC lending increased marginally until it reached 48 percent of total rural lending in 1996. The trend continued into 1997 when commercial banks' total nominal lending actually fell while that of BAAC rose. Lending by agricultural cooperatives has been small by comparison, and represented only 6 percent of the total in 1996.

The number and distribution of banking outlets have a strong influence on access to banking services in rural areas. Transaction costs for savers and borrowers fall when banking outlets expand and move closer to rural businesses and residences. There was a six-fold increase in commercial bank branches from 1970 to 1996 (Table XII.6). The major expansion in BAAC outlets occurred in the 1990s, when the number of provincial and district branches rose from less than 200 to more than 500, and the number of field offices increased from 615 to 875. Not surprisingly, this period coincides with the rapid increase in BAAC market share.

Outreach

The best insights on access to formal rural finance are obtained by analyzing BAAC. It has recently received a great deal of international attention because of its impressive performance in outreach, lending portfolio, savings mobilization, efficiency, profitability, and subsidy independence. The penetration of BAAC in rural areas is more significant

Table XII.5: Outstanding Rural Loan Portfolio of Commercial Banks, 1987–1996
(B Million)

| Year | Loans made to: | | | | | Deposits at BAAC | Total rural loans |
	Farmers	Minor occupations	Small-scale industries	Other target groups	Agri-businesses		
1987	45,838	-	10,026	-	35,988	12,340	104,192
1988	56,765	-	16,446	-	43,357	14,118	130,687
1989	72,490	-	27,493	5,910	51,473	14,486	171,852
1990	96,203	-	37,803	7,328	63,397	14,503	219,234
1991	115,737	-	46,109	34,361	77,756	17,092	291,055
1992	130,138	862	55,944	81,927	94,150	11,488	374,509
1993	141,539	5,456	70,190	136,906	116,075	4,556	474,722
1994	142,268	7,677	79,338	205,213	132,048	7,556	574,100
1995	149,239	8,029	92,859	310,187	151,358	7,137	718,808
1996	151,148	9,246	103,617	375,322	171,380	3,981	814,693

Source: Bank of Thailand.

Table XII.6: Number of Commercial Bank Branches, BAAC Outlets, and Agricultural Cooperatives, 1970–1996

		BAAC		Agricultural Cooperatives	
Year	No. of commercial bank branches	No. of provincial and district branches	No. of field offices	No. of cooperatives	No. of members
1970	647	45	205	1,910	226,526
1975	895	58	317	575	363,115
1980	1,478	58	498	875	778,175
1985	1,835	68	580	1,059	837,434
1990	2,358	168	615	1,464	1,007,637
1994	3,194	365	840	2,461	3,717,609
1995	3,235	494	847	2,832	3,942,416
1996	3,718	535	875	3,097	4,338,095

Sources: Bank of Thailand, BAAC, Office of Agricultural Economics in the Ministry of Agriculture and Cooperatives.

than any other single rural financial institution in Asia. Some 4.7 million of the country's five million plus farm households are registered for its services, although in any one year not all have loans. In 1996, 3.4 million households (72 percent) were registered as individual branch clients, while the remaining 28 percent were registered as members of 877 agricultural cooperatives and 295 farmers' associations that borrowed from BAAC. Therefore, directly or indirectly, it reached about 90 percent of the country's farmers.

The depth of outreach, referring to the wealth or poverty level of the clients, has not been measured and can only be inferred from BAAC loan size information. In 1995, the average disbursement per client for individual loans was B24,176 ($971) or about 35 percent of the country's GDP per capita that year of almost B70,000. This ratio has remained fairly constant during recent years suggesting that the rapid expansion of its portfolio has not occurred only through making larger loans, but also by expanding its client base. Moreover, over 1.1 million (51 percent) of the 2.1 million loans made in fiscal year 1996 were in the loan size category of B30,000 or less. The average loan in this category was about B16,500 ($660) or 24 percent of GDP.

The average size of all BAAC loans outstanding in 1995 was $1,161, or 42 percent of GDP (Muraki, Webster, and Yaron, 1998). These relatively small loan sizes suggest that BAAC must be reaching fairly poor clients, if not the poorest of the poor. Moreover, the cooperatives and associations that on-lend BAAC funds possibly reach members who may be even poorer. Over the past five years, more than 50 percent of BAAC loans have been made in the lower-income northeastern and northern regions, which is further evidence of its support to the poor.[2]

The total BAAC loans outstanding have grown dramatically, especially from 1990 to 1996 when loan volume quadrupled and the total portfolio reached B177 billion (about $6.9 billion) (Table XII.7).[3] The mix of loans has changed considerably. For example, loans to cooperatives and associations represented 64 percent of the total in 1975, but 20 years later that share had fallen to only 8 percent. Overall, the repayment rate rose from about 70 percent to close to 90 percent during this same period. Repayment rates have been much lower on cooperative and association loans; thus, the shift to more individual lending contributed to raising the repayment rate.

BAAC's main loan products include short-term, cash credit, medium-term, and long-term loans. Medium- and long-term loans have been expanding as a reflection of the increased capital intensity of agriculture and several government programs implemented by BAAC. BAAC is fairly unique in rural Asia because of the relatively large share of its portfolio in longer-term loans. In 1995, 60 percent of loan disbursements

---

[2] If the data were available, average loan sizes should be disaggregated by region and compared with regional GDP because of the wide regional disparities in income. From the present analysis, it is impossible to learn how far down into the poverty profile BAAC reaches in the poorer compared to the richer regions.

[3] BAAC is a large institution. According to Asiaweek statistics on the 500 largest Asian banks, BAAC is about equal in size to Thailand's seventh largest commercial bank (Asiaweek, 11 September, 1998.).

Table XII.7: BAAC Loans Outstanding
(B Million)

Year	BAAC clients				Repayment rate (%)
	Farmers	Agricultural cooperatives	Farmers' associations	Total	
1970	754	409	0	1,163	
1975	2,473	1,642	441	4,556	69.0
1980	7,134	3,614	415	11,163	73.3
1985	17,032	4,068	243	21,343	72.5
1990	36,850	4,870	203	41,923	85.8
1991	47,766	5,995	198	53,959	87.9
1992	66,137	6,892	193	73,222	88.8
1993	75,608	7,493	191	83,292	88.6
1994	97,680	8,305	169	106,154	88.2
1995	127,243	10,747	180	138,170	86.1
1996	162,640	14,241	183	177,064	87.2

Source: BAAC

went for short-term and cash credit loans, 20 percent for medium-term and 17 percent for long-term, while 57 percent of loans, outstanding were medium- or long-term (Muraki, Webster, and Yaron, 1998). Short-term loans have maturities of 12 months and are used mostly for agricultural production and related activities such as food processing. Cash credit loans are lines of credit that borrowers withdraw only as needed. Medium-term loans have maturities of more than one year up to three to five years, and are used for purchasing machinery and livestock. Long-term loans have maturities of up to 15 years and are typically used for purchasing agricultural equipment. The arrears rates have been somewhat higher for medium- and long-term loans (Fitchett, 1997).

BAAC administers several policy-based lending programs on a fee basis for the Government. These programs have included the Land Reform Efficiency Improvement Plan under the Land Fund, the Agricultural Rehabilitation Plan under the Ministry of Agriculture and Cooperatives, and the Revolving Fund for Refinancing Old Debts of Poor Farmers under the Office of the Permanent Secretary to the Prime Minister. They have highly subsidized interest rates, each has specific financial policies and procedures and, for some programs, the selection of borrowers and loan approval are not BAAC's responsibility (Sacay, Randhawa, and Agabin, 1996). These loans often have lower recovery rates than BAAC's regular loans.

The problem of access to loans by persons without loan collateral has been resolved by BAAC for working capital loans by making joint liability group loans, in which the farmer-members guarantee each other's loan repayment. The minimum number of borrowers per group is five and the average is 15. First-time borrowers are provided with small loans and loan size is increased with repeat loans. The loan ceiling per borrower is B50,000 but average loan size has been less than half this amount. Group members are also eligible for additional individual loans of up to B50,000 on the basis of two guarantors. Farmers with titled land can also use it as collateral for individual loans. BAAC staff hold group meetings to encourage timely loan recovery and increase peer pressure (Muraki, Webster, and Yaron, 1998). Borrower transaction costs may be lower for BAAC than for commercial bank loans because BAAC loan officers work in the field in closer proximity to their clients, although there are additional transaction costs in attending group meetings. The groups screen their own members and this process plus peer monitoring may reduce lending risks. To qualify, loan applicants need to have been engaged in an agricultural activity for at least one year in the market area of the local branch, should receive more than half their total income from farming, and should not be indebted to an agricultural cooperative, farmers' association, or commercial bank (GTZ, 1997).

Relatively little is known about the outreach of agricultural cooperatives and village credit unions. Supposedly their loans are in addition to those made directly by BAAC to individual farmers. In the mid-1970s some 40,000 informal groups with an average of 15 members borrowed directly from BAAC. Each of the 600-plus agricultural cooperative societies in operation at the time had about 700 members, while each of the 3,000-plus farmers' associations had an average of about 100 members (Meyer, Baker, and Onchan, 1979). This would imply that some

700,000 farmers were reached indirectly by BAAC. The number of agricultural cooperatives oscillated until 1990 as the system went through periods of consolidation and reform. Steady growth occurred in the 1990s, when the number of cooperatives doubled from almost 1,500 to over 3,000, and the membership grew four-fold from one million to over four million. Part of this expansion in cooperative membership may have been because farmers expected to get loans by becoming members.

A recent study by Preedasak and NaRanong (1998) provides some insights into cooperative lending. Lending to members has always been the main activity of general agricultural cooperatives. In 1995, they were reported to have B13.8 billion outstanding, an amount roughly equal to 11 percent of BAAC's outstanding loans to individual farmers that year. The cooperatives rely mostly on loans received from BAAC, which is consistent with BAAC's reported B10.7 billion in loans to cooperatives in 1995. Cooperatives charge interest rates slightly higher than those charged by BAAC, but a few percentage points below those of commercial banks. Most cooperatives require that 5 percent of the loan must be deducted and assigned to the borrower's shares in the cooperative. About 60 percent of the loans are short term, i.e. for one year or less. Most of the rest are intermediate loans of one to three years. Cooperative lending was reported to have grown from B4.4 billion in 1988 to B13.8 billion in 1995, an increase roughly equivalent to the increase in BAAC lending to cooperatives. The cooperatives have had a checkered history. Quality leadership, active participation by members, optimum size and scope of operations, stable income of members, and avoidance of top-down promotion by the Government were factors found to influence their performance.

No comprehensive rural household surveys have been conducted to determine who have and who do not have access to financial services. Some insights are available from two rural household surveys by the Thailand Development Research Institute (TDRI) conducted in northeastern Thailand. The proportion of rural households that reported formal loans in a 1995/96 survey was significantly larger than in a 1986 survey, while the proportion reporting only informal loans declined. It is surprising that the proportion that did not obtain loans was 42 percent in both surveys. The large proportion of the total rural population reportedly served by BAAC makes it hard to interpret this result. Perhaps both the information about BAAC outreach and the level of borrowing reported in these surveys were somehow biased. Or perhaps this particular study area is unique with respect to the rest of the country. If some 40 percent of the rural population regularly do not borrow, in spite of the wide network of BAAC branches and cooperatives, it casts doubt on the argument that additional special institutions and programs are needed to increase outreach.

According to the surveys, most households that demanded credit obtained it somewhere. No evidence was presented on the degree of credit rationing the households experienced from formal or informal sources. The nonborrowing households were not disaggregated so there is no way to determine how access to finance might vary by income or wealth category. The share of loan contracts provided by BAAC increased from 17 to 25 percent of total loans between the two surveys, cooperatives increased their share from 8 to 11 percent, while the commercial bank share declined from 5 to 2 percent. Likewise, the BAAC share of loan volume rose from 19 to 39 percent, that of cooperatives rose from 9 to 14 percent, and that of banks fell from 14 to 5 percent. The average size of commercial bank loans was B71,000 ($2,840). Cooperative loans averaged B25,135 ($1,005), and BAAC loans averaged B23,720 ($949). These results suggest, as expected, that commercial banks serve wealthier clients, but BAAC and cooperatives may compete for a similar market niche. Locational considerations may determine whether BAAC or a cooperative serves a particular client. Cooperatives, however, do not supply the savings services that rural households demand. Poorer rural households and households that engage primarily in nonfarm enterprises probably have less access to formal sector loans.

Data from the 1995/96 TDRI survey in the province of Nakhon Ratchasima in northeastern Thailand also showed the relative loan shares and average loan sizes of the various sources of loans reported by farmers (Table XII.8). As expected, commercial banks made the largest loans (B71,350) but had less than an 8 percent market share. BAAC accounted for more than half the loan volume but the cooperatives actually had slightly larger loans (B25,135 = $1,008). Most cooperatives offer savings and time deposits. Interest rates are slightly higher than commercial banks and interest is tax exempt. Total savings rose rapidly from 1988 to 1995, and the loan-to-savings ratio fell from a high of 2.67 in 1988 to 1.33 in 1995.

Table XII.8: Total Loans and Average Size of Loans in Rural Nakhon Ratchasima, 1995

Source of loan	Total loans (B)	Share (%)	Average size of loan per contract (B)
Formal lenders	5,106,403,059	80.13	25,675
BAAC	3,293,858,210	51.69	23,720
Commercial banks	503,660,339	7.90	71,350
Agricultural cooperatives	1,139,504,182	17.88	25,135
Village credit unions	13,372,040	0.21	3,527
Other cooperatives	132,714,536	2.08	128,705
Government fund	18,119,652	0.28	8,206
Insurance companies	5,174,100	0.08	8,652
Informal lenders	1,265,986,559	19.87	16,264
Lenders inside the village	278,815,987	4.38	13,457
Lenders from other villages	320,795,295	5.03	22,105
Lenders in the district	100,073,152	1.57	20,340
Lenders in the province	6,773,433	0.11	16,401
Relatives	480,394,636	7.54	14,566
Village funds	144,033	0.00	1,000
Others	78,990,023	1.24	19,026
Total	6,372,389,618	100.00	

Source: Preedasak and Naranong (1998).

Sustainability

The issue of sustainability of rural financial institutions largely concerns BAAC and the agricultural cooperatives. BAAC is dependent on subsidies, although not as heavily as many specialized agricultural lending institutions in developing countries. The subsidies include soft loans from donors, preferential interest rates for rediscounting loans with BOT with a guarantee from the Ministry of Finance, exemptions from reserve requirements on deposits, and exemptions from income and other taxes and certain documentation fees (Sacay, Randhawa, and Agabin, 1996). Moreover, the requirement that Thai Government offices hold their deposits in Government-held financial institutions implies an additional subsidy of unknown magnitude.

Muraki, Webster, and Yaron (1998) estimated the subsidy dependence index (SDI) for BAAC for several years. The SDI is a ratio that calculates the percentage increase in the present average on-lending rate required to eliminate all subsidies in a given year, while keeping the return on equity equal to the approximate nonconcessional borrowing cost. In 1995, for example, the average interest rate earned on the loan portfolio was 11.0 percent and the SDI was estimated at 35.4, such that all subsidies could have been eliminated by obtaining an average yield on portfolio of 14.89 percent (11.0 percent x 1.35 = 14.8). That is, if interest rates on loans were 3.89 percentage points higher, all else being equal, subsidies would have been zero.[4] Over the past decade, the SDI rose (i.e., subsidies were greater)

---

[4] This type of analysis ignores the interest rate elasticity of demand for loans. Borrowers of larger loans with better access to commercial banks might reduce their demand for loans if their interest rates were increased by 3–4 percentage points. However, the large number of borrowers of small loans that represent 50 percent or more of the total portfolio have fewer options, so a simple leveling of interest rates across loan sizes would probably have little impact on demand, but a large effect on reducing subsidies. Furthermore, it would tend to bring the interest rate structure more in line with the transaction costs of making smaller loans.

during periods when the rate of inflation rose, and it fell when inflation fell. This pattern was explained as stickiness in lending rate adjustments. As a price taker, when inflation rises, BAAC has to pay competitive rates on deposits, but because of political pressures, it does not immediately adjust lending rates sufficiently upwards. When inflation falls, it doesn't immediately reduce lending rates consistent with falling deposit rates. Using an average- rather than marginal-cost pricing policy for setting lending rates is another explanation for this pattern.

BAAC's need for subsidies cannot be attributed to low levels of efficiency. In fact, it is noted for its high productivity and efficiency and several measures demonstrate improvements made in recent years. Evaluation of staff performance and the awarding of bonuses and promotions are linked to energetic savings mobilization, and some BAAC branches have become self-financing. Although there was a slight decline, from 384 to 363, in loan accounts per employee from 1989 to 1995, the value of loans outstanding rose from B4.24 million ($170,300) to B10.5 million ($421,480).

Three main factors contributed to the growth of BAAC loans. First, inflation represented about one fifth of the total growth. Second, average loan sizes increased because of the larger share of medium- and long-term loans. Third, employees increased their efficiency in response to the incentive systems. The number of accounts per branch fell, but the average loan balance per branch rose while the number of staff per branch stayed roughly constant. During this same 1989 to 1995 period, total administrative and financial expenses as a share of average loan portfolio fell from 16.1 to 12.3 percent. This occurred even as BAAC's resources shifted from large commercial bank deposits toward more expensive savings mobilization from the public. Personnel expenses fell from 2.9 to 2.3 percent of loans outstanding during this same period (Muraki, Webster, and Yaron, 1998).

Incentives are used to improve staff efficiency. Staff promotions are tied to performance. Staff compensation consists of fixed basic salaries plus bonuses based on verifiable indicators. The basic salaries are higher than the payment structure of

Government institutions but lower than banking industry standards. Financial incentives are significant and allow for bonus payments up to a maximum of five months of salary. The system is based on a) number of clients served by the bank, b) the amount of loans made, and c) other criteria related to quality of services and cost control. At the branch level, performance indicators include credit targets, repayment, savings mobilization and profits (Sacay, Randhawa, and Agabin, 1996). Average salaries including bonuses doubled from 1989 to 1995 so that an average salary was roughly 3.5 times GDP per capita. A unique feature of the incentive system is that the Thai Rating Information Service reviews BAAC performance at the end of the year and determines the systemwide level of bonuses to pay.

In 1995, 82 percent of BAAC's revenue came from loans to farmers, 5 percent from loans to cooperatives and associations, 5 percent from deposits and investments, and 8 percent from other income. The share of income from farmers has risen relative to that of cooperatives and associations as the share of farmer loans has risen. In 1995, almost 70 percent of total expenses were due to interest costs and other financial expenses. Administrative expenses made up the other 30 percent with 21 percent attributed to salaries, wages, and bonuses. Return on equity (ROE) ranged from 6.5 to 7.1 percent from 1989 to 1994, then fell to 3.9 percent in 1995. Likewise, returns on assets were low, varying between 0.52 and 0.55 percent, then fell to 0.28 percent (Muraki, Webster, and Yaron, 1998).[5] By comparison, net profits of Thai commercial banks rose from 0.7 percent of total assets in 1989 to 1.58 percent in 1996 (Vajragupta and Vichyanond, 1998).

---

[5] As a generalization, US banks with 8 percent equity can be expected to earn a return on assets of 1 to 1.5 percent and a return on equity of 12 to 20 percent. Another point of comparison is the highly profitable bank for the poor, BancoSol, in Bolivia. It is much smaller, with $63 million in loans in 1997 serving 76,000 clients. Its return on equity ranged from 13.3 to 23.7 percent between 1994 and 1997. What is also problematic about the BAAC returns is that its policy on making provisions for bad debt may not be realistic given the past record of loan losses.

These relatively poor financial results are in part due to five pricing policies of BAAC. First, it tries to maintain low interest rates. On average in 1995, it paid depositors a nominal rate of 7.6 percent on savings but only charged 11 percent on loans. After adjusting for inflation, real deposit rates were 1.7 percent and lending rates were 4.9 percent. Second, it charges higher rates for larger loans and cross-subsidizes its small clients. For example, in 1995, nominal interest rates for short- and medium-term loans were 9 percent for loans of B30,000 or less, 11 percent for B30,000 to B60,000, 12.5 percent for B60,000 to B1 million, and 14.5 percent for more than B1 million.[6] The average rate structure for long-term and agriculture-related loans was a little lower. Third, the interest rate spread of 3.8 percent in 1994 fell to 2.6 percent in 1995 because interest rates were not adjusted enough to cover the rise in inflation.

The fourth pricing policy was the requirement for BAAC in October 1995 to reduce nominal interest rates from 11 to 9 percent for loans less than B30,000. In April 1996, the reduction was extended to loans less than B60,000. As a result, there was a decline in very small loans from 50 percent of total loans made in 1995 to 38 percent in 1996, with a corresponding fall in total loan volume from 17 to 10 percent. BAAC also imposed a surcharge of B500 for loans between B100,000 and B1 million, and B1,000 for loans more than B1 million. Fifth, BAAC charges 3 percent less on wholesale loans made to cooperatives and associations than on retail loans to individual borrowers. Lower transaction costs for these larger loans justify a somewhat lower rate, but a 3 percent discount may be too large to cover costs and risks (Muraki, Webster, and Yaron, 1998).

---

[6] The distribution of volume of loans to individual clients by rate of interest in fiscal 1995-1996 was: 9 percent of clients were paying 36 percent interest; 11 percent were paying 13 percent interest; 12.5 percent were paying 44 percent interest; and 14.5 percent were paying 7 percent interest. In the event of natural calamities, unpaid loans are restructured and no penalty is assessed. Unauthorized arrears are assessed a 3-percent-per-annum penalty.

DEPOSIT MOBILIZATION

Rural savings mobilization has not been a particularly strong feature of financial policy in Thailand. Commercial banks are the most important financial institutions in providing demand and savings services in rural areas. The banking system held about B4.3 trillion (about $140 billion) in total deposits in late 1997 and early 1998 (Table XII.9). Provinces outside Bangkok held 34 to 38 percent of the total deposits from 1980 up to 1997, suggesting that the Bangkok bias of economic activity did not change much during that period. In recent years, the provinces outside Bangkok held proportionately more savings and time deposits, but fewer demand deposits, suggesting a slightly greater preference for savings than for transactions instruments.

BAAC's total deposits are small by comparison with those of the other banks (Table XII.10). At the end of 1997, they totaled about B73 billion (approximately $2.6 billion), which was less than two percent of total bank deposits, or about 5 percent of total deposits of commercial banks outside Bangkok. Total

Table XII.9: Commercial Bank Deposits: Total and for Provinces
Outside Bangkok
(B Million)

		Provinces outside Bangkok			
Year	Total commercial bank deposits	Percentage of total deposits	Percentage of demand deposits	Percentage of savings	Percentage of time deposits
1970	31,885				
1975	86,559				
1980	214,994	38.2	22.9	50.9	38.8
1985	557,044	37.1	21.7	35.7	38.7
1990	1,436,514	35.2	20.8	31.9	37.5
1995	3,227,697	36.9	13.3	38.0	38.2
1996	3,666,028	37.3	15.1	37.7	38.6
1997	4,304,040	34.0	9.9	37.7	38.6
Mar 1998	4,342,407	34.7	16.0	32.9	35.9

Source: Bank of Thailand

Table XII.10:   Sources of BAAC Deposits
(B Million)

Year	Total	Percentage				
		Demand	Savings	Compulsory	Time	Commercial bank
1970	266	0	6.3	21.3	35.3	37.0
1975	2,845	0	10.0	10.8	20.5	58.8
1980	9,079	0	5.1	0.0	17.7	77.1
1985	15,348	0	12.4	0.0	17.9	69.7
1990	32,484	<1	26.7	0.0	31.7	44.6
1995	89,795	<1	52.0	0.0	40.0	7.9
1996	63,809	<1	62.3	0.0	31.3	6.2
1997	73,033	<1	74.6	0.0	26.2	4.9

Source: Bank of Thailand

BAAC deposits actually peaked in 1995 at close to B89 billion (about $3.6 billion at the time). The volume of commercial bank deposits in BAAC has declined in recent years and it has mobilized deposits from other sources. Commercial bank deposits represented over 70 percent of BAAC deposits in the 1980s. These deposits reached a peak of B17 billion in 1991 (equal to 41 percent of BAAC's deposits that year), then started to fall such that at the end of 1997 they totaled B3.6 billion, representing only 5 percent of BAAC deposits. Savings deposits have been the most popular instrument offered by BAAC, and their share now reaches close to three fourths of all deposits. Time deposits have varied from 20 to 40 percent of total deposits.

Information on the source and size of savings and time deposits provides insights into the nature of BAAC depositors, and reveals the potential noninterest costs and risks of savings mobilization. Thai Government offices are required to deposit their funds in Government-owned financial institutions. Because of its aggressive savings campaign and the political preference of some organizations to choose BAAC over other State-owned banks, BAAC has been successful in capturing a large proportion of these deposits (Muraki, Webster, and Yaron, 1998). This represents another implicit subsidy to BAAC. The composition of BAAC savings and time deposits for 1995 (Table XII.11) shows that private individuals held 4.1 million savings accounts with a total balance of B1.1 billion, which represented 99.5 percent of all savings accounts and about 62 percent of total savings. Public sector agencies held less than one percent of total savings accounts, but they represented almost 36 percent of total savings. A similar pattern exists for time deposits.

The size distribution of savings accounts reveals that the very large number of small accounts represents an important but small share of total savings (Fitchett, 1997). At the end of 1995, some 3.4 million savings accounts out of a total of more than 4.1 million (83 percent) were private individual accounts with balances of only $201 or less. These small accounts represented only 6 percent of total savings. The average size of these accounts was $33. More than half a million additional savings accounts in the range of $201–2,008 were held by private individuals. Clearly, poor people must have held some of these small accounts. If each person held just one savings account, then the 4.1 million accounts held

Table XII.11: BAAC Savings and Time Deposits, 1995

Item	Savings	Time	Total
Private individuals			
No. of accounts	4,148,041	246,498	4,394,539
Percentage of total	99.5	99.3	99.5
Amount ($'000)	1,156,638	674,582	1,831,220
Percentage of total	61.7	46.8	55.2
Cooperatives and associations			
No. of accounts	5,366	679	6,045
Percentage of total	0.1	0.3	0.1
Amount ($'000)	47,259	8,759	56,018
Percentage of total	2.5	0.6	1.7
Public sector agencies			
No. of accounts	16,520	1,046	17,566
Percentage of total	0.4	0.4	0.4
Amount ($'000)	671,933	756,698	1,428,631
Percentage of total	35.8	52.8	43.1
Total			
No. of accounts	4,169,927	248,223	4,418,150
Amount ($'000)	1,875,830	1,440,039	3,315,869

Source: Adapted from Fitchett (1997).

by private individuals surpassed the total number of BAAC loans outstanding at the end of 1995 (3.1 million) by about a million. At the other end of the size distribution, BAAC had just under 1,900 private savings accounts in the size category of more than $40,161 that represented over 10 percent of total savings. The situation is even more striking with larger public-sector agency accounts. There were only 787 of these large accounts, but they represented one third of total savings.

A similar size distribution holds for time-deposit accounts. Accounts with $201 or less held by individuals represented 43 percent of total accounts, but only 0.4 percent of total volume of time deposits. Conversely, the 348 larger-size deposits (more than $40,161) for public-sector agencies accounted for only 0.1 percent of total time deposits, but more than 50 percent of the total value of all time deposits. Attracting large public sector accounts may be a cheaper way to mobilize savings but, at the same time, it exposes BAAC to the risk of a large loss in savings if only a few are withdrawn. This occurred in 1997/98 when Government entities and State enterprises responded to the Government's austerity measures by drawing down their BAAC deposits. From 1996/97 to 1997/98, individual deposits grew from 50 to 58 percent of the total while those of Government and State fell from 48 to 40 (BAAC/GTZ, 1998).

BAAC has introduced a variety of specialized savings products tailored to the rural environment including funeral aid associations, personal accident insurance, women's savings programs, and savings for the haj pilgrimage. However, no information is available on how many clients use these products or the volume of savings mobilized. A recently designed product, OM SAP THAWI CHOKE (multiple fortune savings account), was created and marketed by BAAC in conjunction with the GTZ Self-Help Linkage Project. The minimum opening balance is only $2, the interest rate is 4 percent per annum, and the account holder participates in semi-annual lotteries that offer as prizes goods that are popular in rural areas. Savings accounts have unlimited withdrawals but accounts below B2,000 ($79) are not eligible for the lottery

(Fitchett, 1997). By January 1997, the number of savers had risen to more than half a million nationwide with total savings of $70 million. There are questions, however, about the ability of this type of instrument to significantly raise savings in the long run. Since average deposits are close to the minimum level required to join the lottery, the depositors' primary motivation may be to gamble rather than accumulate financial savings in the long run (Poapongsakorn, Ammar, and Charoenpiew, 1998; BAAC/GTZ, 1998).

Since 1974, the Department of Community Development (DCD) of the Ministry of Interior has persuaded villagers to form thousands of village level credit unions (*Kloom Orm Sup*), small-scale financial institutions operated by villagers. Most serve only one village and most successful credit unions do not register because they do not want to follow DCD rules on interest rates. They serve an important market niche by gathering savings from people who want to or can only save in amounts too small to justify a trip to a bank or even a cooperative. Each member pledges to save a certain amount each month. The members meet once a month, accumulate the savings, and almost immediately lend them out; thus, their operation is similar to informal rotating savings and credit associations (RoSCAs). By 1995, there were over 11,000 credit unions with almost 900,000 members (average of 79 members) reporting a total of B1.8 billion in savings (about $74 million). Profits from lending and other businesses are divided among members according to the magnitude of their savings. On average, about half the savings mobilized are lent out and the balance is deposited in the banking system. Many charge borrowers 2 to 3 percent per month on loans and pay interest rates on savings that are higher than banks. Since credit unions require regular savings, they are more successful in southern Thailand where villagers have steadier incomes.[7] Many credit

---

[7] Village-level research in Thailand in 1979/80 showed that households smoothed their seasonal crop expenses and revenues by complex strategies involving nonfarm income, capital sales and purchases, and borrowing (Meyer and Alicbusan, 1984).

unions fail, however, because they are created in a top-down approach and are run by village administrators with little village participation. (Poapongsakorn, Ammar, and Charoenpiew, 1998).

The TDRI surveys of rural households in northeastern Thailand in 1995/96 provide the only recent information available about rural household savings. Some 70 to 90 percent of households reported savings deposits with some financial institution, but savings in kind were much larger than financial savings. The determinants of household savings were found to be income per capita, number of dependents, and social status of household head. Households that purchased property on an installment basis had less savings than other households because of their monthly debt burden. BAAC's branch expansion was found to explain part of its deposit growth, but it is still more convenient for farmers to use commercial banks, particularly if they want to transfer money to and from Bangkok. This is an important service because of the large number of rural households with family members that have migrated to Bangkok. Agricultural cooperatives have few incentives to mobilize savings because of the cheaper sources of funds available from BAAC, and the village credit unions have limited capacity to mobilize savings (Poapongsakorn, Ammar, and Charoenpiew, 1998).

MICROFINANCE

Specialized microfinance services are not important in Thailand. One reason is that BAAC has achieved such a large outreach. A second reason is that poverty is not as serious in Thailand as in some other Asian countries. The poverty that exists is heavily concentrated in rural areas, especially in the northeastern and northern regions. Several cash and in-kind transfers are made to the poor through Governmental agencies, and special support has been given to microfinance for the poor.

Increased attention is now given to microfinance as part of the package of activities directed at easing the social problems associated with the financial crisis (Ammar and Sobchokchai, 1998). The Community Development Department provides funds to villages for on-lending to poor households. By 1995, nearly B1 billion ($40 million) were reported in loans outstanding to nearly 200,000 households. The Government Savings Bank and the Urban Community Development Office of the National Housing Authority provide loans to community organizations (sometimes referred to as savings and credit organizations) for on-lending to individual members. Together they have provided loans to nearly 1,500 community organizations with a combined membership of around 200,000 households. Some of these organizations are registered as cooperatives, but most are not registered. It is unknown how many are in rural areas.

A few private bodies and NGOs are involved in microfinance, but they have a more limited role than in most other countries in the region (McGuire, Conroy, and Thapa, 1998). Presumably these initiatives reach a somewhat poorer clientele than is served by BAAC. However, if they are similar to such programs elsewhere, they have limited outreach, provide subsidized loans, and are not sustainable. Whatever financial services they provide may be useful to the recipients, but will make only temporary, rather than permanent, contributions to poverty alleviation. The GTZ project, which helped develop the OM SAP THAWA CHOKE savings product, began as an effort to develop self-help groups into financial intermediaries, but the concept became obsolete once most of the members had savings accounts in and became borrowers of BAAC (Maurer, 1997).

INFORMAL FINANCE

Various informal financial arrangements have been reported in Thailand but there is little detailed information about total volume or the characteristics of the participants in these financial transactions (Ghate, 1992). Moneylenders, landlords, traders, farmers, input suppliers, friends, and relatives are sources of informal finance in rural areas. People participate in ROSCAs and other types of group saving and lending arrangements. Land pawning or usufruct loans are found in poorer areas where land values are low, local markets are relatively inactive, and cash surpluses are less likely to exist.

Two logical questions can be raised about informal finance in light of the rapid expansion in formal finance. Has informal finance declined in importance? Have interest rates and other terms and conditions improved for informal finance? Onchan (1992) summarized several rural surveys that seemed to show that the proportion of borrowers reporting informal loans and the relative market share of informal loans declined over the period 1961/62 to 1986/87. Loans from friends and relatives were reported most frequently, followed by loans from traders, farmers, and rice merchants. Informal loans were often used for consumption purposes, and the lenders were more likely to make loans without collateral or group guarantees than occurred in formal finance.

Poapongsakorn, Ammar, and Charoenpiew (1998) analyzed information obtained from the two TDRI surveys in the province of Nakhon Ratchasima in 1986 and 1995/96. They concluded that the reported share of informal contracts fell in number from 69 to 50 percent of total loan contracts reported, while the volume of funds lent declined from 56 to 40 percent of the total. Moreover, the proportion of farm households reporting only informal loans fell from 32 to 11 percent, while the proportion reporting only formal loans rose from 16 to 38 percent, and the proportion borrowing from both sources was roughly unchanged at 8 to 10 percent. At the time of the 1986 survey, there was no clear downward trend in informal interest rates (Ammar et al., 1993), but by the time of the second survey, a decline seemed to have occurred. In 1986, the interest rate for cash borrowers was 4.5 percent per month, but it had fallen to 2.8 percent per month in 1995. Likewise, the rate for installment credit fell from 4.45 percent per month to 2.63 percent per month.

There are few reasons to expect that, because of expanded formal finance, informal finance will completely disappear or that informal interest rates will be much lower than their historic levels. First, the transaction costs of getting a small formal loan for emergency or consumption purposes may be so high that it is cheaper for borrowers to use informal lenders for this type of borrowing. Second, although an average of three resident and two nonresident informal lenders were reported per village in 1986, it may be difficult for a borrower to obtain better loan terms by switching lenders because of information costs. It takes time to establish creditworthiness with an informal lender; thus, switching lenders must be done slowly and may involve costs and risks to the borrowers (Ammar et al., 1993). The information accumulated by an informal lender about clients represents a sunk cost so an existing lender can afford to temporarily cut interest rates to forestall the entry of a new informal lender into a local market. The result is highly segmented markets with long-term customer relationships between borrowers and lenders and fairly high interest rates for small, short-term loans.

IMPLICATIONS OF THE FINANCIAL CRISIS

The financial and economic crisis in Asia first began in Thailand, then the contagion spread to Indonesia, Malaysia, and the Philippines in Southeast Asia, then to East Asia, and eventually to Russia and Brazil. The problems in Thailand led international investors to conclude that several Asian countries had similar weaknesses, namely weak financial sectors with poor prudential supervision, large external deficits, appreciating exchange rates, declining quality of investments, export slowdowns, and overexpansion in certain key industries including urban real estate (Goldstein, 1998).

The impact of the crisis has been very severe in Thailand. Real GDP growth was 5.5 percent in 1996, fell to –0.4 in 1997, and was projected at –3 to –5 percent for 1998. The inflation rate was 4.8 percent in 1996, and was estimated to rise to 7.7 percent in 1997, and to around 10 percent in 1998 (Anon., 1998a). Imports were expected to contract sharply while exports were projected to increase slowly, but much of that increase is dependent on the economic performance of its regional trading partners.

The financial sector has been hard hit because of sharp increases in nonperforming loans. The central bank intervened in four banks and 58 finance companies were closed (56 permanently), which is likely to have affected financing for small business and consumer credit (Ding, Domac, and Ferri, 1998; IMF, 1998b). The eventual net cost to taxpayers of the attempt to fiscalize the cost of the financial bailout is large. The amount lent out by the Financial Institution Development Funds (FIDF) to prop up banks and financial companies was reported to be B1 trillion, and the interest cost on this sum alone is B100 billion. Estimates suggest that, at most, half of this money will be recovered through liquidation of seized assets. The eventual cost of this problem and bank recapitalization may total B100–200 billion annually, compared with a total B800 billion budget (Ammar and Sobchokchai, 1998).

Recent IMF estimates of these costs are even larger. It projects the total State obligations for the bail out at the end of 1999/2000 to be B2.1 trillion equal to 38 percent of GDP. The interest cost for servicing this debt is projected to rise from 3 percent of GDP in 1997/98 to about 4 percent in 1998/99 and 1999/2000 (Lane et al., 1999). This fiscal burden can be related to total budgetary support for agriculture of about $4.5 billion in the mid-1990s, when the total Thai GDP, measured in 1987 dollars, was about $100 billion (Rosegrant and Hazell, 1999). Therefore, it would be necessary to wipe out almost all support for agriculture in order to finance the bank problem. Obviously, this will not occur but the example provides a rough order of magnitude of the banking problem and reveals the huge cost that society must bear when inadequate financial and macroeconomic policies are pursued. How these costs are eventually allocated will influence the future development of the rural economy.

The crisis had an impact on savings mobilization in BAAC. Whereas the growth rate in savings and time deposits ranged between 33 and 38 percent in 1996 and 1997, it fell to 5 percent in 1998. The share mobilized by the head office fell relative to other regions of the country and Government and State enterprise deposits fell relative to those of private individuals (BAAC/GTZ, 1998).

Employment and unemployment have been significantly affected by the crisis, and the positive trend of the past few years of declining poverty has been reversed. Analysis of labor-force surveys through the first quarter of 1998 revealed the nature of the problem. After accounting for seasonal and annual trends, it was shown that the crisis contributed to a decline of 1.2 million in wage and salary earners. Employment on farms actually increased by over 600,000, but some of this increase may simply represent disguised unemployment (Kakwani, 1998). Moreover, unemployment increased by over 800,000 with the impact greatest on young men with limited education and recent migrants. The average number of hours worked and average real wages have fallen. There has also been an increase in child labor and a reduction in real income among children in the workforce. Close to 200,000 persons have been identified as return migrants and over half returned to the northeastern region (Chalamwong, 1998).

Depreciation of the baht has boosted prices for some agricultural products, mitigating the effects of the crisis for farm households. Rice farmers in particular have benefited from the currency depreciation and increased demand due to El Niño-impacted production in other countries. Prices for rubber farmers rose for a time but fell to their previous levels (Ammar and Sobchokchai, 1998). As a result, BAAC officials reported that 1997 and 1998 loan repayments were largely unaffected by the crisis (Table XII.12). The BAAC 1997 Annual Report, however, shows that at the end of fiscal year 1997, overdue loans for individual farmers amounted to B19.4 billion, an increase of 58 percent over the previous year. It was assumed that part of this increase was due to the crisis. Debt repayment problems led to demonstrations and petitions for a debt moratorium by an association of farmers in the Northeast. Loan recovery has been negatively affected in the community organizations funded by the Urban Community Development Office (McGuire and Conroy, 1998).

Table XII.12: BAAC Loan Disbursements and Repayments by Quarters for Fiscal Years 1996–1998, Classified by Type of Borrowers[a]
(B Million)

Items	1996			1997			1998		
	Q1	Q2	Total	Q1	Q2	Total	Q1	Q2	Total
Disbursement									
- Individuals	30,562	21,283	51,845	36,406	14,352	50,578	25,168	15,351	40,519
- Institutions	4,359	2,333	6,692	4,863	2,886	7,749	4,489	3,136	7,625
Total	34,921	23,616	58,537	41,269	17,238	58,507	29,657	18,487	48,144
Repayment									
- Individuals	14,357	11,906	26,263	17,228	12,354	29,582	15,584	11,770	27,354
- Institutions	2,957	1,568	4,525	3,251	2,360	5,611	3,085	2,185	5,270
Total	17,314	13,474	30,788	20,479	14,714	35,193	18,669	13,955	32,624

a BAAC Fiscal year is 1 April to 31 March.

Source: BAAC.

The Thai response to the crisis has focused on restoring health to the financial sector and implementing reforms to strengthen the financial system. There have also been several efforts to reduce social impact. Expenditures to support the social safety net were planned to include small infrastructure programs in the agricultural sector, and increases in funds for retraining programs and lending to the unemployed to facilitate self-employment. International agencies are also actively involved in programs to ease social problems (Ammar and Sobchokchai, 1998).

It appears that the short-term impact of the crisis has been felt more by the urban than by the rural financial system. BAAC could face a longer-term negative impact, however, if the Government decides to use it as a channel for relief and emergency funds to rural households as policy directed loans. This could create two problems: it would increase confusion about BAAC's mission and detract staff time from regular lending. Both problems could contribute to reducing BAAC's loan recovery rate and force the Government to subsidize it even more in the future. BAAC could also be affected if savings fall so that it lacks resources for new lending. Borrowers may be less inclined to pay existing loans if they are unable to get new ones.

CURRENT POTENTIAL AND CONSTRAINTS FOR RURAL FINANCE

Until the 1990s, Thailand was a good example for the developing world in financial sector development. State intervention in the financial system was moderate, and the authorities proceeded slowly with deregulation. A desire to support agriculture led to creation of BAAC in 1966, and to establishing the agricultural loan quota for the commercial banks in 1975. Today, BAAC loans represent about half of total agricultural lending and its outreach is reported to be about 90 percent of farm households. Depth of outreach is also impressive with a third to half of recent BAAC loans made for $1,200 or less. The average loan in the small loan category was $660, or 24 percent of per capita GDP. During the 1990s, BAAC began to mobilize savings more aggressively and rely less on commercial bank deposits. It now has roughly a million more depositors than borrowers. Agricultural cooperatives and farmers' associations serve largely as a means to retail loans from funds acquired wholesale from BAAC. Village-level credit unions mobilize small-scale savings and make small loans.

An important issue to understand is how BAAC has largely avoided the problems that undermine many other specialized agricultural development banks. Three factors have been identified by Thai observers. First, regardless of the political party in power, the Minister of Finance has been chosen largely because of technical competence and this has contributed to maintaining a banking vision for BAAC. Second, BAAC has had strong leadership oriented towards professionalism, efficiency, and long-term sustainability. Third, the interest of the workers' union is tied to BAAC performance through annual bonuses. Therefore, the workers argue against BAAC engaging in activities that detract from strong financial performance. Because of these three sets of factors, BAAC maintains a firewall between its regular banking business and the projects it implements for the Government. It strives to identify the full costs of these projects and requires the Government to fully reimburse them.

There are a number of weaknesses in the Thai rural financial system. Rural savings mobilization is not a high priority. BAAC still depends on subsidies, and its low interest policy is a disincentive for searching more aggressively for ways to make smaller loans efficiently. Despite changes by parliament in 1999, BAAC is also constrained by charter and policies from fully serving the rural nonfarm economy. The supply of medium- and long-term loans may be limited compared with future demands, and BAAC staff may lack the skills needed to meet the demands for serving the rural nonfarm sector.

The information available does not permit a complete assessment of the rural financial markets. Information is weak or nonexistent on the following topics:

(i)   How far has formal finance penetrated into all rural regions and the most isolated areas? How far down into the poverty profile do BAAC and the other formal institutions reach in supplying loans and savings services?

(ii)   How well have commercial banks served the financial demands of large farmers and agribusinesses? What has been the impact of the financial crisis on their ability and willingness to continue to serve these clients?

(iii)   If BAAC would be permitted to charge higher interest rates for loans to smaller and poorer clients, how much would it improve access to formal finance? Would there still be a role for special microfinance institutions, or do the problems of the poor require nonfinancial services?

(iv)   What are the sources of finance for rural nonfarm enterprises today, and are they seriously affected by the regulations that constrain BAAC from serving a broader rural clientele? What would happen to the size and riskiness of BAAC's portfolio if it were permitted to serve a broader range of rural nonfarm activities?[8]

(v)   What additional rural financial services (e.g., transfer of remittances, insurance) do rural residents and enterprises demand, and what prevents them from being supplied by the current financial institutions?

(vi)   What constraints must be addressed if the financial system is to make more medium- and long-term loans that are necessary for the further structural transformation of the rural economy?

(vii)   What role does informal finance play in the rural economy and how will that role change as the formal financial system improves and expands?

---

[8] In early 1999, the Thai parliament eased restrictions on BAAC by authorizing it to offer a broader range of financial services in rural areas. However, BAAC still cannot compete in offering the full range of services offered by commercial banks.

Thai agriculture faces some major challenges. How they are resolved will influence the nature of financial services demanded in the future. First, farmers face a cost-price squeeze caused by input-price increases and falling world commodity prices. Governmental research and extension systems have not been very successful in helping the farming sector cope with these problems in the past (Poapongsakorn et al., 1995). Second, the future growth path of farming and its impact on the rural-urban income gap are unclear. In spite of rapid agricultural growth, there has been relatively little change in average farm size. Rather, rural households have increasingly turned to paid employment and income earned from other enterprises to supplement farm income (Table XII.13). If this trend continues, the country will have to become more successful in rural industrialization to create higher-paying nonfarm work in rural areas. This would imply following a Japanese type of rural development based on small, part-time farms. Alternatively, the country could adopt more of a US-type of rural development by consolidating farms and increasing average farm size. Both the Japanese and US models of development require specialized financial services.

Table XII.13: Sources of Income for the Rural Population, 1975–1994[a]
(percent)

Source of Income	Year						
	1975	1981	1986	1988	1990	1992	1994
Wage income	21.38	19.99	26.93	25.99	25.60	30.72	33.39
Farm income	49.99	44.35	36.48	36.11	36.55	30.89	25.24
Income from enterprise	19.44	18.20	23.16	22.34	23.55	23.70	24.86
Property income	1.05	1.63	1.22	1.45	1.72	1.41	1.18
Transferred income	6.94	12.51	10.58	12.10	10.01	10.84	13.35
Other income	1.20	3.31	1.63	2.00	2.53	2.44	1.98
Total (percent)	100	100	100	100	100	100	100

[a] Excludes Bangkok and vicinity.

Source: Unpublished data of the Thailand Development Research Institute. Calculated from the Socio Economic Survey for 1975, 1981, 1986, 1988, 1990, 1992 and 1994, National Statistical Office.

Creating the Policy Environment

The immediate policy concern in Thailand is to restore the country's economic health and stability. Resolving these problems will have an especially important impact on how well commercial banks will serve large farms and agribusinesses in the future, because they are more dependent on banks than on other sources of financial services. There are several important policy concerns regarding BAAC that will affect its future performance and the access of small and medium farm and rural enterprises to financial services. The first, which has obvious political implications, concerns the subsidized interest rate policy on loans. Subsidized rates discourage other financial institutions from trying aggressively to serve agriculture; large segments of the sector are and will continue to be dependent on BAAC. Setting lower rates for smaller loans, although intended to help the poor, actually hurts them by discouraging BAAC from making small loans and searching for innovative ways to serve poorer clients with small loans.

Second, the policy of having BAAC administer policy-based lending is destructive. It creates confusion in the minds of borrowers about its true financial mission, and distracts it from exclusive dedication to the task of becoming the best possible financial institution serving the broadest range of rural clientele.

Third, BAAC's recently expanded lending authority still prevents it from fully serving the rural nonfarm sector. Rural industries and nonfarm enterprises will be better served if commercial banks and BAAC are allowed to compete in serving their financial demands. Moreover, BAAC may be less vulnerable to risks if it develops a less specialized portfolio composed of both farm and nonfarm loans. Fourth, BAAC's special institutional status needs to be reviewed. It may be more prudent for BAAC to be regulated and supervised by the stronger central bank that will emerge with the policy reforms now underway.

Creating and Strengthening the Financial Infrastructure

The financial crisis revealed important weaknesses in the country's financial infrastructure. One weakness is the decline of the technocracy responsible for managing the economy, including the Ministry of Finance and Bank of Thailand (Ammar, 1998). Weaknesses were also identified in the banking sector's ability to analyze and manage risks properly. Banks have traditionally relied on collateral to secure loans to Thai enterprises that were basically family businesses. But foreclosure procedures were not efficient, and it could take three to five years between initiation of proceedings and the time the lenders could realize their funds (Ammar and Sobchokchai, 1998). These and other infrastructure issues need to be addressed in the reforms.

No information is available on how limitations in financial infrastructure may specifically affect rural finance. Since BAAC plays such an overwhelming role in providing rural loans, there is less need for a credit bureau to maintain financial records for use by all institutions than would be the case in a market with many competing institutions. However, as BAAC broadens its mandate and competes more directly with other institutions, there will be a greater need to develop information systems for client credit histories, levels of indebtedness, and the status of collateral offered for loans.

Institutional Development

The major institutional development issue in Thailand concerns improving the capacity of BAAC to meet the future financial needs of the rural economy. The immediate problem is that it is vulnerable because it is undercapitalized. The total of all shareholders' equity in fiscal year 1996 represented about 7 percent of liabilities, but by the end of fiscal year 1997 equity had fallen to just under 3 percent of liabilities. This deterioration in capital resulted from an increase in total liabilities and a sharp decline in equity due to exchange rate fluctuations. The subsequent improvement in the exchange rate eased this problem, but a lending institution with a portfolio heavily concentrated in a sector subject to systemic weather risks and volatile international commodity prices needs larger reserves. Moreover, it is not clear how realistic BAAC current loan loss provisions are, considering that the loans in arrears at the end of 1997 represented almost 11 percent of outstanding loan principal.

Another issue is the ability of BAAC's human capital and lending technology to respond to future challenges. Now that BAAC has achieved a large outreach, it cannot grow by simply lending to more farmers. Its loan portfolio can grow by either increasing loan sizes for existing clients and/or by lending for new types of nonfarm enterprises. Either approach implies more sophisticated loan appraisal and developing loan sizes and repayment terms suited to the demands and capacities of these clients. Peer monitoring will play a lesser role in assuring repayment, and more traditional types of collateral will be needed to reduce lending risks.

Another possible way for BAAC to increase profits would be to expand savings mobilization sharply. This would require the careful design of savings products with more complications in managing funds to earn a high but prudent return, while maintaining sufficient reserves to meet demands for withdrawals. Mobilizing more savings may require expanding the network of branches and field offices, and building linkages with village-level credit unions. Increased savings also implies the representation of new stakeholders in the institution's governance, and closer supervision to protect savers (Fitchett, 1997).[9]

The lower end of the rural financial market needs to be analyzed clearly to determine how village-level credit unions are performing, what risks they represent to local savers, and

---

[9] In 1998, an ADB technical assistance team was working on-site to improve BAAC's loan appraisal and risk management capacity.

how they should be monitored as their savings and lending activities grow. The role of cooperatives and farmers' associations in the financial system should be evaluated. They are not heavily involved in savings mobilization, largely lend the funds provided by BAAC, and are responsible for some of BAAC's loan recovery problems. BAAC may not be adequately pricing loans made to cooperatives and associations to cover full costs and risks. Finally, the performance of subsidized microlenders and governmental programs for the poor need ongoing assessment to determine whether they are meeting financial demands that could be better served through nonsubsidized sources. Programs for the poor should separate training and other activities that require subsidies from financial services that can be provided subsidy free.

REFERENCES

Adams, Dale W. 1988a. Distinctive Features of Rural Financial Markets in Asia. In *Farm Finance and Agricultural Development*. Tokyo: Asian Productivity Organization. p. 25-40.

_____. 1988b. The Conundrum of Successful Credit Projects in Floundering Rural Financial Markets. *Economic Development and Cultural Change* 36(2): 355-367.

_____. 1995. Reforming Development Banks. Unpublished paper. Department of Agricultural, Environmental, and Development Economics. Columbus: The Ohio State University.

_____. 1998. The Decline in Debt Directing: An Unfinished Agenda. Paper presented at the Second Annual Seminar on New Development Finance, Goethe University of Frankfurt, 21-25 September.

_____, Douglas H. Graham, and J.D. Von Pischke (eds.). 1984. *Undermining Rural Development with Cheap Credit*. Boulder: Westview Press.

Adams, Richard H. Jr. 1998. Remittances, Investments and Rural Asset Accumulation in Pakistan. *Economic Development and Cultural Change* 47(1): 155-173.

ADB (Asian Development Bank). 1969. *Asian Agricultural Survey*. Tokyo: University of Tokyo Press, and Seattle: University of Washington Press.

_____. 1978. *Rural Asia: Challenge and Opportunity*. New York: Praeger Publishers.

_____. 1993. Agricultural Credit Policy Paper. Draft. Manila: ADB.

_____. 1996. *Economies in Transition: The Asian Experience*. Asian Development Bank Annual Report 1995. Manila: ADB.

_____. 1997a. *Microenterprise Development: Not by Credit Alone.* Manila: ADB.

_____. 1997b. Report and Recommendations of the President to the Board of Directors on a Proposed Loan to BAAC for the Rural Enterprise Credit Project in the Kingdom of Thailand. Manila: ADB.

_____. 1997c. *Key Indicators of Developing Asian and Pacific Countries.* Manila: ADB.

_____. 1997d. Proposed Loan: Rural Financial Institutions Project. Kyrgyz Republic. RRP: KGZ 28395. Manila: ADB. July.

_____. 1997e. Technical Assistance to the People's Republic of China for the Reform of the Rural Credit Cooperative System. Manila: ADB. December.

_____. 1997f. *Emerging Asia: Changes and Challenges.* Manila: ADB.

AFC (Agricultural Finance Corporation) Limited. 1988. *Agricultural Credit Review: Role and Effectiveness of Lending Institutions.* Vol. V. Bombay: AFC, India.

Ahmed, Zia. 1989. Effective Costs of Rural Loans in Bangladesh. *World Development* 17(3): 357-363.

Akrasanee, Narongchai, Tongroj Onchan, Yongyuth Chalamwong, Pradit Charsombut, Somsak Tambunlertchai, and Chamlong Atikul. 1983. *Rural Off-Farm Employment in Thailand.* Bangkok: United States Agency for International Development.

Aleem, Irfan. 1993. Imperfect Information, Screening, and the Costs of Informal Lending: A Study of a Rural Credit Market in Pakistan. In *The Economics of Rural Organization: Theory, Practice and Policy,* edited by Karla Hoff, Avishay Braverman, and Joseph E. Stiglitz. New York: Oxford University Press. p. 131-153.

Amin, Ruhul, Stan Becker, and Abdul Bayes. 1998. NGO-Promoted Microcredit Programs and Women's Empowerment in Rural Bangladesh: Quantitative and Qualitative Evidence. *The Journal of Developing Areas* 32(2): 221-236.

Ammar, Siamwalla 1998. *Can a Developing Democracy Manage its Macroeconomy? The Case of Thailand.* Bangkok: Thailand Development Research Institute.

_____, Chirmsak Pinthong, Nipon Poapongsakorn, Ploenpit Satsanguan, Prayong Nettayarak, Wanrak Mimgmaneenakin, and Yuavares Tubpun. 1993. The Thai Rural Credit System and Elements of a Theory: Public Subsidies, Private Information, and Segmented Markets. In *The Economics of Rural Organization: Theory, Practice, and Policy*, edited by K. Hoff, Avishay Braverman, and Joseph E. Stiglitz. Oxford: Oxford University Press. p. 154-185.

Anon. 1998a. Mid-Year Economic Review. *Bangkok Post*, 30 June.

_____. 1998b. RBI Chief Asks NABARD to Set Up Panel on Microcredit. *Economic Times*, 7 November, p. 6.

_____. 1998c. Citibank Launches Micro-Credit Scheme. *United News of India*, 19 November, p. 1.

_____. 1998d. Focus on Micro-Credit Pricing. *Business Standard*, 6 November, p. 4.

_____. 1998e. A Capital Idea Goes Sour at China's Investment Trusts. *Asian Wall Street Journal*, 9 November, p. 1, 5.

_____. 1998f. Foreign Lenders Grow Increasingly Wary of China's Reliability as a Borrower. *International Herald Tribune*, 6 November, p. 21.

_____. 1999a. Seeds of Disaster: How China Managed to Lose $25 Billion on its Grain Program. *Wall Street Journal* CIII(17), 26 January, p. 1.

_____. 1999b. *Indonesia Bank Move 'A Big Breakthrough'*. Financial Times, *15 March*.

_____. 1999c. High Savings Rate Cuts into Chinese Economy. *International Herald Tribune*, 7 March, p.15.

Ashok Khanna. 1995. South Asian Financial Sector Development. In *Financial Sector Development in Asia*, edited by Shahid N. Zahid. Manila: Asian Development Bank. p. 261-353.

Assadi, Muzaffar. 1998. Farmers Suicides: Signs of Distress in Rural Economy. *Economic and Political Weekly*, April: 747-749.

Aungsumalin, Saroj. 1990. *Finance, Credit and Provincial Industrialization*. Bangkok: Thailand Development Research Institute.

BAAC (Bank for Agriculture and Agricultural Cooperatives). 1998. *Annual Report 1997*. Bangkok: BAAC.

_____,and GTZ (Deutsche Gesellschaft für Technische Zusammenarbeit). 1998. Savings Mobilization in the BAAC: Analysis of Past Trends, Assessment of Performance and Recommendations for the Future. Bangkok: Bank for Agriculture and Agricultural Cooperatives.

Badu, K. 1998. Project Implementation Manual on Microcredit. Bishkek: United Nations Development Programme Country Office.

Bakht, Farid, and Raisul Awal Mahmood. 1998. Overseas Remittances and Informal Financing in Bangladesh. Studies on Informal Financial Markets in Bangladesh. Working Paper 5. Dhaka: Bangladesh Institute of Development Studies.

Banerjee, Basudeb. 1997. India: New Perspectives on Rural Industrialization. Paper presented at the Asian Productivity Organization (APO) Seminar, July. Tokyo: APO.

Barua, Dipal C. 1998. The Grameen Strategy to Combat the Flood of 1998. Paper presented at the SEEP Network 1998 Annual Meeting, Washington DC, 28-30 October.

Bennett, Lynn, Mike Goldberg, and J.D. Von Pischke. 1998. Basing Access on Performance to Create Sustainable Financial Services for the Poor in Nepal. In *Strategic Issues in Microfinance*, edited by Mwangi S. Kimenyi, Robert C. Wieland, and J.D. Von Pischke. Aldershot: Ashgate Publishing. p. 141-160.

Besley, Timothy. 1994. How do Market Failures Justify Interventions in Rural Credit Markets? *The World Bank Research Observer* 9(1): 27-47.

Bhandari, M.C. 1997. Agricultural Finance Revisited: Using Policy to get Results, a Case of India. Working paper. Rome: Food and Agriculture Organization of the United Nations.

Binswanger, Hans P., and J. McIntire. 1987. Behavioral and Material Determinants of Production Relations in Land-Abundant Tropical Agriculture. *Economic Development and Cultural Change* 36(1): 73-99.

_____, and Shahidur R. Khandker. 1995. The Impact of Formal Finance on the Rural Economy of India. *The Journal of Development Studies* 32(2): 234-262.

_____, Shahidur Khandker, and Mark R. Rosenzweig. 1993. How Infrastructure and Financial Institutions Affect Agricultural Output and Investment in India. *Journal of Development Economics* 41(2): 337-366.

Bloch, Peter. 1997. Central Asia: Second Reconnaissance Mission Report. Madison: Land Tenure Center.

_____, James M. Delehanty, and Michael J. Roth. 1996. Land and Agrarian Reform in the Kyrgyz Republic. Madison: Land Tenure Center.

Bouman, F.J.A., and R. Bastiaansen. 1992. Pawnbrokering and Small Loans: Cases from India and Sri Lanka. In *Informal Finance in Low-Income Countries*, edited by Dale W Adams and D. A. Fitchett. Boulder: Westview Press. p. 181-194.

_____, and H.A.J. Moll. 1992. Informal Finance in Indonesia. In *Informal Finance in Low-Income Countries*, edited by Dale W Adams and D. A. Fitchett. Boulder: Westview Press. p. 209-223.

von Braun, Joachim. 1995. Agricultural Commercialization: Impacts on Income and Nutrition and Implications for Policy. *Food Policy* 20(3): 187-202.

Caprio, Jr., Gerald. 1998. Banking in Crises: Expensive Lessons from Recent Financial Crises. Policy Research Working Paper No. 1979. Washington DC: World Bank.

CARE Bangladesh. 1998. Effects of Flood '98 on Livelihood of Poor Participants and Savings and Credit Programs of 24 Partner NGOs of Income Project. Dhaka: CARE.

Carpenter, Janney. 1997. Bangladesh. In *Regulation and Supervision of Microfinance Institutions: Case Studies*, edited by C. Churchill. Occasional Paper no. 2. Washington DC: MicroFinance Network.

Chalamwong, Yongyuth. 1998. Crisis Impact on Migration in Thailand. Bangkok: Thailand Development Research Institute.

Chandavarkar, Anand. 1998. Book Review: India's Economic Reforms, 1991-2001. *Economic Development and Cultural Change* 47(1): 332-336.

Chant, John, and Mari Pangestu. 1996. An Assessment of Financial Reform in Indonesia, 1983-90. In *Financial Reform: Theory and Experience*, edited by Gerard Caprio, Jr., Izak Atiyas, and James A. Hanson. Cambridge: Cambridge University Press. p. 223-275.

Charitonenko, Stephanie, Richard H. Patten, and Jacob Yaron. 1998. Indonesia, Bank Rakyat Indonesia – Unit Desa 1970-1996. Case Studies in Microfinance. Sustainable Banking with the Poor. Washington DC: World Bank.

Chaves, Rodrigo A., and Claudio Gonzalez-Vega. 1996. The Design of Successful Rural Financial Intermediaries: Evidence from Indonesia. *World Development* 24(1): 65-78.

Cheng, Enjiang. 1997. Market Reforms and Provision of Credit for Grain Purchases in China. *The China Quarterly* 151: 633-653.

————, and Cheng Yuk-shing. 1998. Banking Reform and the Separation of Policy and Commercial Loans in China. Working Paper. Chinese Economies Research Centre. Adelaide: University of Adelaide.

————, and L.R. Malcolm. 1995. Provision of Institutional Credit and Economic Transition in Rural China. Working Paper. Chinese Economies Research Centre. Adelaide: University of Adelaide.

————, Christopher Findley, and Andrew Watson. 1997. We are Not Financial Organizations: Financial Innovation Without Regulation in China's Rural Credit Foundations. Working paper. Chinese Economies Research Centre. Adelaide: University of Adelaide.

Chowdhury, Amirul Islam. 1998. Report on Microfinance Programs for Urban Poverty Alleviation in Bangladesh. Manila: Asian Development Bank.

Christen, Robert P., Elisabeth Rhyne, Robert C. Vogel, and Cressida McKean. 1995. *Maximizing the Outreach of Microenterprise Finance: An Analysis of Successful Microfinance Programs.* Program and Operations Assessment Report No. 10. Washington DC: United States Agency for International Development.

Christensen, Scott, David Dollar, Ammar Siamwalla, and Pakorn Vichyanond. 1993. *The Lessons of East Asia: Thailand – the Institutional and Political Underpinnings of Growth.* Washington DC: World Bank.

Churchill, Craig. 1998. Unconventional Wisdom: The State of the Art of Individual Microlending. Draft paper. Toronto: CALMEADOW.

————. 1999. *Client Centered Lending: The Art of Individual Lending.* Toronto: CALMEADOW.

Claessens, Stijn, and Tom Glaessner. 1998. Internationalization of Financial Services in Asia. Policy Research Working Paper 1911. Washington DC: World Bank.

Corsetti, Giancarlo, Paolo Pesenti, and Nouriel Roubini. 1998. What Caused the Asian Currency and Financial Crisis? Unpublished paper. New Haven: Yale University.

Credit and Development Forum (CDF). 1997. *CDF Statistics*. Vol. 5. December.

Csaki, Csaba, and John Nash. 1998. The Agrarian Economies of Central and Eastern Europe and the Commonwealth of Independent States. Discussion Paper No. 387. Washington DC: World Bank.

Cuevas, Carlos E., and Douglas H. Graham. 1984. Agricultural Lending Costs in Honduras. In *Undermining Rural Development with Cheap Credit*, edited by Dale W Adams, Douglas H. Graham, and J.D. Von Pischke. Boulder: Westview Press. p. 96-103.

De Melo, Martha et al. 1997. Circumstance and Choice: The Role of Initial Conditions and Policies in Transition Economies. Policy Research Working Paper No. 1866. Washington DC: World Bank.

Ding, Wei, Ilker Domac, and Giovanni Ferri. 1998. Is There a Credit Crunch in East Asia? Policy Research Working Paper 1959. Washington DC: World Bank.

Donald, Gordon. 1976. *Credit for Small Farmers in Developing Countries*. Boulder: Westview Press.

Doner, Richard, and Daniel Unger. 1993. The Politics of Finance in Thai Economic Development. In *The Politics of Finance in Developing Countries*, edited by S. Haggard, C. H. Lee, and S. Maxfield. Ithaca: Cornell University Press. p. 93-164.

Donors Working Group on Financial Sector Development. 1995. Micro and Small Enterprise Finance: Guiding Principles for Selecting and Supporting Intermediaries. Washington DC: World Bank.

Dorosh, Paul A., Steven Haggblade, and Peter Hazell. 1998. The Impact of Alternative Agricultural Strategies on Growth of the Rural Nonfarm Economy. Paper presented at the International Food Policy Research Institute Conference on Strategies for Stimulating Growth of the Rural Nonfarm Economy in Developing Countries, Arlie House, Virginia, 17-21 May.

Dreze, Jean, Peter Lanjouw, and Naresh Sharma. 1997. Credit in Rural India: A Case Study. The Development Economics Research Programme. Working paper. London: London School of Economics.

Egaitsu, Fumio. 1988. Rural Financial Markets: Two Schools of Thought. In *Farm Finance and Agricultural Development*. Tokyo: Asian Productivity Organization. p. 111-122.

Eichengreen, Barry, and Michael Mussa. 1998. Capital Account Liberalization and the IMF. In *Finance and Development*. Washington DC: International Monetary Fund.

Esguerra, Emmanuel F., Geetha Nagarajan, and Richard L. Meyer. 1991. Applying Contestability Theory to Rural Informal Credit Markets: What Do We Gain? Paper Presented at the XXI International Conference of Agricultural Economists. Tokyo, Japan, 22-29 August.

European Bank for Reconstruction and Development (EBRD). 1998. *Transition Report 1998: Financial Sector in Transition*. London: EBRD.

Evans, Timothy G., Alayne M. Adams, Rafi Mohammed, and Alison H. Norris. 1999. Demystifying Nonparticipation in Microcredit: A Population-Based Analysis. *World Development* 27(2): 419-430.

Fafchamps, Marcel, and John Pender. 1997. Precautionary Savings, Credit Constraints, and Irreversible Investment: Theory and Evidence from Semiarid India. *Journal of Business and Economic Statistics* 15(2): 180-194.

FAO (Food and Agriculture Organization of the United Nations). 1964. *New Approach to Agricultural Credit*. Rome: FAO.

_____, and CARIPLO (Cassa de Risparmio della Provincie Lombarde). 1975. *Agricultural Credit for Development*. Rome: FAO.

_____, and GTZ (Deutsche Gesellschaft für Technische Zusammenarbeit). 1998. *Agricultural Finance Revisited: Why?* Rome: FAO.

Feder, Gershon, Lawrence Lau, Justin Lin, and Xiaopeng Luo. 1989. Agricultural Credit and Farm Performance in China. *Journal of Comparative Economics* 13: 508-526.

_____. 1990a. The Relationship Between Credit and Productivity in Chinese Agriculture: A Microeconomic Model of Disequilibrium. *American Journal of Agricultural Economics* 72(5): 1151-1157.

_____. 1990b. The Credit Market in Rural China. Working Paper. Stanford: Stanford University.

_____. 1990c. The Determinants of Farm Investment and Residential Construction in Post-Reform China. Policy, Research and External Affairs Working Paper No. 471. Washington DC: World Bank.

_____, Tongroj Onchan, Yongyuth Chalamwong, and Chira Hongladarom. 1988. *Land Policies and Farm Productivity in Thailand*. Baltimore: The Johns Hopkins University Press.

Fernando, Nimal A. 1994. Improving Rural Institutional Finance: Some Lessons. Manila: Asian Development Bank.

FINCA (Foundation for International Community Assistance). 1998. Kyrgystan: Fact Sheet. Washington DC: FINCA.

Fitchett, Delbert. 1997. Comparative Analysis of Savings Mobilization Strategies – Case Study of Bank for Agriculture and Agricultural Cooperatives (BAAC), Thailand. Eschborn: Deutsche Gesellschaft für Technische Zusammenarbeit.

Fleisig, Heywood W. 1995. The Right to Borrow: Legal and Regulatory Barriers that Limit Access to Credit by Small Farms and Businesses. In *Viewpoint*. Washington DC: World Bank.

_____, and Nuria de la Peña. 1998. Romania: How Problems in the Framework for Secured Transactions Limit Access to Credit. Draft report. Washington DC: Center for the Economic Analysis of Law.

Foundation for Development Cooperation (FDC). 1996. *The Policy and Regulatory Environment for Microfinance in Asia*. Brisbane: Banking with the Poor Network, FDC.

Fry, Maxwell J., 1988. *Money, Interest and Banking in Economic Development*. Baltimore: The Johns Hopkins University Press.

Garnaut, Ross. 1998. Economic Lessons. In *East Asia in Crisis: From Being a Miracle to Needing One*, edited by R. H. McLeod and R. Garnout. New York: Routledge. p.352-366.

Ghate, Prabhu. 1992. *Informal Finance: Some Findings from Asia*. Hong Kong: Oxford University Press.

Ghosh, Madhusudhan. 1996. Agricultural Development and Rural Poverty in India. *Indian Journal of Agricultural Economics* 51(3): 374-380.

Goldstein, Morris. 1998. *The Asian Financial Crisis: Causes, Cures, and Systemic Implications*. Washington DC: Institute for International Economics.

Gonzalez-Vega, Claudio. 1982. *Indonesia: Financial Services for the Rural Poor*. Report to the United States Agency for International Development (USAID). Washington DC: USAID.

_____. 1984. Credit Rationing Behavior of Agricultural Lenders: The Iron Law of Interest-Rate Restrictions. In *Undermining*

Rural Development with Cheap Credit, edited by Dale W Adams, Douglas H. Graham, and J.D. Von Pischke. Boulder: Westview Press. p. 78-96.

_____.1998. Microfinance Apex Mechanisms: Review of the Evidence and Policy Recommendations. Paper prepared for the CGAP-OSU Research Project on Microfinance Apex Mechanisms. Department of Agricultural, Environmental, and Development Economics. Columbus: The Ohio State University.

_____, and Rodrigo A. Chaves. 1993. Indonesia's Rural Financial Markets. Department of Agricultural Economics and Rural Sociology. Columbus: The Ohio State University.

_____, and Douglas H. Graham. 1995. State-Owned Agricultural Development Banks: Lessons and Opportunities for Microfinance. GEMINI Technical Report No. 89. Bethesda, Maryland: Development Alternatives International.

Government of India. 1998. *Economic Survey of India: 1997-98*. New Delhi: Ministry of Finance.

van Greuning, Hennie, Joselito Gallardo, and Bikki Randhawa. 1999. A Framework for Regulating Microfinance Institutions. Policy Research Working Paper No. 2061. Washington DC: World Bank.

GTZ (Deutsche Gesellschaft für Technische Zusammenarbeit). 1997. BAAC's Joint Liability Group: Access to Reach the Poor. Paper presented at the Regional Workshop on the Linkage Program, Focus: Assessment of Linkage Projects in Asia, sponsored by APRACA and GTZ, Denpasar, Indonesia, 3-6 December.

Gudger, Michael. 1998. *Credit Guarantees: An Assessment of the State of Knowledge and New Avenues of Research*. FAO Agricultural Services Bulletin 129. Rome: Food and Agriculture Organization of the United Nations.

Halarnkar, Samar. 1998. Harvests of Death. *India Today* 8 June, p. 49-54.

Hassan, M. Kabir. 1997. The Review of Financial Sector Reform in Bangladesh. In *Growth or Stagnation? A Review of Bangladesh's Development 1996*, edited by Rehman Sobhan. Dhaka: University Press Limited. p. 55-98.

Hazell, Peter, and Thomas Reardon. 1998. Interactions Among the Rural Nonfarm Economy, Poverty, and the Environment in

Resource-Poor Areas. Paper presented at the International Food Policy Research Institute Conference on Strategies for Stimulating Growth of the Rural Nonfarm Economy in Developing Countries, Arlie House, Virginia, 17-21 May.

Holt, Sharon L. September 1991. Women in the BPD and Unit Desa Financial Services Programs: Lessons from Two Impact Studies in Indonesia. Technical Report No. 19. Bethesda, Maryland: Gemini Development Alternatives, Inc.

Hospes, Otto. 1992. Evolving Forms of Informal Finance in an Indonesian Town. In *Informal Finance in Low-Income Countries*, edited by Dale W Adams and D. A. Fitchett. Boulder: Westview Press. p. 225-238.

Hossain, Akhtar, and Sabin Rashid. 1997. Financial Sector Reform. In *The Bangladesh Economy in Transition*, edited by M.G. Quibria. Manila: Asian Development Bank. p. 221-274.

Huang, Jikun, Scott Rozelle, and Albert Nyberg. June 1998. Fiscal and Financial Flows from Agriculture to Non-Agriculture and Non-Rural Sector. Beijing: Paper Prepared for China Rural Vision Project.

Hulme, David, and Paul Mosley. 1996. *Finance against Poverty*. Vol. 1. London: Routledge.

Humphrey, John, and Hubert Schmitz. 1998. Trust and Inter-Firm Relations in Developing and Transition Economies. *The Journal of Development Studies* 34(4): 32-61.

International Food Policy Research Institute (IFPRI). 1998. *Rural Finance and Poverty Alleviation: Food Policy Report*. Washington DC: IFPRI.

International Monetary Fund (IMF). 1998a. Kyrgyz Republic: Recent Economic Development. Staff Country Report No. 98/8. Washington DC: IMF.

_____. 1998b. Thailand Letter of Intent, 26 May. Washington DC: IMF.

Iqbal, Farrukh. 1981. Dualism, Technical Change and Rural Finance in Developing Countries. A Rand Note prepared for the United States Agency for International Development (USAID). Washington DC: USAID.

Islam, Reazal, J.D. Von Pischke, and J.M. de Waard. 1995. *Small Firms Informally Financed: Studies from Bangladesh*. Dhaka: University Press Limited.

Jayasuriya, Sisira. 1998. Safe Behind Close Doors: India. In *East Asia in Crisis: From Being a Miracle to Needing One?* Edited by R. H. McLeod and R. Garnaut. London: Routledge.

Jha, Markendeya. 1988. *Lead Bank Scheme and Regional Development.* New Delhi: Deep Publications.

KAFC (Kyrgyz Agricultural Finance Corporation). 1997. Aspects of KAFC. Bishkek: KAFC.

Kakwani, N. 1998. Impact of Economic Crisis on Employment, Unemployment, and Rural Wages in Thailand. Unpublished paper. School of Economics. Sydney: University of New South Wales.

Kalia, Saroj Kumar. 1996. Transactions Costs of Farm Credit in India. Report presented at the Asian Productivity Organization (APO) seminar held in December 1993. Tokyo: APO.

Kawai, Sinji. April 1996. The Second Assessment on Rural Financing System in the Kyrgyz Republic. Tokyo: Agricultural, Forestry and Fishery Finance Corporation of Japan.

Khalily, M.A. Baqui, and Richard L. Meyer. 1992. Factors Influencing the Demand for Rural Deposits in Bangladesh: A Test for Functional Form. *The Journal of Developing Areas* 26(3): 371-382.

_____, and Richard L. Meyer. 1993. The Political Economy of Rural Loan Recovery: Evidence from Bangladesh. *Savings and Development* 17(1): 23-38.

_____, Rasheda Huda, and Fargas Lalarukh. 1997. On the Behavior of Agricultural Credit in Bangladesh: The Role of Bangladesh Bank. *Dhaka University Journal of Business Studies* 18(1): 131-152.

_____, Richard L. Meyer, and Leroy J. Hushak. 1987. Deposit Mobilization in Bangladesh: Implications for Rural Financial Institutions and Financial Policies. *The Bangladesh Development Studies* 15(4): 85-107.

Khandker, Shahidur R. 1998. *Fighting Poverty with Microcredit: Experience in Bangladesh.* New York: Oxford University Press.

_____, and M.A. Baqui Khalily. 1996. The BRAC's Credit Program: Performance and Sustainability. In *Credit Program for the Poor: Household and Intrahousehold Impacts and Program Sustainability,* edited by Shahidur R. Khandker, M.A. Baqui Khalily, and Azhed H. Khan. Dhaka: Bangladesh Institute of Development Studies. p. 135-246.

————, M.A. Baqui Khalily, and Zahed H. Khan. 1996. Grameen Bank: Performance and Sustainability. In *Credit Program for the Poor: Household and Intrahousehold Impacts and Program Sustainability*, edited by Shahidur R. Khandker, M.A. Baqui Khalily, and Azhed H. Khan. Dhaka: Bangladesh Institute of Development Studies. p. 11-134.

Kochar, Anjini. 1997. Does Lack of Access to Formal Credit Constrain Agricultural Production?: Evidence from Land Tenancy Market in Rural India. *American Journal of Agricultural Economics* 79(3): 754-764.

Kochkar, Kalpana, Prakash Loungani, and Mark R. Stone. 1998. The East Asian Crisis: Macroeconomic Developments and Policy Lessons. Working Paper No. 128. Washington DC: International Monetary Fund.

Krahnen, Jan Pieter, and Reinhard H. Schmidt. 1994. *Development Finance as Institution Building: A New Approach to Poverty-Oriented Banking*. Boulder: Westview Press.

Kumar, Anjali et al. 1997. China's Nonbank Financial Institutions. Paper No. 358. Washington DC: World Bank.

Lailieva, Maya D. 1998. Kyrgyz Republic's Financial Stabilization: The Banking Crisis. Washington DC: World Bank.

Lane, Timothy, Atish R. Ghosh, Javier Hamann, Steven Phillips, Marianne Schulze-Ghattas, and Tsidi Tsikata. 1999. IMF-Supported Programs in Indonesia, Korea, and Thailand: A Preliminary Assessment. Washington DC: International Monetary Fund.

Lapenu, Cecile. 1998. Indonesia's Rural Financial System: The Role of the State and Private Institutions. Case Studies in Microfinance. Sustainable Banking with the Poor. Washington DC: World Bank.

Lee, Young, and Patrick Meagher. 1999. Missing Institutions, Misgoverned Markets, Mysterious Reforms: Determining the Law's Role in Financing Enterprise Growth in Central Asia and Beyond. Draft paper. The Institute for Research on the Informal Sector. Maryland: University of Maryland.

Levine, Ross. 1997. Financial Development and Economic Growth. *Journal of Economic Literature* 35(2): 688-726.

Ling, Zhu, Jiang Zhongyi, and Joachim von Braun. 1996. *Credit for the Rural Poor in China*. Project Report to Deutsche Gesellschaft für Technische Zusammenarbeit. Washington DC: International Food Policy Research Institute.

_____. 1998. Credit Systems in the Economic Transformation of China: Institutions, Outreach and Policy Options. Paper presented at the international workshop on Innovations in Rural Micro-Finance for the Rural Poor: Exchange of Knowledge and Implications for Policy, organized by the International Food Policy Research Institute, held in Accra, Ghana, 9–13 November.

MacIntyre, Andrew J. 1993. The Politics of Finance in Indonesia: Command, Confusion, and Competition. In *The Politics of Finance in Developing Countries*, edited by S. Haggard, C. H. Lee, and S. Maxfield. Ithaca: Cornell University Press. p. 123-164.

Macours, Karen, and Johan F.M. Swinnen. 1998. Patterns of Agrarian Transition: Comparing Russia, China and Eastern Europe. Paper presented at the annual AAEA meeting, Salt Lake City, Utah, 2-5 August.

Mahajan, Vijay, and Bharati Gupta Ramola. 1996. Financial Services for the Rural Poor and Women in India: Access and Sustainability. *Journal of International Development* 8(2): 211-224.

Maloney, Clarence, and A.B. Sharfuddin Ahmed. 1988. *Rural Savings and Credit in Bangladesh.* Dhaka: University Press Limited.

Martino, Luigi De, Almaz Japarov, and Erkin Kasybekov. 1997. Rural Finance in the Kyrgyz Republic. Working Paper. Zurich: Swiss Agency for Development and Cooperation.

Martokoesoemo, Soeksmono B. 1994. Small-scale Finance: Lessons from Indonesia. In *Indonesia Assessment 1994: Finance as a Key Sector in Indonesia's Development*, edited by R. H. McLeod. Canberra: Australian National University. p. 292-313.

Matin, Imran. 1998. Limits of Simplicity: Loan Delinquency of Grameen Bank Borrowers in Madhupur. Working Paper No. 3. Poverty Research Unit at Sussex. Brighton: University of Sussex. p. 159-174.

Maurer, Klaus. 1997. Comparative Analysis of Savings Mobilization Strategies – Case Study of Bank Rakyat Indonesia. Draft report. Eschborn: Deutsche Gesellschaft für Technische Zusammenarbeit.

_____. 1997. BAAC/GTZ, Project Linking Self-Help Groups to Banking Services, Thailand. Eschborn: Deutsche Gesellschaft für Technische Zusammenarbeit.

McGregor, J. Allister. 1994. Government Failures and NGO Successes: Credit, Banking and the Poor in Rural Bangladesh, 1970-90. *Poverty, Inequality, and Rural Development*, edited by Tim Lloyd and Oliver Morrissey. London: MacMillan Press. p. 100-121.

McGuire, Paul B. and John D. Conroy. 1998. Effects on Microfinance of the 1997-1998 Asian Financial Crisis. Paper prepared for the Second Annual Seminar on New Development Finance, Goethe University of Frankfurt, 21-25 September.

————, John D. Conroy, and Ganesh B. Thapa. 1998. *Getting the Framework Right: Policy and Regulation for Microfinance in Asia.* Brisbane: Foundation for Development Cooperation.

McKinnon, Ronald I. 1973. *Money and Capital in Economic Development.* Washington DC: Brookings Institution.

McLeod, Ross H. 1998. The New Era of Financial Fragility. In *East Asia in Crisis: From Being a Miracle to Needing One*, edited by R. H. McLeod and R. Garnaut. London: Routledge. p. 333-351.

————. 1999. Control and Competition: Banking Deregulation and Re-regulation in Indonesia. *Journal of Asia Pacific Economy* 4(2): 258-296.

Meyer, Richard L. 1999. Rural Financial Markets and Rural Non-Farm Enterprise Development. In *Strategies for Stimulating Growth of the Rural Non-Farm Economy*, edited by Steven Haggblade, Peter Hazell, and Thomas Reardon. Washington DC: International Food Policy Research Institute. (In press)

————, and Adelaida P. Alicbusan. 1984. Farm-Household Heterogeneity and Rural Financial Markets: Insights from Thailand. In *Undermining Rural Development with Cheap Credit*, edited by Dale W. Adams, Douglas H. Graham, and J.D. Von Pischke. Boulder: Westview Press. p. 22-35.

————, and Carlos E. Cuevas. 1992. Reduction in Transaction Costs of Financial Intermediation: Theory and Innovations. In *Savings and Credit for Development*. Report of the International Conference on Savings and Credit for Development, Denmark. 28-31 May, 1990. New York: United Nations. p. 285-317.

————, and Donald W. Larson. 1997. Issues in Providing Agricultural Services in Developing Countries. In *Promoting Third World Development and Food Security*, edited by Luther G. Tweeten, and Donald G. McClelland. Westview: Praeger, p. 119-151.

_____, and Geetha Nagarajan. 1992. An Assessment of the Role of Informal Finance in the Development Process. In *Sustainable Agricultural Development: The Role of International Cooperation*, edited by G.H. Peters, and B.F. Stanton. Brookfield: Dartmouth Press. p. 644-654.

_____, and Geetha Nagarajan. 1996. *Credit Guarantee Schemes for Developing Countries: Theory, Design and Evaluation*. Report prepared by the Barents Group for the United States Agency for International Development, Washington DC.

_____, Chester B. Baker, and Tongroj Onchan. 1979. Agricultural Credit in Thailand. Research Report No. 6. Center for Applied Economics Research. Bangkok: Kasetsart University.

Morduch, Jonathan. 1998a. Does Microfinance Really Help the Poor? New Burdens from Flagship Programs in Bangladesh. Manuscript. Department of Economies and Harvard Institute for International Development. Cambridge: Harvard University.

_____. 1998b. The Grameen Bank: A Financial Reckoning. Manuscript. Hoover Institution. Stanford: Stanford University.

_____, Albert Park, and Sangui Wang. 1997. Microfinance in China. Department of Economics. Working Paper. Cambridge: Harvard University.

Mudahar, Mohinder S. 1998. Kyrgyz Republic: Strategy for Rural Growth and Poverty Alleviation. Discussion Paper No. 394. Washington DC: World Bank.

Muraki, Tetsutaro, Leila Webster, and Jacob Yaron. 1998a. Thailand, BAAC – The Thai Bank for Agriculture and Agricultural Cooperatives, Case Studies in Microfinance. Sustainable Banking with the Poor. Washington DC: World Bank.

_____. 1998b. The Thai Bank for Agriculture and Agricultural Cooperatives (BAAC): Outreach and Sustainability through 1996. Unpublished paper. Washington DC: World Bank.

Muscat, Robert J. 1995. Thailand. In *Financial Systems and Economic Policy in Developing Countries*, edited by S. Haggard and C. H. Lee. Ithaca: Cornell University Press. p. 113-139.

Nagarajan, B.S., N. Narayanasamy, and S. Ramachandran. 1996. A Financial Appraisal of Rural Financial Institutions in Tamil Nadu. *Journal of Financial Management and Analysis* 3(1): 1-7.

Nagarajan, Geetha. 1998. Microfinance in the Wake of Natural Disasters: Challenges and Opportunities. Paper prepared for the Microenterprise Best Practices Project. Bethesda: Development Alternatives International.

_____, and Claudio Gonzalez-Vega. 1998a. Friends of Women's World Banking: An Apex Organization in India. Working Paper. Department of Agricultural, Environmental, and Development Economics. Columbus: The Ohio State University.

_____, and Claudio Gonzalez-Vega. 1998b. The Palli Kama Sahayak Foundation (PKSF): An Apex Organization in Bangladesh. Manuscript. Department of Agricultural, Environmental, and Development Economics. Columbus: The Ohio State University.

_____, Richard L. Meyer, and Leroy J. Hushak. 1995. Segmentation in the Informal Credit Markets: The Case of the Philippines. *Agricultural Economics* 12(2): 171-181.

National Bank for Agriculture and Rural Development (NABARD). 1990 to 1997. Annual Reports. Bombay: NABARD.

_____. 1998. SHG-Bank Linkage Programme: Status as on March 1998. Micro Credit Innovations Department. Bombay: NABARD.

Navajas, Sergio, Mark Schreiner, Richard L. Meyer, Claudio Gonzalez-Vega, and Jorge Rodriguez-Meza. 1998. Microcredit and the Poorest of the Poor: Theory and Evidence from Bolivia. Unpublished manuscript. Department of Agricultural, Environmental, and Development Economics. Columbus: The Ohio State University.

Nayak, Jayendra P., 1995. Reform of India's Financial System. In *Financial Sector Development in Asia*, edited by Shahid N. Zahid. Manila: Asian Development Bank.

Nayar, C.P.S. 1992. Strengths of Informal Financial Institutions: Examples from India. In *Informal Finance in Low-Income Countries*, edited by Dale W Adams and D. A. Fitchett. Boulder: Westview Press. p. 195-208.

Novak, J.J. 1993. *Bangladesh: Reflections on the Water*. Bloomington: Indiana University Press.

Oliver, Raylynn. 1997. Credit and Microfinance in the Kyrgyz Republic. Bishkek: United Nations Development Programme Country Office.

Onchan, Tongroj. 1992. Informal Rural Finance in Thailand. In *Informal Finance in Low-Income Countries*, edited by Dale W Adams and D. A. Fitchett. Boulder: Westview Press. p. 103-117.

Ong, Shao-er. 1969. Developing the Small Farm Economy in Asia. Report No. 10. In *Asian Agricultural Survey*. Tokyo: University of Tokyo Press, and Seattle: University of Washington Press.

Otero, Maria, and Elisabeth Rhyne (eds). 1994. *The New World of Microenterprise Finance*. Hartford: Kumarian Press.

Oxford Analytics. 1998. China's Economy at Cross Roads. (World Bank Internet site on East Asian Crisis). Available: http://www.worldbank.org.

Park, Albert. 1998. Rural Financial Market Development in China: A Report to the World Bank. Working Paper. Department of Economics. Ann Arbor: University of Michigan.

_____, and Sangui Wang. 1998. Rural Household Credit in China's Poor Areas. Working Paper. Department of Economics. Ann Arbor: University of Michigan.

_____, Changing Ren, and Guabao Wu. 1998. Microfinance with Chinese Characteristics: Preliminary Tables. Working Paper. Department of Economics. Ann Arbor: University of Michigan.

_____, Loren Brandt and John Giles. 1997. Giving Credit Where Credit is Due: The Changing Role of Rural Financial Institutions in China. Working Paper. Department of Economics. Ann Arbor: University of Michigan.

Park, Yung Chul, and Chi-Young Song. 1998. The East Asian Financial Crisis: A Year Later. Paper presented at the East Asian Crisis Workshop, Institute of Development Studies, University of Sussex, 13-14 July.

Patten, Richard H. 1998. The East Asian Crisis and Retail Finance: The Experience of Bank Rakyat Indonesia through August 1998. Paper presented at the Second Annual Seminar on New Development Finance, Goethe University of Frankfurt. 21-25 September.

_____, and Jay K. Rosengard. 1991. *Progress with Profits: The Development of Rural Banking in Indonesia*. San Francisco: ICS Press.

Pingali, Prabhu L., and Mark W. Rosegrant. 1995. Agricultural Commercialization and Diversification. *Food Policy* 20(3): 171-185.

_____, and Shahidur R. Khandker. 1996. Household and Intrahousehold Impacts of the Grameen Bank and Similar Targeted Credit Programs in Bangladesh. Discussion Paper No. 320. Washington DC: World Bank.

_____.1998. The Impact of Group-Based Programs on Poor Households in Bangladesh: Does the Gender of Participants Matter? *Journal of Political Economy* 106(5): 956-996.

Poapongsakorn, Nipon, et al. 1995. *Agricultural Diversification/Restructuring of Agricultural Production Systems in Thailand*. Bangkok: Thailand Development Research Institute.

_____, Ammar Siamwalla, and Patchaneeboon Charoenpiew. 1998. The Rural Finance Market in Thailand and the Role of the Bank for Agriculture and Agricultural Cooperatives. In *The Rural Finance in Thailand*, edited by Nipon Poapongsakorn et al. Bangkok: Thailand Development Research Institute. p. 1-42.

Pomareda, Carlos. 1984. *Financial Policies and Management of Agricultural Development Banks*. Boulder: Westview Press.

Preedasak, Paradorn, and Viroj NaRanong. 1998. Agricultural Cooperatives and Village Credit Unions in Rural Financial Markets in Thailand. In *The Rural Finance in Thailand*, edited by Nipon Poapongsakorn, et al. Bangkok: Thailand Development Research Institute. p. 55-82.

Puhazhendi, V. 1995. Transaction Costs of Lending to Rural Poor: NGOs and SHGs of the Poor as Intermediaries for Banks in India. Working paper. Brisbane: Foundation for Development Cooperation.

Quibria, M.G. 1997. Introduction to *The Bangladesh Economy in Transition*, edited by M.G. Quibria. New Delhi: Oxford University Press.

Quinones, Benjamin. 1997. Evaluation of the Linkage Banking Programme in India. Bangkok: Asia Pacific Rural and Agricultural Credit Association.

Rahman, Aminur. 1999. Microcredit Institutions for Equitable and Sustainable Development: Who Pays? *World Development* 27(1): 67-82.

Rana, Pradumna B. 1993. *Reforms in the Transition Economies of Asia.* Occasional Papers No. 5. Economics and Development Resource Center. Manila: Asian Development Bank.

_____. 1997. Reforms in Bangladesh: A Comparative Assessment in Relation to Other South Asian Countries. In *The Bangladesh Economy in Transition,* edited by M.G. Quibria. New Delhi: Oxford University Press. p. 7-27.

_____, and Naved Hamid. 1995. *From Centrally Planned to Market Economies: The Asian Approach.* Vol. I. Manila: Asian Development Bank, and New York: Oxford University Press.

Rao, Giridhara. 1995. Reaching the Poor: Strategies of Canara Bank. Paper presented at the NABARD-APRACA International Seminar on Development of Rural Poor Through the Self Help Groups, Bangalore, India.

Rao, Hanumantha C.H. 1998. Agricultural Growth, Sustainability, and Poverty Alleviation in India: Recent Trends and Major Issues of Reform. Lecture Series No. 5. Washington DC: International Food Policy Research Institute.

Ravicz, R. Marisol. 1998. Searching for Sustainable Microfinance: A Review of Five Indonesian Initiatives. Policy Research Working Paper No. 1878. Washington DC: World Bank.

Reardon, Thomas, Kostas Stamoulis, Maria Elena Cruz, Arsenio Balisacan, Julio Berdegue, and Kimseyinga Savadogo. 1998. Diversification of Household Incomes into Nonfarm Sources: Patterns, Determinants, and Effects. Paper presented at the International Food Policy Research Institute Conference on Strategies for Stimulating Growth of the Rural Nonfarm Economy in Developing Countries, Arlie House, Virginia, 17-21 May.

Reille, Xavier, and Dominique Gallman. 1998. The Indonesia People's Credit Banks (BPRs) and the Financial Crisis. Paper presented at the Second Annual Seminar on New Development Finance, Goethe University of Frankfurt, 21-25 September.

Reserve Bank of India (RBI). 1982 to 1992. Statistical Bulletins. Bombay: RBI.

_____. 1995. Expert Committee on IRDP: Interim Report. Bombay: RBI.

_____. 1997. Special Issue on the 50th Year of Independence. *Occasional Papers* 18, Nos. 2 and 3. Bombay: RBI.

Rhyne, Elisabeth, and Linda S. Rotblatt. 1994. *What Makes Them Tick? Exploring the Anatomy of Major Microenterprise Finance Organizations.* Cambridge: ACCION International.

Riedinger, Jeffrey M. 1994. Innovation in Rural Finance: Indonesia's Badan Kredit Kecamatan Program. *World Development* 22(3): 301-313.

Robinson, Marguerite S. 1992. Rural Financial Intermediation: Lessons from Indonesia. Development Discussion Paper No. 434. Cambridge: Harvard Institute for International Development.

_____. 1994. Financial Intermediation at the Local Level: Lessons from Indonesia, Development Discussion Paper No. 482. Cambridge: Harvard Institute for International Development.

_____. 1997. Sustainable Microfinance. In *Assisting Development in a Changing World*, ed. By Dwight H. Snodgrass and Joseph J. Stern. Cambridge: Harvard Institute for International Development. p. 255-283.

Rosegrant, Mark W., and Peter Hazell. 1999. The Transformation of the Rural Economy

Rozelle, Scott, Albert Park, Vincent Benziger, and Changqing Ren. 1998. Targeted Poverty Investments and Economic Growth in China. *World Development* 26(12): 2137-2151.

Ruofeng, Niu, and Chen Jiyuan. 1992. Small Farmers in China and Their Development. In *Sustainable Agricultural Development: Role of International Cooperation*, edited by G.H. Peters and B.F. Stanton. Brookfield: Dartmouth Press. p. 620-642.

Ruogu, Li. 1996. The Three Stages of Financial Sector Reforms in The People's Republic of China. In *Creating Resilient Financial Regimes in Asia: Challenges and Policy Options*, edited by Priya Basu. Hong Kong: Oxford University Press, and Manila: Asian Development Bank. p. 49-55.

Rutherford, Stuart. 1996. A Critical Typology of Financial Services for the Poor. Working Paper No. 1. London: ACTIONAID.

Sacay, O., B. Randhawa, and M. Agabin. 1996. The BAAC Success Story: A Specialized Agriculture Bank Under Government Ownership, Draft report. Financial Sector Development Department. Washington DC: World Bank.

Sachs, Jeffrey. 1997. Lessons from the Thais. *Financial Times, 30* July.

Sa-Dhan. 1998. Recommendations for the Promotion of Microfinance in India. Paper Presented at the Policy Forum for Microfinance organized by Women's World Banking, Ahmedabad, November.

SafeSave. 1998. Update. Newsletter of SafeSave Cooperative Ltd., Dhaka, Bangladesh. 31 October.

Sankaranarayanan, R. 1998. A Study of the Problems of Over Dues and Recovery Performance of RRBs in Tamil Nadu State. Unpublished Ph.D. Dissertation. Tamil Nadu: Gandhigram University.

Satish, S., and K.K. Swaminathan. 1988. Lending Costs and Margins. Agricultural Credit Review Report. Bombay: Reserve Bank of India.

Schreiner, Mark. 1999. Aspects of Outreach: A Framework for Discussion of the Social Aspects of Microfinance. Draft paper. Center for Social Development. St. Louis: Washington University.

Seibel, Hans Dieter, and Uben Parhusip. 1998. Microfinance in Indonesia: An Assessment of Microfinance Institutions Banking with the Poor. Economics and Sociology Occasional Paper No. 2365. Department of Agricultural, Environmental, and Development Economics. Columbus: The Ohio State University.

Shaw, Edward S. 1973. *Financial Deepening in Economic Development*. New York: Oxford University Press.

Shylendra, H.S. 1996. Institutional Reform and Rural Poor: A Study on the Distributional Performance of a Regional Rural Bank. *Indian Journal of Agricultural Economics* 51(3): 301-314.

_____, and Orapin Sobchokchai. 1998. Responding to the Thai Economic Crisis. Paper prepared for the United Nations Development Programme in Thailand. Bangkok: Thailand Development Research Institute.

Sinha, Saurabh and Imran Matin. 1998. Informal Credit Transactions of Micro-Credit Borrowers in Rural Bangladesh. Micro-Credit Impact, Targeting and Sustainability. *IDS Bulletin* 29(4): 66-80.

Sobhan, Rehman. 1991. Introduction to *Debt Default to the Development Finance Institutions: The Crisis of State Sponsored Entrepreneurship in Bangladesh*, edited by Rehman Sobhan. Dhaka: University Press Limited. p. 1-9.

_____. 1997. Introduction to *Growth or Stagnation? A Review of Bangladesh's Development 1996*, edited by Rehman Sobhan. Dhaka: University Press Limited. p. 1-41.

Song, Ligang. 1998. China: Behind Closed Doors. In *East Asia Crisis: From Being a Miracle to needing One?* edited by R. H. Mcleod and R. Garnaut. London: Routledge. p.105-119.

Steinwand, Dirk. 1998. KPM Study: Survey on Groups of Micro-entrepreneurs (KPM) Linked with Rural Credit Banks (BPR) in the Framework of PHBK, second draft. Project Linking Banks and SHG. Jakarta: Bank Indonesia, and Eschborn: Deutsche Gesellschaft für Technische Zusammenarbeit.

Stiglitz, Joseph E. 1992. The Role of the State in Financial Markets, IPR Paper 56. Washington DC: Institute for Policy Reform.

_____. 1997. Building Robust Financial Systems. Keynote Lecture at Private Capital Inflows: What Have We Learned? Bogota, Columbia, 1 October.

_____. 1998a. The Role of the Financial System in Development. Presentation at the Fourth Annual Bank Conference on Development in Latin America and The Caribbean, San Salvador, 29 June.

_____. 1998b. The East Asia Crisis and its Implications for India. Commemorative Lecture for the Golden Jubilee Year Celebration of Industrial Finance, New Delhi. Washington DC: World Bank.

_____, and Marilou Uy. 1996. Financial Markets, Public Policy, and the East Asian Miracle. *The World Bank Research Observer* 11(2): 249-276.

_____, and Andrew Weiss. 1981. Credit Rationing in Markets with Imperfect Information. *American Economic Review* 71(3): 393-410.

Swaminathan, Madhura. 1991. Segmentation, Collateral Undervaluation, and the Rate of Interest in Agrarian Credit Markets: Some Evidence from Two Villages in South India. *Cambridge Journal of Economics* 15: 161-178.

Tacis (Technical Assistance for Central Asian Independent States by the European Union). 1996. Policy and Agro-Business Support Project: Input I Report of Rural Credit Specialist. Bishkek: Tacis Office.

_____. 1997a. Policy and Agro-Business Support Project: Input II Report of Rural Credit Specialist. Bishkek: Tacis Office.

_____. 1997b. Terms of Reference for Support of Sustainable Rural Credit Services in Kyrgyzstan. Bishkek: Tacis Office.

Teuku, Hamzah. 1994. Indonesia: Country Study. In *Rural Development Policies and Strategies*. Tokyo: Asian Productivity Organization. p. 214-237.

Todd, Helen. 1997. *Women at the Center: Grameen Borrowers After One Decade*. Dhaka: University Press Limited.

Tomich, Thomas P., Peter Kilby, and Bruce F. Johnston. 1995. *Transforming Agrarian Economies: Opportunities Seized, Opportunities Missed* Ithaca: Cornell University Press.

Townsend, Robert. 1995. Financial Systems in Northern Thai Villages. *Quarterly Journal of Economics* 11(4): 1011-1046.

Tuan, Francis, C. 1993. China's Recent Rural Development: Policy Implications for the 1990s. Paper Presented at the International Conference on China's Rural Reform and Development in the 1990s, Beijing, 3-5 December.

United Nations Development Programme (UNDP). 1998. Proceedings of National Microcredit Summit. Bishkek: UNDP County Office.

Vajragupta, Yos and Pakorn Vichyanond. 1998. *Thailand's Financial Evolution and the 1997 Crisis*. Bangkok: Thailand Development Research Institute.

Vichyanond, Pakorn. 1995. Financial Sector Development in Thailand. In *Financial Sector Development in Asia: Country Studies*, edited by Shahid N. Zahid. Manila: Asian Development Bank. p. 303-370.

Vogel, Robert C. 1984. Savings Mobilization: The Forgotten Half of Rural Finance. In *Undermining Rural Development with Cheap Credit*, edited by Dale W Adams, Douglas H. Graham, and J.D. Von Pischke. Boulder: Westview Press. p. 248-265.

_____, and Dale W Adams. 1997. Old and New Paradigms in Development Finance. *Savings and Development* 22(4): 361-382.

Von Pischke, J.D. 1991. *Finance at the Frontier.* Economic Development Institute. Washington DC: World Bank.

_____, Dale W Adams, and Gordon Donald. 1983. *Rural Financial Markets in Developing Countries: Their Use and Abuse.* Baltimore: The Johns Hopkins University Press.

Wade, Paul, Rizal Djaafaro, Houng Lee, Jong-won Yoon, and Min Tang. 1998. Bangladesh: Selected Issues. Staff Country Report No. 98/130. Washington DC: International Monetary Fund.

Wadwa, S.C. 1998. Operational Guidelines for Suggested Microcredit Model for Kyrgyzstan. Paper presented at the National Microcredit Summit, held by the United Nations Development Programme, Biskek, Kyrgyz Republic.

West, Loraine A. 1990. Farm Household Access to Credit Markets Under the Household Responsibility System in China. Paper Presented at the AAEA Annual Meeting, Vancouver, August.

White, Lawrence. 1995. Structure of Finance in Selected Asian Economies. In *Financial Sector Development in Asia*, edited by Shahid N. Zahid. Manila: Asian Development Bank. p. 51-55.

World Bank. 1989. *World Bank Development Report 1989.* Washington DC: World Bank.

_____. 1993. *The East Asian Miracle: Economic Growth and Public Policy.* Washington DC: World Bank.

_____. 1995a. Kyrgyzstan: The Transition to Market Economy. Country Study. Washington DC: World Bank.

_____. 1995b. The Kyrgyz Republic Agricultural Sector Review. Washington DC: World Bank.

_____. 1995c. Financial Services for the Rural Poor and Women in India: Access and Sustainability. Washington DC: World Bank.

_____. 1996a. Bangladesh Rural Finance. Report No. 15484-BD. Washington DC: World Bank.

_____. 1996b. *From Plan to Market: World Development Report.* Washington DC: World Bank.

_____. 1996c. The Kyrgyz Republic: Financial Sector Technical Assistance Project. Washington DC: World Bank.

_____. 1997a. *The World Development Indicators.* Washington DC: World Bank.

_____.1997b. Kyrgyz Republic: Rural Finance Project, Staff Appraisal Report. Washington DC: World Bank.

_____. 1997c. Financial Services for the Rural Poor and Women in India: Access and Sustainability. Washington DC: World Bank.

_____. 1997d. China 2020: Development Challenges in the New Century. Report No. 17027-CHA.Poverty Reduction and Economic Management Unit. East Asia and Pacific Region. Washington DC: World Bank.

_____. 1997e. Kyrgyz Republic: Country Overview. Washington DC: World Bank. Country Profiles. Available: http://www.worldbank.org. Accessed December 1997.

_____.1998a. *East Asia: The Road to Recovery*. World Bank. Washington DC: World Bank.

_____.1998b. *World Bank Development Report 1998/99*. Washington DC: World Bank.

_____. 1998c. *The World Development Indicators*. Washington DC: World Bank.

_____. 1998d. India: Draft Rural Finance Report. South Asia Region. Washington DC: World Bank.

_____. 1998e. Kyrgyz Republic: Agricultural Support Services Project, Staff Appraisal Report. Washington DC: World Bank.

Wright, Graham A.N. 1999. *Microfinance Systems: Straight-Jackets or Tailored Suits, Designing Quality Financial Services for the Poor*. Dhaka: University Press Limited and London: Zed Books. (In press)

Yadav, S., K. Otsuka, and C.C. David. 1992. Segmentation in Rural Financial Markets: The Case of Nepal. *World Development* 20(3): 423-436.

Yaron, Jacob. 1992. Successful Rural Finance Institutions. Discussion Paper No. 150. Washington DC: World Bank.

_____, McDonald P. Benjamin, Jr., and Gerda L. Piprek. 1997. Rural Finance: Issues, Design, and Best Practices. Environmentally and Socially Sustainable Development Studies and Monographs Series 14. Washington DC: World Bank.

Zeller, Manfred, Gertrud Schreider, Joachim von Braun, and Franz Heidhues. 1997. *Rural Finance for Food Security for the Poor: Implications for Research and Policy*. Food Policy Review No. 4. Washington DC: International Food Policy Research Institute.

AUTHOR INDEX

SUBJECT INDEX

microlending 44
microlevel 209
  information 265
microloans 170, 223
Ministry of Agriculture (Indonesia)
  277
Ministry of Agriculture &
  Cooperatives (Thailand) 325
Ministry of Agriculture and Food
  (Kyrgyz Republic) 216
Ministry of Civil Affairs (PRC) 245
Ministry of Finance (Thailand)
  312, 316
Ministry of Labor and Social
  Protection (Kyrgyz Republic) 219
mobilize savings 22
money transfer 17
moneylenders 26, 340
  traditional 192
monobanking 206, 224, 236
monopolistic behavior 217
moral hazard problem 308, 315
multilateral donors 206
mutual aid societies 26
mutual associations and credit
  groups (MACGs) 243, 245
Myanmar 10

N

NABARD. *See* National Bank for
  Agriculture & Rural Development
Narasimhan Committee 180
National Agricultural Cooperative
  Federation 68
National Bank for Agriculture &
  Rural Development (NABARD)
  78, 171
National Bank of Kyrgyz Republic 214
National Cooperative Development
  Corporation 171

national microcredit summit 218
national savings program 295
national voluntary savings program
  283, 285
negative before-tax profits 249
Nepal 62, 102
Netherlands 272
newly independent republics 203
NGOs. *See* nongovernmental
  organizations
nominal rate 144, 214
nonagricultural-based economy 235
nonbanks
  financial institutions 206, 207, 315
  legal and regulatory frameworks 208
nonfarm economy 11
nonfarm firms 10
nonfarm production activities 242
nonfinancial services 45
nongovernmental organizations
  (NGOs) 2, 59, 79, 130, 139,
  156, 157, 186–187, 286
  Credit and Development Forum
  139
  financial programs 26
nonperforming institutions 166
nonrotating savings 193
nonsubsidized financial institutions
  309

O

obligatory savings 146
Office of the Permanent Secretary to
  the Prime Minister (Thailand) 325
oil-funded subsidized credit system
  273
onfarm investments 217
output-market reforms 236
outreach and sustainability 56
overdues 207